Made in Australia and Aotearoa/New Zealand

Made in Australia and Aotearoa/New Zealand: Studies in Popular Music serves as a comprehensive and thorough introduction to the history, sociology, and musicology of twentieth-century popular music of Australia and Aotearoa/New Zealand. The volume consists of chapters by leading scholars of Australian and Aotearoa/New Zealand music, and covers the major figures, styles, and social contexts of pop music in Australia and Aotearoa/New Zealand. Each chapter provides adequate context so readers understand why the figure or genre under discussion is of lasting significance to Australian or Aotearoan/New Zealand popular music. The book first presents a general description of the history and background of popular music in these countries, followed by chapters that are organized into thematic sections: Place-Making and Music-Making; Rethinking the Musical Event; Musical Transformations: Decline and Renewal; and Global Sounds, Local Identity.

Shelley Brunt is Senior Lecturer in the Music Industry program at RMIT University, Australia.

Geoff Stahl is Senior Lecturer in Media Studies at Victoria University of Wellington, Aotearoa/New Zealand.

Routledge Global Popular Music Series

Series Editors: Franco Fabbri, Conservatorio di Musica Arrigo Boito di Parma, Italy, and Goffredo Plastino, Newcastle University, UK

The *Routledge Global Popular Music Series* provides popular music scholars, teachers, students and musicologists with a well-informed and up-to-date introduction to different world popular music scenes. The series of volumes can be used for academic teaching in popular music studies, or as a collection of reference works. Written by those living and working in the countries about which they write, this series is devoted to popular music largely unknown to Anglo-American readers.

Made in Korea: Studies in Popular Music
Edited by Hyunjoon Shin and Seung-Ah Lee

Made in Sweden: Studies in Popular Music
Edited by Alf Björnberg and Thomas Bossius

Made in Hungary: Studies in Popular Music
Edited by Emília Barna and Tamás Tófalvy

Made in France: Studies in Popular Music
Edited by Gérôme Guibert and Catherine Rudent

Made in the Low Countries: Studies in Popular Music
Edited by Lutgard Mutsaers and Gert Keunen

Made in Turkey: Studies in Popular Music
Edited by Ali C. Gedik

Made in Australia and Aotearoa/New Zealand: Studies in Popular Music
Edited by Shelley Brunt and Geoff Stahl

Made in Greece: Studies in Popular Music
Edited by Dafni Tragaki

Made in Australia and Aotearoa/New Zealand

Studies in Popular Music

Edited by
Shelley Brunt and
Geoff Stahl

NEW YORK AND LONDON

First published 2018
by Routledge
711 Third Avenue, New York, NY 10017

and by Routledge
2 Park Square, Milton Park, Abingdon, Oxon OX14 4RN

Routledge is an imprint of the Taylor & Francis Group, an informa business

© 2018 Taylor & Francis

The right of Shelley Brunt and Geoff Stahl to be identified as the authors of this part of the Work has been asserted by them in accordance with sections 77 and 78 of the Copyright, Designs and Patents Act 1988.

All rights reserved. No part of this book may be reprinted or reproduced or utilised in any form or by any electronic, mechanical, or other means, now known or hereafter invented, including photocopying and recording, or in any information storage or retrieval system, without permission in writing from the publishers.

Trademark notice: Product or corporate names may be trademarks or registered trademarks, and are used only for identification and explanation without intent to infringe.

Library of Congress Cataloging in Publication Data
A catalog record has been requested for this book

ISBN: 978-1-138-19568-4 (hbk)
ISBN: 978-1-138-19569-1 (pbk)
ISBN: 978-1-315-63825-6 (ebk)

Typeset in Minion Pro
by Keystroke, Neville Lodge, Tettenhall, Wolverhampton

Visit http://www. globalpopularmusic.net/

Contents

List of Illustrations	vii
Series Foreword	ix
Preface	xi
Acknowledgments	xv

Introduction: This is My City: Reimagining Popular Music Down Under   1
SHELLEY BRUNT AND GEOFF STAHL

Part I: Place-Making and Music-Making   17

1 Singing about the City: The Lyrical Construction of Perth   19
JON STRATTON AND ADAM TRAINER

2 The Phoenix and the Bootleg Sessions: A Canberra Venue for Local Music   31
JULIE RICKWOOD AND EMMA WILLIAMS

3 Lorde's Auckland: Stepping Out of "the Bubble"   45
TONY MITCHELL

Part II: Rethinking the Musical Event   57

4 Popular Music and Heritage-Making in Melbourne   59
CATHERINE STRONG

5 The "Dunedin Sound" Now: Contemporary Perspectives on Dunedin's
Musical Legacy   69
OLI WILSON AND MICHAEL HOLLAND

6 The Construction of Latin American Musical Identity in Melbourne   81
MARA FAVORETTO

vi • Contents

Part III: Musical Transformations: Decline and Renewal 95

7 Outside the Square: *Songs for Christchurch* in a Time of Earthquakes 97
SHELLEY BRUNT

8 The Making and Remaking of Brisbane and Hobart: Music Scenes in
Australia's "Second-Tier" Cities 111
ANDY BENNETT AND IAN ROGERS

9 Urban Melancholy: Tales from Wellington's Music Scene 121
GEOFF STAHL

Part IV: Global Sounds, Local Identity 131

10 Singing the Lord's Song in a Strange City: An Examination of the Nexus
Between the Southern Gospel Choir and the City of Hobart, Tasmania 133
ANDREW LEGG, CAROLYN PHILPOTT AND PAUL BLACKLOW

11 "I Rep for My Mob": Blackfellas Rappin' from Down-Unda 145
CHIARA MINESTRELLI

12 Technomotor Cities: Adelaide, Detroit and the Electronic Music Pioneers 155
CATHY ADAMEK

13 Giving Back in Wellington: Deep Relations, *Whakapapa* and Reciprocity
in Transnational Hip Hop 167
APRIL K. HENDERSON

14 The Music City: Australian Contexts 179
SHANE HOMAN

Coda 191

15 Site-ing the Sounds: Discovering Australia and New Zealand's Popular Music
in the United States 193
KYLE BARNETT AND ROBERT SLOANE

Afterword 205

16 Negotiating Trans-Tasman Musical Identities: Conversations with Neil
and Tim Finn 207
LIZ GIUFFRE

A Selected Bibliography of Books on Popular Music in Australia
and Aotearoa/New Zealand 219
Notes on Contributors 221
Index 225

List of Illustrations

Figures

2.1	The original Phoenix	32
2.2	A Bootleg Sessions poster	37
2.3	The reunified Phoenix on Monday January 30, 2017	40
4.1	Amphlett Lane	63
7.1	"The Square" and the remains of ChristChurch Cathedral in 2013	99
7.2	Audience members at the stage for the *Songs for Christchurch* CD launch	102
7.3	Selling the *Songs for Christchurch* CD at the merchandise stall	103
10.1	Victoria Dock, the city of Hobart and Kunanyi (Mount Wellington)	134
10.2	Andrew Legg and the audience at Standing in the Shadows of MONA	139
10.3	The Southern Gospel Choir at the Potter's House Church in Dallas	142
12.1	Theo Bambacas and DJ HMC (Cam Bianchetti), *The Face*, July 1995	159
12.2	Claude Young DJing at the "toxic" dance party at Le Rox, Adelaide, 1993	160

Tables

10.1	Total numbers of participants who enrolled in the Gospel stream of Festival of Voices, against all enrollments 2005–2007	138
10.2	Total enrollment numbers for each of the Festival of Voices workshop streams offered in 2007, and from 2010–2014	138

Series Foreword

Popular music studies have progressed from the initial focus on methodologies to exploring a variety of genres, scenes, works, and performers. British and North American music have been privileged and studied first, not only for their geographic and generational proximity to scholars, but also for their tremendous impact. Everything else has been often relegated to the dubious "world music" category, with a "folk" (or "roots," or "authentic") label attached.

However, world popular music is no less popular than rock 'n' roll, r&b, disco, rap, singer-songwriters, punk, grunge, brit-pop, or nu-gaze. It is no less full of history and passion, no less danceable, socially relevant, and commercialized. Argentinian tango, Brazilian *bossa nova*, Mexican *reggaeton*, Cuban *son* and *timba*, Spanish and Latin American *cantautores*, French *auteurs-compositeurs-interprètes*, Italian *cantautori* and electronic dance music, *J-pop*, German cosmic music and *Schlager*, Neapolitan Song, Greek *entechno*, Algerian *raï*, Ghanaian highlife, Portuguese *fado*, Nigerian *jùjú*, Egyptian and Lebanese Arabic pop, Israeli *mizrahit*, and Indian *filmi* are just a few examples of locally and transnationally successful genres that, with millions of records sold, are an immensely precious key to understand different cultures, societies, and economies.

More than in the past there is now a widespread awareness of the "other" popular music: however, we still lack access to the original sources, or to texts to rely on. The *Routledge Global Popular Music Series* has been devised to offer to scholars, teachers, students, and general readers worldwide a direct access to scenes, works, and performers that have been mostly not much or not at all considered in the current literature, and at the same time to provide a better understanding of the different approaches in the field of non-Anglophone scholarship. Uncovering the wealth of studies flourishing in so many countries, inaccessible to those who do not speak the local language, is now no less urgent than considering the music itself.

The series website (www.globalpopularmusic.net) includes hundreds of audio-visual examples which complement the volumes. The interaction with the website is intended to give a well-informed introduction to the world's popular music from entirely new perspectives, and at the same time to provide updated resources for academic teaching.

Routledge Global Popular Music Series ultimately aims at establishing a truly international arena for a democratic musicology, through authoritative and accessible books. We hope

x • Series Foreword

that our work will help the creation of a different polyphony of critical approaches, and that you will enjoy listening to and being part of it.

Franco Fabbri
Conservatorio di Musica Arrigo Boito di Parma, Italy

Goffredo Plastino
Newcastle University, UK

Series Editors

Preface

Both Australia and Aotearoa/New Zealand offer a different set of case studies than what might otherwise be expected from the Routledge *Global Popular Music Series*. As editors, we have deliberately paired these two countries together for this volume for reasons of geographical proximity, as well as their shared status of lying at the outer reaches of the Anglo-American sphere of influence. As this edited collection demonstrates, local music-makers have embraced a myriad of global popular music genres and made them their own. These chapters exemplify how popular music—from rock and hip hop to electronic dance music—can subtly and profoundly articulate the specificity of geographical and historical circumstance. This book aims to speak to a number of these kinds of music issues and musical aspects, many of which are often unknown or invisible to the international reader.

Book Organization

Made in Australia and Aotearoa/New Zealand is divided into four parts, each exploring a different aspect of popular music in one of these countries or sometimes both. It begins with our co-authored historical chapter which provides a context for the volume and its sub-theme of popular music and the city. This Introduction is followed by Part I, "Place-making and Music-making," which considers how places and practices are deeply intertwined, how places gain their identity through popular song, the power of institutions in the musical life of Australia, as well as the power of built form in shaping musical sensibilities. Part II, "Rethinking the Musical Event," considers how events are mobilized by a range of interested parties. They are designed to celebrate locality, to reaffirm or mine the value of its musical past through heritage sites and tourist packages, as well as allowing a moment to reflect on the wax and wane of the eventfulness of a place. Part III, "Musical Transformations: Decline and Renewal" speaks to issues of how music-makers and other stakeholders view music as a valuable resource, one that individuals as well as cities rely on to make places meaningful. Part IV, the final section, is titled "Global Sounds, Local Identity" and indicates a shift from an inward perspective on Australia and Aotearoa/New Zealand to an outward view, addressing in finer detail how the local and the global are enmeshed in musical practice.

The Coda, written "in conversation" by two American scholars—both fans of music from Australia and Aotearoa/New Zealand—considers a number of related questions that are perhaps in the mind of international readers: How is Anglophone music from the Down xii • Preface

Under periphery understood by the center? What are the discourses that are tied to this music, and are articulated via cultural workers, such as musicians, and institutions such as record shops, mail order catalogues, and fanzines? It examines several interrelated dynamics: the role of cultural intermediaries and tastemakers in facilitating first impressions of the music, to whom we sometimes returned for more information; the ways in which recorded music circulates via specific sites of production, distribution, and reception, from record shops to zines to college radio; and the importance of music media as material culture. The authors situate their own consumption and reception of Australian and Aotearoa/New Zealand's pop music via these intermediaries and institutions as key to their understandings of the music. The Afterword presents a reflection on the trans-Tasman flow of music and musicians which we, and the other authors in this book, have broadly argued for as a point of connection between Australia and Aotearoa/New Zealand. The Australian author of the Afterword presents a case study of the internationally known New Zealand brothers Neil and Tim Finn. She looks back on a series of interviews she conducted with them as co-band members in Crowded House and Split Enz, as well as soloists, and the fandom surrounding these transnational musicians. Lastly, we present a curated but by no means comprehensive list of books about popular music in Australia and Aotearoa/New Zealand, to provide the international reader with further routes of exploration into specific issues or themes mentioned in this volume.

Notes on Terms

We would like to point out the deliberate choice of spelling and languages employed in this book, beginning with the Māori name for New Zealand, "Aotearoa" or the "land of the long white cloud." In recognition of this name, and in keeping with local custom, we use the composite term "Aotearoa/New Zealand"—rather than simply the English language "New Zealand"—as an important acknowledgment of te reo Māori as one of the country's official languages. The forward slash (/) is also a significant post-colonial statement that recognizes that two cultures, Māori and Pākehā (the Māori term for white European settlers and their descendants), both occupy this land (and although it is increasingly a multicultural, not simply a bi-cultural, nation, the acknowledgment of the first peoples in this way is important). Like scholars Jo Smith and Sue Abel, we view the term Aotearoa/New Zealand as a "conjunction of signs that demarcate the endlessly contested nature of this settler nation," where

> "Aotearoa" refers to an *iwi*-based [tribe-based] nation and "New Zealand" is that which demarcates the settler nation and those who come after *tangata whenua* [indigenous people of the land]. The slash ... between these two terms is the site that holds in doubt, suspension and fine balance, the potential unity of the two. Accordingly, a critically conscious approach to this conjunction might see Aotearoa/New Zealand as designating a site of endless contestation over what and who gets to count as the nation.
>
> (2008, 9–10)

Australia, however, does not have a government-recognized single indigenous language that is used in a comparable way to te reo Māori in Aotearoa/New Zealand. English is

Australia's official spoken language—even though a multitude of other languages are articulated every day in what is a deeply multicultural society—and there is no alternative indigenous language name for "Australia" commonly in use.

Our contributors have used their preferred configuration of country names in their respective chapters. We, however, have used the title "Aotearoa/New Zealand" in our own writing and in the book's title to signal that this distinction has an important political salience: although the issues of colonizer and colonized may seem out-dated to some people, it is a situation that is—to use post-colonial parlance—far from settled.

Bibliography

Smith, Jo and Sue Abel. 2008. "Ka Whawhai Tonu Mātou: Indigenous Television in Aotearoa/New Zealand." *MEDIANZ: Media Studies Journal of Aotearoa New Zealand* 11 (1): 1–14.

Shelley Brunt, RMIT University, Australia
Geoff Stahl, Victoria University of Wellington, Aotearoa/New Zealand

Acknowledgments

At the outset, we would like to thank the editors of the *Routledge Global Popular Music Series*, Goffredo Plastino and Franco Fabbri, for their patience and advice over the course of assembling this volume. Sincere thanks go to our authors for their insightful chapters which represent months and, in some cases, years of dedicated research. We are particularly grateful to the members of IASPM-ANZ (International Association for the Study of Popular Music, Australia and New Zealand branch) for their advice regarding the Selected Bibliography, as well as their ongoing commitment to the study of popular music in Australia and Aotearoa/New Zealand, without which this book would not exist. We also appreciate the oversight and support generously offered by the editing team at Routledge.

Geoff would like to thank the staff and students of the Media Studies Programme at Victoria University of Wellington for their advice and allowing him to sound out ideas along the way.

Shelley would like thank her colleagues and family for their support during this project, especially Odette Tui, the Australian New Zealander who was on board from the very beginning.

Shelley Brunt, RMIT University, Australia
Geoff Stahl, Victoria University of Wellington, Aotearoa/New Zealand

Introduction
This is My City: Reimagining Popular Music Down Under

Shelley Brunt and Geoff Stahl

Australia and Aotearoa/New Zealand are neighboring countries in the Southern Hemisphere which are often perceived by those in the West and elsewhere as "down under." This colloquialism refers to their position on the globe as being somewhere underneath Asia, below and to the side of America, and on the opposite side of the world to Europe. Furthering this relational concept is the term "Antipodean," used primarily by those in the Northern Hemisphere to reinforce the vast distance these two nations seemingly are from more "established" culture, music, history, and so forth. For Australians and New Zealanders, however, the vast Pacific and Indian Oceans do not entirely separate them from the rest of the world. Australia, for example, has long embraced its close proximity to Asia in general and Indonesia more specifically, while Aotearoa/New Zealand is one of the cornerstones of the chain of Pacific Islands (including Tonga, Fiji, Samoa, and other regional island nations). Importantly, Australia and Aotearoa/New Zealand's geographical closeness—as countries simply "across the ditch" (meaning "over the ocean") from each other—has enabled a unique reciprocity that has long informed the way in which musicians and their music have traversed the adjoining Tasman Sea.

Made in Australia and Aotearoa/New Zealand is intended to introduce international readers to various aspects of popular music from these two countries which share a very special relationship. This chapter sets the scene by providing a historical context and a cursory sketch of a selection of geo-historical specificities that provide the scaffolding for the subsequent chapters. Our specific interest lies in the cities or broader urban areas of these countries—cities are indelibly connected with the production and consumption of popular music. We also collate and synthesize established research in an original manner, with a view to instigating new concepts and understandings of this existing knowledge in such a way as to reimagine popular music "down under." As such, this is the first study that pairs the popular music histories of both Australia and Aotearoa/New Zealand together in relation to cities; a timely inclusion to the academic literature.[1] In doing so, we reveal contemporary concerns born out of Australia and Aotearoa/New Zealand's colonial pasts and post-colonial presents, and how they respond to globalization in relation to popular music in revealing ways.

What is Australian popular music? What is Aotearoa/New Zealand popular music? Of course, an entire country cannot demonstrate a singular sound that can be said to be "Australian" or "Aotearoa/New Zealand."[2] These challenging questions have equally challenging answers that lie beyond any simple description of a genre or style or instrument or concepts of national identity. Instead, as a starting point for the international reader, it is useful to highlight the numerous, globally recognizable Australian and Aotearoa/New Zealand artists who have entered the global rock, pop, and "world music" pantheon via chart success, critical kudos, or their influence on other artists. Australia has introduced the world to Kylie Minogue, Air Supply, Little River Band, AC/DC, Rick Springfield, Helen Reddy, Men at Work, Nick Cave, The Go-Betweens, Midnight Oil, Jet, Yothu Yindi, INXS, Savage Garden, Gurrumul, and, more recently, Courtney Barnett. Aotearoa/New Zealand has produced Split Enz, The Flight of the Conchords, Moana and the Moahunters, The Clean, The Chills, OMC, Shihad (also known as Pacifier), Bic Runga, and Lorde, and (arguably a joint effort between both countries) Crowded House. Indeed, both Australia and Aotearoa/New Zealand have rich musical histories that speak across, as well as beyond, the Tasman Sea. They are bound together, not just because of proximity, but also through their colonial and post-colonial histories, which have indelibly shaped how pop and rock industries, institutions, and imaginaries have unfolded in both countries.

Indigenous Histories, Colonizers and Musical Life

Although this book focuses on the contemporary state of popular music in the post-colonial nation states of Australia and Aotearoa/New Zealand, it is important to note their indigenous pasts which, in no small way, inform the current state of popular music in both countries. Prior to European invasion and colonization, both countries had robust indigenous cultures, which themselves relied on a wide variety of song and dance as part of numerous rituals and ceremonies. Australia has an unusual and complex history, which, of course, does not simply start with the "discovery" of Australia by various European ships in the 1600s, the charting of the east coast by James Cook, the establishment of British penal colonies, and the subsequent expansion of the Empire during the 1700s. Australia was (and is) home to diverse tribes of Aboriginal and Torres Strait Islander people for many millennia; today they are recognized as the oldest living culture on Earth and have strong connections with the land. Indigenous culture is preserved through oral rather than written traditions, and includes songs to pass on values, family histories, verbal maps of the land, and more. Around the time of colonization, it was regarded that these two distinct cultural groups of Indigenous Australians shared over 250 different languages and 700 dialects between them, spread across the vast continent. Today, for many reasons—most notably the brutal and deadly conflict that caused the decline of the Indigenous population by around 90 percent during the first century or so after colonization—perhaps fewer than twenty indigenous languages remain. This may give the perception that now there are only a few Indigenous cultural groups and that these have contemporary musical traditions which are easily defined. On the contrary, Indigenous instruments and performance practices still exist and, importantly, they vary greatly across Australia; the globally-recognizable didgeridoo, for example, is not a traditional instrument for all Aboriginal people—it originates from the very far north of Australia in Arnhem Land. It can be broadly said, however, that sacred and secular ceremonies involving song and dance, as well as Songlines about Creation Stories known as *The Dreaming*; the latter being an integral part of Indigenous culture, whereby a spiritual connection to the land is enacted and reinforced.

Like Australia, Aotearoa/New Zealand was mapped out by James Cook. The local population were Māori—descended from travellers from Polynesia from approximately the thirteenth and fourteenth centuries. In Aotearoa/New Zealand, the extensive network of Māori *iwi* (tribes) that populated both the North and South Island saw song and dance as a central part of their ecosystem. Much of this was centered around life on the *marae* (meeting house), where many life events, for example births, deaths, and marriages, were marked by a culture of song and dance. *Waiata* (songs) take many different forms, from ritual songs such as lullabies, to laments about the death of a family or tribal member, to love songs. *Waiata* have become a part of the wider culture of Aotearoa/New Zealand, and can often be heard as part of any number of ceremonies held by Pākehā (the Māori term for white European settlers and their descendants) and others. Notably, Split Enz's first international hit album, released in 1981, was titled *Waiata*, and in Australia, where it was recorded, it was given the title *Corroboree*, a term from a specific Aboriginal dialect that has been used controversially by British settlers and others to refer generally to all Aboriginal song and dance ceremonies.

What is the historical and current relationship between the colonizers and the indigenous peoples for each country, and how is this played out in popular music?[3] The answer is undoubtedly complex. One of the most influential events in Aotearoa/New Zealand that reveals much about this relationship is the signing of the Treaty of Waitangi between Māori and British leaders in 1840. This founding document recognized the sovereignty of the British over the country and ostensibly extended those same rights to Māori *iwi*. It became clear almost immediately, however, that this was not the case, a point of legal fact which was later recognized with the establishment of the Waitangi Tribunal in the mid-1970s. This was a precedent-setting legal case that sought, and continues to seek, to redress historical wrongs regarding the displacement of thousands of Māori from their land. This particular historical injustice, among many others, has long politicized Māori (and some Pākehā) culture. The Tribunal arrived at a watershed moment in the mid-1970s, when a revival of te reo Māori (Māori language) was well under way, and the *hikoi* (stepping out), or the Land March, of 1975 which saw thousands of protesters, Māori and Pākehā, travel the length of the North Island on foot to raise awareness of the numerous injustices regarding the confiscation of native land. This moment galvanized a disenfranchised Māori population and opened up a space in the national imaginary for what would emerge as a newly politicized indigenous music-making culture, one which over the ensuing decades profoundly shaped popular music in Aotearoa/New Zealand.

There is no similar treaty between Indigenous Australians and the British. The day marking the anniversary of the arrival of the First Fleet of eleven convict ships and the raising of the British flag on 26 January 1788 is today known as "Australia Day"—a controversial day on which the government celebrates the modern nation, while Indigenous Australians (and others) mourn with sorrowful reflection on the invasion, war, stolen land, and resulting bloodshed (it is colloquially also known as either "Invasion Day" or "Survival Day"). Numerous other injustices have been inflicted upon Indigenous Australians since then, most notably government policies of forcibly removing Aboriginal and Torres Strait children from their families as part of a devastating assimilation directive that continued until the 1970s. Those who were removed from their land, families, heritage, and, of course, musical culture, are known as the Stolen Generation. There have been many contemporary songs about the

Stolen Generation; perhaps the most well-known is "Took the Children Away" (1990) by Aboriginal singer/songwriter Archie Roach. Only relatively recently, in 2008, did the Australian federal government formally apologize to the Stolen Generation, via a landmark speech by the then-Prime Minister Kevin Rudd. Today, there are numerous national and community events that recognize and promote Indigenous Australians, such as Sorry Day and NAIDOC (National Aborigines and Islanders Day Observance Committee) Week, however the relationship between government and Indigenous people may still be considered to be fraught with unresolved conflict.

The music made today by indigenous people in Australia and Aotearoa/New Zealand is, of course, influenced by other sounds and traditions, a result of syncretism and hybridization. Some influences come from outside, some come from within. In Australian contexts, "there has ... been a great deal of mutual influence and partial adoption of practices, beliefs and values among different Aboriginal groups. This historical context suggests that anything 'cultural' is better understood as always already 'inter-'" (Ottosson 2009, 100).

Such interplay and cross-fertilization is also seen in Aotearoa/New Zealand, especially with regard to popular music: "the indigenous Māori and the Pacific immigrant communities ... have been major pop music proponents and have utilised and adapted various pop styles over the years, often using them to combat histories of colonisation and oppression" (Zemke-White 2005, 95).

In both countries, indigenous peoples have their own long-established musical traditions and a rich set of wider music-based practices that sit outside accepted popular music histories. However, many aspects of these deep-seated musical cultures have found their way into the popular music mainstream, from song styles to instruments and instrumentation. This has raised issues about cultural appropriation and fetishization, particularly around the category of "traditional" music. Even so, as a number of scholars have noted—including authors in *Made in Australia and Aotearoa/New Zealand*—the spread among indigenous musicians of popular music genres (jazz, folk, country, rock, reggae, pop, and more) has also provided moments of syncretism in which self-determination has been forcefully articulated, reclaiming global genres as tools of protest, solidarity, and sovereignty.

How do Australians and New Zealanders (both indigenous and non-indigenous) regard the popular music from their own country? Sometimes with pride and pleasure. It can also be argued, however, that there is a quiet anxiousness about originality, influence, and appropriation. This includes the incorporation of indigenous sounds and instrumentation into pop and rock songs, of which there is a long and complicated history. This may be expressed as a "cultural cringe," where domestic music is dismissed as "not good enough," or deemed, perhaps, as a pale imitation of an overseas artist. A similar issue is the "tall poppy syndrome," where musicians who are successful, particularly with international audiences, are disparaged at home precisely for their success. Over the last few decades, these sorts of dismissals have been countered in part by a concerted effort to bolster cultural nationalisms in each country through policy initiatives and a pro-active strategy to promote popular music intra-nationally and internationally. At various points in time, from the 1970s onward, governments in both countries have put in place programs and policies designed to cultivate, support, and promote music made locally, all of these with varying degrees of success and not without their critics. The interventions of the state are very much symptomatic of a post-colonial nationalism, a sensibility that has shaped how popular music is seen as a vital part of both a sense of identity as well as a branding tool.

Australia and Aotearoa/New Zealand's separate and joint contributions to popular music have unfolded in relation to each other in senses that give the region a distinctive place in the global musical canon. The history of popular music in each country is one bound up in the complex relationships of syncretism that can only emerge from multicultural nations, ranging from transnationalization, translocalism, hybridization, and creolization. It is a history in which settlers and their descendants have borrowed from indigenous repertoires, and vice versa; where migrants connect with their homelands as well as integrate into local custom and ritual, and it is a history of music-making that taps into international musical idioms and works to domesticate them. This variegated process of localization takes many musical forms and social shapes and it confounds the stock standard cultural imperialism charge that is sometimes leveled at popular music in both countries (see Mitchell 1994; Keam and Mitchell 2011; Shuker 2008). Variations of rock, pop, reggae, soul, hip-hop, and dance music from Australasia have all made important contributions to the global jukebox, often taking the form of musical expression that draws from the region's rich and well-established musical histories and traditions. The following section points out how these myriad sounds—and the individuals, industries, and institutions that made them possible—are products of each country's own complex colonial and post-colonial histories, the unique movements and migrations, and the geo-political configurations which make up this part of the globe, as well as Australia and Aotearoa/New Zealand's deep connection to one another.

Popular Music: Histories, Distance, Genres

> Aotearoa, rugged individual
> Glisten like a pearl
> At the bottom of the world
> The tyranny of distance
> Didn't stop the cavalier
> So why should it stop me
> I'll conquer and stay free.
>
> (Split Enz, "Six Months in a Leaky Boat," 1982)

The "tyranny of distance" referred to here by Split Enz singer Tim Finn, who has spent much of his professional and personal life divided between both Australia and Aotearoa/New Zealand, is a trope that has long bound together both countries. Drawing on the now famous phrase coined by Australian historian Geoffrey Blainey for the purpose of his 1966 book, Finn speaks to a sensibility shared by descendants of European colonizers/settlers in these two nations, claimed by the British as outposts at the edge of the Empire. The "tyranny" has taken hold of each country's sense of an "imagined community" (Anderson 2006 [1983]) in different ways over the course of their recent histories, ranging from a cultural cringe borne of a deep-rooted cultural anxiety, to more muscular, often over-determined, assertions of national identity. Both tyranny and distance take other forms too, in relation to the treatment of each country's indigenous populations and how, when, and where they do and do not figure in this imagined community's sense of national identity. Tyranny and distance also give shape to the particular experiences of migrants, their connections to their new home and their homelands. Popular music has been one site where these fraught notions of post-colonial nationalism are often worked out and upon. In Australia and Aotearoa/New Zealand, the emergence, consolidation, and maturation of popular music industries and institutions have underpinned this in a complicated fashion. As a consequence, the notion of distance resonates and inflects how popular music mediates fundamental sociospatial relationships for both Australia and Aotearoa/New Zealand: the near and the far, the local and global, home and away, the colonized and the colonizer, the settler, the indigenous peoples, and the migrant.

In both Australia and Aotearoa/New Zealand, the manner in which the music and recording industries and popular music cultures and practices unfolded, intra- and internationally, and in relation to one another, can be seen as parables about the emergence and maturation of post-colonial nationalism. The framing of popular music, from jazz to rock to punk and beyond, by the media, the authorities, musicians, and fans (and, it should be noted, popular music scholars) says a great deal about the uneasy ways in which Aotearoa/New Zealand and Australia have evolved into distinctly post-colonial nation states. Jazz and rock, for example, are noteworthy demonstrations of how popular music provides a locus of activity around which it is possible to read not only a "structure of feeling" of a given era (Williams 1977), but also point to the complicated settling in of genres.

In the early days of sound recording, the two countries had few domestic recording studios, let alone pressing plants, which meant that much of the early marketing and sales of recorded music relied upon overseas sources, coming from either the UK or the US. Local markets were thus dominated primarily by voices and musicians from overseas, with only a few exceptions. With the global spread of jazz, through recordings and sheet music, in the late 1910s and 1920s, an important vehicle for local talent appeared. In Australia, although the first international jazz bands would not appear live until the early 1920s, local bands drew from already extant dance bands, vaudeville, and earlier minstrel tours that traveled through both Australia and Aotearoa/New Zealand at the turn of the nineteenth century, music interpreted very much at a distance. As early jazz evolved in Australia, it adopted what could be unkindly called a particular kind of blandness that tempered the American genre's sensuality (as well as its racialized roots) to make it palatable for the predominantly white audiences who were used to European standards of dance music decorum. Jazz in Aotearoa/New Zealand took a different tack, as many local jazz bands were often made up of Māori, Pasifika (a term used to describe the diasporic communities of the Pacific Islands), and Pākehā musicians (and bands were often a multi-ethnic mix). In this case, their reference points were often drawn from Polynesia as much as America, singing in English, sometimes translating these songs into te reo Māori, as well as incorporating Polynesian instruments and instrumentation (see Bourke 2010). A similar sort of "whitening" took place when rock'n'roll emerged in Australia and Aotearoa/New Zealand in the mid-to-late 1950s, in countries characterized by contradictions and tensions which gave the emergence of rock'n'roll in each country its peculiar local flavor. Both countries were still living under the shadow of an oppressive puritanism, in a climate immediately following concern about impending nuclear war, and a fear of the "Yellow Peril" (immigration from Asia). It was also a period which saw waves of immigrants from Europe, often to help build national infra-structures (highways, dams, etc.), as well as rapid suburbanization and urbanization. There was also an expanding, and more affluent, middle class, as well as the appearance of a younger class of consumer. In the latter case, youth culture was heavily scrutinized by the authorities in each country, and as young people adopted subcultural styles and consumed pop culture from local and international sources, much like generations of adults before them, the inevitable moral panics came to possess the local and national press. In Australia, the Church, police, government, and press served to act as cultural gatekeepers, and the appearance of rock'n'roll was seen by those in power as a harbinger of musical and social upheaval. As a result, early attempts at localizing rock'n'roll in Australia followed some of the similar patterns of domesticating jazz, meaning certain aspects of its African American elements were exorcised. This meant that

> mainstream acceptance of rock 'n' roll was premised on transforming it into melodic music without a strong backbeat and sung without emotional emphasis, music derived from the European musical tradition; respectable music, that is, without an African-American 'primitive' rhythm and blues influence. Establishing rock 'n' roll as having a 'jazz' lineage meant, in white Australia, giving it as far as possible a white, dance music heritage. This would justify 'toning down' rock 'n' roll for white, local consumption even more than [Bill] Haley had already done for white, American teenagers.
>
> (Stratton 2007, 390)

The muted emergence of rock'n'roll in each country—both still dominated by a very conservative culture centered around the family and home—was immediately a concern because of threats of youthful rebellion. The case of rock'n'roll, and its evolution into rock, was also met with anxieties about cultural imperialism that paradoxically sat alongside an ongoing fascination with American popular culture. Indeed,

> a common characteristic of most rock'n'roll performers … was the appropriation of 'America' as the source of their style. This 'America' was distilled as we have seen, not only through records, radio, magazines [and] Hollywood films but also, decisively, through the importation of American entertainment.
>
> (Zion 1989, 170)

This particular discursive framing of rock'n'roll was often how two of the era's biggest local stars, Johnny O'Keefe (from Australia) and Johnny Devlin (from Aotearoa/New Zealand, later emigrating to Australia), were sometimes dismissed as lesser knockoffs of American stars such as Bill Haley for O'OKeefe and Elvis Presley for Devlin. The paradigm shift into the rock era signaled a move away from American influence in certain respects, pointing to the manner in which the anxiety of influence was still caught between seeing Britain as a bastion of high/good culture and America as low/bad culture. Jon Stratton makes this clear in another discussion regarding the arrival of Beat music in the 1960s, where the success of local bands in Australia during this earlier period of rock'n'roll was transitioning into rock. He suggests that it is possible to argue for "cultural influence," but that any sort of

8 • Shelley Brunt and Geoff Stahl

meaningful and productive analysis needs get away from simply reasserting charges of cultural imperialism and the power of Anglo-American hegemonies for "nothing is gained in the understanding of Australian popular music by talking simply in terms of derivation and imitation" (Stratton 2003, 332).

Popular Music Industries

Post-colonial nationalism in Australia and Aotearoa/New Zealand often means that the government adopts either an interventionist or a laissez-faire approach to culture. In the case of the former, a broadcast medium such as radio (and later television) proved to be an ideal tool for promoting culture on a wide scale. In each case, the guiding principles for government-funded public radio were very much shaped by John Reith and his vision for the BBC, namely that public radio had a "civilizing" function. This meant that content was made up typically of classical music, new stories, drama, children's programming, and the like, and where high culture was privileged over popular culture (reflecting the prevailing the British cultural legacy). Whereas Australia had a mixed model of commercial and public broadcasting, Aotearoa/New Zealand's airwaves were monopolized by the government for many decades longer, until pirate radio station Radio Hauraki (founded offshore of Auckland in 1966) was given an official license to broadcast on the FM radio band (in 1970). This opening up of the airwaves for commercial broadcasters across the nation provided a new avenue for international and local rock and pop to find a larger audience.

In Australia, where commercial and public broadcasting sat side by side, the appearance of two more stations would further strengthen its connections to global musical flows. Special Broadcast Service (SBS) was an important conduit for local musical content, both in its initial radio format, founded in 1975, and then when it launched its television wing, in 1979. As a member of the European Broadcasting Union, it connected many of the post-war immigrant communities in Australia to televisual content they could not otherwise access, including popular music programing. It also opened up a European market to some of the lesser-known musical artists coming out of Australia in the 1980s. The other development which did much to undergird Australian pop and rock was the emergence of a national network. One of the Australian Broadcasting Corporation's (ABC's) key radio stations aimed at the national youth demographic was Sydney-based Triple J, previously known as 2JJ and launched in 1975 on the AM band. Triple J is an FM station that reached other capital cities from 1989, and was rolled out to Australia's vast regional centers throughout the 1990s as part of the National Youth Network (Australian Broadcasting Corporation 2014). The cultural impact of Triple J on youth and the promotion of popular music in Australia cannot be overstated; some highlights include the annual music countdown "Hottest 100," which the nation tunes in to each January, and "Unearthed," where music from emerging bands is aired (and is now its own digital station).[4]

The freeing up of FM frequencies was paralleled by the rise of popular music on screen. In Aotearoa/New Zealand, where television arrived in the 1960s (which was considered to be "late"), it was highly regulated and offered limited channels for much of its first two decades. Even so, popular music was there at its inception, seen in programs such as *In the Groove* (1962), *C'Mon* (1966), while pop show *Ready to Roll* and music video show *Radio with Pictures* ran from the 1970s until the mid-to-late 1980s. Across the ditch in Australia, a small selection of variety shows appeared on television from the late 1950s and early 1960s. *Your Hit Parade* was one of the first (1958), *Bandstand* (1958) and *Six O'Clock Rock* (1959) were among others. These early formats tended to feature overseas talent, or people miming to recent hits, with only a spare few appearances of local bands and artists, such that the history of rock music on Australian television can be seen as "cultural domination or straight borrowing: in this case, of both the music and the program format" (Stockbridge 1992, 68). The long running ABC music television show *Countdown* (1974–1987) offered a corrective to this through its informative yet unpredictable interviews by the enthusiastic host Ian "Molly" Meldrum, and provided a platform for local talent to perform live (which often meant lip-synching) on stage to a studio audience. *Countdown's* demise coincided with the arrival of the global MTV format to Australia, but the program's cult status today is recognized by the rebroadcast of interesting segments on television and YouTube, as well as a biopic about Meldrum. Beyond *Countdown*, there have been numerous successful music video shows such as *Video Hits* (1987–2011) and the long running *rage* (1987–present), as well as contemporary music quiz shows.[5]

Key Moments in Popular Music

Pop and rock music, as well as the industries associated with them, in Aotearoa/New Zealand and Australia matured substantially during the 1970s and 1980s, though at different rates. This was in large part because each country's government had begun to recognize, to varying degrees, both the value of musical culture to local economies and also its potential to serve as an iconic cultural commodity and thus a viable export in the global marketplace. In 1970s Australia, the ability for a band to gain a national following was aided by numerous factors, including national booking agencies and record labels (Homan 2008, 603), as well as the national pub venue circuit where touring bands could be promoted via capital city radio stations and music television shows. "Oz Rock" was one particular style and scene of music most recognizable at this time and into the 1990s, best described as "a group of (mostly male) performers and bands regarded as identifiably 'Australian' in their performance attitudes and techniques" (ibid, 601), perhaps best characterized by bands such as Cold Chisel. By the mid-1980s, the Australian pop-rock nexus was becoming a global force, courtesy of the international success of Men at Work, INXS, Kylie Minogue, among many others, who were sometimes willing and unwilling ambassadors for Australian culture. Men at Work's famous song "Land Down Under" articulates one experience of being an Australian abroad:

> These lyrics function as a first-person narrative, as in the Oz Rock ballad-based tradition, here about an Australian travelling Europe 'in a fried-out combie.' The chorus, constructed as a response to the first-person narrator, the traveller, operates in a form of a more or less didactic, critical, political statement . . .
>
> (Stratton 2006, 250)

The "statement" mentioned above is, in the words of lyricist Colin Hay, "about celebrating the country, but not in a nationalistic way," while also lamenting "the selling of Australia . . .

overdevelopment ... [and] the plundering of the country by greedy people" (cited in Stratton 2006, 251). A sentiment of discontent was shared by many other artists at the time, and intensified in the lead up to Australia's Bicentenary celebrations, held on Australia Day in 1988. Considering it was a celebration of the First Fleet invasion 200 years previously, the Bicentenary was a flashpoint for Aboriginal and non-Aboriginal musicians who took this as a moment to challenge the status quo. One of the most outspoken to protest the anniversary was Yothu Yindi, a multi-racial band that sang in both English and Yolngu and performed using a mix of indigenous and rock instruments. As they expressed in "Treaty"—a song which had several versions, remixes, and accompanying music videos—the band demanded the immediate fulfilment of then-Prime Minister "Bob Hawke's 1988 promise to conclude a treaty between Aboriginal people and post-Cook colonists" (Hayward 1993, 35).[6] The band achieved global success with this song—and its incarnations—under the industry classification of "world music." This raised some salient questions about the nature of what Karl Neuenfeldt has called "ethno-pop" (1991), and Yothu Yindi's ambassadorial function in relation to cultural nationalism, and how they might be articulated to other global issues, such as the struggle for indigenous rights unfolding elsewhere.

In Aotearoa/New Zealand, the pace of change was slower and anything that might be called "Kiwi rock" in the 1970s is a more complicated notion as a result. As Britain formed new trading relationships with the European Union (EU) and the European Economic Community (EEC), finalized in 1973, the country's access to European markets was substantially curtailed and, exacerbated by the oil crisis, which saw the country plunge into a deep recession for much of the decade. This happened in tandem with a rise in Māori activism, the Treaty of Waitangi Act 1975, a call for a strengthening of te reo Māori, along with environmental and anti-nuclear protests but it was not until punk and the early 1980s that a recording renaissance took hold in New Zealand among Pākehā, Māori, and Pacific Islanders. There were artists at the time who enjoyed local, trans-Tasman, and international success. Split Enz was the most notable export at the time, but bands such as Dragon were leaving significant impressions on the charts and elsewhere. It was the late 1970s into the early 1980s when popular music entered into a much more productive phase. This was also signaled by an embrace of reggae on a large-scale fashion, primarily by Māori and Pasifika artists, who found an affinity with reggae's politics and its sound. Although reggae had some influence on music in the early 1970s, Bob Marley's 1979 concert in Auckland was a watershed moment in the country's music-making, as was the highly anticipated two-week run of *The Harder They Come*, featuring Jimmy Cliff, and released in the same year. Originally released in 1973, the film had been banned in order to prevent "black youth [being given] any encouragement in the wrong direction" (Hawkeswood, cited in Cattermole 2013, 113). Many artists and bands emerged shortly afterwards, comprised mainly of Māori and Pasifika musicians who borrowed from their own local and island musical histories and instruments to create syncretic variants of dub and reggae (and later electronic variants such as jungle and drum'n'bass). The Polynesian band Herbs in particular enjoyed national and international success in taking up an indigenously hybridized reggae as a political tool, at the forefront of Pacific reggae, offering up songs which focused on anti-nuclear, anti-apartheid, and anti-colonialist themes the musical results of which become an important touchstone of Aotearoa/New Zealand's soundscape (see Cattermole 2013; Turner 2011; Henderson 2014).

The early 1980s was a significant moment in Aotearoa/New Zealand musical history, a moment when the laissez-faire approach to culture was at its peak, abetted by the adoption of neo-liberalization of the economy on a scale that was unmatched elsewhere in the world. As the state, under a Labour government, withdrew from its social welfare contract and started selling off its state owned assets, at a moment when political protest reached its most potent moment as a result of the Springboks tour in 1981 and later the Queen Street riot in 1984 (which erupted around a DD Smash concert), pop and rock culture started to find the traction which underpinned its successes throughout the 1980s and beyond. During this lively period, the independent label Flying Nun and its mythical "Dunedin Sound" found chart success locally and a cult following overseas. So too did Patea Māori Club's song "Poi E," which married African American electro-boogie and te reo Māori. The band Moana and the Moahunters also achieved national and international success with songs that melded Māori *haka* (chant) and custom into an amalgam of rap, hip hop, and reggae, among others, dedicated to celebrating and supporting indigenous culture.

In most cases, the local and occasional international success of bands at the time masked a more serious reality: that much of the music industry in Australia and Aotearoa/New Zealand was still beholden to the major record labels, where most of the domestic revenue generated was through the dominance of international artists on television, radio, and in the music press. Although the independent scenes in each country thrived, local mainstream pop on commercial airwaves remained marginalized with only a few exceptions. In Aotearoa/New Zealand, by the end of the 1980s, the government was beginning to recognize the value of its popular music industry and had established NZ on Air (NZOA), to provide seed money for bands and artists to develop locally as well as ensure they got their products heard overseas. This important development was undermined in part by a pop and rock music marketplace that still remained a relatively laissez-faire one, where artists still had to fend for themselves. For example, whereas other countries had introduced quotas for local content on radio, including Australia, in Aotearoa/New Zealand these remained voluntary due in part to global free trade agreements to which the government was bound. By the 1990s, popular music in Australia and Aotearoa/New Zealand had become part of the "promotional state" apparatus (Cloonan 1999). In the late 1990s, Aotearoa/New Zealand's Labour Prime Minister Helen Clark (1999–2008), who was also Minister for Culture and Heritage, looked to the UK's Labour, in particular, Tony Blair's Third Way policies, and assimilated many of those ideas into cultural policy at home. Funding and support for the arts increased dramatically during her tenure, leading to what Michael Scott has called Aotearoa/New Zealand's "pop renaissance" (Scott 2008). Seeing this as a new nexus of state and industry interests, he suggests that:

Within this state-mediated 'institutional ecology' ... of pop production, commercial radio programmers, formats, and genres influence which artists receive NZOA subsidies and plugger assistance ... As most musicians and small labels are unable to afford the time, green fees, or expense accounts required to transact with programmers, NZOA takes the form of a quasi-record label; institutionalising networks, connexity, and social capital ... NZOA manages the supply of artists in partnership with both labels and broadcasters, subsidies become a calculated state investment conditioned by the economic and cultural logics of the commercial broadcast.

(Scott 2008, 304)

From its inception, NZOA was primary backer of the late 1990s and early 2000s pop renaissance. It underwrote a number of musical successes, a period where a Māori and Pasifika renaissance was also being fomented, finding new musical lexicons in hip hop, r'n'b, dub, and electronic dance music with which to enunciate a new kind of identity. Upper Hutt Posse, Scribe, and others articulated a politics around *tino rangatiratanga* (Māori sovereignty) that landed them chart success, fostering a burgeoning hip-hop culture that reached its apotheosis under the auspices of NZOA, while also rearticulating the struggle of Māori (and Pasifika people) by finding an affinity in Māori oral traditions, notably *patere* (rap), *whakarongo* (listen up), and *wainua* (attitude) (Mitchell 1994).

Into the twenty-first century, both Australia and Aotearoa/New Zealand have continued to contribute to the global popular music jukebox in their own unique ways. The overseas success of Aotearoa/New Zealand's Lorde (see Chapter 3) and her rapid rise to fame saw her co-writing with internationally established songwriters, being shoulder-tapped by David Bowie and appearing on the soundtrack for the successful *Hunger Games* film franchise. In a duet collaboration which spanned the Tasman Sea, Australia's Gotye paired with Aotearoa/New Zealand's Kimbra for the Grammy Award-winning song "Somebody I Used to Know" (2011), and brought both countries to global attention. Concomitant with these success stories, has been Australia's participation in the Eurovision Song Contest, sparking a new (or renewed) interest in Australian music by Europeans. As unusual a pairing as it may seem, the Eurovision Song Contest has long been a fixture in the lives of Australians since it was first broadcast locally by public service broadcaster SBS in 1985 (Brunt and Giuffre 2015). To mark the thirtieth anniversary of this broadcast, and also the sixtieth anniversary of Eurovision itself, Australia was granted a wild-card entry to compete on the European/global stage.[7] While this speaks to Australia's ever expanding (multi-)cultural identity, it is not an uncomplicated arrangement, as Jennifer Carniel (2017) recently suggested:

> [A]s a site of European colonization and immigration, Australia is, at least theoretically, ideologically and culturally aligned with the majority of European nation states involved in the contest; that is, despite its geography, Australia has until recent times largely been constructed, and constructed itself, to be of the West, and much of its national psychology has been shaped by the so-called 'tyranny of distance' from its ostensible ideological motherland.
>
> (13)

As Australia and Aotearoa/New Zealand grapple with their status as post-colonial nation states, as their orientations shift more explicitly to the Pacific and Asia, as they deal with ongoing issues with their indigenous peoples, and at the same time they bear witness to demographic changes due to new waves of immigration, that "tyranny of distance" is once more differently inflected, giving popular music cultures in both countries yet another distinctive cast.

Popular Music "Made In" the City

As we have demonstrated in this introduction, the national musical imaginary of both Australia and Aotearoa/New Zealand has been forged through local histories, as well as regional and global relationships. One site where these popular music practices and conversations come to the fore is in these countries' cities, echoing, in some form or other, the urban tropes the legendary Australian band Skyhooks sing about in their classic song "This is My City" (1976).

> Well I'm back in the land of second chances,
> And rock'n'roll shows where nobody dances
> Back in the land of chicken and chips,
> Mars bars and roadside tips
> And if you don't like it,
> Then that's too bad,
> Cos it's the only city that we've ever had.

Such music can take many forms: bands draw inspiration from living, working, and playing in urban centers; songs give emotional contours to cities via sonic and lyrical signifiers; fans and audiences sustain local scenes; rehearsal spaces offer contexts for musical collaboration and performance; large-scale festivals impart a sense of spectacle to cities; and gigs at small venues provide opportunities for moments of shared intimacy. In these and other important respects, popular music gives unique shape to the socio-musical experience of urban life.

In the cities of Australia and Aotearoa/New Zealand, urban music-making comprises a vital part of larger social, material, and symbolic dimensions that have lent definition and meaning to each city's unique identity (for example, "Melbourne: Australia's Live Music Capital" or "The Dunedin Sound"). Music-making in this context is also characterized and strengthened by regionally specific musical networks, where the local, the transnational, and the global intersect in promising as well as problematic fashion. For migrants or diasporic groups, for example, performing popular music associated with national culture can articulate a sense of identity that can be both "here" and "there". Making music in Australasian cities matters, then, in a myriad of ways that take on a distinctive regional cast and significance.

This edited collection is designed to consider many of these issues, focusing on "the city" as a sub-theme. Some of these ideas were first trialed at conferences held in Melbourne in 2013—"This is My City: Popular Music and the Urban Experience" (RMIT University) and "Cultural Economy: The Next Generation" (Monash University). Both events brought together scholars from the region and invited speakers from overseas. The convenors considered the material being discussed to be an important addition to ongoing discussions about popular music and urban culture, from the musealization of rock'n'roll, to guided tours, to changes in policy affecting the live music scene in many cities in both countries. For this reason, this collection is somewhat unique in the *Made In . . .* series, as it does not attempt to provide an overview of each country's popular music culture broadly understood. It does, however, offer an album of snapshots that captures key aspects of what is happening in both Australia and Aotearoa/New Zealand's major urban centers, exploring along the way a number of key issues which speak to the unique nature of popular music in both countries.

When considering the industries that generate, maintain, and promote popular music, a passing mention must be made of the academic infrastructure that enables scholars to research and teach popular music in Australia and Aotearoa/New Zealand. There are a number of popular music-related degrees and courses offered on both sides of the Tasman Sea which have produced Masters and PhD graduates with dissertations and projects devoted to locally germane issues. A cursory glance at the list of the authors for this book and their affiliated institutions in the "Notes on Contributors" provides an indication (albeit an incomplete list) of such universities. The region is also supported by the journal *Perfect Beat: The Asia-Pacific Journal of Research into Contemporary Music and Popular Culture*. It was originally established in 1992 through Macquarie University, with a focus on articles about Aotearoa/New Zealand, Australia, and the Pacific Islands and had a subtitle (*The Pacific Journal . . .*) which reflected this. In 2014, the new editorial team included "Asia" in the title to recognize the growth of Asian popular music studies alongside the Australia and Aotearoa/New Zealand region (Brunt, Wilson, and Strong 2014). Currently the journal is focused on current and historical issues concerning the greater region, and it continues its long-standing tradition of giving voice to local activists, community groups, and artists. This sentiment is shared by the region's key academic body for scholars: the "Australia and New Zealand" (ANZ) branch of the International Association for the Study of Popular Music (IASPM). IASPM-ANZ is an active and vocal advocate for the field of popular music studies, and is represented by strong membership numbers. The executive committee is typically comprised of a mix of scholars residing in either country, and there is an annual conference alternately hosted in Australia and Aotearoa/New Zealand. Many scholars from IASPM-ANZ share their research here in this timely edited collection about popular music from the region.

Notes

1   There are few publications that focus on the popular music from both countries. For a discussion specifically about popular music studies in Australasia and its relationship to ethnomusicology, see Bendrups (2013).

2   Australia and Aotearoa/New Zealand are relatively small countries population-wise. Population clocks in mid-July 2017 estimated that 4.7 million people live in Aotearoa/New Zealand (Stats NZ Tatauranga Aotearoa, 2017) and 24.5 million live in Australia (Australian Bureau of Statistics, 2017).

3   Our brief and incomplete summary here is only intended as an introduction to establish a context for the chapters within the book, which is about popular music, not traditional music. We instead encourage our international readers to investigate the answer to this critical question via the many books about Australian and Aotearoa/New Zealand history.

4   Many scholars and music journalists have documented the history and politics surrounding this notable Australian radio station. See Hope and Turner (2015) and Maalsen and Mclean (2016) as a recent starting point for further investigation, as well as the official ABC website.

5   An important summary of the impact of *Countdown* and its host Molly Meldrum, as well as other music television programs, is provided by Liz Giuffre (2013). An insider's account of the cult late night music video program *rage* can be found in the 2015 PhD thesis by Narelle Gee, the former head programmer.

6   The politics of the song "Treaty" has been well documented by Australian music scholars. For further reading, see Stubington and Dunbar-Hall (1994) and the 1993 first volume and second issue of the journal *Perfect Beat*.

7   Four Australians—Jessica Mauboy, Dami Im, Guy Sebastian, and Isaiah Firebrace—have now represented Australia as contestants or as an interval act.

Bibliography

Anderson, Benedict. 2006 [1983]. *Imagined Communities: Reflections on the Origin and Spread of Nationalism.* New York: Verso Books.

Australian Broadcasting Corporation (ABC). 2014. "Triple J Goes National." *Beat the Drum: Celebrating 40 Years of Triple J.* www.abc.net.au/triplej/events/beatthedrum/40years/milestones/7 (accessed June 29, 2017).

Australian Bureau of Statistics. 2017, 26 June. "Population Clock." www.abs.gov.au/ausstats/abs%40.nsf/94713ad 445ff1425ca25682000192af2/1647509ef7e25faaca2568a900154b63?OpenDocument (accessed June 26, 2017).

Bendrups, Dan. 2013. "Popular Music Studies and Ethnomusicology in Australasia." *IASPM@Journal: Journal of the International Association for the Study of Popular Music* 3 (2) 1–15.

Blainey, Geoffrey. 1966. *The Tyranny of Distance: How Distance Shaped Australia's History.* Sydney: Macmillan.

Bourke, Chris. 2010. *Blue Smoke: The Lost Dawn of New Zealand Popular Music, 1918–1964.* Auckland: Auckland University Press.

Breen, Marcus. 1989. *Our Place, Our Music: Aboriginal Music.* Sydney: Aboriginal Studies Press.

Brunt, Shelley and Liz Giuffre. 2015. "Starring Australia! Performing the Nation in Eurovision Song Contest." Paper presented at the 2015 International Association for the Study of Popular Music Conference, Australian National University, December 6.

Brunt, Shelley, Oli Wilson, and Catherine Strong. 2014. "'Lookin, Searchin, Seekin, Findin': A New Beat." *Perfect Beat: The Asia-Pacific Journal of Research into Contemporary Music and Popular Culture* 15 (2): 105–111.

Carniel, Jessica. 2017. "Welcome to Eurostralia: The Strategic Diversity of Australia at the Eurovision Song Contest." *Continuum* 31 (1): 13–23.

Cattermole, Jennifer. 2013. "Beyond the Black Atlantic: Black Outernationality and Afrocentrism in Aotearoa/New Zealand Roots Reggae." *Musicology Australia* 35 (1): 112–137.

Cloonan, Martin. 1999. "Pop and the Nation–State: Towards a Theorisation." *Popular Music* 18 (2): 193–207.

Gee, Narelle. 2015. "Maintaining Our Rage: Inside Australia's Longest-Running Music Video Program." PhD diss., Queensland University of Technology.

Giuffre, Liz. 2013. "Countdown and Cult Music Television Programmes: An Australian Case Study." *Intensities: The Journal of Cult Media* 6: 31–56.

Hayward, Philip. 1993. "Safe, Exotic and Somewhere Else: Yothu Yindi, *Treaty* and the Mediation of Aboriginality." *Perfect Beat* 1 (2): 33–42.

Hayward, Philip (ed.). 2016. *Sound Alliances: Indigenous Peoples, Cultural Politics, and Popular Music in the Pacific.* London: Bloomsbury Publishing.

Hayward, Philip (ed.). 1992. *From Pop, to Punk, to Postmodernism: Australian Popular Music and Culture from the 1960s to the 1990s.* North Sydney: Allen & Unwin.

Henderson, April K. 2014. "Māori Boys, Michael Jackson Dance Moves, and that 1984 Structure of Feeling." *MEDIANZ: Media Studies Journal of Aotearoa New Zealand* 13 (1): 77–96.

Homan, Shane. 2008. "An 'Orwellian Vision': Oz Rock Scenes and Regulation." *Continuum* 22 (5): 601–611.

Hope, Cathy and Bethany Turner. 2015. "The Battle to Open Australia's Airwaves: The Whitlam Government and Youth Station 2JJ." *Journal of Australian Studies* 39 (4): 494–510.

Johnson, Bruce. 2000. *The Inaudible Music: Jazz, Gender and Australian Modernity,* Sydney: Currency Press.

Keam, Glenda and Tony Mitchell, eds. 2011. *Home, Land and Sea: Situating Music in Aotearoa New Zealand,* Auckland: Pearson Educational.

Keith, Sarah and Giuffre, Liz. 2014. Off-Beat: SBS Music Programming [online]. *Metro Magazine: Media & Education Magazine* 179: 40–43. http://search.informit.com.au/documentSummary;dn=247269345202179; res=IELAPA (accessed August 27, 2017).

Maalsen, Sophia and Jessica Mclean. 2016. "Digging Up Unearthed Down-Under: A Hybrid Geography of a Musical Space that Essentialises Gender and Place." *Gender, Place & Culture* 23 (3):1–17.

Mitchell, Tony. 1994. "Maori and Polynesian Music in New Zealand." In *North Meets South,* edited by Philip Hayward, Tony Mitchell and Ron Shule. Sydney: Perfect Beat Publications, 53–72.

Neuenfeldt, Karl W. M. 1991. "To Sing a Song of Otherness: Anthros, Ethno-Pop and the Mediation of 'Public Problems.'" *Canadian Ethnic Studies* 23 (3): 92–118.

Ottosson, Åse. 2009. "Playing with Others and Selves: Australian Aboriginal Desert Musicians on Tour." *The Asia Pacific Journal of Anthropology* 10 (2): 98–114.

Scott, Michael. 2008. "The Networked State: New Zealand on Air and New Zealand's Pop Renaissance." *Popular Music* 27 (2): 299–305.

Shuker, Roy. 2008. "New Zealand Popular Music, Government Policy, and Cultural Identity." *Popular Music* 27 (2): 271–287.

Smith, Jo. 2011. "Aotearoa/New Zealand: An Unsettled State in a Sea of Islands." *Settler Colonial Studies* 1 (1): 111–131.

Stats NZ Tatauranga Aotearoa. 2017. "Population Clock." 27 June. http://www.stats.govt.nz/tools_and_services/ population_clock.aspx (accessed June 27, 2017).

16 • Shelley Brunt and Geoff Stahl

Stockbridge, S. 1992. "Rock Music on Australian TV." In *From Pop, to Punk, to Postmodernism: Australian Popular Music and Culture from the 1960s to the 1990s*, edited by Philip Hayward . North Sydney: Allen & Unwin, 68–85.

Stratton, Jon. 2007. "'All Rock and Rhythm and Jazz': Rock'n'Roll Origin Stories and Race in Australia." *Continuum: Journal of Media and Cultural Studies* 21 (3): 379–392.

Stratton, Jon. 2006. "Nation Building and Australian Popular Music in the 1970s and 1980s." *Continuum: Journal of Media & Cultural Studies* 20 (2): 243–252.

Stratton, Jon. 2003. "Whiter Rock: The 'Australian Sound' and the Beat Boom." *Continuum: Journal of Media and Cultural Studies* 17 (3): 331–346.

Stubington, Jill and Peter Dunbar-Hall. 1994. "Yothu Yindi's 'Treaty': Ganma in Music." *Popular Music* 13(3): 243–259.

Turner, Elizabeth. 2011. "Whats' be Happen? Analysing the Discourse of Reggae Lyrics" [online]. *Instruments of Change: Proceedings of the International Association for the Study of Popular Music Australia-New Zealand 2010 Conference*. Melbourne: International Association for the Study of Popular Music, 149–156. http://search.informit.com.au/documentSummary;dn=881539798154925;res=IELNZC (accessed August 27, 2017).

Whiteoak, John. 2002. "Popular Music, Militarism, Women, and the Early 'Brass Band' in Australia." *Australasian Music Research* 6: 27–48.

Williams, Raymond. 1977. *Marxism and Literature*. London: Oxford University Press.

Zemke–White, Kirsten. 2005. "Nesian Styles (Re) Present R'n'B: The Appropriation, Transformation and Realization of Contemporary R'n'B with Hip Hop by Urban Pasifika Groups in Aotearoa." *Sites: A Journal of Social Anthropology and Cultural Studies* 2 (1): 94–123.

Zion, Lawrence. 1989. "Disposable Icons: Pop Music in Australia, 1955–63." *Popular Music* 8 (2): 165–175.

Discography

Archie Roach. "Took the Children Away." Aurora, 1990, K10157.

Gotye. "Somebody That I Used to Know." Vertigo, 2011, ELEVENDPRO100.

Patea Maori Club. "Poi E." Maui Records, 1983, MAUI EP 001.

Skyhooks. "This Is My City." Mushroom Records, 1976, K-6487.

Split Enz. *Corroboree*, Mushroom, 1981, RML-53001.

Split Enz. "Six Months in a Leaky Boat." In *Time and Tide*, Mushroom Records, 1982, RML-53012.

Split Enz, *Waiata*, Mushroom Records, 1981 ENZ 2.

Yothu Yindi. "Treaty." Mushroom Records, 1991, K10344.

PART **I**

Place-Making and Music-Making

The first part of this collection is dedicated to exploring how places and music are deeply intertwined and "made" through practice, experience, and history. Popular song, a signature sound, or a landmark scene can significantly add to the identity of places. Cities—and more specifically, particular institutions—can take on a mythical stature in this way. For example, the local pub venue, and the larger pub circuit, so important to fostering music scenes in both Australia and Aotearoa/New Zealand, has been a vital institution out of which a local musical identity can develop over time, giving a scene a kind of ballast of meaning and value for local and trans-local music-making. The success or failure of a pub venue also has both a material and symbolic power that makes it an important barometer of the liveliness of a city's musical culture. In sites like this, the affective charge or the emotional pull of cities is very much bound in how its musical life comes to resonate, for locals and non-locals alike, through these kinds of institutions.

Part I begins with a chapter dedicated to Perth, Australia, in which Jon Stratton and Adam Trainer point to the city's isolation, far from Australia's more populous east coast where the other capitals are in closer contact with one another. Perth's suburban sprawl and its perception as a smaller city often positions the city as conservative and dull. The co-authors argue that Perth songwriters engage with this image in their music, by way of articulating the lived reality of the city. In the next chapter, Julie Rickwood and Emma Williams examine popular music in the Australian capital city, Canberra, through The Phoenix venue. Adopting an ethnomusicological approach, they outline how this one space has been a vital component to the social, material, and symbolic dimensions that have given shape and meaning to Canberra's unique and somewhat undervalued musical identity. Part I then shifts focus towards Aotearoa/New Zealand and one of the country's more recent global popular music stars, Lorde. Author Tony Mitchell argues that Lorde's music is very much a product of her upbringing and sense of "home" in Auckland's North Shore. Her success has underlined its place as a central node in Aotearoa/New Zealand's music industry, as well as added another layer to its musical mythologies.

1
Singing about the City
The Lyrical Construction of Perth

Jon Stratton and Adam Trainer

Perth is the only major city on Australia's west coast. Founded in 1829, it is the capital of Western Australia. Perth is situated on the Swan River inland of the coast. Fremantle, the city's port, and linked as a conurbation with Perth, is twenty kilometres away at the mouth of the river. Much of Perth's wealth is generated from mining in other parts of the state and the expansion in the city's population has been connected with mining booms. It is also a predominantly suburban city, with a population of two million spread across 31,000 hectares. Perth's remoteness from other major Australian cities—Adelaide, the nearest, is over 2500 kilometres away—has meant that Perth's inhabitants have tended to see themselves as different from t'othersiders, those living on the other side of the Nullarbor. In this chapter, we examine the lyrics of songs about the city composed in the period from the late 1970s, the time of punk, which in Perth was often used to express distaste for the city, to the mid-2010s. These lyrics articulate Perth's identity as it has been expressed through the experience of living in the city.

Myths of the City

Every city has its myths. These both convey the experience of that particular city and help to construct that experience. These myths are key elements in the formation of each city's idiosyncratic identity. At least since the early 1960s popular music has played an important role in the reproduction of ideas about cities. As Ola Johansson and Thomas Bell put it: "Popular music . . . is a cultural form that actively produces geographic discourses and can be used to understand broader social relations and trends, including identity, ethnicity, attachment to place, cultural economies, social activism, and politics" (2009, 2).

In thinking more specifically about urban geography, John Connell and Chris Gibson suggest that: "The city was a promise of things illegal and forbidden elsewhere, of drugs and deals and strange liaisons, a place of excitement and danger, of decay and difference, but not a place of boredom and tranquillity" (2003, 74). There are, as we shall see, many music texts about Perth. These produce and reproduce dominant myths of the city. Indeed, one of the most important myths about Perth is that it does not have the kind of city life described by Connell and Gibson.

We are concerned with the mythic construction of Perth in popular music by those brought up in the city and who either lived there when they composed their songs or composed them reflecting back on their experience of life in Perth. For a long time, until at least the advent of the Web and, later, of social media, Perth musicians have often felt it necessary to travel and live elsewhere, usually Melbourne or Sydney in the first instance, to find a place accepting of their creativity and to get their music recorded and heard by an audience outside of Perth. Some would argue that this is still the case. In 1988, the novelist Rodney Hall wrote a travel book called *Home: A Journey Through Australia*. His description of Perth combined the dominant myths about the city:

> People assure me that Perth—the world's remotest city—is vivacious, exciting and beautiful. I have to admit that I find it dull. I returned to the west last year, hoping to encounter the place I still hear reported as being there. For me, it doesn't exist: just a little city fully absorbed with navel-gazing. Its loyal citizens, obsessed with cleanliness and sunbathing, congratulate each other on living in a place so vivacious, so exciting and so beautiful. On weekdays Perth strikes me as half-dead—and totally dead on Sunday. The location is fine, the Swan River describes a broad sweep around parklands and freeways, which usurp all the most interesting sites. People are friendly, this cannot be denied, and the pace is leisurely. Yet the city seems to have no heart, no shape, no character.
>
> (1988, 119–120)

Here, Hall reproduces four of the myths that shape the experience of Perth; that it is isolated, that it is inward-looking, that it is small, that its inhabitants are concerned with superficial things and with having a good time; that Perth is, as he puts it, dull.

A chapter dealing with the reproduction of myths is not the place to debunk those myths but it is worth pointing out, if only to show how the strength of myths can overwhelm empirical reality, the fallacies in some of these claims. On the matter of Perth's mythic isolation, it is worth quoting David Whish-Wilson from his book on Perth:

> Perth is often described as the world's most isolated capital city. It's a title less relevant than it was for most of the twentieth century, when flying interstate was expensive and the Nullarbor Plain was crossed via dirt track. Before the 1890s gold rush, people didn't see themselves as being isolated from the eastern states, where almost nobody came from (because nobody wanted to come). Instead they measured distance from the mother country, and of course Perth is closer to Britain than either Sydney or Melbourne. Perth became by definition an isolated capital after Federation in 1901, only eleven years after the colony had been granted self-government, and only thirty-odd years before it tried to secede from Australia.
>
> (2013, 12)

Perth's isolation is relative to where one is describing Perth in relation to. Perth is also closer to south-east Asia, to Bali and to Singapore than are the eastern cities of Australia. Even as a capital city Perth is not the most isolated; that prize goes to Honolulu. Perth's distance from the eastern cities has led to a certain self-sufficiency as Whish-Wilson indicates, which can easily be read by Australian visitors from "over east" as navel-gazing.

In 1980 Perth's population was a little under 900,000. This was not small. For comparison, in 1980 in the United States, Dallas had just over 900,000 inhabitants and San Diego just under. In Britain, Sheffield at this same time had a much smaller population of rather over 500,000, which was roughly the same as that of Liverpool. By 2000, Perth's population had increased by about a million to nearly 1,900,000 and by 2014 the population had climbed to a little over 2,000,000. Nevertheless, the rhetoric that Perth is small has, as we shall see, been perpetuated in a number of song lyrics, which arguably connect to its status as a suburban and predominantly middle-class city. These labels can connect smallness with conservatism, and on occasion a kind of colloquial ennui. Smallness is a central theme in the Bank Holidays' "The City Is Too Small" released in 2004. Here they tell us that: "The city is too small for honesty / I guess I'll keep it quiet now." Lyricist and vocalist Nat Carson is perhaps referring here to the small-town mentality that becomes part of the myth of Perth as small—an assertion that in a town with a close-knit population personal grievances are best left unsaid for fear of causing social disharmony. In relatively contained music scenes, which have become a feature of Perth's music industry,[1] and to which the Bank Holidays arguably belonged, such secrecy becomes not only an internalized personal characteristic, but one that has implications for an entire community. Carson's lyrics describe well the experience that keeping honesty hidden smooths over the problems that could rupture Perth's pleasant lifestyle in a city experienced as small but, as we shall see, doing this also generates a feeling of claustrophobia.

It is in addition important to comment on Hall's description of Perth as dull. In the early 2000s dull became a key negative rhetorical trope for the experience of Perth. It was most probably popularized in the form of Perth being labelled "dullsville" by the Lonely Planet's travel guide in which in 2000 Rebecca Chau and Virginia Jealous wrote:

> When many a traveller came to visit in the 1990s, the city was dismissed as 'dullsville.' The streets were dead, there was nowhere to party. Locals were just too lackadaisical, at home, in their boardshorts and desert boots, tinkering with the barbecue.
>
> (52)

Most likely in response to the travel guide's use of the term, Perth's daily paper *The West Australian* started a debate about its applicability in their November 16 issue of that year. Tara Brabazon has critiqued this perception arguing that: "The problem confronting Perth planners in particular is that the denizens like living in the suburbs and have no great need to travel to 'the centre'" (2014, 55). She writes that:

> A key weakness [in policy discussions of Perth] is the excessive policy attention to Perth's Central Business District. It is—as with many modern cities—a dead centre. The impact of this dead centre is that the suburbs become more important to social cohesion and the building of identity. The majority of Perth's population hugs the coast and creates clusters of community from Mandurah to Mindarie Keys. The water is blue. The local shopping is adequate for both the weekly grocery shop and the occasionally [sic] extravagant purchase.
>
> (53)

Here, Brabazon is celebrating the suburban lifestyle that Hall, and then Chau and Jealous, deride as dull. This celebration of the city's relaxed pace and leisurely lifestyle is echoed in a later publication by *Lonely Planet*, which in suggesting that "easy-going Perth rivals its east-coast brethren for quality of life" (Holden and Metcalfe 2009, 306), seems to have sought to rectify its initial assessment.

Depicting Life in Perth: The Triffids and the Panda Band

Post-punk band The Triffids' second single, released in 1982, was "Spanish Blue." Although it doesn't mention Perth, the lifestyle described fits well with the ways, both positive and negative, that have been linked to Perth being dull (for a discussion of The Triffids as a Perth group see Stratton 2008). Spanish Blue is a color. In Dave McComb's lyrics the color becomes a code for Perth. Technically, Spanish Blue is 100 percent saturated and 75 percent bright. It is the color of the sea that Brabazon mentions. In are McComb's lyrics we are told: "Nothing happens here / Nothing gets done / But you get to like it / You get to like the beating of the sun / The washing of the sun / In Spanish Blue." Whish-Wilson comments on the quality of Perth's light:

> Ask many Perth expatriates what they miss about the city and the answer is often the light. It's not a romantic or a nostalgic light, not the playground light of our childhoods, but a light so clean and sharp that it feels like an instrument of grace, seeing a new world with new eyes.
>
> (2013, 217)

It is this light that creates the Spanish Blue of Perth's coastal sea. For Whish-Wilson and others including, it would seem, McComb, it is a cleansing light, a light that washes away cares and, perhaps, sins.

In 2004, the Panda Band released "Sleepy Little Deathtoll Town." It won the West Australian Music Industry Song of the Year award two years later. The track's refrain carries a similar idea of being scoured clean: "And it rains down so damn hard in this city / Don't it cleanse our souls man / Don't they shine pretty like a crown / In my sleepy little deathtoll town." Here it is not light but the heavy winter rain that cleanses people. Grace is achieved through the commutation of sin. What the Panda Band's track signals in its titular use of "deathtoll" is the sense of a Gothic substratum to Perth's cleanliness. Although it seems that the band wanted to make a statement about Perth's road toll, the track is pervaded by uneasiness. The deathtoll can be read as referring to the Bell Tower, which is centrally positioned on Riverside Drive overlooking the river. Twelve of the bells were a gift to Perth during the Australian Bicentennial Year of 1988. They come from the London church of St Martin-in-the-Fields. Combined with a further six bells they are now known as the Swan Bells. They hang in a purpose-built tower and are rung four times a week. The tower was opened in 2000. In describing the tower as having a deathtoll, analogous to a death knell, there is a suggestion of the understanding of Perth as stultifying. The bells in the tower toll for death rather than life. Perth's grace, its cleaniness, overlays the city's darker history from dubious mining deals to the treatment of Aborigines to the reoccurrence of serial killers from Eric Edgar Cooke who was hung for murder in 1964, to the Birnies who in 1986 raped five women and murdered four, the fifth managing to escape, to the Claremont Serial Killer, responsible for at least two deaths of young women and one disappearance in the mid-1990s.[2] The Claremont Serial Killer has never been brought to justice. Yet Perth offers a pleasant and mundane face to the world. As the Panda Band's lyrics tell us: "And all the girls are dreaming / Of screen stars and health spas / Of facials and massage / And all the boys / The boys just want the girls to settle down." Here is the Perth life scrubbed clean, indeed in a state of grace. There is no suggestion of the terrible things that have happened, and continue to happen, in the city. The girls fantasize about unobtainable film stars and making themselves look pretty while the boys want to marry them and settle down in suburban respectability. In this town the worst that people think can happen is, "Crash your cool cars kids and watch the citizens all gather round." This can be read as referring to Western Australia's proportionally high number of road deaths. Indeed, in 2007 Western Australia, a state of just over two million residents recorded 235 deaths, over half of the number recorded in New South Wales (435), a state of seven million ("Road Safety Report" 2007). In a sleepy town such as this the only attraction is the number of people killed in cars. We should also note that in this song Perth is not only sleepy, it is not included in the world of cities described by Connell and Gibson, but, again, it is a town—not a city of nearly two million people.

Perth and Suburbia

At the core of the experience of Perth's dullness is the myth of Perth's suburbia. Central to any discussion of the Perth music scene in the 1970s and 1980s is the question of whether Perth had an inner city—or, better for our purposes here, whether Perth musicians and fans experienced Perth as having an inner city. The reason for this is that in the eastern cities of Sydney and Melbourne inner cities were where the alternative rock scene, which in general terms we can say began with punk, was situated. One of the problems for Perth was the lack of an appropriate built environment for an inner city lifestyle, with its comparably smaller population spread across vast suburban sprawl (Trainer 2016). Kate Shaw argues that:

> Alternative cultures have a curious relationship with place . . . . They find [space] in the interstices of the urban form: in the disinvested inner city; in the derelict buildings, deindustrialized sites, under-used docks and railway yards of advanced capitalist economies; in unregulated, unpoliced 'no-man's lands.' Underground clubs have low overheads; empty sheds and warehouses often come at low or no rent, bars and pubs in run-down inner city areas do not charge at the door and drinks are cheap. The low costs create for interaction and formation, and economic space for experimentation and flexibility.
>
> (2005, 149)

In Perth, as in other Australian cities, the beginning of alternative rock is the true beginning of musicians writing songs about their own cities. However, in other cities, the songs were about parts of the city. Perhaps the best example is the Melbourne group Skyhooks, a glam precursor to the more radical inner city groups, on whose first album, *Living in the 70s*, were songs located in Carlton, Balwyn and Toorak. In Perth, in the main with a crucial exception to which we will return later, the songs were about Perth as a city, about the experience of living in Perth. Perth punk rejected Perth entirely.

The Exterminators, a group which only existed for a few months in late 1977, used to perform a track about Perth of which unfortunately there is no record of the lyrics, titled "Arsehole of The Universe." The criticism of Perth's suburban life is clear from the title. Around 1977 and 1978 the Victims used to perform "Perth is a Culture Shock." It was written by James Baker and Dave Faulkner, both of whom would go on to higher profile careers in Australian popular music. The story goes that Baker had gone abroad to New York and London where he had been in contact with the evolving punk scene. Faulkner suggests that: "James was familiar with all that, so returning to Perth, he felt was a long way down from the excitement he had been feeling elsewhere, so he wrote that lyric" (Wilkinson 2010). The lyrics of the first verse describe how the singer has to spend his time at home watching television. The refrain repeats "Perth—it is a culture shock" three times followed by "But this is where I'm born" suggesting that, in the end, there is no escape. The song's narrator will always carry the taint of Perth's blandness. The second and final verse is a more direct attack: "Everyone says this town is right / But I'm telling you it's so wrong / No-one wants to change a thing / You're all so content with nothing!" What is unsaid is that what is wrong with Perth is its suburban self-satisfaction and the effect of this is the lack of any intensity and desire for change described in the lyrics. The track suggests that Perthites are prepared to accept anything so long as it does not interfere with their suburban lifestyle.

These punk attacks on Perth form the beginning of a tradition. In 1984, the Perth pop group Eurogliders released "Heaven (Must Be There)." As a single the track reached number 2 on the Australian chart and number 21 on the American chart. Written by band members Grace Knight, a recent immigrant to Perth from Britain, and Perth-born Bernie Lynch, it was the group's most successful international hit. Often read as a song about striving for somewhere different, or something better, it is more appropriately understood as, in the first instance, an expression of the dislike of living in Perth. The song has few lyrics. It insists that: "I want to find a better place" and "I'm searching for a better place." We are then told: "I'm tired of living in the sand" and "I'm searching for a better land." Notoriously, Perth is built on sand. Perthites are known colloquially to those in the eastern states as Sandgropers. This lyrical repetition of the search for somewhere better to live emphasizes the singer's desire to leave where she is. The refrain makes this desire even clearer: "Heaven must be there / Well, it's just got to be there / I've never, never seen Eden / I don't wanna live in this place." If Heaven, or Eden, are elsewhere then in binary logic where she is may well be Hell. The rest of the lyrics repeat these motifs. The total effect is a yearning to escape the present place— Perth, where the group was formed, which goes undescribed but which the lyrics imply is a Hellish place to live.

And yet, as with Baker and Faulkner's lyric for "Perth is a Culture Shock," there is a sense in "Heaven" that Perth cannot be left. If it is left then it follows you and, like Baker, people return. From at least the late 1970s, Perth musicians, along with other creative artists, left the city. James Baker and Dave Faulkner reconvened in Sydney to found the Hoodoo Gurus in 1981. That same year, the Scientists, Kim Salmon's group, for another example, also went to Sydney. Salmon observes in his liner notes that: "My main memories of [Perth] feature a huge inferiority complex about what was referred to as the "Eastern States." i.e. not some hierarchy of levels of enlightenment but all that was to the east in fact, everywhere in Australia!" (Salmon 2004). In 1983, the Eurogliders relocated to Sydney. In 1984, the Triffids went to London. This leaving of Perth by young creative artists continued into the twenty-first century. In an article in *The Australian* in 2011, Guy Allenby noted that:

> Perth's educated young adults have been leaving the city in significant numbers and relocating to Australia's eastern states. In fact, between 2001 and 2006, while Western Australia's population grew by 157,000 people, the net loss of 25 to 34-year-olds with a university degree was 3 per cent from Perth. During that period the most popular destination among people who left Western Australia's capital was Melbourne, at 39 per cent. Sydney followed with 32 per cent.

What the article does not talk about is the large number of these diasporic Perthites who return after a shorter or longer period of time to make their life, often their family life, in suburban Perth. On this topic there is Sleepy Township's track, "S.T. Song," released in 1996. As the title suggests, the lyrics describe Perth as sleepy, as does the Panda Band's track six years later, for which we might read dull, or at least not vibrant, and as small, as a township. The first two verses sum up precisely the relationship to the city we have been outlining: "It's been 3 months / Since I left Perth / And in that time I've come to see how much my time there was worth / I've been back twice / Can't keep away / I know I'll probably end up living there some day." Perth's lifestyle may not suit Perth's creatives but, it seems, it is a great place to settle down. Sleepy Township's lyricist and vocalist Guy Blackman did not return to Perth to live, settling in Melbourne and building the independent record label that he established in Perth, Chapter Music. In "S.T. Song," he namechecks a number of Perth bands from the 1990s, suggesting that part of what he misses, despite Perth's sleepiness, is the connectedness of the social groups and sense of community that the city's music scene provides. Blackman wrote about Perth again in 2008, in the song "Carlton North," a love song with lyrics about moving from Perth to the titular Melbourne suburb, where he refers to Perth yet again as a "sleepy town," and suggests that "(B)oys / In sunny Perth / Oh what a waste / With a bucket in every lounge room." These lyrics again reinforce Perth as a town where there are few options but to pass the time smoking pot, echoing Baker and Faulkner's reliance on television as an escape from Perth's blandness.

It is the ambiguity of the Perth experience, often played out as an ambivalence towards the Perth lifestyle, which permeates many lyrics about the city. We have already seen some of this ambiguity in Dave McComb's lyrics for the Triffids. Released in 1986, *Born Sandy Devotional* was the group's second album not counting the anthology *Love in Bright Landscapes*, a title which, as we have already seen, was very apt. The cover of *Born Sandy Devotional* is a photograph of Mandurah taken in 1961. It shows the Peel Estuary and a few shacks. By the late 1980s the town was already becoming suburbanized and in the 2000s it has become swallowed up in Perth's coastal suburban spread. Recorded in London, the album is often said to capture a particular understanding of the Perth experience. Whish-Wilson writes that:

> The sound was, as described by Butcher [Bleddyn Butcher wrote a biography of the Triffids], "both spacious and claustrophobic," exactly how I'd felt as a teenager in a city where it seemed that the brightness was always turned up but the volume turned down.
>
> (2013, 148)

The album is perhaps best understood as an expression of love for a city that rejects all excessive expressions of emotion; a city that people experience as claustrophobic and leave, or want to leave, but to which they almost inevitably return—for the lifestyle.

The Perth Suburban Life

There has been one more way that musicians have related to the experience of Perth as suburban. This has been to become immersed in the suburban life and write songs expressing that suburbanism. The most important Perth artist to take this course was Dave Warner, who released the song with which he is most readily associated: "Suburban Boy" in 1978. Warner might best be described as the troubadour of suburbia. On his website Warner writes that he

> set out to do what a couple of years earlier I would have thought of as impossible and certainly un-artistic—to make art from mundane suburban Australian life. Before Howard Arkley or Neighbours I decided to celebrate my ordinariness as a young white middle-class Australian male, not using the fake iconography of Meat Pies and Holden Cars, or an outback I had never known but Football. Bus Stops. Rejection. My life. For me the key was to make it really local.
>
> (2013)

Warner was born in Bicton, a Perth suburb between Perth and Fremantle. He formed his first band, Pus, in 1973 and performed songs influenced by the American group the Fugs. His later band, the one with which he is most associated, plainly states his creative interests in its name, Dave Warner's From the Suburbs.

Warner's songs offer a sympathetic exploration of middle-class suburban life in Perth during the 1970s. Sometimes the lyrics directly reference roads, suburbs or places in Perth, at other times Warner uses his own experience to make more general comments on suburban life. In some songs he was pointedly political. "Phantom" is one example, critiquing Perth life under Premier Charles Court. Most particularly, Warner is critical of the equation of development with progress. Talking to the comic strip superhero Phantom, he asks: "What you gonna do / If the MRPA builds a freeway through your skull cave / Where you gonna screw, Diana and Guran?" The MRPA is the Metropolitan Regional Planning Authority, which came into existence in 1963, taking on responsibility for establishing Perth's transport network. Warner asks Phantom to come to Perth to save us: "And, I know you'll just love Garden City / Though Devil might have to stay outside / Still Hero can become a police horse / Providing you teach him how to take a bribe / The capitalists are ripping out our jungle." Garden City is a large shopping mall in the southern suburb of Booragoon which opened in 1973 with almost a hundred shops. Indeed, Garden City is part of the suburban expansion of Perth in the 1970s discussed earlier. Warner's sardonic lyric emphasizes the disjunction between name and reality. The reference to bribes is a commentary on the many dubious transactions that took place during the building boom of the 1970s.

Warner also wrote songs about the, predominantly male, suburban experience. "Suburban Boy" is a description of this life, of waking up and being roused by his mother, watching television on Saturday nights rather than going out, supporting the local Aussie Rules team and getting rejected by the girls he asks out. As Warner sings in the lyrics: "I'm sure it must be, easier for boys from the city." The city here is that inner city of bright lights and liberated life about which, it seems, Warner's suburban boy fantasized. Warner's ordinary suburban boy can only watch and envy what he views as the sophistication and bohemian progressivism of the city in comparison to his stultifying suburbs (on Warner see Stratton 2005).

Following Warner almost a generation later in writing about Perth suburbia from within has been Kevin Mitchell in his alter ego as Bob Evans. Mitchell was one of the founders of the alternative rock group, Jebediah. He was brought up in the suburb of Bull Creek which he describes as follows:

> Bull Creek is a very ordinary little suburb. And I'm not saying that in a negative way. But yeah, it's a little brown brick 1970s kind of southern suburb, working to middle class. There was nothing incredibly unusual about my existence there.
>
> (Mitchell 2009)

Jebediah's first album, *Slightly Odway*, was released in 1997. The lyrics show little obvious Perth influence, however the cover of their first album features a photograph of Kardinya Bowls Club. Above it flies a Futuro house that for a long time was positioned next to Leach Highway on the border of Rossmoyne and Willetton. Kardinya is a suburb of Perth on the southside of the city, a little south of Leach Highway and to the west of Bull Creek. Like Bull Creek, and indeed Warner's Bicton which is just up the road, there is nothing special about the suburb. *Slightly Odway's* cover image emphasizes this mundanity with white-dressed bowlers going about their pastime. The Futuro house is a Finnish design from the late 1960s and 1970s. It was prefabricated and planned for easy transport and construction. It looks very much like a 1950s idea of a flying saucer and this, indeed, is realized on *Slightly Odway's* cover. The suburbs, the cover suggests, can generate strangeness that is ignored and unseen by the suburban inhabitants. In 1999 Mitchell started performing as Bob Evans. His purpose was to acknowledge more fully his suburban origin. His first album as Evans was *Suburban Kid* (2003), a reference back to Warner's track "Suburban Boy." One track on the album was titled "Ode To My Car," which celebrates an old, blue Mitsubishi which should be taken to the wrecking yard but which continues faithfully to get the singer from one place to another. This is the same kind of suburban ordinariness which interested Warner.

Mitchell's second album as Evans was *Suburban Songbook*, his third, released in 2009, was *Goodnight Bull Creek!*, an assertion of Mitchell's/Evan's Perth suburban background. Mitchell has said that this album would be the final of a trilogy set in the suburbs. The album's title is taken from the first line of the first track on the album, a song called "Someone So Much." The lyrics personify Bull Creek: "Goodnight Bull Creek / You were the world to me / Now you're just a well-worn postcode for the memories." Mitchell/Evans sings about driving "down your road" and of taking "[t]he road less travelled." He is leaving Bull Creek and Perth's suburbia behind but, as we have seen, leaving Perth's suburbia is very difficult, it is, as Mitchell implies, like leaving someone you love: "When you love someone so much it hurts." There is an echo here of McComb's anguish in The Triffids' "Wide Open Road." In the Perth experience, affect appears at the moment the suburbs and their lifestyle are left behind.

Conclusion

Public discourse surrounding Perth's character as a city continues. In 2014 *New York Times* travel writer Baz Dreisinger, in reference to the city's trend towards boutique bars and restaurants, labeled Perth "hipster heaven" (2014). This led to a heated online discussion featuring a flurry of opinion pieces from Perth expats (Jimmy the Exploder 2014) and current residents (Barron 2014) debating whether Perth had truly shrugged off its status as a dull city. With Western Australia having sustained an almost decade-long mining boom, debate was concerned with Perth's resulting gentrification, the price of beer and quality of coffee as markers of its status as a world city rather than its fundamental character, or that of its inhabitants. The fervor of this discussion suggests a continuing sense of inferiority—a pervasive desire for Perth to be considered alongside or in competition with other cities.

The myth of Perth's remoteness continues to be a defining feature of the way in which the city is thought about. Despite its sizeable population, Perth still maintains a perception as a small and insular city. The exodus of musicians and other creatives, mostly to Melbourne and Sydney, persists as a constant drain on the city's cultural profile. In song Perth artists have often lamented the city's limitations, but there also remains an acceptance of the positive aspects of small towns and suburbs—be it Sleepy Township's uncertainty about the finality of moving away or Bob Evans' nostalgic acceptance that despite leaving the insularity and relaxed atmosphere of Perth have shaped him. This is arguably where the truest sense of the city emerges in song. Perth can here be viewed not as a wasteland or a vacuum, but as a home, and a place that despite or perhaps indeed because of its flaws has provided a birthplace for creativity. That creativity is founded in Perth's identity as lived through the naturalized myths of its inhabitants and expressed by its artists.

Acknowledgments

We would like to thank Dave Faulkner for providing us with the lyrics to "Perth is a Culture Shock."

Notes

1   For a discussion of Perth's alternative music scenes of the late 1990s and early 2000s as close-knit and socially connected see both the documentary *Something in the Water* (O'Bryan 2008) and Christina Ballico's PhD thesis "Bury Me Deep in Isolation: A Cultural Examination of a Peripheral Music Industry and Scene" (2013).
2   On Eric Edgar Cooke see Estelle Blackburn *Broken Lives: The Complete Life and Crimes of Serial Killer Eric Edgar Cooke* (2005); on the Claremont serial killings see Debi Marshall *The Devil's Garden: The Claremont Serial Killings* (2007). Since this chapter was written police have charged a man with three murders identified as the Claremont serial killings

Bibliography

Allenby, Guy. 2011. "Southern Capital Shows the Way." *The Australian*, April 22. www.theaustralian.com.au/executive-living/home-design/southern-capital-shows-the-way/story-fn6njxlr-1226043411093?nk=df94775e5d353f213c43c885173bae6b (accessed November 12, 2015),

Ballico, Christina. 2013. "Bury Me Deep in Isolation: A Cultural Examination of a Peripheral Music Industry and Scene." PhD diss., Edith Cowan University.

Ballico, Christina. 2012. "Music and Place: The Case of Perth." Paper presented at CCI Winter School Paper Jam Conference, Brisbane, Australia, June 21–27.

Barron, Nik. 2014. "Do Hipsters Go to Heaven?: Perth and Its Place in the World." *The Yarn*, March 6. www.theyarn.net.au/pop-culture/do-hipsters-go-to-heaven-perth-its-place-in-the-world (accessed November 11,2015).

Blackburn, Estelle. 2005. *Broken Lives: The Complete Life and Crimes of Serial Killer Eric Edgar Cooke*. Melbourne: Hardie Grant.

Brabazon, Tara. 2014. *City Imaging: Regeneration, Renewal and Decay*. Dordrecht: Springer Netherlands.

Bracewell, Michael. 1998. *England Is Mine: Pop Life in Albion from Wilde to Goldie*. London: Flamingo.

Chau, Rebecca and Virginia Jealous. 2000. *The Lonely Planet Guide: Perth & Western Australia*. Melbourne: Lonely Planet.

Connell, John and Chris Gibson. 2003. *Sound Tracks: Popular Music, Identity and Place*. London: Routledge.

Dreisinger, Baz. 2014. "Catching Perth's Wave in Western Australia." *New York Times*, February 27, 2015. www.nytimes.com/2014/03/02/travel/catching-perths-wave-in-western-australia.html?_r=0 (accessed November 11, 2015).

Gregory, Jenny. 2014. "Scoping Perth as an Energy Capital." In *Energy Capitals: Local Impact, Global Influence*, edited by Joseph Pratt, Martin Melosi and Kathleen Brosnan. Pittsburgh, PA: University of Pittsburgh Press, 95–110.

Gregory, Jenny. 2003. *City of Light: A History of Perth Since the 1950s*. Perth: City of Perth.

Hall, Rodney. 1988 [1990]. *Home: A Journey Through Australia*. Port Melbourne: Minerva.

Holden, Trent and Anna Metcalfe. 2009. *The Cities Book: A Journey Through the Best Cities in the World*. Footscray: Lonely Planet.

Jimmy the Exploder. 2014. "Mate, Perth is not a Hipster City." *Guardian*, March 5. www.theguardian.com/commentisfree/2014/mar/05/mate-perth-is-not-a-hipster-city (accessed December 10, 2015).

Johansson, Ola and Thomas Bell. 2009. *Sound, Society and the Geography of Popular Music*. Farnham: Ashgate.

Marshall, Debi. 2007. *The Devil's Garden: The Claremont Serial Killings*. Milson's Point: Random House.

Mitchell, Scott-Patrick. 2009. "It's Not me, It's You … Bull Creek." *Out in Perth: Gay & Lesbian Life & Style*, April 3. www.outinperth.com/its-not-me-its-you-bull-creek (accessed November 11, 2015).

"Road Safety Report." 2007. *Road Deaths Australia: 2007 Statistical Summary*. https://infrastructure.gov.au/roads/safety/publications/2008/pdf/Ann_Stats_2007.pdf (accessed December 5, 2015).

Shaw, Kate. 2005. "The Place of Alternative Culture and the Politics of its Protection in Berlin, Amsterdam and Melbourne." *Planning Theory & Practice* 6: 149–169. doi: 0.1080/14649350500136830

Shedden, Iain. 2009. "The Name's Bob Evans, For Now." *The Australian*, April 3. www.theaustralian.com.au/news/the-names-bob-evans-for-now/story-e6frg6n6-1225697652001 (accessed November 11, 2015).

Stratton, Jon. 2008. "Suburban Stories: Dave McComb and the Perth Experience." *Continuum: Journal of Media and Cultural Studies* 22 (2): 255–267.

Stratton, Jon. 2005. "'Pissed on Another Planet': The Perth Sound of the 1970s and 1980s." *Perfect Beat: The Pacific Journal for Research into Contemporary Music and Popular Culture* 7 (2): 36–60.

Trainer, Adam. 2016. "Perth Punk and the Construction of Urbanity in a Suburban City." *Popular Music* 35 (1): 100–117.

Warner, Dave. 2013. "The Importance of the Local in Literature." *Thoughts of a Suburban Boy Blog*. http://davewarner.wordpress.com/category/uncategorized/page/5 (accessed November 11, 2015).

Whish-Wilson, David. 2013. *Perth*. Sydney: New South Publishers.

Wilkinson, Christian. 2010. "Gurus Break Dullsville Hoodoo." *In My Community*, April 12. www.inmycommunity.com.au/going-out/gig-guide/Gurus-break-Dullsville-hoodoo/7553416 (accessed November 12, 2015).

Discography

Salmon, Kim. Liner Notes for *Pissed on Another Planet*. Citadel, 2004, compact disc.

Filmography

O'Bryan, Aiden (director). 2008. DVD edition: *Something in the Water*. Perth: WBMC Productions.

2

The Phoenix and the Bootleg Sessions
A Canberra Venue for Local Music

Julie Rickwood and Emma Williams

Introduction

Canberra, Australia's national capital, is the largest inland city in Australia. It is a young city compared to Sydney and Melbourne, celebrating its centenary in 2013. Its current population of approximately 390,000 is comparatively well educated and middle-class (see, for example, Visit Canberra and Australian Bureau of Statistics). Civic, the name of the city center, is currently witnessing a rapid inner urban vitalisation which is outing Canberra's "hipster underbelly" (Riordan 2014). A core venue in Civic is The Phoenix, an intimate and hugely decorative pub in the historic Sydney Building (see Figure 2.1). The Phoenix was shut down due to a fire on 17 January 2014. Its closure was deeply felt by many of its customers and the musicians who played there. The Phoenix partially rose from the ashes in March 2014, re-opening in the recent (pre-fire) extension, a section that lacked the iconic charm of the original venue. Consecutive concerts at that time promoted the venue as "literally the hottest live music venue in Canberra": a humorous reference to the recent fire. Generations of musicians have played at The Phoenix and generations of music lovers have flocked there. In particular, the Monday night Bootleg Sessions have been supporting live music, particularly local musicians, and nurturing local audiences since 2003. The affection given to the venue is reflected in its website url lovethephoenix.com.

Canberra is a city maligned by many Australians. Little has been written about Canberra within popular music studies although some research has been carried out on the city's popular music history. The resulting publications have largely focused on documenting particular bands and musical genres (Spencer 2001; Sharpe 2006; Shakallis 2013; Starr 2014) which was also demonstrated in "Head Full of Flames: Punk in the Nation's Capital 1977–1992" held at Canberra Museum and Gallery in 2013. The Phoenix, however, has been critical in the productive interaction of musicians and audiences that has given shape and meaning to Canberra's musical sensibilities. Moreover, it plays a vital role in cultivating the social, material and symbolic dimensions that reflect the popular music culture of Canberra, as a place separate from and different to its site as the national capital. This chapter explores how "The Phoenix" demonstrates the role pub culture plays in the musical life of Australians and how its identity has given shape and meaning to popular music in Canberra. In doing so, we first briefly outline how place and practice are deeply intertwined, and then investigate the history of local popular music in Canberra and The Phoenix as a venue within that

Figure 2.1 The original Phoenix. Image from the front screen of the venue's website. Photograph by Adam Thomas.

context. The chapter then more closely examines the Bootleg Sessions. It draws on conversations with Phoenix staff members, organizers of past and present Bootleg Sessions, local musicians, as well as audience members, all of whom contribute to the "anecdotes and commentaries ... in relation to music [which emanates] from a common stock of understandings concerning music's relationship to the local" (Bennett 2004, 3). The chapter concludes with a reflection on why the tagline lovethephoenix represents the productive interaction created in The Phoenix.

Place-Making and Music-Making

The place of origin of a band or musician is an important reference point for Australian popular music fans and commentators (Williams 2007). This consciousness is also reflected within the academy. Homan recognizes that regional difference in Australia is "actively sought and played out within a variety of production/consumption contexts and (mis) perceptions" (2000, 32). Hesmondhalgh argues similarly, noting that "in spite of the global circulation of musical commodities, place matters" (2013, 123). Indeed, there has long been an association between a city and its music, most notably New Orleans in the first two decades of the twentieth century (Hesmondhalgh 2013), Liverpool after the Beatles (ibid), and in the Australia-New Zealand region, Dunedin (Bannister 1999), Perth (Stratton 2008; Trainer 2015), Brisbane (Stafford 2006; Rogers 2010), Wollongong (Gallan 2012). Many cities have their "sounds" (see also Connell and Gibson 2003) but also Shank's (1994) study of the

1980s rock scene in Austin showed the vitality of popular music in a place derives from a productive interaction of musicians and audiences. This interaction is often facilitated by a venue. It could even be argued that the "interaction between the artist and the audience is understood and controlled by the venue" (Webster 2010, 25). How the venue then understands and meets the expectations and requirements of its audiences is fundamental to the realization of shared cultural knowledge, style (Turino 2008, 2) and meaning within the interaction.

Canberra: Local Popular Music

Though officially named as the new Federal Capital in 1913, Canberra was slow to develop in a built sense. The fledgling city's population had reached a mere 6000 by 1927 (*Canberra Times* 1927, 4), largely made up of construction workers and public servants uprooted from their lives in Melbourne or Sydney and tasked with the job of creating a national capital city. The delivery of municipal services and infrastructure lagged well behind demand, and accommodation for new residents remained in short supply for many decades.

As the site of Federal Parliament, it is the political debates, decisions and debacles made in Canberra which dominate national media. This discourse also colors the city's reputation, often appearing to be insular, austere and aloof to outsiders. This insider/outsider dichotomy can be seen in the sense of inclusiveness and tight networking among those that live in Canberra, a city that has been recently named one of the most liveable in the world (Riordan 2014), contrasting with the perception held by many Australians that it is full of bureaucrats and culturally vacant. As long-time residents of the city, we find that the disconnect between popular perception of the cultural scene and its lived reality is stark (see Sharpe 2006, 11, who also concurs). Canberra as a living, vibrant, growing, spirited place is little understood. It is not just a geographic space but also a cultural experience. It has unique social, cultural, political, economic and geographical quirks, from its territory status and relative isolation within regional New South Wales, to the hardships recognized in the growing numbers of homeless people, the city's reputation as the sex capital of Australia,[1] its legendary standing amongst outsiders as a rare place in Australia where one could legally purchase fireworks (until 2009), as well as an active arts community.

Today, music contributes significantly to the wider arts community through a variety of genres including classical, jazz, community and popular music. Performances take place in a wide range of venues, from theaters, pubs and clubs to community halls, street festivals and local parks. Even though Canberra is not a city that is often included on touring schedules in Australia, it attracts its fair share of significant international acts. The music scenes have been vibrant for generations and are best described as diverse and eclectic, as opposed to a unified or distinctive localized "sound" based on subcultural or stylistic conventions. It is useful to provide a brief historical overview of musical life and its associated venues in Canberra, to provide a context for The Phoenix today. Canberra and surrounds produced a "surprisingly active music scene" in the 1920s (Starr 2014, xiii) where forms of entertainment included picture theaters and dances held at local halls (Sharpe 2006; Starr 2014). The Albert Hall, opened in 1928, became a mainstay for Canberra's musical entertainment, hosting all manner of concerts, recitals, dances and performances including the regular ABC Concert series. The first rock'n'roll dance in Canberra took place here in 1956 (Starr 2014, 5), starting a wave that supported tens of venues and hundreds of bands. Alternative venues included The Tomb, a folk venue in the basement of St John's Church in Reid, and the Lemon Tree discotheque (Starr 2014; Spencer 2001). For the more successful Canberra bands of the 1960s, the limited size of the Canberra music scene often meant moving on to a bigger city, particularly Sydney or Melbourne (Williams 2007, 63–64). A punk rock scene thrived from the 1970s, which sharply contrasted with the popular perception of Canberra as a city full of be-suited public servants. In the same decade and the early 1980s, The Floyd was "the" music venue hosting local, national and international bands. The latter decades of the twentieth century saw a broad range of popular music played across venues that included the Australian National University bar, The Asylum, Stakeout Tavern, Lizard Lounge, Gypsy Bar and Toast. Music festivals, including the National Folk Festival, the now defunct Indyfest and Corinbank and the annual regional touring music festival Groovin The Moo often take place outdoors or at one of the university campuses. Today, the popular music landscape is dotted with well-loved regulars like The Fuelers, The Cashews and the Brass Knuckle Brass Band. In addition to large venues like the Canberra Theatre Centre, the city is currently home to a handful of intimate, free spirited, iconic performance venues, including the Transit Bar, The Front and, more recently, Smith's Alternative. The Phoenix, the subject of the next section of this chapter, is arguably seen as Canberra's iconic venue for popular music.

The Phoenix

> The Phoenix, which has always been my personal favorite, has been having a rough patch what with the fire and all, but has maintained its status as Canberra's best and most interesting small venue and will soon redouble itself with the promise of expanding their program of entertainment.
>
> (McRae 2015b)

Nigel McRae, one of the founders and organizers of the Canberra Musicians Club, wrote a report on the state of local music venues in Canberra in late 2015. With decades of participation, McRae is well aware of the frequency with which bands and venues have come and gone, but maintains a positive view of the contemporary music scene overall. He declared that it had "seldom been in rudder health" and noted that there were now upwards of twenty live music venues throughout Canberra (McRae 2015b). As the quote above indicates, the Phoenix is and has been a popular favorite, and not only for McRae. The Phoenix has produced, reproduced and been "inflected by the imaginative and the sociological" (Whiteley 2004, 1–2) dynamics of the live music scene in Canberra for over two decades.

The Phoenix is first and foremost a pub. It is regarded as a comfortable "melting pot" (Hannigan pers. comm. 2015) of diverse people and held with much affection because of its "non-judgemental tendency" (McRae pers. comm. 2015a). Adam Hadley, a former MC of the Bootleg Sessions, agrees: "I love the Phoenix because it is the only pub I've ever been to that fits into the weird mythic idea of a 'local.' It's like a person. A huge cavernous person that you get drunk inside" (Hadley pers. comm. 2015). Hadley's statement captures and reflects the comfort that many feel within The Phoenix, a comfort that is indeed often prompted by drinking but as readily by the engaging, welcoming, friendly, self-regulating nature of the venue. Just as important is the "junky" décor; the "old furniture with holes in it" and "old jugs" (Ingall pers. comm. 2015). One social media user commented that The Phoenix is "One of the best pubs I've ever been to. Writers on the walls, Guinness on tap, a well-stocked whiskey bar and they treat touring bands like human beings" (Facebook user, July 16, 2015). Another declared "At @PhoenixThePub for the first time since the fire and though it has changed it still feels like coming home" (Twitter user, October 4, 2014).

The rolling chapters of locals, aged anywhere between 85 and 18, all proudly assume the title of being a regular. "Everybody owns the Phoenix," said McRae (pers. comm. 2015a). The Phoenix is a key resource in terms of the ways in which [the regulars] make sense of and negotiate the everyday (as observed by DeNora 2000 and Bennett 2004). The Phoenix creates a narrative space for the relationships developed with the venue. The regulars represent not one particular demographic, but an attitude that contributes to and promotes a sense of place that is at once safe, inclusive and tolerant, and, frequently, a "rich experiential [setting] in which music is consumed" (Bennett 2004, 2). Its Monday night Bootleg Sessions, which are discussed in detail below, clearly "demonstrate how locally produced music interacts with the 'local structure of feeling'" (Bennett 1997, 28).

Sean Hannigan has co-owned and managed The Phoenix since 1993. The Phoenix caters to a cross section of the local arts community which includes musicians, poets, trivia nerds and visual artists. Hannigan suggests the venue builds cultural capital because it is the antithesis of gentrification and the sterile development that is more common in Canberra, as in other cities. Musically, it is a venue for those wanting an alternative to clubs and he sees the investment in local music-making as an important function of The Phoenix. With twenty-two years association, the publican and co-owner Kieron Clohessy also understands that The Phoenix generates cultural capital, especially as a venue for emerging local musicians that can then go on to establish themselves more widely. As an example, he recalled knowing the members of Peking Duk, the electronic music duo, Adam Hyde and Reuben Styles, who have had Top Ten success in Australian charts, "since they were children" (Clohessy pers. comm. 2015). He views their success on national public radio station Triple J's *Unearthed* as being supported by their early appearances at the Bootleg Sessions. Fiete Geier, currently the venue's music manager, has been working at The Phoenix since 2001, initially on sound and later as a booker from 2005. All three are audience and artist aware and astutely attend to both, conscious of the nurturing role the Bootleg Sessions have within the Canberra music scene.

We have our own insights into the socio-musical activities undertaken inside the venue. There are, for example, similarities between this venue and the renowned Scottish venue King Tut's Wah Wah Hut (see Webster 2010), particularly in the way overt and covert, aural and visual signals between the musicians, the audience and the staff influence behavior within the parameters and conventions of the venue. An important difference, however, is that The Phoenix is a locally owned and operated venue that fundamentally maintains a local, grass-roots image. Like all popular music venues, it too has to deal with local legislation and red tape and is equally "bound up with new, increasingly global, technological, cultural and economic shifts" (Connell and Gibson 2003, 1). While acknowledging these wider influences on The

Phoenix, including government regulations and adherence to statutory control, they are not dealt with in any great depth within this chapter. Rather, our primary attention is given to the dynamic interactions within The Phoenix itself and the musical culture which "evolves out of the everyday" (Stratton 2008, 1) and is implicated in the social order of Canberra.

Not long before the fire, The Phoenix had expanded. The acquisition of the adjoining Shooters Bar had enabled The Phoenix to double in size in late 2013. The need for expansion was multifaceted and beyond the mere need to cope with its popularity: The Phoenix had been losing bands to bigger venues. The expansion accommodated a new stage and new sound system which meant that musicians were better serviced. In addition, there was greater flexibility to provide sectioned off, discrete spaces.[2]

The twenty-first anniversary celebration of The Phoenix in 2013 was held in its expanded iteration which accommodated double its original capacity, enabling 250 people to be "jumping up and down together" (Ingall pers. comm. 2015). When the fire closed the venue in 2014, its absence was greatly felt. People "were forlorn" and there were many "discussions about what to do" (Liz Kirwan pers. comm. 2015). Posts to The Phoenix Facebook page also demonstrated this with comments ranging from "Dear Phoenix, When will you be re-opening? I am thirsty. Love, Hayley" (Facebook user, February 4, 2014) and "Am greatly missing this place" (Facebook user, February 16, 2014).

These comments demonstrate some of the loss, grief and nostalgia that circulated among the music community and bolstered The Phoenix's reputation as a venue without equal, contributing further to its almost mythic existence. When the venue re-opened, Kirwan was thankful and relieved and "found a piece of furniture and gave it a kiss" (Liam Kirwan pers. comm. 2015). Other fans also celebrated: "Oh is it really true that @PhoenixThePub is open again??? Please let it be true! #bestlivemusicvenueever" (Twitter user, July 22, 2014).

The Phoenix continues in its limited post-fire location, the original door beside it still boarded up, and has cobbled together a sense of itself with its regular program. Despite the removal of the scaffolding that shadowed the new entrance for many months, it has been understandably challenged by the extreme delay in repairing the damage to the Sydney Building and the loss of its short-lived expansion in which significant investment had been placed. Nevertheless, it continues to provide the familiar sense of place that its community had missed and for which it is highly valued. When it expands again in 2017 it will do so in a new set of circumstances which include an increased capacity and a greater potential to re-present its unique atmosphere.

The Bootleg Sessions

"Monday WOOT! If you love Canberra music then you already know about this legendary night! http://lovethephoenix.com/bootlegs/" (Twitter user, 2012). The Bootleg Sessions began in 2003 when Pete Gare "put in a lot of effort [to] promote it ... because Monday nights were dead" (Hannigan quoted in Nourse 2013). Where once local musicians could simply show up, it quickly became a programmed event with, at times, bookings up to three months in advance because it is "so popular amongst musicians and punters alike" (Nourse 2013). Although Monday nights remain a quiet night for many music venues in Canberra, the Bootleg Sessions continue to be "the thing to do" (Geier quoted in Nourse 2013).

Figure 2.2 A Bootleg Sessions poster.

Gare is credited as the founder and first host of the Bootleg Sessions, fundamentally playing the role of a booking agent. Ben Drysdale took over that role in 2004/2005 and facilitated what has come to be regarded as the Bootleg Sessions' "golden years." Drysdale felt that the success of that period was because the Bootleg Sessions were a coming together of old and emerging musicians. It was a time when some of the more established bands such as The Fuelers and Dubba Rukki were "still willing to play" and there was "a massive insurgence of really solid newer bands" (Drysdale pers. comm. 2015) such as Dahahoo, Vorn Doolette, Julia and the Deep Sea Sirens and Inflatable Ingrid. There were bands, he said, that would pull their own crowd but were favorites beyond that immediate circle and it was this merging of two generations of bands that created the uniqueness of that time. Drysdale also felt that as a single point of contact, performers knew who to approach and this enabled some stability to the booking process.

One of the central features of the Bootleg Sessions is MC, a role that greatly contributed to the success of Monday nights during Drysdale's term when Adam Hadley took on that position. Hadley's contribution to the Bootleg Sessions was one of the key factors in the "golden age." Hadley, a musician and a theater performer, was unique, as described by Hannigan:

> Hadley's reign over The Phoenix on a Monday night [was] akin in spirit to the most confusing, erratic, but nevertheless thrilling of absurdist comedies. He encapsulates the excitement of live music perfectly when he's in front of a microphone and he makes it just a really entertaining night for everybody.
>
> (Hannigan, quoted in Nourse 2013)

During the heights of the Bootleg Sessions the queue was not so much an indicator of the popularity of the musicians performing but simply the popularity of the Bootleg Sessions as an event. During this time, queues were often longer than those on a Friday and Saturday. Sometimes there were "two-hour line ups in the dead of winter" recalled Drysdale (pers. comm. 2015). McRae (pers. comm. 2015a) recalls those "glory days" being "before they banned smoking; before overcrowding was policed." He wryly remarked that had an emergency situation occurred it would have "wiped out Canberra's cultural community" (McRae pers. comm. 2015a).

Following Drysdale's departure, the Bootleg Sessions became a curated event by local independent organizations such as *BMA Magazine*, Landspeed Records and others. Current Bootleg Sessions are hosted by 2XX Radio Local'n'Live, Canberra Institute of Technology and Canberra Musicians Club. The Canberra Musicians Club (CMC) was launched in late 2008, although the informal network among musicians in Canberra had been previously well established. There had been significant change in attitude to local music in Canberra, claims McRae, who adds that most local musicians are "over the ingrained idea that everything in Canberra is shit" (pers. comm. 2015a). The Phoenix played a vital role in that mind shift. McRae has curated the CMC Bootlegs since 2011 although he was involved in both playing gigs and curating live music events at The Phoenix before that.

The Phoenix has supported "anything from a metal band to a quiet solo artist; from someone's first gig to a national touring band who's [sic] stopping by . . . There's no genre—except no cover bands, of course" (Geier quoted in Nourse 2013). As a group of regulars commented, the Bootleg Sessions organizers do not turn away any original music and part of its attraction is the random nature of the bands. McRae (pers. comm. 2015a) also remarked on the diversity present in Canberra's live music scene. He suggested that the city's small population and the influence of diverse genres from the Australian National University's School of Music, including the Jazz School, and other random bands meant that different genres and styles could be brought together. That eclecticism, he suggested, drove artistic ideas.

The opportunity to play a first gig is particularly potent to the success of, and affection for, the Bootleg Sessions. Over the years, hundreds of local bands and performers have played their first gig on the Phoenix stage.[3] The bands capture the diversity of local popular music genres including contemporary folk and metal which are solid styles popular in Canberra. The bands are local "because of social and geographical proximity—not because of any innate musicological distinctiveness" (Gallan 2012, 1). Gallan argues that live music at the Oxford Tavern in Wollongong, a small city in the state of New South Wales, is "associated with local meanings of what it [means] to play and support local music—a place to drink, socialise, dance, mosh, sing and belong" (ibid). The same could be said of the Bootleg Sessions and, in a similar way to the local bands performing in the Oxford Tavern sessions, some of the Canberra bands would come to regard their gigs at The Phoenix as the best thing they did.

The accommodation of a diversity of musical taste is a highlight of the Bootleg Sessions. Whatever the genre being played, audiences can often be "a rowdy crowd" (Geier quoted in Nourse 2013). Others also commented on this, suggesting that even when the music could be "shit, someone's always loving it" (Liz Kirwan pers. comm. 2015). The success of the Bootleg Sessions is embedded in an acceptance of wild behavior. Two well-remembered gigs highlight the delight audiences take in these animated nights. The band Inflatable Ingrid, for example, "went off" (Liam Kirwan 2015) at their reunion show. Not only was lead singer Paul Kelloway drenched in sweat and wearing his "stage face" (Liam Kirwan pers. comm. 2015), he fell into a glass. The blood smeared across his chest. Lead guitarist Reuben Ingall remembers cutting his finger open, blood flowing over his pink Hello Kitty guitar. Excitement built and the audience spontaneously stood on tables which became covered with broken glass and beer. "It felt as if bombs were dropping on the building" and that "destruction was raining on the place" (Liam Kirwan pers. comm. 2015). Equally exhilarating was Dahahoo's last gig, described by Drysdale (pers. comm. 2015) as "epic." The Phoenix was filled beyond capacity, "jam packed [and] queued out the door ... People standing on any room, including tables and seats ... Everything going up and down" (Ingall pers. comm. 2015).

Gallan (2012), Cohen (1994) and others have argued that a local popular music scene is constituted by the people, organizations, events and situations associated with the production and consumption of the music. In fact, examination of the social meanings of music, its significance, whether banal or unique, and the factors guiding participation is highly localized (Gallan 2012, 38; see also Bennett 1997; Homan 2000), even within the context of national and global influences. In Canberra, this is best demonstrated by the Bootleg Sessions which have contributed enormously to the reputation of the Phoenix. It is those Monday nights in particular that produce and reproduce "the circumstances and location" (Mitchell 2009, vi) for the production and consumption of popular music, consciously creating a connection to local music through its own distinctive set of social networks and drinking practices.

Conclusion: Loving The Phoenix

Ben Drysdale, former organizer of the Bootleg Sessions, noted that while they no longer capture the capacity audiences and excitement of their pinnacle days in the mid to late 2000s, the Bootleg Sessions still do "well by any standards on a Monday night" (pers. comm. 2015). Now curated by different organizations each week on a regular cycle, the various networks of musicians and audiences nevertheless remain central to the production and consumption of local, live music in Canberra.

The Phoenix remains the most successful of Canberra's live music venues, and the Bootleg Sessions a central feature of its success. Some of the success can be attributed to the venue in many ways "flying under the radar" (McRae pers. comm. 2015a) of not only visitors but also many Canberrans. That's part of the reason why it works, suggested McRae (2015b), as "people only find it if they're looking for it." It contains "technological,

Figure 2.3   The reunified Phoenix on Monday January 30, 2017. Photo by Patrick Cox.

architectural and ideological accounts of what people have understood as a good sound, a good performance, a good listening experience, a good night out" (Frith 2010, 3). The Phoenix demonstrates the power of a built form to create music sensibilities.

Without doubt, the fire enabled a richer appreciation of The Phoenix, exhibited through loss, grief and nostalgic recollections of the venue as "the coolest, alternative place to go" (Liz Kirwan pers. comm. 2015), especially on a Monday night. And it is those Monday nights, the Bootleg Sessions, that have helped to shape Canberra's eclectic popular music identities created through the productive interaction of musicians, audiences and the venue for over a decade. They have also prompted a sense of belonging to and investing social, material and symbolic meaning in The Phoenix. It was therefore appropriate that it was a Monday night when the reunified Phoenix finally opened, a little over three years after the fire. The occasion was joyously celebrated in the venue and on social media (see Figure 2.3).

Canberra has often been described as a place without soul but this is not the case. Its soul is embedded in community which is rarely aligned to national politics but rather anchored in the local; the social, cultural, intellectual, political and economic networks that can merge and intermingle. In a similar way, The Phoenix holds the "soul" of place for many, one that can be hard to access from without but once found becomes meaningful. There is no other live music venue in Canberra that would have seen the outpouring of emotion that occurred during the closure of The Phoenix after the fire of early 2014. And, it seems, those who come to know its intimacy, ultimately #lovethephoenix.

Postscript: Phoenix Rising: An Acoustic Evening for the Love of The Phoenix

In late March 2017, social media and local news were ablaze (pun intended) with the news that The Phoenix had unexpectedly closed on Wednesday March 29, 2017. An official notice on one window indicates that the lease has been terminated. On another window, there is a different message from The Phoenix staff: "due to unforeseen circumstances the pub is shut until further notice. Hang in there, see you on the other side x." The Phoenix community was shattered and they went into action. The gig "Phoenix Rising: An Acoustic Evening for the Love of The Phoenix" was rapidly organized for the evening of Friday March 30. It was intended to "let The Phoenix and everyone in Canberra see just how dang much we love them and hope they get through this current shit storm," posted hosts Canberra Music Blog. One of the authors of this chapter, Rickwood, joined in. As I arrived in East Row the first musician, Alec Randles, began to play and an audience was gathering immediately outside the pub. Clusters of friends circled the performers throughout the evening and the audience grew. Most of the audience were regulars of the Bootleg Sessions—musicians and audiences both, including Ben Drysdale who performed with his band, East Row Rabble. Their performance lifted the energy of the evening. Local favorites Helena Pop followed, with many singing along with their well-known original songs, and later the Brass Knuckle Brass Band created a big sound that got people dancing. Rumors abounded about the legal situation concerning the closure and the threat to the pub's existence. Anger was readily expressed not only on the night but also in social media, which is still live with conversation. The most notable impression from the evening—and from the reviews that are currently flooding onto The Phoenix Facebook page—is, not surprisingly, that the pub is enormously appreciated as a pivotal institution in Canberra's live music scene. It is, indeed, loved by many. On the footpath, in front of the musicians, chalk art was growing, including the hashtag #phoenixrising. While The Phoenix's future was uncertain at that time, its community fervently hopes that it does, indeed, rise from these ashes.

Postpostscript: We're Broke. The Community Built This Place, They Love This Place, so We're not Going to Let It Die.

The Phoenix fortunately did re-open soon after the above campaign. The Bootleg Sessions and the venue's other regular events continued to draw in its committed community. And the gigs continue and audiences attend, currently in droves. The reason? Yet again The Phoenix community is campaigning to save the venue. Once again, social media and local media have been and continue to be ablaze with activity. Various action is being taken, including a gofundme campaign and many fundraising gigs at the pub. Local Greens leader, Shane Rattenbury, has shown support, stating that it would be a disaster for Canberra's music scene if The Phoenix was forced to close (Groch 2018). Indeed it would, but as this publication goes to press, the future of The Phoenix remains uncertain.

Notes

1 In 2015, Canberra Museum and Gallery exhibited an historical and musicological exploration of that industry, entitled "X-Rated: The Sex Industry in the ACT."
2 Nonetheless, for many of its regulars there was at first an odd engagement with its new dimensions because of the "ghosts from Shooters" (McRae pers. comm. 2015a).
3 See http://lovethephoenix.com/bootlegs for an overview of the various bands that have played at the Bootleg Sessions. See also https://www.facebook.com/groups/canberramusiciansclub for other local bands.

Bibliography

Australian Bureau of Statistics. 2015. www.abs.gov.au/ausstats/abs@.nsf/mf/3101.0 (accessed July 11, 2015).
Bannister, Matthew. 1999. *Positively George Street*. Auckland: Reed Books.
Bennett, Andy. 2004. "Music, Space and Place." In *Music, Space and Place: Popular Music and Cultural Identity*, edited by Sheila Whiteley, Andy Bennett and Stan Hawkins. Aldershot and Burlington: Ashgate, 2–8.
Bennett, Andy. 1997. "'Village Greens and Terraced Streets': Britpop and Representations of 'Britishness.'" *Young* 5 (4): 20–33.
Brand Canberra CBR. 2015. www.brandcanberra.com.au (accessed July 11, 2015).
Canberra Music Blog. 2017. "Phoenix Rising: An Acoustic Evening for the Love of the Phoenix." https://www.facebook.com/events/1666511463360778 (accessed March 31, 2017).
Canberra Musicians Club. 2017. https://www.facebook.com/groups/canberramusiciansclub (accessed February 6, 2017).
Canberra Times. 1927. Canberra's Population. 19 July, p. 4. http://trove.nla.gov.au/newspaper/article/1215326 (accessed February 6, 2017).
Clohessy, Kieron. 2015. Interview with authors. Recording. Canberra, February 9.
Cohen, Sara.1994. "Identity, Place and the 'Liverpool Sound.'" In *Ethnicity, Identity and Music* edited by Martin Stokes. Oxford: Berg Publishers, 117–134.
Connell, John and Chris Gibson. 2003. *Sound Tracks: Popular Music, Identity and Place*. London: Routledge.
Counihan, Bella. 2015. Interview with author JR. Recording. Canberra, January 11.
DeNora, T. 2000. *Music in Everyday Life*. Cambridge: Cambridge University Press.
Drysdale, Ben. 2015. Interview with author JR. Recording. Canberra, March 13.
Evans, Mark and Denis Crowdy. 2008. "Introduction." *Perfect Beat: The Pacific Journal for Research into Contemporary Music and Popular Culture* 8 (4): 1–2.
Frith, Simon. 2010. "Analysing Live Music in the UK, Findings One Year into a Three-Year Research Project." *Journal of the International Association for the Study of Popular Music* 1 (1): 1–3. www.iaspmjournal.net (accessed October 7, 2014).
Gallan, Ben. 2012. "Gatekeeping Night Spaces: The Role of Booking Agents in Creating 'Local' Live Music Venues and Scenes." *Australian Geographer* 43 (1): 35–50. http://dx.doi.org/10.1080/00049182.2012.649518 (accessed February 8, 2015).
Geier, Fiete. 2015. Interview with authors. Recording. Canberra, February 9.
Goodfellow, Mitchell. 2015. Interview with author JR. Recording. Canberra, January 13.
Groch, Sherryn. 2018.'May the Phoenix Rise Again': Canberra Rallies Behind Pub Facing Closure." *Canberra Times*, 11 January. www.canberratimes.com.au/act-news/may-the-phoenix-rise-again-canberra-rallies-behind-pub-facing-closure-20180111-h0gmqi.html (accessed January 25, 2018).
Hadley, Adam. 2015. Facebook message to author JR. March 28.
Hannigan, Sean. 2015. Interview with authors. Recording. Canberra, February 9.
Hayward, Diana. 2017. "Phoenix Pub Closed Due to 'Unforseen Circumstances' Leaving Bands, Patrons Confused." *ABC News*. https://www.facebook.com/Mordd.IndyMedia/posts/1935856506634282;0, (accessed March 30, 2017).
Hesmondhalgh, David. 2013. *Why Music Matters*. Chichester: Wiley Blackwell.
Hesmondhalgh, David. 2002. "Popular Music Audiences and Everyday Life." In *Popular Music Studies*, edited by David Hesmondhalgh and Keith Negus. London: Arnold/Hodder Education, 117–130.
Homan, Shane. 2000. "Losing the Local: Sydney and the Oz Rock Tradition." *Popular Music* 19 (1): January. www.jstor.org/stable/853710 (accessed October 2, 2015).
Ingall, Reuben. 2015. Interview with author JR. Recording. Canberra, February 16.
Kirwan, Liam. 2015. Interview with author JR. Recording. Canberra, January 11.
Kirwan, Liz. 2015. Interview with author JR. Recording. Canberra, January 11.
McRae, Nigel. 2015a. Interview with author JR. Recording. Canberra, February 14.
McRae, Nigel. 2015b. *State of the Local Music Venues Report 2015*, Loadedog Email, May 8, 2015.

Mitchell, Tony. 2009. "Music and the Production of Place: Introduction." In *Transforming Cultures eJournal* 4 (1): i–vii. http://epress.lib.uts.edu.au/journals/TfC (accessed October 10, 2012).

Mordd IndyMedia. 2017. April. https://www.facebook.com/Mordd.IndyMedia/posts/1935856506634282:0 (accessed May 5, 2017).

Nourse, Gemma. 2013. "The Bootleg Sessions." In *BMA Magazine*. www.bmamag.com/articles/features/20120213-bootleg-sessions (accessed January 26, 2015).

Riordan, Primrose. 2014. "Canberra Named the Best Place in the World ... Again." *Canberra Times*, October 7. www.canberratimes.com.au/act-news/canberra-named-the-best-place-in-the-worldagain-20141006-10r5sp.html (accessed July 14, 2015).

Riotact. 2017. "The Phoenix is Here to Stay: Proprietors." http://the-riotact.com/the-phoenix-is-here-to-stay-say-proprietors/199292 (accessed March 31, 2017).

Rogers, Ian. 2010. "'You've Got to Go to the Gigs to Get Gigs': Indie Musicians, Eclecticism and the Brisbane Scene." *Continuum: Journal of Media & Cultural Studies* 22 (5): 639–649.

Shakallis, Chris, Robina Gugler, Cody Anderson and Steve Nebauer. 2013. *Head Full of Flames: Punk in the Nation's Capital 1977 to 1992 – Alternate Sub-Kulture and Tribal Interaction*. Canberra: Robina Jane Gulger Publications.

Shank, Barry. 1994. *Dissonant Identities: The Rock'n'Roll Scene in Austin, Texas*. Hanover: University Press of New England.

Sharpe, John. 2006. *A Cool Capital: The Canberra Jazz Scene 1925–2005*. Torrens, ACT: J. Sharpe.

Spencer, Chris. 2001. *Rockin' and Rollin' in Canberra: A Documentation of Bands that Emanated from Canberra and the A.C.T.* Golden Square, Victoria: Moonlight Publications.

Stafford, Andrew. 2006. *Pig City: From the Saints to Savage Garden*. St Lucia: University of Queensland Press.

Starr, Val. 2014. *Rock & Roll Comes to Canberra Next Saturday Night*. West Geelong, Victoria: Echo Books.

Stevenson, Lucy. 2015. Interview with author JR. Recording. Canberra, January 13.

Stratton, Jon. 2008. "The Difference of Perth Music: A Scene in Cultural and Historical Context." *Continuum: Journal of Media & Cultural Studies* 22 (5): 613–622.

The Phoenix. 2015a. #lovethephoenix. https://twitter.com/search?q=%23lovethephoenix&src=typd (accessed July 26, 2015).

The Phoenix. 2015b. http://lovethephoenix.com (accessed July 15, 2015).

The Phoenix. 2015c. . https://www.facebook.com/thephoenixcanberra (accessed July 15, 2015).

The Phoenix. 2015d. https://twitter.com/PhoenixThePub (accessed July 26, 2015).

The Phoenix. 2017a. http://lovethephoenix.com (accessed April 1, 2017).

The Phoenix. 2017b. https://www.facebook.com/thephoenixcanberra (accessed April 1, 2017).

Trainer, Adam. 2015. "Sleepy Township, Perth Indie Rock in the 1990s." In *Continuum, Journal of Media & Cultural Studies*. doi: 10.0180/10304312.2015.1025364.

Trask, Steven. 2017. "Popular Phoenix Pub in the Sydney Building 'Shut Until Further Notice.'" www.canberratimes.com.au/act-news/popular-phoenix-pub-in-the-sydney-building-shut-until-further-notice-20170329-gv9j76.html (accessedMarch 30, 2017).

Tully, Beth. 2015. Interview with author JR. Recording. Canberra, February 14.

Turino, Thomas. 2008. *Music as Social Life: The Politics of Participation*. Chicago and London: University of Chicago Press.

Visit Canberra: Canberra Facts and Figures. 2015. http://visitcanberra.com.au/visitor-information/canberra-facts-and-figures (accessed July 11, 2016).

Webster, Emma. 2010. "King Tut's Wah Wah Hut: Initial Research into a 'Local' Live Music Venue." *Journal of the International Association for the Study of Popular Music* 1 (1): 24–30. www.iaspmjournal.net (accessed October 7, 2014).

Whiteley, Sheila. 2004. "Introduction." *Music, Space and Place: Popular Music and Cultural Identity*, edited by Sheila Whiteley, Andy Bennett and Stan Hawkins. Aldershot and Burlington: Ashgate, 1.

Williams, Emma. 2014. "Taking the 'Next Step' with Web 2.0: Social Media as a Research Tool for Museums." *Museums Australia Magazine* 22 (4): 16–19.

Williams, Emma . 2007. "States-Minded: Local Identity in Australian Pop Music Scenes 1962–1971." Unpublished Hons. thesis, University of Sydney.

3

Lorde's Auckland

Stepping Out of "the Bubble"

Tony Mitchell

In this chapter, I examine Auckland, and in particular the suburbs of Devonport and Morningside, as the environment in which the multi-award winning and chart-topping female New Zealand alt-pop singer Lorde's global music career flourished in 2013 and 2014, and her move away from it in 2015 and 2016. Lorde (real name Ella Yelich-O'Connor) relied heavily on internet outlets such as YouTube, Facebook, Twitter, Tumblr, Soundcloud and Instagram to forge her links with the rest of the world and to achieve an unprecedented success in popular music, but was also able to rely on a highly supportive environment in both Devonport and Auckland.

My study is grounded in a specific understanding of "place" that has been adopted in popular music studies. In his 1995 chapter "(Dis)located? Rhetoric, Politics, Meaning and the Locality," John Street explains manifestations of locality in music-making according to six broad categories: industrial base, social experience, aesthetic perspective, political experience, community and scene (Street 1995, 256–257). To break these categories down further, "place" arguably has a direct impact on music-making, providing: (a) space, outlets and institutions for performance, recording, broadcasting, marketing and distribution of music; (b) an environment and network (e.g. school) for social interaction through music; (c) an experience and appreciation of the cultural and educational elements and opportunities of a locality; (d) either a normative or oppositional experience of one's local environment; (e) a network of people, beginning with family, with which one interacts, and including friends and local institutions; and, finally, (f) what Will Straw has defined as "that cultural space in which a range of musical practices coexist, interacting with each other within a variety of processes of differentiation, and according to widely varying trajectories of change and cross-fertlilisation" (Straw 1991, 368). Both of these accounts occurred before the internet became a major factor in defining musical environment, but I argue that the non-virtual aspects of place have remained concrete. It has been widely asserted that place is still an important source of musical identity, as well as providing links with a global music culture.

Success: Stepping Out of the Bubble

Even if there are few perceptible New Zealand influences in her music, Lorde has clearly been shaped by her upbringing. She cites, in particular, "the bubble" of Devonport as being a significant site from her childhood, "because it's so insular and closed off from everything" and it is "the kind of suburb that people make movies about, there's quite weird mums everywhere" (Petridis 2013). The bubble refers to the enclosed nature of Devonport, where only one road leads into the suburb, Lake Road on Auckland's North Shore, and the only other way out is by boat or ferry to the city center.

By the time she was eighteen and had achieved musical success, Lorde had rapidly passed through a number of personal and professional changes. On the day of Lorde's eighteenth birthday in November 2014, the *New Zealand Herald* estimated she had earned NZ\$11 million from record sales and royalties, from the sale of 2.7 million copies of her album and a combined 17 million singles, and compared her earnings "to winning a Lotto jackpot every year" (Nippert 2014), which meant no more "Counting our dollars on the train to the party," as her song "Royals" had put it in 2013. Victor O'Connor, the singer's father and director of her holding company, Sackful of Squirrels, declined to comment at the time on the estimate, or whether his daughter would take over directing the company having turned eighteen (ibid).

In May 2015, Lorde was reported to have split with her manager, Scott Maclachlan, and his company, Saiko Management (Anon. 2015b), and taken over her own management. In a further move towards independence, she split from her long-term boyfriend, 26- year-old photographer James Lowe, who "had been there for every step of Lorde's transformation from a shy Auckland teen to a globe-trotting chart-topper" (Anon. 2016b). In August 2015, she was reported to have bought a NZ\$2.84 million house in inner city Auckland, "a villa on a quiet street on the border of Herne Bay, Ponsonby and Grey Lynn" (Nippert 2016). The house, bought mortgage free, was in "the hottest city in a country which ratings agency Fitch . . . said was the most expensive housing market in the world" (ibid). Earlier she had been quoted in the *New Zealand Herald* as saying that "if the first record was about living in the bubble of your hometown [i.e. Devonport], the second record will be about stepping out of that bubble for the first time." This related to a previous comment she had made:

> All the kids call this [Devonport] the bubble because everyone knows everyone and it feels very shut off from the rest of the city . . . I feel like you can hear where I'm from in the music, I feel like I write about the place a lot.
>
> (Anon. 2015a)

But by March 2016, in the long hiatus between her first and second albums, she revealed that she was writing song lyrics at the house of US singer-songwriter Jack Antonoff, who co-wrote a number of songs on her friend Taylor Swift's album *1989*, but also continuing to work in Joel Little's Kingsland studio in Auckland (Anon 2016a). And by September 2016, three years after the release of *Pure Heroine*, there was still no sign of a second album(Anon. 2016b).

Lorde and Devonport

The borough of Devonport had an important influence on Lorde's development as a teenager and burgeoning singer/songwriter, along with her mother's influence on her reading. In an interview given when she was fifteen, Lorde commented on the two suburbs near Devonport on Auckland's North Shore, where she lived during her early life, as well her literary upbringing:

I was born on Hororata Road in Takapuna, and I grew up on Beresford Street in Bayswater. We had a big backyard and a sandpit and a lot of animals and books and paints. It was good ... I guess my mum influenced my lyrical style by always buying me books. She'd give me a mixture of kid and adult books too, there weren't really any books I wasn't allowed to read. I remember reading *Feed* by M.T. Anderson when I was six, and her giving me Salinger and Carver at a young age, and [New Zealand Author] Janet Frame really young too. We'd always discuss what I had read, which helped me form this really strong understanding of what I did and didn't like about the ways different writers used words. I think that's a smart thing to raise kids on, and I'm glad she did.

(Fell 2013)

She later lived in Devonport, and attended Belmore Intermediate School, between Devonport and Takapuna, and then went to Takapuna Grammar School, where she topped year 11 in English. Lorde's other achievements at an early age include coming third in the Bank of New Zealand Short Story Competition, winning the North Shore Primary Schools Speech Competition and coming second in the 2009 World Literary Quiz in Johannesburg with a team from Belmont Intermediate School, at the age of twelve. She also won Belmont Idol, her intermediate school talent contest, along with school friend Louis McDonald on acoustic guitar, and was invited back as a judge of the competition in November 2013. Their duo—titled "Ella and Louis," because she was not using the stage name Lorde at that time—later played covers in cafes around Auckland, and at Devonport's Victoria Theatre, an historic art-deco building built in 1912 as a cinema, rescued from demolition and re-opened in 2010, thereafter functioning as a cinema complex, concert venue and playhouse. She performed some of her own songs there in November 2011. The duo also performed at the annual Devonstock festival on Mount Victoria in December 2010. They were interviewed on Radio New Zealand in 2008, where she sang a version of the Kings of Leon single "Use Somebody," and two other songs (Mulligan 2009), and McDonald's father sent a video of their Belmont performance to Scott Maclachlan of Universal Music, who subsequently engaged Ella Yelich-O'Connor in 2009 as a recording artist "under development." She also sang with the band Extreme at Belmont Intermediate in 2009, competing in the covers category of the Intermediate Schools Battle of the Bands finals. They were placed third in the North Shore Battle of the Bands finals at the Bruce Mason Centre, Takapuna in November 2009. She later sang with And They Were Masked at the age of fifteen: a "future noir" band influenced by P.J. Harvey, Massive Attack and others (Thomas 2014). She worked under the tutelage of a singing coach and a number of New Zealand songwriters, with unsuccessful results, before teaming up with Jason Little in December 2011, and working with him in her school holidays on producing tracks, which eventually led to the 2012 EP *The Love Club*, including the song "Royals."

Lorde's parents are far from wealthy, her father being an Irish-born civil engineer and her mother a Serbian-born poet, although as Lorde told the *NZ Listener* in 2014:

I've said from the beginning I'm not poor. I'm extremely lucky. I haven't had times in my life when I've been hungry or anything like that. But I don't have a Rolex and I don't have a credit card to use with abandon.

(Wichtel 2014)

48 • Tony Mitchell

As she stated in a series of video clips she recorded as interviews about her formative years and influences:

> I think you can kind of hear where I'm from in my music. I feel I write about the place a lot. I don't know if it's New Zealand in particular but it definitely is this place. . . . I'm happy I grew up here. Everybody knows me here and they have since I was a little kid. I am Ella here.
>
> (Lorde 2013)

Devonport: A Brief History

In 2014, the Depot Artspace—consisting of two art galleries, as well as a music venue and recording studio in Clarence Street, Devonport—published the book *Tūrangawaewae: Sense of Place*, about Devonport. *Tūrangawaewae* is a te reo Māori word which literally means "a place to stand," and denotes a powerful Māori concept often defined in relation to a local mountain and river. The book defines it as "a standing place from where you gain the authority to belong" (Mackillop 2014, n.p.). Devonport is noted for being the first borough in Auckland to grant women the vote in 1893 and also the first to be declared nuclear free in 1981. It was first settled by the Ngāti Pāoa tribe in the fourteenth century with fortified *pā* (hill forts or village strongholds) on the slopes of Takarunga (Mount Victoria). Other vestiges of Māori presence in the area include the Te Taua Moana marae, established in 2000 under the jurisdiction of the New Zealand Navy, on the foreshore of Ngataringa Bay, near the largest naval base in the country. In the 1970s and 1980s, the book reports, Queenie Karami ran a center for homeless people in her garage on Rutland Road, indicating that at that time it was by no means a prosperous area.

The book, which has a seal on the cover denoting the incorporation of Devonport as a borough in 1866, features profiles of prominent figures and institutions in the local community. Present day institutions include the Devonport Folk Club, run by Roger Giles and Hilary Condon on a site known as the Bunker, and a military command post built in 1891 on the slopes of Takarunga for surveillance of possible Russian invasion. Maungauika (North Head), the other extinct volcano in the area, was used as a military coastal defence installation from 1885, and is riddled with underground tunnels, bunkers and three gun batteries. The Devonport Museum of the Vernacular, at the foot of Takuranga, is a non-traditional museum devoted to "cultural mapping." One notable quote in the book is from the father of Mary Williamson, made when Devonport was still a "poor" suburb: "anywhere else in the world this would be a millionaire's paradise" (Mackillop 2014, n.p.). This is in fact what parts of Devonport have become, with wealthy businessmen and an increasing number of Chinese immigrants settling in the area, and house prices verging on NZ$1 million.[1] In 2009 Stephen Hart, the author of *Where to Live in Auckland* (2011) and *The Streetwise Homebuyer* (2006), reported in the *New Zealand Herald* that

> Devonport came top [of the Auckland house prices market] by a comfortable margin, having shown an 18.5 per cent price increase over the past two years. In October,

Devonport cracked the [NZD]$800,000-plus average sales price ceiling for the first time, with 94 homes selling collectively for more than [NZD]$89 million.

(Hart 2009)

Representing Devonport

Lorde's music videos also articulate Devonport as a very personal place for her. The music video for "Royals" features a number of her peers and friends, and although there are few direct references to place in her lyrics, apart from slightly derogatory comments such as "we're not proud of our address" in "Royals," and the patently untrue chorus of "Team": "We live in cities you'll never see on screen/Not very pretty, but we sure know how to run things)<[2] there is a more intangible sense of her origins and upbringing in her music. As she told Jason Lipshutz in *Billboard*:

> In that song, there are a few lines which are kind of me being the 'realistic' pop star: "We live in cities you'll never see onscreen," which is like, no one comes to New Zealand, no one knows anything about New Zealand, and here I am, trying to grow up and become a person. I've been countering that with going to New York and seeing this place that's in every movie and every TV show. Part of me wanted to go back to writing for me and for my friends, and write something that I felt related to us a little bit.
>
> (Lipshutz 2013)

But as she told Tavi Gevinson of *Rookie* magazine, describing North Head and Cheltenham Beach in Devonport, where one gets a spectacular view of Rangitoto Island, as featured on the cover of Stephen Barnett's *A Picture Book of Old Auckland* (1981):

> I live by the beach near a mountain, and if you walk around the side of the mountain, there are lots of succulents and kind of aqueous plants that grow on the rock base and they all drift in the water, and there's always sound there but it's also always quiet. Walking along the beach over a bunch of rocks and just hanging out there is really nice for me. I walk heaps and heaps and heaps, and sometimes just a good two-hour walk through my neighborhood listening to some rollicking music will make me feel happy.
>
> (Gevinson 2014)

She recalled her schooldays in Devonport as a rebellious pre-teen in *Billboard*:

> I live in a beach town, and there are these boats that sit on land, and we would break into them ... We'd sit in them all night, doing Ouija boards and telling secrets. I remember that feeling so vividly, like, "We are here. It's us against everything else."
>
> (Lynch 2014)

Experiencing Devonport

My own experience in Devonport is worth recounting. I lived there for six months in 2011, and found peace and inspiration on North Head, with its numerous gun turrets, strategic

50 • Tony Mitchell

tunnels and underground passages dating from the nineteenth century. Inspiration was also provided by the picturesque Cheltenham Beach, with its pohutukawa trees and views of Rangitoto, and by spectacular views all around Waitemata Harbour from Mount Victoria, where the Devonstock festival was originally held – in 2011 it was headlined by a local rock/electronic group the Naked and Famous, and Lorde performed there as Ella in 2010. Other favorite haunts were the Devonport Folk Club, also known as the Bunker, an Aladdin's cave of folk music memorabilia, and the Devonport public library, now completely rebuilt and re-opened as a spectacular NZ$7.8 million Māori-styled, open-plan, timber edifice (Barton 2015), after much debate, in February 2015. It was described in *Metro* magazine by Chris Barton as

> [a] pavilion in the park. It opens to the outside via a high verandah around two sides and the transparency of its glazed and ventilating, louvred façade brings the park inside. In places, you can view straight through. The mezzanine level has quieter study spaces, including a perimeter desk that looks out through the pohutukawa of Windsor Reserve to the harbour. Everywhere are comfortable places to sit, including lounge chairs and sofas around gas fireplaces on each level. Just like home.
>
> (Barton 2015)

When I revisited Devonport in early 2015, I spotted a teenage girl on the ferry wearing a Cramps T-shirt, in apparent emulation of Lorde on the cover of *Rolling Stone* (March 2014) where Rob Tannenbaum had described Lorde, rather ludicrously, as "Judith Butler in Doc Martins, with a Tumblr" (Tannenbaum 2014, 77). The Evergreen second hand bookshop, a treasure trove for local historical books, had been replaced by a bookshop from neighboring Takapuna, equally as well-stocked, and extensions to the Devonport wharf were in progress, which some local people were not happy about. The suburb continues to have an air of affluence, with numerous art galleries dotted around the center, and Victorian, colonial style, timber mansions lining the road to Torpedo Bay and North Head. According to Duncan Greive in *Metro*:

> [Lorde's] school, Takapuna Grammar, celebrated the [Grammy] wins with a vast banner across its main building. In nearby Devonport, they altered the sign to read 'We're now proud of our address,' a cute rewording of a "Royals" lyric which actually goes 'We're not proud of our address.'
>
> (Greive 2013)

This managed to combine Devonport's pride for their location with their pride for their native daughter.

Morningside (for Life)?

The other significant location in Lorde's musical career in Auckland is Morningside, an inner-city suburb. This place was popularized on television via the New Zealand animated comedy series *Bro'Town*, which ran from 2004 to 2010, and was devised by Elizabeth Mitchell and theater group The Naked Samoans. Influenced by the US series *The Simpsons* and especially *South Park*, it deals with the misadventures of five school kids, four Pacific Islanders and one Māori. It was very popular with young people, and it presented the fictional Morningside as "one of Auckland's grungier suburbs." However, as Matthew Bannister has pointed out, its location is much more fluid:

> Morningside (which is the Auckland innercity suburb of the creators' childhoods) does triple service as South Auckland, which is popularly identified with Polynesian culture (for example OMC standing for Otara Millionaires Club), and also Waitakere (West Auckland), as in 'Survival of the Fattest' when the boys enact a 'Lord of the Flies' scenario in the Morningside (Waitakere) Ranges.
>
> (Bannister 2008, 7)

As Bannister points out, the show was much attacked for its ethnic stereotyping and politically incorrect humor as regards Māori and Pacific Island people, but nonetheless the catchphrase "Morningside for life!" took hold, and images from the series were featured on Morningside railway station.[3] The station, where some spectacular graffiti art is featured, including a large copy of a Tretchikoff painting, and art work by noted Auckland female graffiti artist Misery (Matt L. 2014), is where Lorde took the train to Britomart in downtown Auckland after a day's work at Golden Age studio in Morningside, prior to taking the ferry across to Devonport. The station was also featured (very fleetingly) in the video clip for "Royals." As Lorde noted in an article she wrote for the Auckland *Sunday Star Times*:

> We wrote, as we always have, at Golden Age, Joel [Little]'s studio in Morningside, Auckland. I'll always remember this so vividly—walking to the same few places to get lunch or dinner every day; moments outside the studio when we hurried back, or let our feet drag, either terrified or elated at the prospect of that room; listening back at the end of a day, the fairy lights winking, and both feeling this weary but budding excitement. Each day I'd take the train. The night-time rides were my chance to breathe, relax for a few minutes. Then I'd pull out my laptop and hit play on whatever we'd worked on that day. For a few seconds with a new song there's always this thudding amnesia, like it's not your work, and you get to listen with fresh ears to this thing that's still newly born. For months and months I took that night train and listened to my voice and the beats over and over, silvery, suspended. I'd grin like a creep from Kingsland to Grafton, face all moony under the white light. It's the best thing I've ever made.
>
> (Yelich-O'Connor 2013)

It was where she returned in late March 2015 to begin recording her second album with Little, despite the producer having recently married and bought a house in Los Angeles, after his celebrity from the *Pure Heroine* album (Newman 2015; Duff 2014).

Silo Park: Lorde's Post-Grammy "Homecoming Concert"

Lorde suffered the pains of New Zealand celebrity media exposure. Her family was almost pushed over by the media scrum on her return to Auckland after winning two Grammy

52 • Tony Mitchell

Awards in Los Angeles in January 2014. She was welcomed by a Māori haka by Air New Zealand crew when she got off the plane, but she later complained about the local media's "constant lecherous gaze," and her family being jostled by them (Theunissen 2014). Lorde also told the New Zealand press that she had been far more nervous at the New Zealand Music Awards, whereas the Grammys were "business as usual" (ibid). This is despite having said

> That's the good thing about starting off in New Zealand, there is absolutely no concept of 'celebrity' or fame ... people are starting to recognize me now, which is kind of weird. But in New Zealand, it's easy to hide from that stuff ... I think growing up in New Zealand, it's easy to keep grounded.
>
> (Gevinson 2014)

In 2014, Lorde staged a special one-off homecoming concert in Auckland the day after the Grammy Awards. This festival, which originated in Detroit USA, and in Auckland in 2014 featured mainly indie rock performers including Cat Power, Chvrches, Savages and a number of Australian and New Zealand artists, on January 27, Auckland Anniversary Day. When that date coincided with her appearance at the Grammy Awards, she re-scheduled a solo concert in the same venue, Silo Park, the day of her return to Auckland on January 29. Named after the giant silos situated nearby, originally used for storing cement, Silo Park is in Auckland's Wynyard Quarter, not far from Britomart, in an area also known as the Western Reclamation (which took place in 1930) or the Tank Farm, on Auckland's waterfront. It is the site of a summer night market, an open-air cinema where films are projected on one of the silos, concerts, community events, restaurants and an annual vinyl record fair. The entire Wynyard Quarter was extensively redeveloped for the America's Cup when it was hosted in Auckland in 2000 and 2003, an event which entrenched Auckland's nickname "city of sails."

I went to the site early, and was fortunate enough to be able to see Lorde's sound check, where she performed about four songs in a long, white T-shirt, through gaps in the covered wire netting fences surrounding Silo Park. During her performance, I saw a number of parents holding pre-teens and toddlers on their shoulders, instead of the usual concert-going young men holding women of a similar age on their shoulders. Free glow sticks were handed out to the audience, and a number of teenage girls present were emulating Lorde's hairstyle and dress sense. Her support artists on the night included Christchurch group Doprah,[4] a band that she named at the 2014 Vodafone New Zealand Music awards in November 2014 as one of her favorite New Zealand recording artists, along with the Joel Little-produced brother and sister duo Broods, Tiny Ruins (aka Hollie Fullbrook), transsexual rapper Randa and Dawn Raid Samoan hip hop artist David Dallas. At Silo Park they were followed by Watercolours, aka Chelsea Jade Metcalf, a former art student. As expected, neither support artist in any way measured up to Lorde.

The New Zealand Herald reviewer, Chris Schulz, described her twenty-minute late start as her "only diva moment," and the audience of almost 10,000 as "full of parents, teens, kids and leftover Laneway hipsters" (Shulz 2014).[5] In my view, however, it was an atmosphere of family celebration and local pride reminiscent of Split Enz reunion concerts, but with a much younger demographic. Lorde appeared with two relatively anonymous backing musicians—keyboard player Jimmy Macdonald and drummer Ben Barter—who have been with her since her first public performance, and she opened with the song "Bravado." Her fourteen-song set list included cover versions of Son Lux's "Easy" and James Blake's "Retrograde," both performed live by her for the first time—as well as all her most well-known songs from the album *Pure Heroine*. These included "Tennis Court," "Buzzcut Season," "White Teeth Teens," "Royals," which she performed in the US Grammy version style, "Team," "Ribs" and, finally, "A World Alone." Her long black dress, jerky movements and hair-flinging gave a slightly awkward sense to her performance, but the audience was totally in support of her.

Conclusion

Subsequent to her Grammy Awards, Lorde became much in demand as a touring musician in the USA and to a lesser extent the UK. She made numerous trips to the USA in 2013 and 2014 and has made several since, spending increasing amounts of time there, but her Grammy Awards appearance with "black death"-styled smudged fingertips for her Grammy performance of "Royals," which scandalized US fashion gossips, caused local music writer Russell Baillie to muse that:

> [it] might … have been its own little comment. Something about being an outsider to the US of A? Because if you've spent much of the 17th year of your life undergoing the joys of US immigration formalities, as you've crossed the Pacific again and again, you've been fingerprinted more than most. Or could it have been something about getting one's artistic, idealistic hands dirty in what is the American, most mainstream, often most baffling, biggest televised music event on the planet?
>
> (Baillie 2014)

Despite having acquired traces of a US accent in her speech, she appears to remain committed to her base in Auckland, her parents and family in Devonport, the New Zealand music scene, which she has commented on at New Zealand music awards Anon. 2014), and the community she came from. Although her aesthetic perspective has arguably shifted from New Zealand towards the USA, her political experience embraces feminism and speaking out for teenagers universally (Gevinson 2014), and she still appears to regard her career in New Zealand as all important, at least at this early stage, despite her having made numerous celebrity appearances in the USA with friends such as Tavi Gevinson, Taylor Swift and Jack Antonoff. Her second album has been a re-defining moment "outside the bubble," but until then, she continues to nurture her roots in Auckland.

Notes

1   There is also a residue of Englishness about the place, one of the few suburbs in Auckland to have a UK grocer, Bramptins, specializing in imported goods, including sweets, from the UK, next door to a pub called The Patriot, "Devonport's only British pub."

2   Ian Brodie's 2006 book *A Journey Through New Zealand Film* indicates that a number of significant New Zealand films have been shot in Auckland, including Roger Donaldson's *Sleeping Dogs* (1997), Geoff Murphy's *The Quiet Earth* (1985), Peter Jackson's *King Kong* (2005), which used the 1929 Civic Theatre in Queen Street, and Japanese director Nagisa Oshima's *Merry Christmas Mr. Lawrence* (1983), while Karekare Beach, outside of

54 • Tony Mitchell

Auckland, was the setting for Jane Campion's Cannes and Academy Award-winning film *The Piano* (1993). Another notable film set in Auckland city was Bruce Morrison's *Queen City Rocker* (1986), about street kids. Jonathan King's film *Under the Mountain* (2009), based on the children's fantasy novel by Maurice Gee, was set on the volcanic Lake Pupuke on Auckland's North Shore, near Takapuna, and on Mount Eden in Auckland. Segments of Jane Campion's award-winning film of Janet Frame's *An Angel at My Table* (1990) were set in writer Frank Sargeson's house at Takapuna.

3   The previously closed station was re-opened in 2009 in the lead up to the 2011 Rugby World Cup because the station is close to [rugby ground] Eden Park (Horrell 2009).

4   Doprah describe themselves on Bandcamp as a "sinister and evil cult which lures young people into drug-taking." They are a six-piece trip hop ensemble featuring gyrating "little girl" singer Indira Force (aka Indi), seemingly even younger than Lorde (she was in fact age twenty at the time), who had worked with Joel Little, and instrumentalist Steven Marr. The group had released their debut single in September 2013 and an EP in June 2014.

5   It was clear to me that he was not aware that Lorde had been vomiting prior to the start of the concert, due to severe jetlag and nerves.

Bibliography

Anon. 2016a. "Lorde Shacks Up with Famous Faces for New Album." *New Zealand Herald,* March 29. www.nzherald. co.nz/entertainment/news/article.cfm?c_id=1501119&objectid=11613121 (accessed May 25, 2016).

Anon. 2016b "Lorde Hits Back at Impatient Fans: 'Give Up on Me If You Want To.'" *New Zealand Herald* August 25. www.nzherald.co.nz/entertainment/news/article.cfm?c_id=1501119&objectid=11700175 (accessed May 25, 2016).

Anon. 2015a. "Lorde's New Record Will Be About Leaving Auckland." *New Zealand Herald*, June 23. www.nzherald. co.nz/entertainment/news/article.cfm?c_id=1501119&objectid=11469882 (accessed May 25, 2016).

Anon. 2015b. "Lorde Splits from Manager Scott Maclachlan: Pop Star and Man Who Discovered Her Part Ways." *New Zealand Herald*, May 18. www.nzherald.co.nz/entertainment/news/article.cfm?c id=1501119& objectid=11450459 (accessed May 25, 2016).

Anon. 2014. "Lorde: My Favourite NZ Artists." November 21. http://m.nzherald.co.nz/nz-music-awards/news/video.cfm?c_id=1500975&gallery_id=146829&gal_objectid=11361733 (accessed May 20, 2015).

Baillie, Russell. 2014. "Diva with Smudged Fingertips Shows Up Showgirls of Pop." *New Zealand Herald*, January 28. www.nzherald.co.nz/entertainment/news/article.cfm?c_id=1501119&objectid=11192827 (accessed May 20, 2015).

Bannister, Matthew. 2008. "Where's Morningside?" *NZ Journal of Media Studies* 11 (1), June. https://medianz.otago.ac.nz/medianz/article/download/55/58 (accessed May 20, 2015).

Barnett, Stephen. 1981. *A Picture Book of Old Auckland*. Takapuna: ROSS.

Barton, Chris. 2015. "Pavilion in the Park." *Metro*, April. www.metromag.co.nz/city-life/urban-design/pavilion-in-the-park (accessed May 20, 2015).

Brodie, Ian. 2006. *A Journey Through New Zealand Film*, Auckland: Harper Collins.

Duff, Michelle. 2014. "Joel Little: The Man Behind Lorde." *Sunday*, November 16. www.stuff.co.nz/entertainment/music/63161125/Joel-Little-The-man-behind-Lorde (accessed May 20, 2015).

Fell, Grant. 2013. "Lorde of Takapuna." *Blacklog,* May 2. http://blacklognz.blogspot.com.au/2013/05/blk-19-lorde-of-takapuna.html (accessed May 20, 2015).

Gevinson, Tavi. 2014. "Super Heroine: An Interview with Lorde." *Rookie*, February 1. http://rookiemag.com/2014/01/lorde-interview (accessed May 20, 2015).

Greive, Duncan. 2013. "Storm Singer." *Metro*, October 2013, 54–60, 135. www.fasterlouder.com.au/headliners/lorde (accessed May 20, 2015).

Hart, Stephen. 2011. *Where to Live in Auckland*. Auckland: Barbican Publishing Limited.

Hart, Stephen. 2009. "Devonport Leads in House Price See-Saw." *New Zealand Herald*, December 6. www.nzherald.co.nz/business/news/article.cfm?c_id=3&objectid=10613671 (accessed May 20, 2015).

Hart, Stephen. 2006. *The Streetwise Homebuyer*. Auckland: Barbican Publishing Limited.

Hayes, Samantha. 2013. "The Story of Lorde." TVNZ *Channel 3 News*, September 18. www.3news.co.nz/tvshows/3d/the-story-of-lorde-2013091816#axzz3b6kXM4A3 (accessed May 20, 2015).

Horrell, Rhiannon. 2009. "Morningside for Life." *Auckland City Harbour News*, August 14. www.stuff.co.nz/auckland/local-news/auckland-city-harbour-news/2748769/Morningside-for-life (accessed May 20, 2015).

Lipshutz, Jason. 2013. "Lorde Q&A: New Zealand Star On Next Single, Nicki Minaj & Staying Mysterious/" *Billboard*, September 10. www.billboard.com/articles/columns/pop-shop/5687330/lorde-qa-new-zealand-star-on-next-single-nicki-minaj-staying (accessed May 20, 2015).

Lorde. 2013. "Under the Influence." YouTube, November 13. https://youtu.be/YftTq4XXTg8 (accessed January 14, 2018).

Lynch, Joe. 2014. "Billboard Cover Sneak Peek: 5 Things You Didn't Know about Lorde Before She was Famous." *Billboard*, October 30. https://www.billboard.com/articles/news/6304078/billboard-cover-sneak-peek-lordeg (accessed January 18, 2018).

Mackillop, Lia Kent. 2014. *Tūrangawaewae: Sense of Place*. Devonport: Depot Artspace. n.p.

Matt, L. 2014. "Photo of the Day: Morningside Art." http://transportblog.co.nz/2014/03/20/photo-of-the-day-morningside-art (accessed May 20, 2015).

Mitchell, Tony. 2009. "Sonic Psychogeography: A Poetics of Place in Popular Music in Aotearoa/New Zealand." *Perfect Beat: The Pacific Journal for Research into Contemporary Music and Popular Culture* 10 (2): 145–175.

Mulligan, Jesse. (2009). "Ella Yelich-O'Connor." RNZ, August 13. www.radionz.co.nz/national/programmes/afternoons/audio/2033420/ella-yelich-o'connor (accessed January 18, 2018).

Newman, Melinda. 2015. "Joel Little Gives Update on Lorde's Second Album at ASCAP Pop Music Awards." *Billboard*, April 30. www.billboard.com/articles/news/6553085/lorde-new-album-ascap-pop-music-awards (accesssed May 20, 2015).

Nippert, Matt. 2016. "Lorde Pays $2.84m for Her City Villa." *New Zealand Herald*, January 16. www.nzherald.co.nz/business/news/article.cfm?c_id=3&objectid=11574655 (accessed May 20, 2015).

Nippert, Matt. 2014. "Birthday Girl Lorde's Earnings Estimated at $11m-Plus." *New Zealand Herald*, November 7. www.nzherald.co.nz/business/news/article.cfm?c_id=3&objectid=11354524 (accessed May 20, 2015).

Petridis, Alex. 2013. "Lorde: 'I'm Just a Freak.'" *Guardian,* October 11. www.theguardian.com/music/2013/oct/10/lorde-just-freak-royals-pure-heroine (accessed May 20, 2015).

Shulz, Chris. 2014. "Concert Review: Lorde, Silo Park, Auckland." *New Zealand Herald*, January 30. www.nzherald.co.nz/entertainment/news/article.cfm?c_id=1501119&objectid=11193929 (accessed May 20, 2015).

Straw, Will. 1991. "Systems of Articulation, Logics of Change: Communities and Scenes in Popular Music." *Cultural Studies* 5 (3): 368–388.

Street, John. 1995. "(Dis)located? Rhetoric, Politics, Meaning and the Locality." In *Popular Music: Style and Identity*, edited by Will Straw et al. Montreal: Center for Research on Canadian Cultural Industries and Institutions, 256–257.

Tannenbaum, Rob. 2014. "Lorde: The New Girl." *Rolling Stone* 748, March: 74–79.

Theunissen, Matthew. 2014. "Lorde Slams NZ Media Welcome as 'Sad.'" *New Zealand Herald*, January 29. www.nzherald.co.nz/entertainment/news/article.cfm?c_id=1501119&objectid=11193590 (accessed May 20, 2015).

Thomas, Sarah. 2014. "Lorde's Early Work Unmasked." *Sydney Morning Herald*, August 8. www.smh.com.au/entertainment/music/lordes-early-work-unmasked-20140808-101rem.html (accessed May 20, 2015).

Wichtel, Diana. 2014. "Lorde on High." *NZ Listener*, January 26. www.listener.co.nz/culture/lorde-on-high (accessed May 20, 2015).

Yelich-O'Connor, Ella. 2013. "Our Lady Lorde: The Kiwi Schoolgirl Turned Pop Royalty." *Sunday Magazine, Sunday Star Times*, September 29. www.stuff.co.nz/entertainment/music/9208190/Our-Lady-Lorde-The-Kiwi-schoolgirl-turned-pop-Royalty (accessed May 20, 2015).

Discography

Lorde, *Pure Heroine*, Universal Music, New Zealand, 3751900, 2013.
Lorde, *The Love Club* EP, Universal Music, New Zealand, 3738955, 2013.

PART **II**

Rethinking the Musical Event

This part offers considerations about how events are mobilized by a range of interested parties, from music-makers and historians, to tourists and city brand managers. Recasting cities as "eventful" sites through music festivals and museums, for example, situates them as the locus for and repository of musical moments and memories that are designed to celebrate locality. They become at once cultural, social, and semiotic resources. The reorganization of musical activity (in terms of both its past and present) through heritage sites and tourist packages (which memorialize at the same time as they monumentalize) is designed to reaffirm and simultaneously mine the value of a city's musical legacy. This is done as a way of maximizing its symbolic, cultural, and—it is hoped—economic capital. As the contributors here suggest, this raises some important issues in terms of how music is staged in urban settings.

Melbourne is a key musical hub in Australasia. The city is the pinnacle of all popular music destinations for musicians residing elsewhere in Australia, as well a site of pilgrimage for Aotearoa/New Zealand musicians and a key destination in the global circuit—all factors that firmly reconfirm Melbourne's official status as a "music city." Both Catherine Strong and Mara Favaretto explore Melbourne in this capacity, albeit through different lenses. In the case of Strong's chapter, there is a clear attempt (on behalf of music fans) to influence the shape that "heritagization" has taken in Melbourne, and she outlines the strategies that have been successful and what other interests are at stake. The chapter also considers the way this inclusion of popular music as an aspect of cultural memory reflects global trends and processes of commodification. Favaretto, by contrast, presents Melbourne, as a multicultural city which has long appealed to immigrants from Europe, Asia, and elsewhere. It offers a space where festivals can exist as a space where ethnic identity can be consolidated and can also become caught up in clichés. Her chapter explores the discourse surrounding the festival Clave Contra Clave and the case of the "Aussie-Latins" who are committed to the creation of an alternative sound that both represents distant homelands and incorporates alternative or negotiated identities that arise from their current Australian context. Oli Wilson and Mike Holland take a different tack, exploring how Dunedin, on Aotearoa/New Zealand's South Island, and its particular musical mythology are both a boon and a problem for music-makers there. Noting the tenacious legacy of the indie record label Flying Nun, and the various bands associated with it and the so-called "Dunedin Sound," Wilson and Holland offer a more critical take on how musicians in the city can get trapped in its mythology, while others do their best to try and escape it, in the process presenting an intriguing study of how differing sociomusical experiences of place can generate complicated yet sometimes productive tensions.

4

Popular Music and Heritage-Making in Melbourne

Catherine Strong

Introduction

The city of Melbourne has long had a reputation for having a strong musical culture. In recent years this has increasingly been recognized and emphasized politically. State and local politicians have been promoting Melbourne as a "music city" (Homan and Newton 2010; see also Chapter 14); as not just a national but global center for the creation and performance of popular music, where music is central to the life of the city, as well as central to tourism and economic growth. One aspect of this has been the inclusion of popular music in heritage discourses. This is in line with trends in other Western cities such as Berlin, Germany and Austin, Texas in the USA, and reflects a major shift in how popular music is regarded. From being very much considered a low-brow, "throw-away" form of culture with little lasting significance, it is now being incorporated into the stories that nations, cities and communities tell about what is important about their past (Bennett 2009; Roberts 2014).

In Melbourne, the formalization of popular music as part of the city's heritage is in its early stages, but it is clearly an area where more development is on the way. In the 2014 state election,[1] for example, "celebrate and promote Melbourne's rich music heritage" was a criteria by which Music Victoria (the peak body for the music industry in the state) assessed political parties' performance (Music Victoria 2014). Indeed, the victorious Labor Government has committed up to AUD10 million to the establishment of the Australian Music Vault, a hall of fame which opened in late 2017 (Andrews 2015; Creative Victoria 2016). This is, then, a pivotal moment when the shape of popular music heritage in the city will be debated and moulded at an official level. Given the way in which incorporating something into a heritage discourse can shape the collective memory of it in specific ways, or "freeze" the form that it takes (Weiss 2007), the question of whose voices are privileged in the processes that link popular music to heritage, and the strategies that are successful in doing this, are important questions to consider.

In order to do this, this chapter will use three case studies of heritage-making in relation to popular music in Melbourne that have been taking place in the mid-2010s. These are the establishment of Amphlett Lane, the campaign to save the Palace Theatre and the Melbourne Music Walk created by the Melbourne City Council. I will use Cohen and Roberts' framework for analysing music heritage practices to examine these case studies, in order to understand how claims to authority are made in relation to heritage, and when these are successful.

60 • Catherine Strong

Furthermore, I will argue that in addition to demonstrating different types of heritage-making at work, these case studies also show different relationships between memory and the built environment of the city, and connections between these and how heritage is conceptualized. When heritage is strongly connected to physical locations then the permanence of heritage is only as reliable as the permanence of the sites it is connected to, and this relates back to a key function it has been argued memory performs in late modern society—to act as an anchor against continuous change. I will show how in the cases of Amphlett Lane and the Palace Theatre heritage is used as a way to reach for permanence, but in the case of the Melbourne Music Walk an impression of underlying instability is presented that is at odds with the ostensible aims of the walk. The following section will detail the theories that will be used to support these arguments, after which the case studies will be discussed.

Understanding Popular Music as Heritage

Heritage is not an easy concept to pin down, and is also one that has changed in recent decades. It is usually associated with representations of the past, including custom and tradition, that help define the collective identity of a group in the present (often on the national level) (Bennett 2009). As such, heritage is often contested. Increasingly, the concepts of "heritage" and "collective memory" have overlapped, as "the right to narrate the past is no longer reserved solely to political elites or academics" (Neiger, Meyers and Zandberg 2011, 973). As such, pronouncements about what is important about the past come to incorporate input from a wider variety of groups than was previously the case. This is part of what has been described as the "democratisation of the past" (Foote and Azaryahu 2007), which has seen not only the incorporation of the memories of many previously marginalized groups into discourses about what should be remembered, but has also seen forms of culture previously considered low-brow included as part of heritage for the first time. In the case of popular music, as fans have aged and gained more authority in society, they have championed the importance of music to not just their own identities, but to the shaping of the character of cities and nations. The exemplar of this is Liverpool, where the Beatles have become emblematic of the city, and Beatles-related tourism is an important industry (Cohen 2013).

The different aspects of popular music heritage have been theorized by Sara Cohen and Les Roberts (Cohen and Roberts 2015; Roberts and Cohen 2014). Their extensive work on heritage and popular music in the UK has allowed them to develop a tripartite framework elaborating on different aspects of this, as a way of enabling analysis of "the various ways in which popular music heritage is not simply practiced but also authorized and ascribed with value, legitimacy and social and cultural capital" (Roberts and Cohen 2014, 243). They have identified the following types of popular music heritage, all of which are identifiable in the current Melbourne context:

Official authorized music heritage: this is an aspect of the past that has been formally legitimized as heritage using structures of authority recognized and agreed on within a society (often governments and government-sponsored bodies). This type of heritage often takes tangible and physical form, such as monuments or plaques.

Self-authorized music heritage: claims to heritage status are not only legitimated through official and formal channels. Media, local tastemakers, fans and commercial entities (such as tourism industries) can act in a way that grants authority to certain types of heritage, particularly at more local levels. Self-authorized heritage is more grassroots and DIY, and as such can provide a place for the inclusion of versions of the past that might otherwise be left out of official heritage. However, the distinction between official and self-authorized heritage can often be blurred, as "they are part of an ongoing process of negotiation and dialogue in which the value and legitimacy attached to the act of *authorization* informs their role as part of a wider cultural politics of memory, place and identity' (Roberts and Cohen 2014, 230). As such, self-authorized heritage can take on a more official aspect given the right sort of support.

Unauthorized music heritage: this category allows us to think about heritage as something that can be engaged with by every music fan, and as something connected as much to individual memories and practices as to grand narratives about what makes a national identity. Unauthorized music heritage incorporates heritage-as-praxis more than heritage-as-object (Cohen and Roberts 2015, 16), as well as providing space for resistance to the heritagization of popular music, or anti-heritage discourses.

This framework allows for a better understanding of the complexities involved in popular music heritage. In particular, it provides an opportunity for the input of non-official groups to be fully incorporated. This is particularly important when it comes to popular music, as for a long time popular music's history has been mainly curated by fans. Indeed, one of the concerns that has arisen about the heritagization of popular music is that it has the potential to remove its vibrancy—whatever it is that people experience when listening to the music, whether alone or in groups—and turn it into just another museum exhibition (Leonard 2010). Using Cohen and Roberts' framework provides a way to include manifestations of heritage that may not always be recognized as such (although, as they themselves note, this approach does raise the question of the meaningfulness of heritage as a concept).

The heightened focus on—and expanding definition of—heritage can also be connected to the acceleration of time and change in late modern society (Harvey 1989). Many scholars have documented an increasing fascination with the past in Western cultures, sometimes dubbed the "memory boom" (Huyssen 1995). This can be seen in an increased popularity of cultural items relating to the past, and heightened interest in ancestry and heritage-related tourism. In the case of popular music, this manifests most clearly as the continued dominance of a music canon mostly created between the 1960s and 1990s. It is this canon that is often central to popular music heritage, leading Bennett to argue that despite the inclusion of more voices in the construction of the past,

> [p]opular music heritage . . . is at one significant level a self-servicing exercise, committed among other things to the uncritical reproduction of a heritage canon inextricably bound up with a white, middle-class, baby-boomer understanding of musical authenticity . . . that threaten[s] to expunge vast tracts of musical production, performance and reception from popular memory.
>
> (2014, 20)

62 • Catherine Strong

Although writers like Reynolds (2011) are critical of our fascination with the past, and the ability of certain groups to shape heritage must always be interrogated (and, indeed, the people involved in the three case studies under consideration in this chapter are over-whelmingly white, and mostly middle-aged), the function that a focus on the past has also needs to be considered. At a time when "all that is solid melts into air" (Berman 1988), the past can be a source of consistency and surety that is otherwise lacking (Huyssen 1995). In cities, where change is constant and urban landscapes can be altered dramatically in short periods of time, finding ways to connect physical locations in the city to the past—through this concept of "heritage"—can provide a way to create a sense of permanence, or to try to protect sites from inevitable alteration.

The Establishment of Amphlett Lane

On February 3, 2015, Amphlett Lane was officially dedicated in the Melbourne CBD. The laneway was named after the lead singer of rock band The Divinyls, who had died of breast cancer in April 2013. In the week that followed Amphlett's death, journalist Jessica Adams set up an online petition asking Melbourne City Council (MCC) to "please dedicate and name a laneway (or other Melbourne city landmark) for Chrissy Amphlett." The petition quickly gained support, and was presented to the Council in July with over 6000 signatures (Masanauskas 2013). The proposal also had backing from music celebrities (for example, well-known music TV presenter Molly Meldrum) and Amphlett's family.

The process of establishing the laneway was, relatively speaking, fairly straight-forward. Neither the MCC nor the community presented any objections to the laneway. This stands in contrast to the establishment of AC/DC Lane in 2004, where council received a number of submissions from the public objecting to the naming, and councillors themselves came very close to backing away from the dedication (Frost 2008). A laneway was found that was close to the Princess Theatre and directly behind the Palace Theatre, which were both venues that Amphlett had performed at, thus creating a physical connection between the laneway and the singer (see Figure 4.1). (The proximity to the Palace was also somewhat political, as having Amphlett Lane physically connected to the Palace was seen as potentially giving more weight to the arguments of the Save the Palace campaign, discussed below.) The laneway was officially opened in a formal ceremony for invited attendees, including Amphlett's family, Council officials, journalists and various key players in the Melbourne music industry.

The dedication of Amphlett Lane represents an example of official authorized popular music heritage. There was, in this case, a convergence between the ideas of the Amphlett Lane campaigners about how to best commemorate Chrissy, and the objectives of the MCC in terms of how to utilize heritage, which led to the quick authorization of the project. The Council had already identified the laneways of the CBD as a point of difference for the city that could be used as a drawcard for tourists, promoting them as representing both Melbourne's heritage and various aspects of the city's modern culture (Strong 2015). The turn towards emphasizing music as a drawcard more generally meant that a suggestion that brought "laneways" and "music" together was likely to be looked upon favorably, and the pre-existing example of AC/DC Lane meant the proposal was not too novel or controversial. The laneway was also seen as having economic benefit, in that it would potentially make music fans more likely to visit Melbourne. The dedication of this laneway was also a "safe"

Figure 4.1 Amphlett Lane. Photograph by author.

investment in popular music; a gesture that formalizes the MCC's commitment to music without inviting any of the problems that can be associated with actual music, such as noise complaints or undisciplined behavior in public places.

The dedication of a physical place in this case also gives the impression of permanency. This was noted by Amphlett's husband Charlie Drayton in his speech opening the laneway, where he said "You know, nothing really lasts forever but today's a lot different." The message from the campaigners was that a physical place—not just an object like a grave marker, but a location in and of the city—would in effect immortalize Amphlett. The fact that the naming had official and legal backing and approval enhanced this sense.

Save the Palace

The Palace Theatre, located in the Melbourne CBD, originally opened in 1912 and functioned as a live music venue and nightclub since the 1970s. The building was sold in 2012 to Jinshan Investments, who planned to demolish the building and replace it with a luxury hotel (Dow 2014). As a result, the venue was closed, and the Save the Palace (STP) group was established by community members to try to stop the redevelopment going ahead, and to restart the venue. The group held rallies and vigils at the venue, engaged in challenges to the demolition via official bureaucratic channels offered by the Council and ran an extensive social media campaign designed to build and make visible community support for the venue (see, for example, the *Save the Palace* Facebook page).

Although STP was initially responding to the immediate loss of the contribution the Palace made to live music in Melbourne, the campaign very quickly incorporated heritage discourses in their arguments. This centered on two areas: the Palace as a symbol of both Melbourne's popular music heritage and its ongoing music scene; and the physical building itself and its connection to Melbourne history *beyond* contemporary music. One of the key tactics pursued by campaigners (in conjunction with other heritage related bodies such as Melbourne Heritage Action) has been to argue that the building itself has historical significance, and as such should be preserved. This argument mainly focused on the physical attributes of the building (for example, its staircase and decorative features) rather than the music related uses of the venue as such. The main organizer of STP, Rebecca Leslie, explained that the campaigners felt this approach was necessary because the Palace was no longer being used as a venue at the time of the debate (interview with Rebecca Leslie, 23 July 2014). The campaigners put extensive work into exploring and trying to utilize many different options for protecting the building using heritage-related bureaucracy. An initial attempt to have the Palace listed as being of heritage value at the State level was unsuccessful, so the focus shifted to gaining protection at the local level (administered by Melbourne City Council). This has been partially successful, with heritage protection being given to the outside of the building in December 2014 (Melbourne City Council 2014). However, this was the only concession the campaigners were able to gain. At the time of writing the Palace site remains empty, and it seems highly likely that it will be redeveloped completely with only the façade being retained.

STP and the response to it can be interpreted as relating to all three types of heritage discussed by Cohen and Roberts. It is a self-authorized form of heritage struggling for recognition as official authorized heritage as a way of preserving ongoing music-making, and, in the course of this, highlighting the ongoing tension between "progress"/change and permanence/preservation in the city. The response of Councillors to the STP campaigners demonstrated this, as the campaigners were characterized on the one hand as "passionate" but misguided, and legitimate voices of the community on the other. At the same time, the campaign was partly sustained by community-building acts of memory-sharing, whether during the rallies at the site of the venue, or on the STP Facebook page, which could be understood as heritage-as-praxis.

The way the story of the Palace is connected to many different strands of politics playing out in Melbourne at the moment, and the way this has enabled the campaign to acquire allies (and hence enhanced authority) in a number of different areas, also needs to be considered. The campaign was supported by Melburnians opposed to new high-rise development, and those opposed to the destruction of old buildings, as well as people connected to the specific venue at stake. As such, the campaign had elements of anti-globalization and anti-commercialization, which are themselves in many ways about the preservation of particular versions of the past as well as the built environment of the city. The campaign also needs to be understood in the context of ongoing tensions between the promotion of culture as an economic good for the city and development trends that threaten, in particular, live music. Gentrification of the inner city since the 1990s, and the ever-outward spread of this gentrification, has had an adverse impact on live music, with a number of key venues closing as a result of either noise complaints or increasing rates (Shaw 2009). By positioning the closure of the Palace as a part of this trend, STP was able to draw on the "Melbourne as music city" rhetoric to highlight the disjunction between what councils and governments *said* was important and the actions they took. In this way, STP both draws upon and disrupts official discourses about the role of music, and music heritage, in Melbourne. This can be read as anti-heritage, insofar as heritage and live music cultures are positioned in opposition to each other in this element of STP's narrative. The case of the Palace also disrupts ideas about certainty in relation to the built environment, in that its attempts to gain permanence for the Palace draw attention to the impermanence of city structures, and the way they are constantly changing.

Melbourne Music Walk

In July 2017, the Melbourne City Council launched its Melbourne Music Walk (MMW) (City of Melbourne 2017). This is an addition to an existing group of "guided walks and maps to help you explore Melbourne by foot," including walks focusing on laneways, sports and parks. The music walk—outlined in an online brochure that contains a map and written narrative that guides the walker through the points of interest plotted—covers three and a half kilometers in the CBD. It emphasizes Melbourne's status as a city known for its music scene by taking a route that incorporates many current venues. These venues service a wide range of music genres, such as a number of rock-focused venues and also a jazz club and theaters that stage musicals. This foregrounding of current musical activity is supported by many details about Melbourne's music heritage in the brochure that outlines the route. Some points of interest are included mostly because of their value in terms of music heritage; for example, the portico on the Melbourne Town Hall is highlighted because of its historical use by acts such as The Beatles, Lionel Rose and ABBA on tours during the 1960s and 1970s.

The walk can be considered an example of authorized heritage, in that the official, government-sponsored nature of the project lends legitimacy to the idea that the chosen sites and historical examples are indeed important. A walk, however, has different effects than more tangible markers of authorized heritage such as plaques or street names (although some of these are incorporated into this walk). While the brochure provides a framework for how walkers might think about the sites they encounter, it is likely that they will also come into contact with other aspects of music heritage. Those who venture into the venues on the route will find the unauthorized heritage-as-praxis used by venues to help create a sense of identity at play (Strong and Whiting 2018). Self-authorized heritage is also likely to be evident at various points. For example, the street art in AC/DC Lane often changes and usually represents something music-focused, for instance, a portrait of Prince that appeared not long after his death in April 2016. By placing participants in a changing musical and visual land-scape, the walk includes the possibility of encountering representations of music heritage in Melbourne that offer alternatives to, or may even directly challenge, the narrative presented by the Council.

One notable element of the MMW that relates to this is how it positions the other two case studies discussed in this chapter. Amphlett Lane is one of the stops on the walk, with the discussion of the lane providing a quick overview of its history, as well as a description of an event held in the laneway that allows the inclusion of information on Melbourne Music Week, which is described as "an annual event held in November dedicated to celebrating and

66 • Catherine Strong

supporting Melbourne's music industry." This linking of music heritage, the built environment of the city and ongoing musical activity is typical of the walk's focus. On the other hand, despite the route that the walk takes being very close to the Palace site (as described earlier, the end of Amphlett Lane is at the back of the Palace) the venue is not mentioned. At first glance, it is hardly surprising that a walk with a strong focus on promoting Melbourne's current musical activity would not (deliberately) take participants to a closed venue, regardless of its historical significance. However, elsewhere the walk does refer to some of the problems with the music scene in Melbourne described elsewhere in this chapter. The walk notes that "[s]upport for the musical heritage of Melbourne is increasing as the gentrification of the dusty corners of the city rolls on and venues close down" before directing participants to the steps of Parliament House. This was where the Save Live Australian Music (SLAM) rally took place in 2010, where, as described in the walk pamphlet, "20,000 people marched to protest rules and regulations that were forcing the closure of inner-city venues." Although the characterization of gentrification as taking place in undesirable-sounding "dusty corners" may be an attempt to put a positive spin on the changes taking place in the city, the immediate juxtaposing of this with the account of community opposition to venue closures destabilizes the otherwise confident picture being presented in the brochure. For walkers on the route, this impression of instability may be reinforced by, for example, discovering that one of the venues marked on the map, Bennett's Lane Jazz Club, has closed since the walk was published or by the presence of construction sites near venues (as observed on the walk in July 2017). The walk and the information accompanying it also have an ephemeral quality. Although it is deemed "official," the walk is not marked physically by signs in the streets but instead only exists online on a website, and is thus presumably either easily changed or deleted. Therefore, the walk does not speak to permanence in the same way a specific site such as Amphlett Lane might.

Conclusion

The above case studies show different strategies being employed in Melbourne in relation to claiming space for popular music in heritage discourses. These strategies can be understood as representing versions of official, self-authorized and unauthorized heritage, and the case studies show how these overlap as well as interact with each other. Amphlett Lane very quickly became official heritage, due to the alignment of those in favor of the naming with the goals of those who wield political power. In this case, MCC granted legitimacy to Amphlett Lane, and could later draw on the existence of the lane in their music walk to further promote Melbourne as a music city. Political will was divided, however, in the case of the Palace Theatre, with the clash of business and planning with heritage considerations preventing the shift from self-authorized/unauthorized to official heritage, despite this being the aim of STP campaigners. This demonstrates how the shape that heritage takes, and the extent to which it can be considered "successful," is strongly dependent on the goals and influence of those engaged in its creation, as well as accepted ideas about what forms heritage should take. The case studies also demonstrate how heritage can be used to pursue goals that are actually more future-oriented than only being about the past, as in the case of the Palace Theatre and the Melbourne Music Walk.

In addition to this, these case studies illustrate different ways that people connect heritage to the built environment of the city, and hence to the preservation of the past. I have argued that the Amphlett Lane project pursued the illusion of permanence, and those involved expressed faith that the built environment of the city can act as a permanent keeper of memory. The Palace Theatre campaign, on the other hand, is about stopping change, and in attempting to do so brings to light the inevitability of change, especially in the accelerated, globalized world that the campaign is clearly situated within. Finally, despite its attempt to focus on the strength of music in Melbourne, the Melbourne Music Walk inadvertently highlights the inevitability of change in the urban environment (despite some melancholy relating to this). This is emphasized further by the way the memories of participants become part of the tours, meaning each tour is unique but also ephemeral and cannot be captured for preservation—much like the missing and threatened venues the tour visits. As the city of Melbourne increasingly attempts to position itself as a global "music city," ideas about music heritage will become more important and probably more contested. This move will almost certainly involve a shift towards the incorporation of more official heritage in the landscape of the city. As this happens, those involved in self-authorized and unauthorized heritage-making will be called upon to reposition their activities, and more such activities may arise as a response to the story that official heritage-makers are telling. As this occurs, the city itself—the buildings, laneways and even its absences—has the capacity to become a tool, an ally or a liability to the stories different groups try to tell. Exactly how this plays out will provide insights into our relationship with the past—do we hold on tight, fight change or accept that inevitably "all that is solid melts into air"?

Note

1 Australia has a three-tiered system of government: federal (which will not be discussed in this chapter), state, and local (which includes Melbourne City Council).

Bibliography

Andrews, Daniel. 2015. "Music Works Secured to Support Local Acts and Local Jobs." Press release, May 5. www.premier.vic.gov.au/music-works-secured-to-support-local-acts-and-local-jobs (accessed June 9, 2015).

Bennett, Andy. 2015. "Popular Music and the 'Problem' of Heritage." In *Sites of Popular Music Heritage: Memories, Histories, Places,* edited by Sara Cohen, Robert Knifton, Marion Leonard and Les Roberts. New York: Routledge, 15–27.

Bennett, Andy. 2009. "'Things They Do Look Awful Cool:' Ageing Rock Icons and Contemporary Youth Audiences." *Leisure/Loisir* 32 (2): 259–278.

Berman, Marshall. 1988. *All that is Solid Melts into Air: The Experience of Modernity.* New York: Penguin.

City of Melbourne. 2017. *Melbourne Music Walk.* https://whatson.melbourne.vic.gov.au/visitors/Documents/Melbourne_Music_Walk_June2017.pdf (accessed July 11, 2017).

Cohen, Sara. 2013. "Musical Memory, Heritage and Local Identity: Remembering the Popular Music Past in a European Capital of Culture." *International Journal of Cultural Policy* 19 (5): 576–594.

Cohen, Sara and Les Roberts. 2015. "Unveiling Memory: Blue Plaques as In/tangible Markers of Popular Music Heritage." In *Sites of Popular Music Heritage: Memories, Histories, Places,* edited by Sara Cohen, Robert Knifton, Marion Leonard and Les Roberts. New York: Routledge, 1–13.

Creative Victoria. 2016. "Australian Music History: Straight from the Vault." Press release, December 13. http://creative.vic.gov.au/news/2016/australia-music-history-straight-from-the-vault (accessed February 20, 2017).

Dow, Alisha. 2014. "Palace Theatre Enters Last Chance Saloon as the Bulldozers Warm Up." *The Age,* December 7, www.theage.com.au/victoria/palace-theatre-enters-last-chance-saloon-as-the-bulldozers-warm-up-20141206-121beo.html

Foote, Kenneth E. and Maoz Azaryahu. 2007. "Toward a Geography of Memory: Geographical Dimensions of Public Memory and Commemoration." *Journal of Political and Military Sociology* 35 (1): 125–144.

Frost, Warwick. 2008. "Popular Culture as a Different Type of Heritage: The Making of AC/DC Lane." *Journal of Heritage Tourism* 3 (3): 176–184.

Harvey, David. 1989. *The Condition of Post-Modernity.* Oxford: Blackwell.

Homan, Shane and Dobe Newton. 2010. *The Music Capital: City of Melbourne Music Strategy,* Melbourne: City of Melbourne.

Huyssen, Andreas. 1995. *Twilight Memories: Marking Time in a Culture of Amnesia.* New York: Routledge.

Huyssen, Andreas. 2003. *Present Pasts: Urban Palimpsests and the Politics of Memory.* Stanford, CA: Stanford University Press.

Leonard, Marion. 2010. "Exhibiting Popular Music: Musuem Audiences, Inclusion and Social History." *Journal of New Music Research* 39 (2): 171–181.

Masanauskas, John. 2013. "Melbourne City Councillors Support Creation of Amphlett Lane in CBD in Honour of Divinyls Frontwoman," *Herald Sun,* 10 (September): 7.

Melbourne City Council. 2014. *Future Melbourne Planning Committee Minutes.* December 2. www.melbourne.vic. gov.au/AboutCouncil/Meetings/CouncilMeetingAttachments/1044/DEC14%20FMC1%20MINUTES%20 OPEN%20%28CONFIRMED%29.pdf (accessed July 27, 2015).

Music Victoria. 2014. "2014 Victorian State Election Report Card." Music Victoria. www.musicvictoria.com.au/ projects/election-report-cards (accessed May 3, 2015).

Neiger, Motti, Oren Meyers and Eyal Zandberg. 2011. "Turned to the Nation's Mood: Popular Music as a Mnemonic Cultural Object." *Media Culture Society* 33 (7): 971–987.

Reynolds, Simon. 2011. *Retromania: Pop Culture's Addiction to Its Own Past.* London: Faber and Faber.

Roberts, Len. 2014. "Talkin Bout My Generation: Popular Music and the Culture of Heritage." *International Journal of Heritage Studies* 20 (3): 262–280.

Roberts, Les and Sara Cohen. 2014. "Unauthorising Popular Music Heritage: Outline of a Critical Framework." *International Journal of Heritage Studies* 20 (3): 241–261.

Shaw, Kate. 2009. "The Melbourne Indie Music Scene and the Inner City Blues." In *Whose Urban Renaissance?,* edited by Libby Porter and Kate Shaw. London: Routledge, 366–385.

Strong, Catherine. 2015. "Laneways of the Dead: Memorialising Musicians in Melbourne." In *Death and the Rock Star,* edited by Catherine Strong and Barbara Lebrun. Aldershot: Ashgate.

Strong, Catherine and Sam Whiting. 2018. "'We love the bands and we want to keep them on the walls': Gig posters as heritage-as-praxis in music venues." *Continuum* 32 (2): 151–161.

Weiss, Lindsay. 2007. "Heritage-making and Political Identity." *Journal of Social Archaeology* 7 (3): 413–431.

5

The "Dunedin Sound" Now
Contemporary Perspectives on Dunedin's Musical Legacy

Oli Wilson and Michael Holland

Introduction

What is "Dunedin music"? As in many other small cities, musical cultures in Dunedin are diverse and varied. A number of recent publications, both scholarly and in the popular press, have sought to emphasize this, and provide an eclectic range of examples (Gorman 2008; Saunders 2011; Bendrups and Downes 2011). Such publications serve as counter-narratives to the discourse about Dunedin music that has dominated representations of the city's music and musical culture. We are referring here to the "Dunedin sound." This term refers loosely to the output of a number of acts affiliated with the Flying Nun label during the 1980s, whose legacy is celebrated among indie rock circles internationally. This chapter explores the idea of the "Dunedin sound" in a contemporary setting, and examines how discourses associated with this concept manifest in a variety of mediated and ethnographic contexts. Our analysis draws from our own perspectives, as we have resided in Dunedin for most of the last decade, and have been active in the local music community. We are also both closely involved with The Chills,[1] a group recognized as "pioneers of the 'Dunedin sound'" (Uncredited 2015a).[2] Discourses about the "Dunedin sound" are therefore extrapolated from media reports that focus mainly on The Chills. These include press coverage of The Chills' 2015 album *Silver Bullets*, as well as the group's 2014 and 2016 international tours, and have been chosen as being reflective of broader media trends. Much of the press is via indie rock oriented publications, mostly based in the UK and across Europe – such as *New Musical Express* (*NME*) and *Pitchfork* – but also includes mainstream publications such as the *Guardian* (UK).

The narratives extrapolated from the media are cross-referenced with interviews undertaken by the authors with fans across the USA, UK and Europe, where both authors have toured with the band. This section also interpolates existing scholarly narratives, which assist in identifying key themes that underpin the mediatized "Dunedin sound" discourse. These themes include: nostalgia for the 1980s; Dunedin's perceived geographic isolation; the artists' perceived authenticity; the Flying Nun label; and the artists' subversive approach to music production, all of which are believed to underpin the supposed influence that "Dunedin sound" musicians have had on the international indie rock canon.

70 • Oli Wilson and Michael Holland

Following this discussion, we explore how musicians operating in the local music community perceive their own practice, considering why local musicians tend to reject direct comparisons to the "Dunedin sound," and the various ideological positions and activities of some "Dunedin sound" artists. This discussion draws on our own experience, as well as the views – further evidenced through local media coverage – of younger Dunedin musicians, who actively dissociate themselves from the "Dunedin sound." The final section of the chapter problematises mediatized narratives about the "Dunedin sound," and evinces a growing awareness of how the "Dunedin sound" discourse perpetuates an essentialised view of Dunedin and its musical cultures, both past and present.

The Imagined Sound: Perspectives from Abroad

The association of The Chills and other Flying Nun bands in the 1980s scene to the city of Dunedin has been explicit since the label's early releases (see, for example, the *Dunedin Double EP 1982*). A 2005 *Stylus* magazine article reflects on this release, and cites it as evidence of the "sound's" very existence:

> With the release of the Dunedin Double there was no longer any discussion in the NZ music press, to wit: there WAS a 'Dunedin sound,' it resided on Flying Nun, and it required records to be made in the most appalling of locales on the most primitive of equipment. And, somehow, the magic happened.
>
> (McGonigle 2005

Flying Nun is routinely celebrated as being instrumental in the dissemination and success of the "Dunedin sound" bands of the 1980s and early 1990s, and coverage of The Chills almost always mentions their historical ties to the label.[3] Fans also reiterate this connection. The following quotation, from "Jeff," a fan based in Brooklyn, New York, links his personal discovery of The Chills to Flying Nun, and positions it in opposition to new musical trends that were happening at the time:

> A lot of my friends, we all looked to the UK for our music ... we just thought it would never end, and then it ended! We felt a void, how could all these riches come from this one country and fall flat? ... then we saw this beacon coming from the other side of the world, from the South Island of New Zealand, and it really resonated with the parts that were missing from the UK scene at that time, and it really reconnected you to music that you felt had gone adrift over the last couple of years. It was Flying Nun ... It came by the UK press ... [through] NME, Melody Maker ... They would present whoever they felt was important at that time, and at that time, in 1984 or 1985 it was New Zealand's South Island.
>
> ("Jeff" 2016)

Several academic publications highlight the city's position as peripheral to the global music industry, though it is not always clear if this is used to justify the existence of a sonically unique "sound," or the "sound" as a social construct (Shuker and Pickering 1994; see also McLeay 1994, 43). According to Mitchell, Dunedin is remote: it is located in the "bleakly isolated and uninhabited southern part of the South Island" (Mitchell 1994, 38). Flying Nun label founder Roger Shepherd suggests that this seclusion meant that Dunedin musicians "were a bit more inclined to write and perform the music they wanted to hear ... like different dialects, a unique style definitely emerged" (Shepherd, quoted in Mitchell 1996, 225).[4] A fan interviewed in Cologne, Germany, also nuances this perspective: "I love how everything developed back then in this isolated city, I mean, the best fact I heard about Dunedin in the 80's was the first Joy Division record arrived there after Ian Curts had died" (Unnamed Fan 2016a). The idea that the "Dunedin sound" is a product of isolation has also been perpetuated by members of other Flying Nun-era Dunedin bands. The Verlaines songwriter and singer Graeme Downes (now a university lecturer) once stated:

> in Dunedin we were extremely isolated and it took a long time for musical trends to filter down this far. You have to appreciate the pre-globalisation technological environment that existed back then (at least for us) ... Being something of a backwater meant there was something of a disincentive to follow trends (why bother when they were moribund at their source by the time we knew about them).
> (Graeme Downes, by email, 2005, cited in McGonigle 2005)

The tendency to disregard trends is also noted by other scholars. Mitchell (1996) succinctly summarizes Robertson's delineation of the Dunedin "aesthetic of sorts" (1991, 44), suggesting that:

> The musical aesthetic involved a total disregard for musical fashions and trends, as well as commercial recognition, expressed in the idea of authentic music, which legitimised the ignorance of contemporary musical trends. An adherence to authentic music involved stepping outside the confines of musical fashion and justified an ignorance of any boundaries of what was considered popular.
> (Robertson, cited in Mitchell 1996, 229)

Virtually all of the scholarship on the "Dunedin sound" discusses it in retrospect, implying that it is not a contemporary phenomenon. Fans also discussed their engagement with the "Dunedin sound" as evoking a sense of nostalgia, which was often based on a deep personal connection that was forged in their youth. For many fans, experiencing The Chills several decades after their first experience with the band was highly emotional. A fan in Brighton noted: "It's the resonance. The first track [tonight] gave me goose bumps and it brought back wonderful memories of my youth. It was beautiful" (Unnamed Fan 2016b). Similarly, "Jeff" from Brooklyn New York further explains:

> [the late 80s] was an important time of my life, when I really felt affiliated to a band ... and being so far away here in New York, I felt a real kinship with the Southern Island of New Zealand.
> ("Jeff" 2016)

The appeal for other fans, however, was not necessarily related to nostalgia, and many fans believe that Dunedin is still a haven for indie rock creativity. For example, a German fan described Dunedin as a utopian musical "microcosm," citing the contemporary Dunedin artists that he follows:

> If I could dig a hole through the earth right now I would end up somewhere like east of Dunedin. It is the farthest place away from Germany, and that's pretty amazing. It's still a microcosm that happened back then . . . and [now] there is still a lot of stuff going on there down there . . . so I am really curious to see what cool bands come out of Dunedin next.
>
> ("Thomas" 2016)

However, for the following fan, and others we spoke with, the "Dunedin sound" is both far away in distance, and in time:

> So much of the music is intangible, it has a place and a time, and especially when you are younger, it takes you back, and you have an emotional connection . . . maybe nostalgia is the right or maybe the wrong thing to say, it's an emotion that comes through, a real connection to it.
>
> (Unnamed Fan 2016c)

Fans and media alike substantiate their celebration of Dunedin bands by emphasizing their perceived influence on more successful international artists. The notion that the "Dunedin sound" has "a vital legacy still felt to this day" (Welsh 2014a, see also Welsh 2014b) permeates the music press. For example, when *NME* listed The Chills at number 55 on their "100 Most Influential Artists" list, it stated that "you only have to hear Palma Violets . . . or The Shins to see how well that model [The Chills' approach to the use of the organ] has been honed in recent years" (Barker 2014). Creation Records founder Alan McGee has also discussed The Chills' influence in the *Guardian's* music blog, noting that: "People often ask me about Creation acts, and for the past two years The Chills have come up a lot in conversation. I have been hearing their influence more and more" (McGee 2008). Similarly, in a *PopMatters* feature article, the Flying Nun artists are collectively celebrated for their influence on other, more commercially successful artists: "Groups like The Clean and The Chills have influenced other stalwart indie bands such as Yo La Tengo and Pavement, the latter band having their music distributed by the label during their initial run" (Crowley 2015). New York fan "Jeff" also echoed this sentiment:

> Martin has something that . . . other bands have, but Martin has sustained it, and even though he has gone through changes in his sound, when you hear a Chills song, it is always The Chills, though countless bands sound like them now. Over the last five years, there have been so many bands who are using The Chills as a stepping off point, or pivot point, that you hear just how important they are.
>
> ("Jeff" 2016)

"In Dunedin, Everyone Wants to Get Away from the 'Dunedin Sound'"

The narrative outlined above constructs idealized imaginings of place that are often discord-ant with current local experiences. The following section explores how local musicians – including those also associated with the "Dunedin sound" period – perceive discourses around the "Dunedin sound" as both problematic and prescriptive. We should note that there are, nonetheless, some commonalities of practice and environment that exist across the decades. As one local musician and author suggests:

> The Dunedin sound phenomenon not only generates an 'imagined' effect of similarity between the current and historical scenes of Dunedin originals music-making, but is also a reification of similar scene-values that are re-constructed by contemporary musi-cians and mediatised representations of them. These values emphasise a DIY ethos, impecuniousness, a pared-down arrangement of instruments that feature guitar as a main instrumental carrier of sonic qualities and structure for songwriting, and a notion of authenticity constructed around these aspects.
>
> (McMillan 2016, 41)

Although many of the musicians' creative practices discussed below evoke the characteristics identified by McMillan (which could also broadly underpin many other indie guitar-based scenes), their personal engagement with the "Dunedin sound" discourse is more hostile. This hostility is evident in media coverage surrounding the release of a recent local compilation entitled *Temporary: Selections from Dunedin's Pop Underground, 2011–2014* (Various Artists 2015). The compilation gained national press, and was promoted as a marker of the health of the current indie music scene in Dunedin. The compilation features mostly contemporary artists, whose work is described by Fishrider Records' motto: "psych-pop and no wave from beneath the underground" (Smith 2014). The media coverage around this release repeatedly highlights local artists' struggle to assert their value from beneath "the weight of tradition" (Smithies 2014). In reviewing this release, prominent New Zealand music critic Grant Smithies succinctly evokes this tension:

> It is, I imagine, no fun to have your creative endeavours endlessly defined in relation to everybody else's 80s nostalgia trip. But this is what has happened, again and again, to any young musician daring to make music in contemporary Dunedin.
>
> (Smithies 2014)

Fishrider Records' founder Ian Henderson's attitude regarding the relationship between contemporary Dunedin indie pop and its predecessors is less confrontational. He notes: "Everyone goes on about the 80s being Dunedin's golden decade, but there's precious metal being formed here right now, as indeed there was in the 90s and the 2000s" (Henderson, cited in Smithies 2014).

Henderson discusses this further in another article in a national newspaper, the sole purpose of which appears to be the celebration of more international press outlets covering the "Dunedin sound." While quoted as being, "pleased that two of [his label's] bands – Males and Opposite Sex – were also name checked" in a 2015 *NME* article, he nonetheless notes that "They find it limiting ... it is cool that bands gets recognised but it perennially links them to the past" (McNeilly 2014).[5] This uneasy relationship with Dunedin's history is recurrent among young musicians in the city. Millie Lovelock, of the local band Astro Children, who featured on the *Temporary* compilation, links preconceptions about Dunedin's musical history to local venues, arguing that the closure of one such establishment may have positive outcomes:

> [The music venue] Chick's has been such a staple of the Dunedin music scene for so many years, so it's kind of a bastion of the 'Dunedin sound.' Maybe if we've lost that then we can finally move on, finally progress as a scene to be more than just Dunedin and the 'Dunedin sound.'
>
> (Callister-Baker and Bollen 2016)

Other musicians have publically expressed frustration that their creative output is associated with the "sound," rather than assessed on its own merits. For example, on receiving a favorable review of his latest album in *Pitchfork* magazine (Berman 2016), the then Dunedin based musician Kane Strang tweeted: "I honestly would have been fine with a 3 [star review] as long as they still didn't mention the 'Dunedin sound' lol" (Strang 2016).

Another review of *Blue Cheese* validates Strang's complaint, while pointing out stylistic and timbral similarities to that of 1980s Dunedin artists:

> At first listen, Blue Cheese fits neatly into the legacy of record label Flying Nun and his hometown's "Dunedin sound"—indie guitar-pop popularised by The Chills and The Clean in the early 1980s that was largely jangly, but with a bit of punk and a touch of the psychedelic.
>
> (Kerry 2016)

Despite these similarities, (arguably some of Lovelock's output could also be described as guitar-led indie rock), these artists reject the suggestion that their "sound" represents in any way a continuation of the "Dunedin sound" as a tradition. Importantly, this highlights how the "sound" is less of a sonic or musical phenomenon, and more an institution underpinned by a set of ideas that do not resonate with many young musicians.

As musicians, we also share Strang's frustration with the media, because our own creative endeavors have also been benchmarked against the "Dunedin sound." This has happened despite, and because of, our outputs being highly dissimilar musically and stylistically. For example, participants in an online local music forum discussed an interview in which Holland's sludge-metal band was compared to the "Dunedin sound." One musician (who was performing in a hip hop group at the time) noted:

> The stigma of the "Dunedin sound" is an issue that a lot of us have to deal with when it comes to the media; I personally grew pretty tired pretty quickly of having to answer questions about my band's "relationship to the 'Dunedin sound.'" (Vibrasics – if you ever heard us, you'll know it's a pretty irrelevant angle to take; we didn't even have a guitarist, pretty defining element in the "D.S." really).
>
> (L.W. 2008)

In another example, Wilson's band Knives at Noon gained national media attention after signing with an Australian label in 2010. At the time, one headline read: "Knives at Noon Shun Dunedin Sound." The article claimed that the band "have shunned the typical 'Dunedin sound' to incorporate more keyboards" (Schulz 2010), while overlooking Wilson's role as keyboardist in The Chills, who are, ironically, cited in other press for their distinctive use of the very same instrument.[6]

These tensions highlight the burden of historical precedent in cities with well-known musical histories. Musicians in Liverpool, for example, reportedly felt a similar frustration regarding the legacy of The Beatles. As Sara Cohen notes, "Many local rock musicians also felt excluded by the dominance of the city's Beatles heritage, and were irritated by the way that they and their music were continually situated and judged in relation to it" (Cohen 2007, 197). This frustration, however, is particularly interesting in the case of Dunedin, where a number of musicians are engaged in musical activities that both reinforce and contradict the "Dunedin sound" ideals.

A deeper understanding of the ambivalence towards the "Dunedin sound" can be gained by examining contemporary musical activities that overtly associate themselves with the "sound." One significant recent local celebration of the "Dunedin sound" involved an orchestral concert in the Dunedin Town Hall in 2015 (Various Artists 2015). This event was the brainchild of The Verlaines' songwriter Graeme Downes, who arranged a number of Flying Nun-era songs for the city's amateur orchestra, the Southern Sinfonia (now the Dunedin Symphony Orchestra). The performance also featured Martin Phillipps, Shayne Carter and classical and pop musicians studying at the University of Otago. Both the concept of orchestrating pop songs for performance in a concert hall and the subsequent media framing of "Dunedin sound" period songs as "classic" (Alexander 2015) suggest a transition from mainstream media associations (as discussed above) towards a form of canonization that is both "political and selective" (Bannister 2006, 78).[7] In a similar vein to international fans' reification of the "Dunedin sound" as a key influence on mainstream indie pop, the orchestral project seems to be an attempt to locate the songs within a tradition of high art. In our view, this embodies the transformation that lies at the heart of contemporary musicians' anxieties about the "sound." The music and mythology of that era appear, in some instances, to have shifted the term away from simply denoting musical and social practice, towards the perception of the "Dunedin sound" as a hegemonic "standard of excellence" (see Thornton 1996, 8; also quoted in Bannister 2006, 80).

These anxieties about the nature of the "Dunedin sound" discourse are echoed by some in the local and national media, who critique the unproblematic notion of the "Dunedin sound." For example, a review of Roger Shepherd's 2016 autobiography is highly critical of the broader notion that Flying Nun's output dominates international perceptions of New Zealand music:

> What an odd, distorted reality, that one raggedy alt-rock label could represent New Zealand in the eyes of the world . . . [Flying Nun's] prominence has sadly obscured all the great music that happened outside of its orbit, and all of the great bands that didn't quite fit its post-punk alt-rock/indie aesthetic . . . The label's classic sound was . . . as cutting edge as a toddler's plastic cutlery set.
>
> (Steel 2016)

The reviewer also goes on to critique the predominantly white, male-dominated Dunedin scene. This issue has been previously taken up by Bannister, who suggests, "Canonism in popular music has historically been identified with men, and indie was also overwhelmingly masculine" (2006, 84). Recent trends in both the local and national music scenes point to a heightened awareness of power dynamics. In one notable example, prominent indie song-writer Emily Edrosa recently publicly discussed her abusive experiences in the New Zealand indie scene, declaring, "I wanna make music for girls to feel comfortable to go to the shows and to feel like they want to dance to. Not for dudes in Flying Nun shirts to stroke their chins" (Greive 2016).[8]

It is also worth pointing out that uncritical perspectives on the "Dunedin sound" are not accepted by all artists associated with the "sound." In the case of The Chills, frontman Martin Phillipps frequently resists attempts to historicize the group and their musical output. During the 2014 international tour with the group, the authors became interested in the number and type of media engagements that Phillipps was involved in, not least because they frequently interrupted sound-check schedules. To entertain ourselves, we (the tour party) began privately reviewing the performance of the journalists who would interview him. On one such occasion, Phillipps noted that "those questions were really good. Not just the usual stuff ... [like] yet another "Dunedin sound" question!" (pers. comm., 2014). Phillipps also resists audiences' attempts to frame him as a solitary emblem of the Dunedin sound era. Towards the end of the final show of the 2016 tour, one fan yelled, "we love you Martin!" To which Phillipps pointedly replied, "[A]nd the *band* loves you all too," before introducing each member of band, thanking the crew and not mentioning himself in any way. Phillipps' desire to situate The Chills' musical practice as having more to do with a band performing new music in 2016 than his association with an historical era is significant. Those participating in The Chills' current creative endeavors – and other contemporary musicians in Dunedin – appear to share a diversity of practice, and a desire to exist beyond historical associations. These tensions are particularly observable in the touring activities of The Chills, whose current endeavors (both physically and aesthetically) transgress boundaries between the historically and geographically distributed conceptualization of Dunedin music, reflecting the global scale upon which local identity is negotiated (see Frith 1993, 11; Cohen 2007, 198).

Conclusion

Upon reflection, the first mobilizations of the "Dunedin sound" discourse by international fans and media appear to be largely nostalgic, unproblematically celebratory and linked to exoticised visions of Dunedin's musical and cultural legacy, and in some cases, current scene. Seemingly in opposition to this, contemporary local musicians rail against the discourse, linking it to reductive preconceptions that conflate their work with that of a prior generation. Their opposition towards the "sound" is also underpinned by a perception that the "standard of excellence" the term has come to embody is representative of institutions and an ideology with which young musicians do not identify (see Bannister 2006, 80). We have also observed a number of anomalies within the discursive frame. The preceding sections, for example, highlighted local and national media's increasingly critical outlook on the monolithic nature of the "Dunedin sound" discourse. So, how might we interpret this multitude of perspectives? One possibility involves recourse to the cyclical nature of popular music culture that is renewed through a repeated process of rebellion and co-optation. In this way, one person's historical subversion of mainstream culture is another's accepted (and acceptable) historical context against which to react and/or rebel. We should also consider the relationship between music, geography, history and determinism: without Dunedin, the music and discourse would not exist. One can argue, however, that the place now has less effect on the music made there than the historical discourse does in constructing (and imposing itself upon) contemporary musicians' conceptualization of the geographical space. This reinforces Cohen's assertion that "popular music ... influences how cities are perceived, experienced and made meaningful" (Cohen 2007, 226). Furthermore, post-modern and post-structuralist interpretations may account for these fluidities of meaning, and the disconnect between the term and its many referents. There exists, for example, a certain irony in contemporary musicians' public rejection of the "Dunedin sound" discourse, and the ways in which the very act of mentioning it in this manner guarantees the association. Our own experiences reinforce this interpretation, as both musically and in text, we are simultaneously attempting to define, and being defined by a discourse whose meanings are constantly shifting. The current state of the "Dunedin sound" appears to reflect Jacques Derrida's notion of a discourse that "borrows from a heritage the resources necessary for the deconstruction of that heritage itself" (Derrida 1978, 416). It is this paradox, however, that will likely preserve the discourse in some form or other, as the term ultimately functions as a linguistic and cultural trace—as already and always beyond signification.

Notes

1   Oli Wilson moved from Dunedin to Wellington in November 2015, but still plays keyboards with The Chills. Michael Holland has worked in Dunedin as an audio engineer for the past ten years, and has recorded a wide range of Dunedin artists. He currently works as front of house engineer and production manager for The Chills, as well as several other Dunedin artists.

2   The linking of the band to the label and the city is most succinctly evident in the subtitle of a brief announcement by *Pitchfork* of the bands then forthcoming album: "The Chills—the Dunedin, New Zealand-based band whose early records were released by Flying Nun" (Uncredited 2015b). In a similar vein, a *Pitchfork* review of *Silver Bullets* simply states the band were "the breakout band from the Dunedin indie scene" (Keyes 2015).

3   For example, when *Pitchfork* listed The Chill's song "Pink Frost" (1984) as 169 in their "the 200 best songs of the 1980s," they explained that the song had been "released just as Phillipps and his band were emerging as part of the thriving scene in Dunedin, New Zealand, most of which was being documented by the lauded Flying Nun label" (Uncredited 2015c). The band is not currently releasing new material through Flying Nun.

4   Similarly, in an article published in the *Guardian* (UK), remoteness and smallness is pointed to in the description of Flying Nun as "the label with the highest quality output per capita in pop history" (Hann 2014).

5   The authors of this article produced and engineered Males' contribution to the compilation (see Males 2013).

6   For example, see an *NME* article (Barker 2014).

7   It is also worth noting that the Dunedin Settlers Museum currently houses an exhibit on the "Dunedin sound," which includes Phillipps' leather jacket – the subject of the well-known song, "I Love My Leather Jacket," from the *Kaleidoscope World* (1986) album encased in a glass cabinet. For more information on the exhibit and song respectively, see http://www.toituosm.com/whats-on/exhibitions/creative-dunedin.

8   The indie music scene in New Zealand has also been the subject of recent discussions around the safety of their participants. Wellington collective Eyegum released a statement on safer spaces in April 2016, which began by noting: "women have been leaving Eyegum. There have been men taking advantage of their position in the scene to harass and abuse our audience/guests (Eyegum 2016). On a local level, 2016 saw the first iteration of Yes! Fest, whose press declared: "Yes! Fest aims to provide an alternative to uninclusive and inaccessible music events. Yes! Fest will be a live music event with a focus on safety, inclusivity and community" (Undertheradar 2016).

Bibliography

Alexander, Mike. 2015. "Dunedin Sounds Coming Back." stuff.co.nz. www.stuff.co.nz/entertainment/music/66139131/dunedin-sounds-coming-back (Accessed July 16, 2017).

Bannister, Matthew. 2006. "'Loaded': Indie Guitar Rock, Canonism, White Masculinities." *Popular Music* 25 (1): 77–95.

Barker, Emily. 2014. "100 Most Influential Artists." *New Musical Express*, July 30, 22–45. http://www.nme.com/photos/nme-s-100-most-influential-artists-50-1-1411863 (accessed June 14, 2017).

Bendrups, Dan and Graeme Downes, eds. 2011. *Dunedin Soundings: Place and Performance.* Dunedin: Otago University Press.Berman, Stuart. 2016. "Kane Strang: Blue Cheese. *Pitchfork.*" http://pitchfork.com/reviews/albums/21623-blue-cheese (accessed July 16, 2017).

Callister-Baker, Loulou and John Bollen. 2016. "Farewell to Chick's Hotel." *The Wireless.* http://thewireless.co.nz/articles/farewell-to-chick-s-hotel (accessed July 16, 2017).

Cohen, Sara. 2007. *Decline, Renewal and the City in Popular Music Culture: Beyond the Beatles.* London: Ashgate.

Crowley, Andrew. 2015. "Part Past Part Fiction: A Conversation with The Chills' Martin Phillipps." *Popmatters.* www.popmatters.com/feature/part-past-part-fiction-a-conversation-with-the-chills-martin-phillips (accessed July 15, 2017).

Derrida, Jacques. 1978. *Writing and Difference.* London: Routledge & Kegan Paul.

Eyegum Music Collective. 2016. "Eyegum Statement about Safer Spaces Process and Practice." https://eyegum.co.nz/2016/04/20/eyegum-statement-about-safer-spaces-process-and-practice (accessed July 13, 2017).

Frith, Simon. 1993. "Popular Music and the Local State." In *Rock and Popular Music: Politics, Policies, Institutions,* edited by Tony Bennett, Simon Frith, Larry Grossberg, John Sheperd and Graeme Turner. Abingdon: Routledge, 14–24.

Greive, Duncan. 2016. "'Rock Music: I Don't Know What's Wrong with It': An Interview with Street Chant's Emily Edrosa." *The Spinoff.* http://thespinoff.co.nz/featured/27-04-2016/its-a-mans-world-the-music-industry-an-interview-with-street-chants-emily-edrosa (accessed July 7, 2017).

Hann, Michael. 2014. "The Chills: The Band Who Fell to Earth." *Guardian.* https://www.theguardian.com/music/2014/nov/24/the-chills-martin-phillipps-comeback (accessed July 15. 2017).

"Jeff." 2016. Interview with OW, digital audio recording, Brooklyn, New York, May 22.

Kerry, Laura. 2016. "REVIEW: Kane Strang – Blue Cheese." Thrdcoast. www.thrdcoast.com/read/2016/2/23/review-kane-strang-blue-cheese (accessed July 15, 2017).

Keyes, J. Edward. 2015. "The Chills Silver Bullets." *Pitchfork.* http://pitchfork.com/reviews/albums/21055-silver-bullets (accessed July 15. 2017).

L.W. 2008. "Made in China Feature on Christchurch News Show." Dunedinmusic.com. http://forum.dunedinmusic.com/viewtopic.php?t=3091 (accessed July 15, 2017).

McGee, Alan. 2008. "The Chills: Ready for a Comeback?" *Guardian*, August 5. https://www.theguardian.com/music/musicblog/2008/aug/05/thechillsreadyforacomebac (accessed July 15, 2017).

McGonigle, Dave. 2005. "In Love with Those Times: Flying Nun and the Dunedin Sound." *Stylus Magazine.* www.stylusmagazine.com/articles/weekly_article/in-love-with-those-times-flying-nun-and-the-dunedin-sound.htm (accessed July 22, 2017).

McLeay, Colin. 1994. "The 'Dunedin Sound': New Zealand Rock and Cultural Geography." *Perfect Beat: The Pacific Journal for Research into Contemporary Music and Popular Culture* 2 (1): 38–50.

McMillan, Paul Andrew. 2016. "Why Cover? An Ethnographic Exploration of Identity Politics Surrounding 'Covers' and 'Originals' Music in Dunedin, New Zealand." *MEDIANZ: Media Studies Journal of Aotearoa New Zealand* 15 (1). doi: 10.11157/medianz-vol15iss1id136. https://medianz.otago.ac.nz/medianz/article/view/136/134.

McNeilly, Hamish. 2014. "British Music Mag Loves 'Songs in the Kiwi of Life'." *The New Zealand Herald* July 24. www.nzherald.co.nz/entertainment/news/article.cfm?c_id=1501119&objectid=11298481 (accessed July 15, 2017).

Mitchell, Tony. 1996. *Popular Music and Local Identity: Rock, Pop and Rap in Europe and Oceania.* London: Leicester University Press.

Mitchell, Tony. 1994. "Flying in the Face of Fashion: Independent Music in New Zealand." *Perfect Beat: The Pacific Journal for Research into Contemporary Music and Popular Culture* 1 (4): 28–72.

Phillipps, Martin. 2014. Interview with MH and OW, London, May 22.

Robertson, Craig. 1991. "It's OK, It's All Right, Oh Yeah: The 'Dunedin Sound'? An Aspect of Alternative Music in New Zealand 1979–85." BA (Hons) thesis, University of Otago.

Saunders, Trish. 2011. *The Other Dunedin Sound: The Acoustic Community of Southern New Zealand.* Dunedin: Trish Saunders.

Schulz, Chris. 2010. "Knives at Noon Shun Dunedin Sound." stuff.co.nz October 12. www.stuff.co.nz/entertainment/music/4222964/Knives-at-Noon-shun-Dunedin-sound (accessed July 15, 2017).

Shepherd, Roger. 2016. *In Love with These Times: My Life with Flying Nun Records.* Auckland, Harper Collins Publishers.

Shuker, Roy and Michael Pickering. 1994. "Kiwi Rock: Popular Music and Cultural Identity in New Zealand." *Popular Music* 13 (3): 261–278.

Smith, Emma. 2014. "Alive Beneath the Weight of Tradition." *New Zealand Listener.* September 11.www.listener.co.nz/culture/music/alive-beneath-the-weight-of-tradition (accessed July 15, 2017).

Smithies, Grant. 2014. "Dunedin's Beautiful Sound Lives On." stuff.co.nz. www.stuff.co.nz/entertainment/music/10598655/Dunedins-beautiful-sound-lives-on (accessed July 15, 2017).

Steel, Gary. 2016. "Flying Nun: In Love with the Sound of their Own Voice, More Like." *The Spinoff* June 14. http://thespinoff.co.nz/featured/14-06-2016/flying-nun-in-love-with-the-sound-of-their-own-voice-more-like (accessed July 15, 2017).

Strang, Kane. 2016. "I honestly would have been fine with a 3 as long as they still didn't mention the Dunedin sound lol." Twitter. https://twitter.com/kanestrang/status/707299336971886592 (accessed July 14, 2017).

"Thomas." 2016. Interview with OW, digital audio recording, Cologne, June 23.

Thornton, Sarah. 1996. *Club Cultures: Music, Media, and Subcultural Capital.* London: Wesleyan University Press.

Uncredited. 2015a. "The Chills – Hear Their Brilliant Comeback Album Silver Bullets." *Guardian,* October 23. https://www.theguardian.com/music/musicblog/2015/oct/23/the-chills-comeback-album-silver-bullets-listen (accessed July 15, 2017).

Uncredited. 2015b. "The Chills Announce First Album in 19 Years, Share 'America Says Hello.'" *Pitchfork,* July 29. http://pitchfork.com/news/60559-the-chills-announce-first-album-in-19-years-share-america-says-hello (accessed July 14, 2017).

Uncredited. 2015c. "The 200 Best Songs of the 1980s" *Pitchfork.* https://pitchfork.com/features/lists-and-guides/9700-the-200-best-songs-of-the-1980s/?page=2 (accessed June 14, 2017).

Undertheradar. 2016. "YES! Fest – Otago Women's Pioneer Hall, Dunedin." Undertheradar www.undertheradar.co.nz/gig/50095/YES-Fest.utr (accessed July 13, 2017).

Unnamed Fan. 2016a. Interview with OW, digital audio recording, Cologne, June 31.

Unnamed Fan. 2016b. Interview with OW, digital audio recording, Brighton, May 29.

Unnamed Fan. 2016c. Interview with OW, digital audio recording, New Jersey, May 23.

Various Artists. 2015. "Tally Ho: Dunedin Songs and Singers." Music concert. *Tally Ho: Dunedin Songs and Singers,* orchestrated by Graeme Downes. Dunedin Town Hall.

Welsh, April Clare. 2014a. "Listen: 17 Must-Hear Dunedin Sound Classic Tracks." *New Musical Express,* July 16. www.nme.com/blogs/nme-blogs/listen-17-must-hear-dunedin-sound-classic-tracks (accessed August 21, 2017).

Welsh, April Clare. 2014b. "Songs in the Kiwi of Life." *New Musical Express,* July 19, 32–35.

Wilson, Oli and Kirsten Johnstone. 2016. "The Chills Audio Diary." Radio program. *Music 101.* Wellington: Radio New Zealand.

Videography

Gorman, Pete. 2008. *The Other Dunedin Sound: Hardcore 1985–1995.* videorecording. Dunedin, NZ: Pete Gorman and Variant Media.

Discography

Males. *Run Run Run/MalesMalesMales.* Fishrider Records, FISH 011, 2013, compact disc and 33⅓ rpm.

The Chills. *Kaleidoscope World.* Flying Nun FN COLD005, 1986, 33⅓ rpm.

The Chills. *Pink Frost.* Flying Nun FN COLD2, 1984. 33⅓ rpm.

The Chills. *Silver Bullets.* Fire Records FIRELP382, 2016, compact disc and 33⅓ rpm.

The Chills, Sneaky Feelings, The Stones, The Verlaines. *Dunedin Double EP.* Flying Nun DUN 1, 1982, 33⅓ rpm.

6

The Construction of Latin American Musical Identity in Melbourne

Mara Favoretto

Introduction

With around 140 cultures represented, including established Chinese, Greek and Italian communities, Melbourne is one of the most multicultural cities in the world (Melbourne City Council 2016). For this reason, it forms an ideal site to explore the formation of hybrid identities, in-between culture dynamics and transculturation processes. Interestingly, despite Australia's acknowledged diversity, the promotion and celebration of Latin-American popular music in Australia has been filtered through an Anglo perspective and, more specifically, a US lens, limiting the vast variety of Latin-American rhythms to a few Caribbean and New York genres including salsa, Afro-Cuban jazz, cha cha cha and merengue. Evidence of this can be seen in the numerous fiestas and festivals that celebrate what is typically called "Latin music," such as the nation-wide Clave Contra Clave competition, which took place in 2011, 2012 and 2013. However, a new generation of musicians is managing to circum-navigate these constraints on what Latin music comprises, and in doing so it is creating a hybrid Australian-Latin-American identity that is more inclusive and dynamic. This chapter draws on the theory of Latinamericanism (Plesch 2012), the history of Latin-American music in Melbourne (Bendrups 2000) and the idea of the third space (Bhabha 1994) to explore, as a case study, the Melbourne-based band Madre Monte's popular music song lyrics as a canny reinterpretation of the Clave Contra Clave competition's narrow definition of Latin music.

Through a series of interviews with Melbourne-based musicians, including Madre Monte band members, and a close reading of the lyrics of their songs against the official discourse that promotes their music, mainly the three consecutive (2011, 2012, 2013) Clave Contra Clave competitions, I argue that Latin-American-Australian musicians are developing ways to move forward and inhabit a hybrid third space where labels cease to matter, far from market-dictated stereotypes. They are instead making the most of market opportunities and cultural events to celebrate multiculturalism and honor traditions and heritage, while also creating an inclusive and attractive performance. The term Latinamericanism is an appropriate way to characterize the discursive formation created by the West to represent, stereotype and fantasize about Latin America, and it has a similar meaning to Said's term "Orientalism" (Said 1978). Without a doubt, Latin America has been construed as an "idea" (Mignolo 2005) and as an "invention" (O'Gorman 1958). The construction of an exotic, idealized, naturalized and eroticized Latin-American "Other," prevalent in the Western imaginary, is nowhere more evident than in the idea of Latin music. Appropriating and reshaping elements from the music genres of the new continent into a series of stereotypical attributes, the West has constructed a musical image of Latin America for its own consumption. Most events that promote Latin music (or food, or popular art, etc.) in Australia incorporate echoes of such a construction, particularly the aforementioned talent competition Clave Contra Clave (CCC). In this chapter, I examine the promotional material used by CCC during three consecutive years—2011, 2012 and 2013—with the aim of exploring the rhetoric employed and the transition towards US Latino culture observable in that period of time. As a consequence of that transition, bands like Madre Monte drew on a threefold strategy to develop their music: appealing to Australian audiences; nurturing traditional Latin-American popular music genres that fall outside the Australian concept of Latin music; and fostering hybrid compositions.

Musical Latinamericanism and the Clave Contra Clave Competition

CCC competition was created "as part of Gift Abroad's culture and community program to support Latin culture in Australia through providing a platform where musicians can share their music nationally in a collaborative, positive and nurturing environment" (Gift Abroad 2013). Gift Abroad, the organizer, is a private company that counts on the cultural partnership of Multicultural Arts Victoria, Bemac (Brisbane Multicultural Arts Centre) and IDA (Inspire & Develop Artists Educational Program, a US-based company that recruits artists in several countries), as well as the support of a number of companies such as Latin Percussion (a brand of percussion instruments). As described on Multicultural Arts' website, the competition is an initiative "aimed at helping build a sustainable Latin music industry propelling creativity and industry growth. The event strongly emphasizes 100% live music performance, original music, and a collaborative approach involving local Latin dance schools, community organisations, and local businesses" (Multicultural Arts Victoria 2013).

In this chapter, I point to a few elements in the 2011–13 competitions' discursive dynamics that operate as a reinforcement of Western discourse on Latin-American culture. At the same time, some Melbourne-based bands such as Madre Monte have managed to incorporate stereotypical images attractive to Western audiences and mix them with traditional elements from their countries of origin, creating a hybrid popular music product. Their creative bicultural and bilingual songs inhabit a third space in the heart of Melbourne.

As suggested above, "there is no doubt that an archive of texts comparable to Orientalism exists with relation to Latin America" (Plesch 2012, 4). This archive, called *musical Latinamericanism*, is one that "the West has built for its own consumption, within its own epistemological logic and to serve its own interests" (ibid), and is particularly observable in Australia where the promotion and consumption of Latin-American music has an impact on the way Latin-American musicians present themselves in order to survive in a system that reduces them to an exotic Other.

My exploration of how Latin-American culture is represented in Australia is not concerned with pointing out misrepresentations or distortions "because that would imply that we believe there is an 'authentic,' 'real' and 'accurate' Latin American music against which these representations can be measured" (Plesch 2012, 5). Rather, I take up Plesch's contention that Latin-American scholars should

> examine the conditions by which stereotypes of Latin American music are reproduced in Western mainstream consciousness. We should perhaps analyze these schemes of difference, explore how they were invented, and how Latin American musicians have negotiated, co-opted with, transacted, or subverted them.
>
> (ibid)

Events like the CCC competition have been embraced and celebrated in Australia, and it is by no means my intention to diminish the importance of such talent competitions. However, it is also necessary to draw attention to some issues that seem to contradict the competition's stated mission, which, according to their website (which has, in 2018 since been deleted),, was expressed in the following terms:

> We believe in:
>
> 1. Creating opportunities to increase exposure for Latin culture and musical talent
> 2. Engage [sic] people and organizations from a diverse background in a common ground venue
> 3. Fostering the traditions of Latin music culture while nurturing emerging young artists
> 4. Stimulating profile and growth of Australian Latin music on a global platform
> 5. Educating wider Australian community of the richness of Latin culture
> 6. The power of music to overcome language and cultural barriers, and build community ties through acceptance of cultural diversity.
>
> (Clava Contra Clave 2014, Homepage)

It is clear from this statement that diversity and inclusion are what motivates the competition organizers, however, the participation criteria for bands interested in the competition dictates certain types of genres, favoring those resembling US Latino music more than an inclusive range of Latin-American genres, as will be taken up below. This coincides with the fact that one of the major supporters of the event, Inspire & Develop Artists Educational Program, is a US-based private business that recruits artists for the North-American popular music industry, and offers them workshops and mentorship opportunities to work in the US.

To be accepted as a participant in the CCC competition, there are series of pre-requisites. For example, bands need to have a minimum of seven members and a maximum of fourteen, a requirement that clearly favors genres such as salsa, which rely on a large number of instruments and thus are comprised of at least seven members. Right from the name chosen for the competition, "clave" refers to Afro-Cuban rhythms. At the same time, there is a list of "rhythms permitted" (Gift Abroad 2014) in the competition that includes genres such as bolero, cha cha cha, merengue, cumbia, Latin jazz, rumba, salsa, plena and vallenato; sub-genres guaguancó and son montuno; and blended styles such as bomba, changüí, danzón, descarga, guajira, mambo, bachata, son and timba. Although original music is encouraged

84 • Mara Favoretto

but not mandatory, the bands that make it to the grand finale are required to perform one piece of original music.

Limiting the scope to genres, sub-genres and blended styles that belong to the Caribbean and New York groups of Latin-American music genres ignores a vast range of genres from other parts of Latin America. Moreover, there are several other indicators of a misconception of Latin-American culture and music. But first, it is necessary to briefly recall what the term Latino implies and revise how it entered the Australian imaginary. In his well-known book *The Idea of Latin America,* Walter Mignolo, by means of a thorough exploration of the discourses that produced this idea, explains how the term "Latin America" has become pre-scriptive rather than descriptive. For him, there was a second historical transformation in the history of Latin America after its colonization in the fifteenth century: the period after the Second World War, when the US became the new imperial leader of the world (Mignolo 2005, 4). How did this affect Australia and our perception of Latin-American music and culture?

There are No Latinos in Australia

Australia has witnessed numerous waves of immigration from several countries in Latin America. People originating from different Latin-American countries who identify as Brazilians, Argentines, Chileans, Colombians, Cubans, etc. face a particular challenge in Australia. Their identity of origin might come to play a secondary role as a new primary identification takes over: once outside their home countries they become "Latin Americans." Globally, understandings of what it means to be a Latin-American migrant have emerged predominantly from the US, a phenomenon that has occurred not only because the US is home to the world's largest and longest-standing Latin-American diasporic communities, but also because of the global reach of US film, television and music industries, which have circulated around the world for close to a century. Thus, an idea of Latin music preceded any significant Latin-American immigration to Australia, with incoming Latin Americans encountering an identity that already existed in Australians' imagination. Latin-American musicians have had to negotiate this prefabricated cultural positioning, at the same time as they have had to deal with the tension between their specific national-cultural identity and a more generic Latin-American one, and with the expectation that they will ultimately assume an identity as Australians.

Prior to the 1966 abolition of the White Australia Policy, which had enabled "the Executive Government of Australia to prevent the immigration of persons deemed unsuitable because of their Asiatic or non-European race" (Robertson, Hohmann and Stewart 2005, 241), the Latin-American population size in Australia was negligible, preventing the emergence of significant language, culture or economic communities. White-only immigration policies eventually clashed with the perception of a strong need for population growth in Australia, especially after the Second World War, when the country was under the paranoia of Japanese invasion and saw the need to "populate or perish" (Martin 2002).

Yet well before the arrival of the first Latin-American immigrants in the 1960s, an interest in Latin-American music and dance had begun in Australia. By the end of 1913, the tango attracted attention as a stage and social dance. Other Latin-American dances—including the rumba and, by 1941, the conga and the samba—were particularly popular with audiences. Furthermore, Hollywood movies with South-American and South Seas settings heightened interest in dancing to Latin-American- and Hawaiian-style music (Whiteoak and Scott-Maxwell 2003, 618), including the tango. As such, Latin-American popular music existed in Australia *before* the arrival of large numbers of Latin-American migrants, due to the influence of the North-American recording industry. Rather than an expression of migrant culture, "Latin music" in this context was a "continuation of mainstream Anglo-Australian popular culture" (Bendrups 2000, 31). When immigrants from Latin-American countries started to arrive in Australia, they not only found a stereotyped construction of a Latin-American identity that homogenized regional varieties, but also a pre-existing Latin music which ignored a vast range of genres.

Large-scale immigration from Latin America began in the 1970s. Most of these immigrants were from major cities such as Buenos Aires (Argentina) and Santiago (Chile) and brought their local music genres with them, thus enriching the variety of popular music and dance that was already found in Australia. Because of its popularity throughout Latin America, performances of cumbia (originally Colombian) were integral to the early establishment of a Latin-American community, becoming a feature of social gatherings in the 1980s (Whiteoak 2003, 393). Community centers at the time started to welcome new immigrants from different countries. Latin-American music genres, together with the Spanish language, became socially binding tools. There was folkloric music and traditional dances such as cueca (Chile), huayno (Peru, Bolivia), tango (Argentina) and, of course, cumbia (Colombia). Brazilian communities also had carnival celebrations, with samba dancers, batucadas and capoeira demonstrations. Peruvian folkloric groups such as Ukamau and Así es Peru were significant in helping people stay connected to their traditions and roots. Spanish clubs were established in Sydney and Melbourne, with Spanish language as their main connecting thread. La Peña in Sydney and Café Bohemia in Melbourne, together with several other small clubs, provided a public space for performance opportunities where Latin-American musicians could share their music with Australian audiences and possibly increase public awareness of the rich variety of genres that existed outside the stereotyped Latin label. As interest in Latin-American music and culture increased in Australia, several festivals were born, such as the Festival del Sole and the Bondi South-American Festival in Sydney and the Johnston Street Fiesta in Melbourne (Dio 2010).

During the 1990s, a different migrant trend from Latin America to Australia emerged. As Latin America embraced democracy, it experienced major economic growth fueled by a commodity trade boom. As a consequence, the number of immigrants motivated by political reasons decreased while economic imperatives and other considerations evidently became more compelling reasons to migrate. Within this later wave of immigration, a new generation of musicians and artists arrived in Australia with the desire to embrace the new cultures while also honoring their own. They found a particular context and audience: a heavily influenced US-Latino music industry, an interest in dance and a variety of opportunities to perform and maybe make a living.

It is important to note that until the year 2000, there were almost no original compositions being produced in Australia, and Latin-American popular music lacked an Australian voice. This has indeed changed in recent years as there is now a large number of bands composing their own music, releasing albums and producing new hybrid forms of alt-Latin music.[1] Indeed,

> the act of music performance creates an environment where Latin-American migrants and other non-Latinos can meet on common ground, where important personal and professional networking opportunities are pursued, where some small economic benefit is afforded to the bands who play the music, and which, most importantly, is rewarding and enjoyable.
>
> (Bendrups 2000, 37)

In the city of Melbourne, in particular, migrant and mainstream music co-existed and negotiated a common space, a "third space," as I will suggest. Music and dance provided people of different national origins from any of the twenty countries of Latin America a space for building relationships and social context. Migrant musicians found some stereotyped ideas of what Latin music should sound like. Far from resisting those stereotypes, they turned them into opportunities and created new alternative sounds, blending market expectations with their homeland music.

Melbourne's Third Space

Whereas Latin festivals in Australia are intended to celebrate locality and embrace multiculturalism, they can fall into the trap of constructing a homogenous Latin-American identity devoid of specificity in the Australian context. As Barry Carr and John Sinclair put it, "in Australia, Latin America is cool" (2016, 67). At least for urban-dwelling young adults, they explain, Latin America has come to mean an imagined landscape of attractive and colorful though indistinct cultural otherness, quite dislocated from the realities of Latin-American immigrants' homelands. In the case of Melbourne in particular, "Latin" or "Latino" are terms used to refer to Latin-American-inspired music, regardless of the origin of musicians. Of course, the term "Latino" is problematic. It is a reductionist category imposed by US policy that delegitimizes regional identity. It has been exported to several other countries, including Australia, where Latin-American immigrants call themselves "Latinos" even if they have never been to the US. This phenomenon has caused a number of reactions from different Latin-American popular musicians,[2] but such a reaction does not seem to have reached Australia, where the term "Latins" or even "Latinos/Latinas" seems to work more often than not as a short form of "Latin American."

However, there is a new generation of artists who are creating an alternative voice that blends pre-conceptions and market expectations with traditions from their countries of origin. The result is a promising third space that moves away from stereotypical images of Latin Americans. Homi Bhabha's notion of hybridity is useful in this context because it describes that alternative space that transcends both "home" and "host" cultures, which he calls a third space (Bhabha 1994). Cultural hybridity results in the creation of a new space in border situations and thresholds as the sites where identities are performed and contested— a space which is not itself hybrid, but which emerges from a hybrid or mixed community. Such an understanding helps to avoid the perpetuation of antagonistic binarisms such as "home" and "host," and posits a more dynamic conception of culture, no longer linked to place of origin. Migrants from Latin America in Australia provide a special case for the investigation of how social and cultural identities can be transformed under the contemporary circumstances of migration. The global movement of people coincides with the global movement of capital, technology, images and ideas, in which context imagination is "a key component of the new global order" (Appadurai 1996, 31). It thus becomes a significant task in itself to delineate the individual and collective self-imaginings of Latin-American Australians in a transnational context. In the case of relatively newly arrived Latin-American migrants negotiating their transnational circumstances, such concepts enable us to observe and analyze how their "symbolic geographies" are imagined (Jackson, Crang and Dwyer 2004, 3), and how their identities are performed and expressed in practice, particularly observable in the field of popular music.

The Discourse of Clave Contra Clave

One could argue that CCC seems to have been principally concerned with US Latino culture from the outset, but with space for some broader Latin-American culture. By its final year, however, CCC narrowed this scope to an almost exclusively Latino focus. In the first two years, performances represented a variety of Latin-American genres, with some South-American musicians invited to perform. For example, in 2011, Gonzalo Porta, an Australian-born musician who lives in Uruguay where his family is from, was one of the main guests, together with Legends of Cuba. Other guests have included, in 2012, Willie Colón, Bronx-born of Puerto Rican grandparents, and Fonseca, a Colombian musician and activist strongly committed to social causes and the promotion of Colombian culture. CCC's scope was narrowed in 2013 when the guest bands were Grupo Niche and Sal Salvador All Stars: two salsa bands. The choice of salsa guest bands, combined with the new selection criteria favoring large participant bands, signaled a move towards Caribbean and New York Latin genres, leaving aside the vast range of Latin-American genres.

In 2011, Latin-American music representation in the CCC competition was indeed more varied and inclusive. Among the participants we can mention Celestino, an instrumental ensemble of five members (not a minimum of seven, as was required in 2013), comprising Andean, Afro-Cuban and Western influences. Their music is presented as "traditional South American instruments sikus (panpipes) and quenas (flutes) accompanied by rhythm section guitar, charango (Bolivian native string instrument) and keyboard" (Celestino Music 2012). They play several genres such as salsa, jazz, funk, reggae, bossa nova, merengue, rock, lounge, and disco. Orulas, another group that participated that year, is described as a band that

> epitomizes world class quality, by bringing to life *what it means to be Latin Australian*, and to share with the rest of the world the diversity of the Australian music industry. Orulas' songs are based on experiences of migrants growing up in Australia, within the larger-than-life backdrop of their Latin-American heritage. As Keko blends these two unique experiences together, his musical and lyrical compositions are an honest representation of one's transformation *from the Latin American to the Latin Australian social identity.*
>
> (Band Together & Scorcher Fest 2012, author's emphasis)

In 2012, among several salsa bands, there were others such as La Mezcla, formed in Melbourne in 1997 by six Chilean musicians playing original songs influenced by Chilean rock and urban music, and Canberra-based Mi Tierra, known for its fusion of diverse musical genres and cultural backgrounds, bringing together musicians from Peru, Chile, Cuba and Australia. Evidently, there has been a move away from these somewhat diverse beginnings, with a narrowing of focus since the competition started.

Furthermore, the majority of the Australian sponsors of CCC are dance schools: the Salsa Foundation (Melbourne), Rio Rhythmics (Brisbane), Ruedisima (Sydney and Newcastle), Buena Vista Dance (Sydney) and Phoenix Dance Studio (Melbourne) to mention just a few. When asked about the popularity of salsa in Melbourne, Melbourne-based musician Eyal Chipkiewicz explained that "salsa as an urban expression is misinterpreted here, where salsa is like a sport for some athletes that have learnt to dance as a type of physical exercise and not as an urban form of expression" (Rossano 2013).

As CCC is to some extent a commercial initiative, a great emphasis is placed on the demands of the audience. In fact, on its social media website, CCC asks its viewers to submit their preferences: "Let us know what you would love to see at Clave Contra Clave 2014" (Clave Contra Clave 2014). These sorts of strategies recall Antonio Gramsci, who many years ago recognized that social power is not a simple matter of domination on the one hand and subordination or resistance on the other. Instead, rather than imposing their will, dominant alliances, coalitions, or blocs within democratic societies generally govern with a good degree of consent from the people they rule, and the maintenance of that consent is dependent upon an incessant repositioning of the relationship between rulers and ruled (Jones 2006, 4). Though in this context we are not talking about "rulers and ruled," Gramsci's concept applies just as readily to the market's model of supply and demand, a two-way street particularly observable in Australia with regard to Latin-American music and its popularization. Here, the dynamics that determine the genres that are performed and consumed are influenced by sponsored festivals such as CCC, individual interests and the public in general.

Indeed, instead of seeing the economy as determining culture and politics, Gramsci argues that culture, politics and the economy are organized in a relationship of mutual exchange with one another, a constantly circulating and shifting network of influence (Jones 2006, 6). Hybridity is not a synonym for fusion (García Canclini 1995, xxiv); rather, it is the result of "sociocultural processes in which discrete structures or practices, previously existing in separate form, are combined to generate new structures, objects, and practices" (ibid, xxv). In the case of the image of Latin-American music in Australia, there is no doubt it has been pervasively influenced by US perceptions of Latin-American musicians, and by the US's influential market.

Stereotypes

Analyzing the representation of Latin Americans in music, Plesch mapped a series of recurrent stereotypes and came up with five tropes, which are as follows: *danger, erotic-exotic, irrationality, excess* and *homogeneity* (Plesch 2012). These tropes have a double function: they provide the West with sexual titillation and a vicarious experience of its fantasies and obsessions, while at the same time reinforcing the ideas of the superiority of reasonable, restrained and law-abiding individuals who, of course, inhabit the West (Plesch 2012, 6).

These tropes are clearly observable and identifiable in the discourse used on the CCC website where the bands are promoted. To take one example, the 2013 events in major cities in the country had a suggestive name: "heat" [*erotic-exotic*]. Indeed, the competition nights held in three of the major capital cities in Australia were called the Melbourne Heat, the Brisbane Heat and the Sydney Heat. Throughout the three consecutive years of CCC analyzed in this chapter, the various bands were presented using expressions that are fully charged with the aforementioned tropes. For example, the band Furia (which means "rage" in Spanish) [*irrationality; danger*] was introduced as "Australia's *hottest* international Latin sensation ... that enables audiences to escape to *the exciting and exotic atmosphere of Latin American countries [homogeneity; erotic-exotic]*. Furia's musicians move and groove with *unstoppable energy*, whilst *pumping* Latin rhythms [*excess*]" (author's emphasis). Chilean musician German Silva, according to the information about him on the website, grew up in *vibrant* Latin America (though he only lived in Chile), "playing soccer to the beats and rhythms of people on the street" [*exotic*]. Furthermore, Los Chavos are referred to as seasoned musicians from Australia and South America, who can make you "*sway hips from Canberra to Colombia*" [*erotic-exotic*]. Other expressions used to present bands and their performances are "sweaty crowds," "pack the dance floors and get the clubs pulsing," "passionate performances," "authentic big band sound," "fiery, rich, passionate." Furthermore, San Lazaro, the winning band in 2012, is described in the following terms:

> How does a band from Melbourne, Australia, come to sound like this? blending old school salsa, reggae and funk with Latinoamerican [sic] folk styles so effortlessly and convincingly? How did this continent of kangaroos and deserts produce such emotive and raw Spanish language songwriting? ... tales of love and loss, injustice and rage, fate and redemption ... like some kind of bizarre lovechild of Ruben Blades and Victor Jara, or a latino incarnation of Johnny Cash backed by the Fania all stars ... Migrants from Latin America and Australian musicians found themselves playing together ... No longer a bunch of songs from across oceans and decades but real home grown Australian Latin music, reflecting the experiences and culture of yet another wave of migrants to wash up on this vast island. Even if you don't understand the lyrics, this music works. It works for the heart [sic] the soul and the hips ...
>
> (Gift Abroad 2013)

This text is also found on other sites that have featured the band, such as Triple J Unearthed (ABC 2009). Similar kinds of descriptions abound in many other bands' promotion material. In other words, the musicians themselves use these tropes, a point that became evident during interviews and fieldwork in music venues in Melbourne during 2013. When asked if they were a Latin-American or a Latin musician, interviewees sometimes used the terms as synonyms. However, the terms "Latin" and "Latin-American" are not interchangeable with "Australian Latin" and "Australian Latin-American."

Towards a Melbournian Sound of Latin-American Music

Even though Latin-American and Latino music entered Australia via the US market and was filtered through a US lens, it is highly likely that the most recent immigration waves of people (including musicians) coming directly from Latin-American countries will give the music scene the variety and inclusion it has been lacking.

Some interviewees suggested that in order to survive in the industry they needed to adapt to the demands of the market, which meant playing music that people could dance to. For scholars such as Simon Frith, music and identity are closely related, and a musical experience makes sense only by taking on both the collective and the subjective identity. In his words, "identity is *mobile*, a process, not a thing, a becoming not a being … and our experience of music—of music making and of music listening—is best understood as an experience of this *self-in-process*" (Frith 1996, 109, emphasis in original). This process, as described by Frith, is clearly observable in some alt-Latin bands that are trying to survive in Australia by making music that negotiates dance genres. Such is the case, for instance, with Madre Monte, a band that made it to the CCC semifinals in 2013.

Madre Monte is a nine-member band, three members of which are Colombian, the rest Australian. Madre Monte[3] musicians say they believe they have discovered "the perfect unison between Afro-Colombian styles and their cousin and neighbour, reggae" (Madre Monte 2015). Colombia's culture comprises an interesting mixture of European, Indigenous and African ancestries, as a result of a long history of slavery, colonization and migration. The band members describe themselves as a South-American Roots outfit that "finds inspiration in the myths, folklore and music of Colombia, with a focus on taking these ideas and making art that is contemporary and that expands the Latin-Australian musical and mythical connection" (Madre Monte 2015). In an interview in *Beat Magazine*, one of the band members, Mauricio Peña, explains that

> after a few songs we decided to make it—well, not really like a concept band, but to have an underlying theme in the lyrics of myths from South America. So we use that as the basis then create characters that play parts in the myths. It's not just telling the stories again but modernising them and including these characters we created to play a part in the stories.
> (Hodgson 2012)

An example of what Peña describes is found in the song "Vincente," in which a mythical character, while running through the jungle, hears a spirit. Running away from the spirit, he gets lost, and he keeps crying, screaming at night. The myth suggests that people can still hear his screams at night.

Their second album *Raza Madre* (which means "mother race") starts with a song called "Breaking News," sung in English with only a few words in Spanish. The lyrics of the song seem like a concoction of words, all mixed up to portray the varied nature of the actual world, while at the same time stating that "the world is changing." The second song, "Subidero," is a traditional Colombian story told in Spanish. The song alerts the audience to the importance of remembering oral tradition. The hybridity of the album is shown not only in its musical styles but also in its bilingualism. While "Miranda" is a song completely sung in Spanish, "El Diablo" (The Devil) is sung in English. The last song, "Cumbia March," is again a bilingual combination.

Language, indeed, plays a pivotal role in the construction of identities. People of different national origins and traditions have over the decades joined together in Australia to become a community, united through common language and other aspects of shared culture and experience (Kath 2016, 7). Undoubtedly, bilingual songs are a tangible sign of hybridization. This is observable in the choice of language spoken in each song in the order they appear on the *Raza Madre* album. At first, "Breaking News" points to the process of hybridization taking place. Then oral tradition is recalled and brought into the present in the song "Vincente," sung in Spanish. Soon after, the album introduces Miranda, a girl whose nationality is unclear. Finally, "El Diablo," a name that signals a change of language in the lyrics of the song, goes back to English words. Amid this apparent linguistic confusion, by the end of the album, cumbia music has completely entered the world and the hybridization process is now clear and obvious.

Madre Monte's track, released September 15, 2015, "Lo que hay" is one in which an interesting symbolic encounter of cultures takes place. In the song, spoken in English and in Spanish by mixing words of both languages in the same line, the Colombian mythical character Caimán meets the Australian Aboriginal Dreamtime serpent. "Lo que hay" means "that what is there" in English, pointing to a reality made up of historical heritage, traditions and multiculturalism that is "out there" before everybody's eyes.

In a personal interview, Mauricio Peña explained how the band envisioned the encounter of the mythological characters from Colombia and the Australian Dreamtime Serpent in the space of multicultural song. Symbolic fusion of the ancient indigenous cultures of both continents in the creative space of a nomadic, hybrid, bilingual pop song is an example of a celebration of multiculturalism and avoidance of stereotyping categories, and illustrates Tony Bennett's conceptualization of culture as "an arena in which dominant, subordinate and oppositional cultural values meet and intermingle . . . vying with one another to secure the spaces within which they can [frame and organize] popular experience and consciousness" (Bennet 1986, xix).

Conclusion

When Latin-American musicians began arriving in Australia, they found a pre-existing idea of Latin-American music. As a result, Latin-American music in Australia has been reduced to a "musical Latinamericanism" which, as I have explained, is evident in the CCC competition. Even so, in Australian society—or, at least, in the city of Melbourne—there are some indicators that signal a probable move away from stereotyping categories towards a third space where hybridity and multiculturalism become a reality. A clear example is found in the hybrid band Madre Monte, which seems to be moving towards a space where labels cease to matter.

Notes

1   These include Los Cabrones, an Afro-Cuban Latin-jazz band that combines original and traditional songs; Funkalleros, self-described on its website as an Alt-Latin band; and The Electric I, a band that consists of a Colombian, a Cuban, two Australians and a New Zealander. Other mix-origin bands are Oz Locos, The Partners, Los Cougarmen, Del Barrio, Bataola, Miss Colombia, Los Diablos, Kunataki, and many more. There have also been cases of solo artists that embrace Latin-American music, such as Maya Jupiter, an Australian-born woman with Turkish and Mexican heritage. In her songs, Maya Jupiter mixes Latin-American rhythms into her hip hop beats, with lyrics that combine Spanish and English language. Finally, Carlito's Way, Los Rumberos, Matanza,

Armandito y su Trovason and Oz Locos y Watussi are bands that embrace a mixture of Latin-American with non-Latin-American players.

2   The Uruguayan band Cuarteto de Nos, for example, have recorded "No somos latinos" (We are not Latinos), a song that directly rejects this categorization. Los Prisioneros, from Chile, ironically sing "Latinoamérica es un país al sur de los Estados Unidos" (Latin America is a country south of the USA).

3   "Madre Monte" is the name of a popular mythical feminine character that generally brings bad news. It is said that if the Madre Monte bathes in a river, its waters turn muddy, it causes flooding and massive damage. The indomitable Madre Monte punishes those who are unfaithful, vengeful, evil or invasive of someone else's territory by sending dreadful plagues that affect their cattle.

Bibliography

ABC. 2009. "San Lazaro." *Triple J Unearthed*. www.triplejunearthed.com/artist/san-lazaro (accessed October 9, 2016).

Appadurai, Arjun. 1996. *Modernity at Large*. Minneapolis and London: University of Minnesota Press.

Band Together & Scorcher Fest. 2012. "Orulas Played at Melbourne—Autumn 2012." *Scorcher Fest*. www.scorcherfest.com.au/v1/band/profile/602-3807-ODJ (accessed October 9, 2016).

Bendrups, Daniel. 2000. *Music of Multiple Migrations: Salsa, Cumbia and Merengue in Melbourne*. Bachelor of Music thesis, University of Melbourne.

Bennet, Tony. 1986. "Popular Culture and the Turn to Gramsci." In *Popular Culture and Social Relations*, edited by T. Bennett, C. Mercer and J. Woollacott. Buckingham: Open University Press, vii–xi.

Bhabha, Homi. 1994. *The Location of Culture*. London and New York: Routledge.

Carr, Barry and John Sinclair. 2016. "The 'Tequila Effect' or 'How the Taco Won Australia': The Appropriation of Mexican and Latin American Culture in Australia." In *Australian-Latin American Relations. New Links in a Changing Global Landscape*, edited by Elizabeth Kath. New York: Palgrave Macmillan, 67–84.

Celestino Music. 2012. "Profile." *Celestino Music Blog*. www.blogger.com/profile/15549566315783750917 (accessed October 9, 2016).

Clave Contra Clave. 2014. Clava Contra Clave Homepage. www.clavecontraclave.com (Accessed July 11, 2014).

Del Rio, Victor. 2014. "Latinos in Australia." In *Australia and Latin America. Challenges and Opportunities in the New Millennium*, edited by Barry Carr and John Minns. Canberra: The Australian National University Press, 167–222.

Dio, Angelica Cristina. 2010. "What is Latin Music? A Journey through Latin American Music in Australia." In *World Music. Global Sounds in Australia*, edited by Seth Jordan. Sydney: University of New South Wales Press, 64–84.

Frith, Simon. 1996. "Music and Identity." In *Questions of Cultural Identity*, edited by Stuart Hall and Paul du Gay. Los Angeles, London, New Delhi, Singapore, Washington DC: Sage, 108–122.

García Canclini, Néstor. 1995. *Hybrid Cultures. Strategies for Entering and Leaving Modernity*. Minneapolis and London: University of Minnesota Press.

Gift Abroad. 2013. *Clave Contra Clave*. www.clavecontraclave.com (accessed January 10, 2014).

Hodgson, Peter. 2012. "Madre Monte." *Beat Magazine*, June. www.beat.com.au/music/madre-monte (accessed October 9, 2016).

Jackson, Peter, P. Crang and C. Dwyer, eds. 2004. *Transnational Spaces*, London and New York: Routledge.

Jones, Steve. 2006. *Antonio Gramsci*. London and New York: Routledge.

Kath, Elizabeth, ed. 2016. *Australian-Latin American Relations. New Links in a Changing Global Landscape*. New York: Palgrave Macmillan.

Madre Monte. 2015. "Bio." *Madre Monte*. madremonte.com.au/wordpress/wp-content/uploads/2014/08/MM-Bio.pdf (accessed October 9, 2016).

Martin, Mario Daniel. 2002. "El Español en Australia." In *Anuario del Instituto Cervantes*. http://cvc.cervantes.es/obref/anuario_02/daniel (accessed August 2, 2014).

Mato, Daniel. 2006. "Identidades transnacionales en tiempos de globalización: el caso de la identidad latina (estadounidense)-latinoamericana." In *Colección Monografías*, No. 33. Caracas: Programa Cultura, Comunicación y Transformaciones Sociales, CIPOST, FaCES, Universidad Central de Venezuela. www.globalcult.org.ve/monografias.htm (accessed November 20, 2013).

Melbourne City Council. 2016. "Multicultural Communities." *City of Melbourne*. www.melbourne.vic.gov.au/about-melbourne/melbourne-profile/pages/multicultural-communities.aspx (accessed October 9, 2016).

Multicultural Arts Victoria. 2013. "Clave Contra Clave." *Multicultural Arts Victoria*. www.multiculturalarts.com.au/events2013/clave.shtml (accessed October 9, 2016).

Mignolo, Walter. 2005. *The Idea of Latin America*. Malden, MA and Oxford: Blackwell Publishing.

O'Gorman, Edmundo. 1958. *La invención de América; el universalismo de la cultura de Occidente*. México: Fondo de Cultura Económica. Published in English as *The Invention of America: An Inquiry into the Historical Nature of the New World & the Meaning of Its History*. Westport, CT: Greenwood Press, 1961.

Plesch, Melanie. 2012. "Musical Latinamericanism: Some Notes Towards the Deconstruction of a Discursive Formation." Discussion paper for the Round Table "Latin American Musical Identities 'for Export': Negotiations, Confrontations and Resistance" (M. Plesch, convenor) at the Nineteenth Congress of the International Musicological Society, Rome, July 1–7.

Robertson, Kel, Jessie Hohmann and Iain Stewart. 2005. "Dictating to 'One of Us': The Migration of Mrs Freer." *Macquarie Law Journal* 5: 241–275.

Rossano, Salvatore. 2013. Interview with Eyal Chipkiewicz from Funkalleros. Melbourne. October 15.

Said, Edward. 1978. *Orientalism*. New York: Vintage Books.

Whiteoak, John. 2003. "Latin-American Influences." In *Currency Companion to Music and Dance in Australia*, edited by John Whiteoak and Aline Scott-Maxwell. Sydney: Currency House, 393–397.

Whiteoak, John and Aline Scott-Maxwell. 2003. *Currency Companion to Music and Dance in Australia*. Sydney: Currency House.

Discography

Madre Monte. 2012. *Reaction*. Sing Sing South Studios, released December 11, 2010. https://madremonte.bandcamp.com/album/reaction (accessed June 7, 2016).

Madre Monte. 2013. *Raza Madre*. Recorded at Sound Park Studios. Mastered at Sing Sing Studios. soundcloud.com/madre-monte (accessed June 7, 2016).

PART **III**

Musical Transformations:
Decline and Renewal

The third part of this book is framed by issues related to popular music and urban policy, noting how music industries and institutions together choreograph musical practice in such a way as to give places their unique identity. The politics of decline and renewal—of cities, of genres, of music scenes, and so on—are particularly significant sites of exploration when it comes to these sorts of efforts, and point to the ways in which some musical practices become valued over others. There is clearly one vision of urban music-making that is produced by musicians and fans alike and emerges "from below," while another vision can be imposed "from above" by policy-makers, urban developers, planners, and promoters. As the chapters in this part indicate, these tensions and the ways in which they may or may not be easily reconciled can be tellingly illustrated when considered around so called "second-tier" cities, or cities seeking to revitalize musical life after a disaster.

Shelley Brunt examines the musical life of Christchurch, Aotearoa/New Zealand, after the September 2010 earthquake and the subsequent deadly quake in February 2011. Looking at particular efforts to memorialize as well pay tribute to the musical and creative resilience of the city, Brunt considers various compilations, live performances, and events that were designed to foster a sense of community in a situation where many of the city's key performance venues had been destroyed. She then turns to the case study of the *Songs for Christchurch* project, a compilation album and launch concert to mark the two-year anniversary of the 2011 earthquake. Part III then shifts to the Australian cities of Brisbane and Hobart, which are presented here as smaller, second-tier cities compared with Sydney or Melbourne. Brisbane is located on the country's east coast and has historically been a vibrant musical city (notably producing the Go-Betweens, among many other bands). Hobart, by contrast, is the capital of the country's southernmost state of Tasmania, which is also a discrete island. As Andy Bennett and Ian Rogers argue, these are two 'marginal' or 'fringe' cities and they remain rapidly changing urban spaces. The music scenes that reside within these cities are steeped in notions of this discontinuity, fracture, and rejuvenation. As such, the authors argue that the music practice described in these places comes to closely mirror the core issues driving the scene concept itself. The final chapter in this part returns to Aotearoa/New Zealand. The current state of affairs in the nation's capital, Wellington, has been marked by a disappearance of venues. Geoff Stahl explores the impact of this on the city's music scene, looking at how the closure of two venues in particular opened up a space for a civic discussion about what matters musically to the city. Drawing on the concept of "urban melancholy," he considers how differing perceptions of the city can catalyze a form of engaging with decline and disappearance in meaningful ways.

7

Outside the Square

Songs for Christchurch in a Time of Earthquakes

Shelley Brunt

We have to think outside the square, because The Square collapsed.
(Paul McLaney from Aotearoa/New Zealand band Fly My Pretties,
cited in Smyth, Moon and McNeill 2012)

On September 4, 2010, the Canterbury region of Aotearoa/New Zealand was severely shaken by a 7.1 magnitude earthquake. The quaint Garden City of Christchurch—at the time, the country's second largest city—experienced extensive damage to the land from liquefaction. Only a few months later on February 22, 2011, a smaller but more destructive 6.3 earthquake rose from underneath the city and toppled buildings, destroyed homes and businesses, collapsed roads, killed 185 people and left many more injured. The sheer force and surprise attack of this second earthquake and subsequent aftershocks left residents of Christchurch frightened, exhausted and on tenterhooks. The skyline permanently changed. The central city shifted into a mix of rubble and precariously standing buildings, and authorities declared "approximately 80% of inner city buildings have been, or will be, demolished" (Vallance and Carlton 2014, 5).[1] For a nation literally in shock, the visible symbol of the physical and emotional destruction of these earthquakes became Cathedral Square—known by locals as "The Square"—and its iconic Anglican ChristChurch Cathedral lying gutted in the heart of the CDB, cordoned off and declared an unsafe Red Zone (see Figure 7.1).

Looking back, it is clear that the earthquakes deeply affected the popular music industry and the local scene in Christchurch and its surrounding towns. There was anxiety and uncertainty about what musical life would look like in the aftermath and long term. The collapse of CBD infrastructure had the most immediate impact, with the prompt closure or demolition of important band venues such as Dux De Lux, artistic precincts like Poplar Lane (home to bars, cafes, venues and artists' studios), as well as record stores, instrument shops and music education facilities. In the months after the quakes, coordinated efforts were needed for regeneration, as noted by Marc Royal, the manager of the city's representative body CHART (Christchurch Music Industry Trust):[2]

Our local artists, live performance venues, sound and lighting companies and music industry personnel have all felt the stress and hardship that the past 18 months has delivered ... the recovery of these groups and organisations is vital to the future of our

98 • Shelley Brunt

> music culture in Christchurch ... The city's local music community need all the leverage and assistance that they can get as we try and rebuild our once thriving scene.
>
> (Marc Royal pers. comm. 11 July 2012)

Financial "leverage and assistance" was available in the form of competitive Earthquake Recovery Grants from Creative New Zealand, Aotearoa/New Zealand's arts council, and other newly created funding opportunities from organizations such as Christchurch City Council to bring music back to the city. The unfunded initiatives, however, make up a greater representation of popular music revival in post-quake Christchurch. It was a time when local musicians were playing anywhere they could and, in the case of the well-known band The Eastern, these locations included

> outside tattoo parlours [and] in makeshift backyards, knee-deep in liquefaction and despair ... They played for the elderly, the USAR [Urban Search and Rescue], the police and the average joe who needed The Eastern to show them that the city had not lost its voice.
>
> (Anderson 2012)

This hands-on approach relied on action from an existing musical community and the sharing of labor amid an inhospitable environment. The kinds of activities—from performing in lounge rooms to simply raise the spirits of a city's downcast residents, to raising money via public gigs to help those in need—also required artists to be creative and "think outside the square," as noted in the quotation at the beginning of this chapter.[3] After all, "The Square" as everyone knew it, had collapsed.

This chapter focuses on one such DIY creative regeneration initiative: a music-driven fundraising project called *Songs for Christchurch* which chiefly ran from 2011–2013 and was designed to assist the post-quake Christchurch community. In doing so, I consider the project's many facets—the publicity for the project; the insider's view from the architect of the project, Barnaby Bennett; the compilation CD and liner notes; the crowd-funding webpage; the promotional video; the live concert for the launch which I attended; and selected song lyrics. The heart of the project is the resulting compilation album *Songs for Christchurch* (released in 2013) featuring twenty-one songs donated by local and global artists including Tim Finn (see Chapter 16 in this collection) and Grammy-award recipients Flight of the Conchords, as well as lesser-known Aotearoa/New Zealand bands.

What does the *Songs for Christchurch* project tell us about the relationship between popular music and the city in a time of earthquakes? I approach this question through the lens of popular music ethnomusicology, while considering my own status in this context as an ethnographer, a resident (at the time) of the nearby city of Dunedin and as someone who experienced the September 2010 earthquake. This chapter begins by providing a context for the *Songs for Christchurch* project, by outlining other music fundraising albums for Christchurch at the time, followed by a discussion of the two-year development of the album and its launch at a free public concert in 2013. The final section is a textual analysis (chiefly of interview responses, song lyrics and liner notes) of materials used in the *Songs for Christchurch* project.

Figure 7.1 "The Square" and the remains of ChristChurch Cathedral in 2013. Photograph by author.

Fundraising for Christchurch: Compilation Albums

Music and musical activities are often commodified for the purpose of fundraising, from purchasing tickets to a charity concert to donating money online after watching a promotional music video (see Davis 2015; Harrison and Palmer 1986).[4] The sale of pre-recorded, yet newly compiled, albums were one such fundraising activity that could be organized quickly after the quakes, and it is useful to provide a summary of the most visible of these releases to contextualize the *Songs for Christchurch* album. The first album considered here is *Christchurch Quake Relief Album 2011* (2011), which was an online-only digital compilation available via download on Bandcamp—an efficient format compared with a physical CD, the latter of which requires additional time for manufacturing and distribution. This album, headed by the Melbourne DJ Pauly Fawcett (aka DJ ShiKung) began simply as a global call out to the dance/electronic community to donate a track by 3 March 2011—only a few weeks after the second major quake—as "a way for the people of Christchurch to know that there are those of us worldwide that wish we could help and we are doing what we can to make a difference" (*Story: Christchurch Quake Relief Album 2011*). It showcased sixty-three artists from around the world (but mainly from Australia and Aotearoa/New Zealand), with profits to be evenly split between the New Zealand Red Cross Earthquake Appeal and

The Prime Minister's Christchurch Earthquake Appeal (*Christchurch Quake Relief Album 2011* 2011). Another online-only release was the eighteen-track dance album *Operation Restore* (2011) by the Aotearoa/New Zealand online record label Empathy Recordings. The promotional material for this album highlighted the artists' direct connection to Christchurch by stating that "Many artists on this release have been personally affected by the earthquake and ALL have been struck by the magnitude of the disaster" (*EMPD023 Operation Restore* 2011; caps in original). This album was also rapidly assembled and released three months after the deadly quake, and comprised donated tracks (from mainly Aotearoa/New Zealand artists and a few from the UK and Russia) with all proceeds donated to the Red Cross Christchurch Earthquake Appeal. On the ground at a local level, musicians from Lyttleton—the port town just outside of Christchurch that was directly affected by the quakes—banded together as a newly formed collective named "The Harbour Union," and produced an online album and physical CD. The self-titled thirteen-track release, *The Harbour Union* (2011), comprised newly composed or "reimagined" songs by prominent musicians The Eastern (mentioned previously), Delaney Davidson and Lindon Puffin among others who had a specific goal in mind, as made clear in the album's online description:

> They have come together to make a record, of, for and about their community, the profits and proceeds of which will find their way back to Lyttleton and the people that need it. [The] first project is paying for children's rides that the Christchurch City Mission hired for a post quake community day!
>
> (The Harbour Union 2011)

Unlike other fundraising compilations, the DIY manner in which this album was created is a direct reflection of the instability of post-quake life that the musicians endured in Lyttleton. They borrowed equipment and recorded the songs in the lounge room of The Eastern's shared home, with production by Ben Edwards from Christchurch's Sitting Room recording studio amidst "aftershocks inadvertently captured during the recording process" (Anderson 2013). In contrast with this DIY self-funded compilation, a local fundraising album, titled *Love Christchurch: A Seismic Selection of Music from Christchurch*, did receive considerable support from funding bodies and institutions to facilitate the compilation process and the physical production of the CD. Described as the co-effort of the New Zealand Music Commission, the Christchurch Music Industry Trust CHART and the REAL NZ Festival, the album was financed by grant money from the New Zealand 2011 Lottery Fund and the REAL New Zealand Festival with proceeds going directly towards the construction of the BEATBOX music rehearsal facility in the central city. This multi-room space was designed to be earthquake-proof and would serve as a replacement for the many other music rehearsal facilities (both professional and home-based) that were lost due to building damage. The success of the *Love Christchurch* may be measured by the number of CDs purchased but, as CHART Manager Marc Royal notes, "selling physical CDs in the current digital age is no easy task" and

> most importantly [the CD] has drawn attention to the cause that it represents and has also provided a great promotional opportunity for all of the talented local artist[s]

involved in the project. Concepts such as this record are really important for uniting people with a shared cause and stimulating positive growth.

(Marc Royal pers. comm. 11 July 2012)

Developing *Songs for Christchurch*

The *Songs for Christchurch* album began in a not dissimilar way to these music-driven fundraising projects. The idea came from the San Francisco-based architecture and design not-for-profit organization Architecture for Humanity a few days after the 2011 earthquake. Melbourne resident Barnaby Bennett, who was embarking on a PhD in architecture and was also connected with the organization, offered his assistance.[5] It was a slow process.

> After about a month no-one had really got anyone, [and] I'd picked up two or three bands that were friends. Then after three or four months still no-one else had got anyone and I'd picked up another five or six, then after about five months one of the other guys … who helped out a lot said "Why don't you finish off the project you've done most of the heavy lifting so far?" So it ended up being transferred over to me and then took a really long time because it was just me as a side project and without a huge amount of experience sort of feeling my way through it.

(Bennett 2013)

The album ended up as a compilation of donated songs by Aotearoa/New Zealand artists: four from greater Christchurch (AHoribuzz, Delaney Davidson, The Eastern and The Unfaithful Ways) and one from the UK (Imogen Heap).[6] It took a lengthy two years for Bennett to organize and eventually release the CD in 2013, in time for the two-year anniversary of the February 2011 earthquake, and soon after it was available as a digital download.[7] The *Songs for Christchurch* CD did not receive any financial support despite Bennett approaching "pretty much everyone for funding for the album," including CHART, Creative New Zealand and the New Zealand Music Commission (Bennett 2013). As such, Bennett turned to the Aotearoa/New Zealand crowd-funding platform, PledgeMe, to

> raise about [NZD]$5,000 or $6,000 to pay for a publicist and to pay for the printing of [500] CDs and just costs involved … so that we didn't ever spend any of the money from the album sales on getting the project together.

(ibid)

The key promotional feature for the PledgeMe campaign was a video featuring many of the musicians speaking to camera about why *Songs for Christchurch* was important to them, and why people should support the project by donating money (Smyth, Moon and McNeill 2012). This, and a series of contribution incentives—such as donated merchandise including band posters, T-shirts and drawings—helped the project reach and exceed the target of NZD$7,700. With production costs taken care of, Bennett found funding for the launch of the CD through Christchurch City Council's Transitional City Projects Fund, which was created to assist "the attraction and retention of creative and innovative talent, by increasing support available for testing new ideas, enlivening places and creating opportunities to meaningfully contribute to a vibrant and innovative city" (Christchurch City Council n.d.). The launch was presented as the final event in the Art Beat program: a series of free music and art events that had been taking place in Christchurch's Re:START mall. This mall was known as the makeshift retail center of the city, neighboring the collapsed Cathedral and literally "outside The Square," and today it still houses food and clothing stores and pop up venues operating from shipping containers. I attended the launch, which was held on a sunny summer afternoon on Sunday February 22, 2013 in an empty block which had been used as a makeshift unpaved car park adjacent to the mall. Over the course of six hours, five of the artists from the album—as advertised on the promotional poster which also featured artwork from the album cover— took to the small stage. Audience members came and went, with a few hundred people at a given moment and around 3,000 in total during the afternoon (Bennett 2013), all seated on borrowed AstroTurf, benches and chairs (see Figure 7.2). A tent at the back of the space operated as a sales stall, where merchandise such as the *Songs for Christchurch* CD, a book about other community-based arts projects and promotional posters were sold (see Figure 7.3).

The *Songs for Christchurch* album received significant chart success in Aotearoa/New Zealand: it debuted at number 1 on the Independent Music New Zealand chart (Independent

Figure 7.2 Audience members at the stage for the *Songs for Christchurch* CD launch. Photograph by author.

Outside the Square • 103

Figure 7.3 Selling the *Songs for Christchurch* CD at the merchandise stall. Photograph by author.

Music New Zealand 2013) and number 17 on Aotearoa/New Zealand's Top 40 chart (Recorded Music New Zealand 2017). It also raised money. At the conclusion of the project, the total funds achieved through the sale of the CDs at the launch concert, at independent retailers and through international online purchases was approximately NZD$10,000. This seems like a small amount considering the time and effort put in to the project, not to mention it was half of the private goal of NZD$20,000, but Bennett remains "quite happy to just go 'Okay we did a good project and it's out there.'... It's not like there's any shortage of other things in Christchurch that are exciting and in need of attention" (Bennett 2013). Most importantly, the project met its three stated goals, which were widely announced via the media (see Andersen 2012a; Bennett et al. 2012) and through the official press release:

> [1] raising as much money as possible for the projects in Christchurch, [2] promoting Christchurch and New Zealand artists to overseas audiences, and [3] putting on a free live concert in Christchurch's CBD.
>
> (Johnson pers. comm. February 25, 2013)

With regard to the first goal, the funds have been allocated to "community projects that are focused on reconstituting Christchurch" which are run by Gap Filler, The Festival of

104 • Shelley Brunt

Transitional Architecture, Life in Vacant Spaces and Architecture for Humanity—all relatively low-key organizations dedicated to providing arts-based creative experiences primarily in the city (Bennett et al. 2012). The second goal was realized through the inclusion of Christchurch and Aotearoa/New Zealand artists on the album, and for the digital version to be distributed via iTunes international, thus reaching a global audience. Lastly, the third goal, the free live concert, was staged successfully.

Earthquake Themes: Music and the City

The *Songs for Christchurch* project provides unique insights into the relationship between popular music and the city in a time of earthquakes. The promotional video, in particular, is a demonstration of the "commodification of suffering" (Ibrahim 2011) which is often seen in disaster situations; a format of media which typically "take[s] us into the intimate details of pain and misfortune ... [where] images of suffering are appropriated to appeal emotionally and morally both to global audiences and to local populations" (Kleinman and Kleinman 1996, 1). Certainly, the video is designed to elicit sympathy and ergo donations from local, national and international viewers, as per the first goal for the project, but it is done in a manner that is "outside the square." Certainly, we do not see the images of suffering which had appeared on high rotation in conventional news broadcasts or bystander accounts via video streaming platforms at the time of the earthquakes—the fallen cathedral, a crushed bus, liquefaction swallowing homes or families mourning the dead. Instead, a calm spectatorship is offered through a montage of interviews with musicians and creatives involved with the *Songs for Christchurch* project, speaking directly to camera, filmed in Wellington and Auckland in their homes or band rooms, "telling it like it is" about rebuilding Christchurch and the magnitude of work needed in the future. The participants express a quiet urgency for assistance tempered by a weariness for the city's rebuild, which has dragged on for years (alongside an unspoken distain for authorities charged with this task):[8]

> "The rebuild of Christchurch and the creative scene is going to take a long time, and ... every little bit [of money] counts". (Mikee Tucker);
>
> "The buildings have been pulled down, but nothing has been erected in their place yet" (Mara TK);
>
> "they're having to start from scratch ... it's [going to take] longer than just two years" (Lisa Tomlins);
>
> "They're saying 'oh everything [is] back to normal down there'. Forget it man, it's a totally new city and it's going to take at least ten years or longer before normality is reached you know" (Delaney Davidson);
>
> "it's still only half a city. So, you know, I don't think people should really stop supporting it until it's back on its feet and functioning like a true city" (Ryan Prebble);
>
> "it's not better yet and it won't be for a long time" (Joe Lindsay).
>
> (Smyth, Moon and McNeill 2012)

The *Songs for Christchurch* CD launch and the PledgeMe campaign video emerged during the final "Recovery" stage of the city's four stage disaster management plan. The key concern during Recovery is the "immediate, medium and long term holistic regeneration of a community following a disaster"' (Ministry of Civil Defence and Emergency Management n.d.). The term "community" is challenging to define, but in disaster scholarship it is considered both "an aggregation of individual persons ... with limited capacity to act effectively or make decisions for themselves [as well as] ... an autonomous actor, with its own interests, preferences, resources, and capabilities" (Patterson, Weil and Patel 2010). But, as I have argued elsewhere in relation to other Aotearoa/New Zealand cities (Brunt 2011, 2010; Bartleet et al. 2013; Brunt and Johnson 2011), projects about music are often used by communities to confirm a sense of collective belonging when identity is threatened. There are many communities addressed in the *Songs for Christchurch* video (and in other promotional material)—a community of musicians and creatives who are at the core of the project; the community of affected musicians in Canterbury; the Christchurch community at large; and, by further extension, the nation of Aotearoa/New Zealand as an imagined community (Anderson 1991 [1983]) in its broadest sense. Together, the individual stories about the effect earthquakes have had on the interviewees' own lives, their families and friends form a cohesive narrative about collective suffering that is linked to a loss of buildings/homes and local identity:

> "The house that I was born and raised in has all but fallen down and needs to be rebuilt" (Jessie Moss);

> "[I've got an] uncle and his family whose house was red-zoned" (Ryan Prebble);

> "My brother's house is sinking into the ground, and it's the on-going question of ... things taking such a long time to get sorted out" (Delaney Davidson);

> "You know, this is my hometown, this is where I grew up." (Mara TK)
> (Smyth et al. 2012)

As mentioned earlier in this chapter, the physical destruction of the city has also meant the loss of music performance spaces. The liner notes to the *Songs for Christchurch* album (2013) describe the loss of two band venues in particular, after the first earthquake, which affected two Aotearoa/New Zealand touring bands. These stories, printed in the CD booklet, bring to light the effect the earthquakes have had on the infrastructure that supports the music industry, as well as the loss of well-known and loved venues (the Wunderbar and the Bedford) which hold memories for audiences and musicians alike:

> Spartacus R were in Lyttelton on the night of the September 4th 2010 earthquake which struck not long after they'd gone to bed at 4am. The next day they got their gear from the rubble of the Wunderbar, checked on their friends, collected their thoughts, counted their blessings, and went on to perform a legendary set with accompanying aftershocks at the now demolished coffee company ... The Black Seeds were set to tour the South

Island in September 2010 but due to the September 4th earthquake their Christchurch show at The Bedford was rescheduled till the end of October. The devastating February 2011 earthquake took the building and meant that The Black Seeds gig was their last at the old Bedford.

(*Songs for Christchurch* liner notes 2013)

Personal accounts such as these are also articulated though song lyrics on the *Songs for Christchurch* album.[9] Some songs were previously written and given new meaning as repurposed for the compilation. British singer Imogen Heap, for example, drove into Christchurch after the second quake and saw "a steeple sitting on the pavement," which prompted her to donate her song "Neglected Space" because, to her, it spoke to "all the tumbled, crumpled buildings crying out again for human connection" (ibid). Jessie James, from Wellington band Jessie James and the Outlaws, also donated a specific song, "In the Still," because the lyric themes were an appropriate fit for the new situation in Christchurch.

I wrote this in 2008, overseas and homesick for my family home in Christchurch. It talks of being grounded to solid family land and all that means to me. I would say I'm more grounded to it now, but a lot has changed. Christchurch soil may not be solid but the people are.

(ibid)

Only a few songs were purposefully written about the earthquakes. These make specific references to landscapes and heritage landmarks that define Christchurch, which is in keeping with Tony Mitchell's perspective that Aotearoa/New Zealand's "landscape and 'sonic geography'" is tied to concepts of home and belonging (2009, 145). LA-resident Greg Johnson, for example, is a New Zealander abroad who had "many rockin times in the old city over the years" and wanted to give an "imagined stoic middle finger to the forces of nature" (*Songs for Christchurch* liner notes 2013). He knew the symbolism of the ChristChurch Cathedral in The Square, and was prompted by "the traumatic scenes on TV" (RadioLive.co.nz 2011) to write the song "Take Me to the Old Cathedral." Even a small excerpt of lyrics from this song points to a sense of community that is unshakable, despite the physical destruction of the city's landmark: "Take me to the old Cathedral / No-one can knock her down / Well God can break every stained glass window / It's still our same old town." Other songs inspired by the debilitating earthquakes, such as "Burden of Relief" by Wellington trio The Nudge, were less literal and, in the band's words, more about "the inevitability and necessity of geological change, and the debilitating affect it has on society" (*Songs for Christchurch* CD liner notes 2013). The songwriter Ryan Prebble, whose other band Spartacus R also appears on the album, had been playing gigs in Christchurch a few days prior to the February 2011 quake. He notes that in the early hours that it hit, "a lot of our friends and favourite places were pretty badly affected … I remember it being pretty unnerving playing in a brick building with all these aftershocks happening. It was difficult to relax into the music" (pers. comm. February 25, 2017). The lyrics of "Burden of Relief" are specifically about geography and landscape, and capture the effect of the shaking land on the buildings as mountains come into relief.

Tumbling rocks / Opening streets / Rumbling shocks / The burden of relief
Under these parts / Tectonic tensions are squeezing the last / Of the space
Mountains are made / Mountains cascade / Reshape the scape
The burden of relief / The urgence of relief.

(The Nudge 2013)

Conclusions

Songs for Christchurch is a multifaceted case study of music-based fundraising for an Aotearoa/New Zealand city. As a charitable project, it has raised money to further arts initiatives for affected communities at the site. As a music project with discrete outcomes—an album and a live concert—it brings together disparate global and local musicians to form a community united through goodwill. As a DIY project, it aptly demonstrates the metaphor of thinking "outside the square" via creative self-sufficiency, crowd-funding and online distribution. As a songs project, it conveys themes that express an insider's view of the hardship and the resilience needed to rebuild a broken city, its buildings and its popular music scene. At its broadest level, however, the *Songs for Christchurch* project speaks to the capacity of music initiatives to aid with recovery in a time of earthquakes by engaging with the social ramifications of post-disaster life.

Acknowledgments

I gratefully thank Ryan Prebble for the permission to print the full lyrics to "The Burden of Relief," and Barnaby Bennett for his generosity in providing detailed insights into the *Songs for Christchurch* project.

Notes

1 Since then, other earthquakes have occurred nearby, most recently the 7.8 magnitude quake on November 14, 2016, known as the Kaikoura earthquake which was situated approximately ninety kilometres north of Christchurch.
2 In January 2018, CHART announced in a press release that the organization would be drawing to a close after eleven years of working with the local and national music industry.
3 The phrase "thinking outside the square" is commonly used in New Zealand to mean a new perspective or creative approach in order to achieve a task. A similar phrase in the United States is "thinking outside the box".
4 Live popular music concerts were one of the first music fundraising activities to be staged after the February 22, 2011 earthquake. These were, arguably, the fastest and easiest to organize, perhaps because of the eagerness of artists to donate their time. All around the world, concerts raised money for charities that would assist with Christchurch's recovery, and ranged from a band and raffle night hosted by a blues society in Ontario, Canada, to the "From London with Love" gig in West London featuring UK and Aotearoa/New Zealand performers. At a national level, prominent Aotearoa/New Zealand websites such as Amplifier.co.nz and Undertheradar.co.nz created special web pages dedicated to the many fundraising shows held across the North and South Islands as they were announced. In Christchurch, understandably, there were comparatively fewer fundraising concerts because of the closure of established band venues.
5 Architecture for Humanity is now closed, after declaring bankruptcy in 2015. In my interview with Bennett, he stated that his connection with Christchurch was mostly via family members who were from the city, whereas he had been raised in Aotearoa/New Zealand's northernmost city, Whangerei, and had also spent eight years in Wellington. In the months that followed the earthquake, Bennett became keenly interested in the architectural and social changes underway in Christchurch and moved there later in the year (Bennett 2013).

108 • Shelley Brunt

6   The full list of musicians on the album is: Mara TK, The Unfaithful Ways, Tim Finn, Electric Wire Hustle, AHoriBuzz, The Nudge, Ladi6, Sparticus R, Flight of the Conchords, The Yoots, The Black Seeds, Dear Frontier, Imogen Heap, L.A. Mitchell, Jessie James and the Outlaws, Greg Johnson, Delaney Davidson, The Eastern, Fat Freddy's Drop, Giles McNeill and Fly My Pretties (*Songs for Christchurch* 2013).
7   Although it became Bennett's project, it was presented as a collaborative effort between Freerange Cooperative Ltd (Bennett's publishing platform via projectfreerange.com) in association with Architecture for Humanity, Gap Filler, Life in Vacant Spaces and the Festival of Transitional Architecture (Bennett, Boidi and Boles 2012, 374).
8   This chapter does not address the extensive issues concerning the city's official recovery strategy, nor the widespread challenges faced by community arts organizations when dealing with the powerful government agency CERA (Canterbury Earthquake Recovery Authority) which controls access to cordoned off areas, as well as plans for demolition and reconstruction. Swaffield (2013) presents a solid introduction into this area of research.
9   In general, Bennett's vision was for an album that articulated an Aotearoa/New Zealand perspective but he left the artistic choice of song up to the artists: "Sometimes they nominated [songs], sometimes they said 'pick one,' sometimes they said 'pick one out of two or three.' For me I always quite strongly was like whatever happens with this I want the album to sound really good and be something that flows well and the music's all really good" (Bennett 2013).

Bibliography

Anderson, Benedict. 1991 [1983]. *Imagined Communities: Reflections on the Origin and Spread of Nationalism.* Second edition. London: Verso.
Anderson, Vicki. 2013. "The Sound of Christchurch: Songs that have Arisen from Chch Post-Quake." *The Press,* August 4. www.stuff.co.nz/entertainment/music/8523755/The-sound-of-Christchurch (accessed September 5, 2013).
Anderson, Vicki. 2012. "Hope and Wire Inspired by The Eastern." *The Press,* September 11. www.stuff.co.nz/the-press/opinion/blogs/rock-and-roll-mother/7656214/Hope-and-Wire-inspired-by-The-Eastern (accessed September 12, 2013).
Bartleet, Brydie-Leigh, Shelley Brunt, Anja Tait and Catherine Threlfall. 2013. "Community Music in Australia and New Zealand Aotearoa". In *Community Music Today,* edited by Kari K. Veblen, Stephen J. Messenger, Marissa Silverman and David J. Elliott. Lanham, MD: Rowman & Littlefield Publishers, 79–98.
Bennett, Barnaby. 2013. Interview with author. Skype. April 17.
Bennett, Barnaby, Eugneio Boidi and Irene Boles, eds. 2012. "Songs for Christchurch Launch." In *Christchurch: The Transitional City Pt IV.* Wellington: Free Range Press, 374–375.
Bartleet, Brydie-Leigh, Shelley Brunt, Anja Tait and Catherine Threlfall. 2013. "Community Music in Australia and New Zealand Aotearoa". In *Community Music Today,* edited by Kari K. Veblen, Stephen J. Messenger, Marissa Silverman and David J. Elliott. Lanham, MD: Rowman & Littlefield Publishers, 79–98.
Brunt, Shelley. 2011. "Performing Identity and Place in Wellington's Cuba Street Carnival." In *Home, Land and Sea Situating Music in Aotearoa New Zealand,* edited by Glenda Keam and Tony Mitchell. Auckland: Pearson, 161–173.
Brunt, Shelley. 2010. "Sounding Out the Streets: Performance, Cultural Identity and Place in Wellington's Cuba Street Carnival." In *Many Voices: Music and National Identity in Aotearoa/New Zealand,* edited by Henry Johnson. Newcastle upon Tyne: Cambridge Scholars Publishing, 39–49.
Brunt, Shelley and Henry Johnson. 2011. "Southern Gold Bars: The Gamelan Community in Dunedin." In *Dunedin Soundings,* edited by Dan Bendrups and Graeme Downes. Dunedin: University of Otago Press, 39–49.
Christchurch City Council. n.d. "Transitional City Projects Fund." https://www.ccc.govt.nz/culture-and-community/community-funding/transitional-city-funding/transitional-city-projects-fund (accessed April 20, 2017).
Davis, Louise. H. 2015. "Commodity Substitution: The Charity Music Video as Effective Fundraising Tool." *The Journal of Popular Culture* 48 (6): 1211–1231.
Harrison, Paul and Robin H. Palmer. 1986. *News Out of Africa: Biafra to Band Aid.* London: Hilary Shipman.
Ibrahim, Yasmin. 2011. "Bearing Witness through Technology." In *Global Media Convergence and Cultural Transformation,* edited by Jin Dal Yong. Hershey, PA: Information Science Reference, 123–138.
Independent Music New Zealand. 2013. "IMNZ Newsletter & Charts to March 3." www.indies.co.nz/imnz/imnz-charts-to-march-3 (accessed March 30, 2013).
Johnson, Emma. 2013. "Media Release: Songs for Christchurch." Pers. comm. Email to author February 25.
Kleinman, Arthur and Joan Kleinman. 1996. "The Appeal of Experience; The Dismay of Images: Cultural Appropriations of Suffering in Our Times." *Daedalus* 125 (1): 1–23.
Ministry of Civil Defence and Emergency Management. n.d. "Recovery." www.civildefence.govt.nz/cdem-sector/cdem-framework/the-4rs/recovery (accessed February 1, 2017).

Mitchell, Tony. 2009. "Sonic Psychogeography: A Poetics of Place in Popular Music in Aotearoa/New Zealand." *Perfect Beat: The Pacific Journal for Research into Contemporary Music and Popular Culture* 10 (2): 145–175.

Patterson, Olivia, Frederick Weil and Kavita Patel. 2010. "The Role of Community in Disaster Response: Conceptual Models." *Population Research and Policy Review* 29 (2): 127–141.

Prebble, Ryan. 2017. Pers. comm. Email to author February 25.

RadioLive.co.nz. 2011. "Greg Johnson – Take Me to the Old Cathedral." www.radiolive.co.nz/Greg-Johnson---Take-Me-To-The-Old-Cathedral/tabid/506/articleID/19534/Default.aspx (accessed April 5, 2016).

Recorded Music New Zealand. 2017. "The Official NZ Music Charts." 2013. http://nztop40.co.nz/index.php/chart/albums/pages/06/chart/nzalbums?chart=2134 (accessed March 4, 2016).

Royal, Marc. 2012. Interview with author. Email. Christchurch, July 11.

Story: Christchurch Quake Relief Album 2011. 2011. Facebook. https://www.facebook.com/pg/Christchurch-Quake-Relief-Album-100138186735832/about (accessed November 25, 2015).

Swaffield, Simon. 2013. "Place, Culture and Landscape after the Christchurch Earthquake." In *Space, Place & Culture*, edited by H. Sykes. Melbourne: Future Leaders, 1–27.

Vallance, Suzanne and Sally Carlton. 2014. "First to Respond, Last to Leave: Communities' Roles and Resilience Across the '4Rs.'" *International Journal of Disaster Risk Reduction* 14 (2): 27–36.

Discography

The Harbour Union. *The Harbour Union.* CD. Social End Product, 2011. www.forteastern.com/store/22.

The Nudge. "The Burden of Relief." In *Songs for Christchurch*, Freerange Co-Op/Southbound Distribution, 2013.

Various Artists. *Christchurch Quake Relief Album 2011.* Digital album. Bandcamp, 2011. https://christchurchquakerelief.bandcamp.com/album/christchurch-quake-relief-album-2011.

Various Artists. *EMPD023 Operation Restore.* Digital album. Empathy Records, 2011. www.empathy.co.nz/2011/03/empd023-operation-restore.

Various Artists. *Love Christchurch: A Seismic Selection of Music from Christchurch.* CD and digital album. CHART, 2011. https://chchmusic.bandcamp.com/album/love-chch-a-seismic-selection-of-music-from-christchurch.

Various Artists. *Songs for Christchurch.* CD and digital album. Freerange Co-Op/Southbound Distribution, 2013. https://songsforchristchurch.bandcamp.com/album/songs-for-christchurch.

Videography

Smyth, Gerard, Gareth Moon and Giles McNeill (director/producer). *Songs for Christchurch.* Promotional video. YouTube, 2012, posted by Jessie Moss. Accessed April 2, 2017. https://www.youtube.com/watch?v=h3dx9WVWK_o.

8

The Making and Remaking of Brisbane and Hobart
Music Scenes in Australia's "Second-Tier" Cities

Andy Bennett and Ian Rogers

Introduction

The respective and closely connected interpretations of the term "music scene" offered by Straw (1991) and Shank (1994) each recognize and strive to articulate the spatial interactivity of music places, namely how ideas transit through, around and between physical spaces. As such, urban spaces have become a major focus for work interrogating music scenes, provoking a range of studies that investigate how a city's cultural, physical and political environments shape—and are shaped by—music practice (see, for example, Stahl 2004; Grazian 2004). To date, however, much of the research carried out on music scenes has focused on scenes located in urban centers and with strongly articulated, historical legacies, which often extend to established trans-local connections with other urban music scenes also centrally positioned within flows of cultural production, performance and consumption (see, for example, Bennett and Peterson 2004). Another notable feature of the scene narratives typically presented in academic work is that they are often largely historical. To put this another way, music scenes are often recalled from the memories of respondents actively trying to describe events of the past as a means of making sense of the present. Indeed, as the work of theorists such as DeNora (2000) has revealed, in recollecting their musical past, individuals are able to use music as a part of what she describes as a "technology of the self" in order to reproduce themselves in the present. Through extrapolating DeNora's argument to the collective memory work embedded in music scenes, we suggest that a similar process can be observed. Moreover, we propose that, just as DeNora's participants articulated both positive and negative perceptions of music in their memory work, so this can be observed in the collective memory work embedded in scenes. Thus, in this chapter, we analyze a number of scene stories taken from two smaller Australian cities: Brisbane (the capital of Queensland) and Hobart (the capital of the island state of Tasmania). Drawing on fieldwork conducted in 2012 and 2013, and encompassing over twenty participant interviews, this chapter examines how the aspirant, developing and unstable nature of these two cities appears in various ideologies surrounding music practice. These are two "marginal" or "fringe" Australian capitals and they remain rapidly changing urban spaces. The music scenes that reside within these cities are steeped in notions of this discontinuity, fracture and rejuvenation. As such, we

Music Scenes and Peripheral Cities

As observed above, in most of the current academic accounts of music scenes, the latter are regarded as largely healthy, vibrant clusters of production, performance and consumption. A notable exception here is seen in the work of Barone (2016) on the Tunisian metal scene. As Barone explains, this is a scene beset by critical issues of deficit with respect to the lack of both hard and soft infrastructures (Stahl 2004) for the development of a base for the production of metal music in Tunisia. As such, argues Barone, the scene is being physically pushed to the point of extinction. A central point of Barone's argument, however, is that such a malaise of the scene is more likely to be observed in the case of music scenes in developing nations which, by their very nature, typically occupy a position on the periphery in comparison to more economically robust western(ized) nations. While there is obviously significant merit in Barone's argument, it could also be argued that such a clear-cut distinction between center and periphery remains problematic. Thus, while westernized nations are, by definition, more economically stable, they often manifest internal disparities in terms of cultural production and consumption. Indeed, in a nation the size of Australia, while its urban centers may bristle with the product of local cultural industries and consequently offer a range of opportunities for cultural consumption, such features become increasingly less prevalent as one moves further away from urban centers. This point is exemplified in Farrugia's (2015) work on rural youth in Australia whose desire for a greater choice of popular leisure and consumption opportunities results in their construction of the "urban" as a cultured other, as an idealized "cool" space. Thus, observes Farrugia:

> If young people wish to take up the subjectivities offered by contemporary youth culture, they must become mobile, either imaginatively or through actual migration. Both imaginative mobilities and actual migrations are embedded within, and articulate a complex relationship to, these metrocentric cultural distinctions.
>
> (2015, 843)

As we argue in this chapter, however, such projected desires for a preponderance of cultural choice and activity do not necessarily respond to a neatly drawn urban/regional/rural binary. In many parts of the world, including Australia, cities themselves often occupy a peripheral position. Although first and foremost a facet of geographical location, this invariably also produces a perception (inwardly and outwardly) of being on the margins of cultural life. Bennett's (2014) study of Perth, the capital city of Western Australia, is telling in this respect and is worth briefly revisiting here to provide a context for Brisbane and Hobart. Perth is often referred to as the most geographically remote city in the world, a title that quickly breaks down under comparison with a number of other cities, including Honolulu, Anchorage and Reykjavik, which are technically more isolated in a geographical sense. It is, nevertheless, geographically isolated in an Australian context. Large areas of desert separate Perth from the cities on Australia's eastern seaboard and even Adelaide, the capital of the state of South Australia and the closest Australian city to Perth, is 2,793 kilometres away. The geographical isolation of Perth has also had an impact on its access to live music. Until quite recently national and international bands would typically leave Perth off their touring schedules while local Perth bands seeking a bigger audience and greater access to recording and promotion deals would head east to Melbourne or Sydney. As Bennett observes, faced with this situation, the local Perth popular music scene has adopted a highly reflexive perception of itself

> as a scene on the periphery ... Although not popularly used to describe this situation by local people then or currently, a strong sense of DIY (do-it-yourself) practice fed the local Perth music scene and this trend has continued. Indeed, over the years this 'survival instinct' understanding of Perth popular music, borne of the city's geographic isolation, has emerged as a key factor through which locals both account for and in many ways 'celebrate' what they perceive to be the distinctiveness of the popular music produced in Perth.
>
> (2014, 111)

Again, however, one is never safe to assume that there will be symmetry in the scene stories that flow from peripheral cities. Like the overall characters of cities themselves, the nature and identity of the specific music scenes located there are both distinctive as well as highly contingent on a range of other local and trans-local factors. In the second part of this chapter we will explore this aspect of local music scenes in two other peripheral cities in Australia: Brisbane and Hobart. As we will illustrate, in each case the marginal status and peripheral location of each city has resulted in quite different responses on the part of their respective local music scenes. Thus, Brisbane has assumed a position of relative "independence," celebrating, in a manner not dissimilar to Perth, its status as a city on the edge. This quality of Brisbane is bolstered by an emergent appreciation among the local of population of the city's rich popular music heritage (see Bennett and Rogers 2014). In the case of Hobart, by contrast, the city's proximity to Melbourne (the capital city of Victoria) and the convenience of low cost flights has seen an increasing number of Hobart musicians and other music industry workers relocating "across the water," namely, the Bass Strait that separates Tasmania from the Australian mainland. This allows them the opportunity to draw on the greater pool of resources available in Melbourne and thus take advantage of its established status as a center for cultural production both in Australia and the wider Asia-Pacific region.

Background to the Study

The data presented in the following section of the chapter is based on fieldwork conducted in Brisbane and Hobart between 2012 and 2013.[1] In total twenty-two participants took part in the research conducted in Brisbane and Hobart. Participants ranged between the ages of 18 and 80 with seventeen of these being male and five female. Most of the participants were heavily involved in some way in the local music industry, often musicians but also incorporating dedicated fans, ancillary music workers and critics. The participants remain anonymous and are cited here with aliases. The primary purpose of the project was to give a voice to local musicians, music industry workers, archivists and music fans regarding their memories of popular music and its place in their lives. The overarching rationale of the project was that, although stories of popular music history and heritage are in wide circulation these are often more "official" representations that do not take into account more localized and vernacular renderings of popular music history and heritage, including the role therein of local popular music scenes.

Brisbane as an Emerging Music Capital

Brisbane is a city harboring a revitalized music scene. Post-World War II, the city endured parochial state governance and systemic corruption leading to both a diminished migrant influence and an exodus of Anglophone musicians and creative workers. Although Brisbane provided notable additions to the punk and post-punk canon of the late 1970s (featuring bands such as The Saints and The Go-Betweens), the city was generally considered something of a police state where local musicians clashed with authorities and worked in an entertainment sector often administered by organized crime. The narrative of Brisbane as a more cosmopolitan and arts-friendly city begins in earnest in the late 1980s: the city hosted the 1988 World Expo while the Fitzgerald Inquiry (1987–1989) cleaned out organized police corruption. For Brisbane music, the early 1990s alternative/grunge boom raised the city's profile significantly. That moment in rock history refocused commercial attention on localized music scenes and Brisbane—something of a perennial rock city—delivered successful bands such as Powderfinger, Regurgitator and Custard. As these acts rose to national prominence, Brisbane began to access new forms of cultural and financial capital. The multiple-platinum selling Powderfinger were one of the first major success stories to come from this and they remained residents of Brisbane, leading to the foundation of a label, management company and music festival (Splendour in the Grass) by the band's entrepreneurial manager Paul Piticco. The Big Sound music industry conference—one of the biggest in Australia today—was founded not long after and its home in inner city Fortitude Valley was "protected" as an entertainment precinct for music and clubbing. Added to which, one of the biggest international pop acts of the late 1990s, Savage Garden, was from suburban Brisbane. By the 2000s, the city had changed, as illustrated by Brisbane music biographer Andrew Stafford's ecstatic, hyperbolic description:

> [Brisbane was not] just a warm, comfortable, laid-back city. No, it was a creative, exciting, happening pace. The weather wasn't just beautiful one day and perfect the next. Frankly, it was hot out there. Now you can go to a gallery, go to a restaurant, go see a band, play in one yourself. No one was about to stop you trying.
>
> (2004, 276)

This century, Brisbane has progressed further. Widely perceived as a hub for radio-ready indie pop and rock bands, Brisbane music is no longer considered culturally isolated in the north. It is now a part of the eastern coast network of commercial touring with both an active industry and a blossoming, widely regarded underground substrata. It remains geographically distant—a ten-hour drive north of Sydney—but in an era of discount airfares, its remove has diminished in significance.

Yet Brisbane remains an aspirant city music scene in many other regards. In comparison with Australia's two music capitals Melbourne (a culturally diverse scene home to a dense network of performance venues) and the populous Sydney (a hub for electronic music and commercial industry) Brisbane is still distinctly second-tier. The story of Brisbane, as told by our respondents, is the story of a place still "catching up." The city is now considered a type of cultural equal, albeit a slightly wilder northern counterpart, but lacks the formalized and strategic comforts of the southern music scenes. Brisbane may be rapidly modernizing and expanding (with notable negatives evident, namely real estate escalation and oppressive traffic congestion) but the music scene is still more tactical than strategic in terms of how it occupies the city. The music that comes from Brisbane now circulates on a hugely diverse set of pathways both international and national but within the city, the week-to-week performance of local music and hosted touring music is hampered by an almost ever-present sense of instability within the city's venue infrastructure. This is felt to such a degree that some (see Spencer 2012) consider it an important part of Brisbane music's sound and social organization, especially in its playful and ragged experimental/ underground rock communities. It is the central factor by which the city remains on the periphery of Australian music more generally. The development of Brisbane music has been aided by a large number of state and academic initiatives[2] but the immaturity of the venue business sector, and its comparison to Melbourne in particular, seems to suggest that only so much stimulation can counteract the city's problematic past and the longer arc of cultural disinvestment.

In the field, our respondents spoke directly to this. Our data set is rich in stories of how Brisbane "makes do" in ways Melbourne and Sydney do not. What emerges are concepts of Brisbane music as a type of resilient practice, energized by rapid change and the close-knit socialization that stems from a type of forced collaboration. When we interviewed Chris, a local venue operator and musician, he spoke of Brisbane's venue circuitry as hybridized from his very early engagements with it as a customer:

> back in those days you'd have ... The Troubadour, The Rev, Ric's Cafe and 610 pretty much doing good shows almost every night ... you used to go into [Fortitude] Valley, and you'd just move between shows ... you'd flick between four shows, you'd sort of pick your favourite couple of bands ... so there was always a whole bunch of different places to go to, and so that was a pretty big time.
>
> (Chris 2012)

In the above passage, Chris describes both official license venues and what we have previously called "unofficial venues" (Bennett and Rogers 2016) such as DIY unlicensed performance sites (for example, 610 was a centrally located band rehearsal building that hosted parties). Chris recalled these early experiences to contextualize his own working life, running his own multi-purpose space containing a venue, practice space and recording studio in Brisbane's

West End. This was a theme that could be found elsewhere in the Brisbane scene. Another respondent, John, operated a hybridized practice as well:

> I run [a business] which is a multi-arts organization. [It] has three streams—one is the label, one is a kind of promotions and concert touring [operation with] festival capacity, and the other one is more of a gallery-based sound art thing. I also make work under my own name and run a number of other small activities that all help accumulate into an amount of cash that I'm dreaming will appear at some point.
>
> (John 2012)

Over time, these tactical approaches to Brisbane music-making and business appeared over and over. The city's tenuous grasp on hard infrastructure was present but far from crippling; it forced music workers into entrepreneurial and hybridized roles to diversify their activities and this in turn diversified their audience and the communal pathways around which they navigated the Brisbane scene.

Hobart

> We scoff at your concern about our cold weather and supposed isolation ...
>
> (Teakle 2010)

The city of Hobart is located in the south of Tasmania, Australia's southernmost island state. Settled as a penal colony and subject to a boom-and-bust cycle of post-World War II economics, Hobart—like Brisbane—is a city still emerging as an arts hub. State policy initiatives around contemporary music alongside private investment (in the form of the Museum of Old and New Art (MONA) and its attendant festivals) have helped solidify Hobart's reputation as a city for music, but the commercial success that made Brisbane still eludes Hobart for the most part. The two cities have a common trajectory regarding the 1990s: both saw a rise in prospects as localized rock music scenes came momentarily to the public fore, but for the most part Hobart ceded its talent to mainland Melbourne (located 600 kilometers north). As one Hobart respondent told us, it's "just a rite of passage for a lot of Tasmanian (musicians), they move to Melbourne" (Anonymous Respondent 2013). The Australian Bureau of Statistics data bears this out; in the last census (2011) twenty- and thirty-year-olds lived in reduced numbers in Hobart by way of comparison with Brisbane and in dramatically reduced numbers compared to Melbourne. Empirically, the city's music scene appears either very young (university aged) or older, with many respondents in their late-thirties and above, a great many of whom had returned to the island after a stint in Melbourne. This migration of music-making young people has only recently started to wane and its effects are compounded by an already reduced population size with Hobart housing roughly a tenth of the population of Brisbane.

The specifics of Hobart are such that a small cohort of local musicians work in the city, and like Perth to the west, touring to Melbourne quickly becomes a focus for bands and artists looking for even a moderately expanded audience. Regular touring to other capital cities on the mainland is, however, something of a step beyond many local Hobart acts, as respondent

Matt describes, "We did a lot of touring for a band from Hobart, really, we went everywhere" (Matt 2013). For the most part, Hobart bands seem to travel to Melbourne for a small run of shows and then return home. This is somewhat typical of Australian artists more generally—where much of the industry is constricted by national population size and density, and a diminished access to capital—but in Hobart, few bands enter the sorts of touring networks that take them regularly beyond Melbourne. What is far more prevalent is that individual musicians leave the island and find footing in Melbourne-based projects that later find significant attention for their work. What remains is a scene where the tone is centered around a social flux of predominantly young adults, playing in a small handful of venues (The Brisbane Hotel, The Grand Poobah) with a scattering of very temporary DIY spaces. The music workers we encountered in Hobart were resolutely part-time and, for many, the idea of deriving a wage from localized music practice seemed remote. That type of aspiration was strictly for the mainland.

What Hobart's music scene does seem interested in is representation. At interview, one respondent, Michael, touched on some of the community-led responses to the issues surrounding Hobart music. One of the few music workers we encountered in a music management role, Michael pointed to a lack of formal industry in Hobart:

> The way I describe Tasmanian artists and the activity down here, it's a music community building into a micro business kind of industry, it's the way I describe it, because there's ...still a lot of pillars of representation or types of roles that aren't serviced, aren't present to support artists' growth. But there's so many artists in Tasmania and so many artists that have a whole different style of genre. I think it's very broad ...so you've got these ... different creative sort of pathways in terms of different artists, but a lot of them have central players that play in a lot of bands as well, so there's this camaraderie I think within ... genre areas. There's that collective kind of approach, but the music and the performances ... are just as well classed as anywhere else I think, it's sort of the other stuff to support those artists' growth that isn't quite present in Tassie [Tasmania].
>
> (Michael 2013)

Issues of representation are also of concern to the city's more DIY and independent/experimental communities. In recent years, Rough Skies Records has taken snapshots of the city's scene, releasing a number of compilation albums, some of which have circulated broadly within the international music press. These compilations reveal the rapid churn of individuals and bands within Hobart. Curator Julian Teakle observes that the second volume is:

> the best we can do to capture a few still moments in this constant state of flux. They share equipment, recording studios, rehearsal spaces, even members. Some of the bands have since broken up or been stripped down to solo projects. Some of the solo projects have since been built up into bands.
>
> (Teakle 2010)

This is the challenge of Hobart in a nutshell: How does one represent and build upon a community so subject to change? Within a place as small as Hobart these changes have a

118 • Andy Bennett and Ian Rogers

tangible impact. Unlike Brisbane's diverse array of tactical approaches to infrastructure issues, Hobart's problem appears another step removed. The people facing these challenges are only ever around for a relatively short period. The music communities themselves appear more tactical and short-term, even in comparison to Brisbane.

Discussion: Hobart and Brisbane as Peripheral Music Scenes

Contrasting these two Australian cities provides valuable lessons in how notions of periphery and center operate in local music scenes. Popular music studies and music journalism have long reported on the effects of geographic isolation within city scenes with issues of distance pervading a huge array of popular music research on places like Milton Keynes (Finnegan 1989) Liverpool (Cohen 1991), Montreal (Stahl 2004) and Perth (Brabazon 2005), with similar music journalism mythologies surrounding places like Reykjavik and Seattle. Yet these narratives are complicated in recent decades by the virtual layer bolstering and occasionally re-routing of the vectors of music scenes. Within the Australian context, we see the powerful effects of geographic remove and social mobility adding further complication and further dismantling linear narratives of center/periphery as they relate to distance. Both Brisbane and Hobart cede musicians to Melbourne and the city remains formidably central to Australian music: a place of greater opportunity, industry and attention. The difference between Brisbane and Hobart is the ease of transit and effect to which individual departures affect community, practice and localized industry. In Brisbane, people leave and an already networked and ready community quickly recover ground: they replace band members, move unofficial venues into new locations, start different club nights and so on. The network is strong enough to sustain broken links. Brisbane's various scene-related identities shift slowly. In Hobart, the city music scene feels vibrant and active today in 2017—perhaps more so than Brisbane—but there's no escaping the degree to which the city's musicians are on pathways that, more often than not, circulate *through* Melbourne. Hobart may be one of the most isolated city music scenes in Australia but it falls under Melbourne's cultural annex. In many ways, it is not on the periphery at all. Socially, culturally and historically, Hobart sits very close to the center of Australian music, with both positive and negative ramifications.

Viewing the two cities as case studies in peripheral or second-tier music scenes also provides lessons in the scene concept itself, especially regarding viewpoint and positioning. Scene is a spatial concept (particularly when viewed through Straw's lens), and demands that the researcher investigate the power and affects of self-reflexivity and subjectivity, both collective and individual. Cultural memory comes into play here, providing a much more grounded and adaptive concept of what scene-research data often records. The results of scene research likewise produce thermalized stories more so than history, and scene's core value as a concept is that it steps away from the essentialism of music history and allows both very focused and nuanced accounts of smaller, group-based music practice, as well as the sort of bold and broad narratives of whole cities utilized here. Both are subject to change and reappraisal as the field rapidly shifts and both are deeply tied to who is interviewed and when. In our data set, there are hugely conflicting accounts of these cities but, for the most part, they conform to a cohort of communal positions. To the musicians of Hobart, the city is isolated, on the periphery and all the better for it. The links the city maintains with

The Remaking of Brisbane and Hobart • 119

Melbourne do not dramatically alter this mythos. In Brisbane, the city's musicians feel north of the center but not on the margins; those days of the city's cultural exclusion are over. Yet Brisbane is a long way from Melbourne: a long drive, a two-hour flight and decades away from the type of venue and policy infrastructure that bolsters Melbourne's continued prominence. As such, both Brisbane and Hobart contain elements of center and periphery, trading off experiential negatives against positives and "making-do" with what remains. Under the virtual layer in which all scenes now have clear and visible trans-local elements, Brisbane and Hobart can also be seen to be no longer as far from any notion of cultural center as they once were. What remains is their distance from each other. If there is an isolation at work here, it is the lack of solidarity experienced between these two city scenes. They rarely cross paths in any meaningful way. This adds a final dimension to the making and remaking of Brisbane and Hobart. It is undeniable that no matter what stage of localized development these cities experience, their experience of the national music culture is still one of looking in. The degree to which this is communally experienced differs but the empirical data recorded in our fieldwork points to the presence of this sensation. Brisbane still volleys to be taken seriously. Hobart still seeks representation. These activities are the work of emerging music cities that no matter the flow and networks of their constituents still mark them as spaces on the periphery.

Notes

1   This study is part of a broader research project funded by the Australian Research Council, titled "Popular Music and Cultural Memory: Localized Popular Music Histories and their Significance for National Music Industries." It was funded under the Australian Research Council's (ARC) Discovery Project scheme for three years (2010–2012, DP1092910). Chief Investigators on the project were Project Leader Professor Andy Bennett (Griffith University), Associate Professor Shane Homan (Monash University), Associate Professor Sarah Baker (Griffith University) and Dr Peter Doyle (Macquarie University). The Research Fellow on the project was Dr Alison Huber (Griffith University) and additional support was provided by the Research Associate Dr Ian Rogers (formerly based at Griffith University during his work on the project and now at RMIT University). The primary form of data collection was through semi-structured interviews. All interviews were recorded using a digital voice recorder and later transcribed. Interviews took place in a range of settings such as residential homes, pubs and community spaces. The fieldwork received ethical clearance from Griffith University's Human Research Ethics Committee (HREC) and was carried out in accordance with the HREC code of practice.
2   In the late 1990s and early 2000s, the Queensland state government entered into a prolonged engagement with Richard Florida's Creative Cities research, spawning an array of studies into popular music clusters and ensuing policy to preserve or bolster the city's cultural capital. For a good example of research from this era, see Flew et al. (2001).

Bibliography

Anonymous Respondent. 2013. Interview with author. Digital recording. Hobart: September 4.
Australian Bureau of Statistics. 2011. "2011 Census QuickStats." www.censusdata.abs.gov.au/census_services/getproduct/census/2011/quickstat/601.
Barone, Stefano. 2016. "Fragile Scenes, Fractured Communities: Tunisian Metal and Sceneness." *Journal of Youth Studies* 19 (1): 20–35.
Bennett, Andy. 2014. "Popular Music, Cultural Memory and the Peripheral City." In *Music City: Musikalische Annäherungen an die »kreative Stadt«*, edited by Alenka Barber-Kersovan, Volker Kirchberg and Robin Kuchar. Bielefeld: transcript, 105–119.
Bennett, Andy and Richard A. Peterson, eds. 2004. *Music Scenes: Local, Trans-Local and Virtual.* Nashville, TN: Vanderbilt University Press.
Bennett, Andy and Ian Rogers. 2016. "In the Scattered Fields of Memory: Unofficial Live Music Venues, Intangible Heritage, and the Recreation of the Musical Past." *Space and Culture* 19 (4): 1–12.

Bennett, Andy and Ian Rogers. 2014. "In Search of Underground Brisbane: Music, Memory and Cultural Heritage." In *Sounds and the City: Popular Music, Place and Globalisation*, edited by Brett Lashua, Karl Spracklen and Stephen Wagg. Basingstoke: Palgrave, 302–316.

Brabazon, Tara, ed. 2005. *Liverpool of the South Seas: Perth and Its Popular Music*. Perth: University of Western Australia Press.

Chris. 2012. Interview with author. Digital recording. Brisbane: January 4.

Cohen, Sara. 1991. *Rock Culture in Liverpool*. Oxford: Clarendon Press.

DeNora, Tia. 2000. *Music in Everyday Life*. Cambridge: Cambridge University Press.

Farrugia, David. 2015. "The Mobility Imperative for Rural Youth: The Structural, Symbolic and Non-Representational Dimensions of Youth Mobilities." *Journal of Youth Studies* 19 (6): 836–851.

Finnegan, Ruth. 1989. *The Hidden Musicians: Music-Making in an English Town*. Middletown, CT: Wesleyan University Press.

Flew, Terry, Gillian Ching, Andrew Stafford and Jo Tacchi. 2001. *Music Industry Development and Brisbane's Future as a Creative City*. Brisbane: Queensland University of Technology.

Grazian, David. 2004. "The Symbolic Economy of Authenticity in the Chicago Blues Scene." In *Music Scenes: Local, Trans-Local and Virtual*, edited by Andy Bennett and Richard A. Peterson. Nashville, TN: Vanderbilt University Press, 31–47.

John. 2012. Interview with author. Digital recording. Brisbane: March 29.

Matt. 2013. Interview with author. Digital recording. Hobart: September 6.

Michael. 2013. Interview with author. Digital recording. Hobart: September 3.

Shank, Barry. 1994. *Dissonant Identities: The Rock'n'Roll Scene in Austin, Texas*. Hanover, NH: Wesleyan University Press.

Spencer, Daniel. 2012. "Global Ear." *The Wire*, January, 335: 16.

Stafford, Andrew. 2004. *Pig City: From The Saints to Savage Garden*. Brisbane: University of Queensland Press.

Stahl, Geoff. 2004. "'It's like Canada Reduced': Setting the Scene in Montreal." In *After Subculture: Critical Studies in Contemporary Youth Culture*, edited by Andy Bennett and Keith Kahn-Harris. Basingstoke: Palgrave, 51–64.

Straw, Will. 1991. "Systems of Articulation, Logics of Change: Communities and Scenes in Popular Music." *Cultural Studies* 5 (3): 368–388.

Discography

Various Artists. *Community: A Compilation Album of Hobart Music*. Rough Sky Records RSKYR 001, 2010, compact disc.

9

Urban Melancholy
Tales from Wellington's Music Scene

Geoff Stahl

In 2012, Air New Zealand launched an advertising campaign showcasing a number of New Zealand cities and regions, stretching north to south, from Auckland to Christchurch. This series of short films, aired on YouTube and other social media, was aimed at convincing so-called "Kiwi sceptics," code for "Australians," of the appeal of Aotearoa/New Zealand as a tourist destination. Flying them over to tour around various cities and regions the Wellington episode, entitled "Hipster," focused on the bohemian culture of the nation's capital city courtesy of a Sydney "hipster" named Patrick, who trotted out well-worn stereotypes of hobbits and dubstep when asked to describe Aotearoa/New Zealand culture (Kiwi Sceptics: Hipster, 2012). Led around Wellington hotspots by a Aotearoa/New Zealand ex-pat fashion writer, the itinerary included a number of local landmarks—from the refurbished Art Deco-era Roxy Cinema, to a number of local nightspots, including cocktail bars such as Duke Carvell's, the Hawthorne Lounge, The Matterhorn—and ending the night, looking rather debauched, at local rock'n'roll bar Mighty Mighty, the ad saw Wellington unfold as a revelation in hip to our Kiwi sceptic.

Although the subject of much local derision, and no small amount of cultural cringe, this ad is significant for marking one of the first times urban culture in Aotearoa/New Zealand has been represented by the nation's major airline. Eschewing the usual images—such as fiords, mountains, rivers, and outdoor sporting activities—that have been the airline's stock and trade in the past, the Wellington episode in particular signaled this move from landscape to urban space, from scenery to scene, which sought to package the Aotearoa/New Zealand capital as youthful, modern, and up-to-date. Wellington, and its myriad spaces of consumption, the ad wants to suggest, has matured enough to appear almost cosmopolitan, a city ready now to take its place on the world stage as a dynamic antipodal urban hotspot.

This efflorescence of Wellington as a city of scenes, and the conditions that made possible the city's emergence as the country's marketable hipster haven, was undermined by the eventual closure of some of the musical venues shown off in the ad. The last stop on that evening of urban exploration and excess, Mighty Mighty, closed in the middle of 2014, and it was followed not long afterwards by the closure of another important live space, Puppies. The disappearance of both within weeks of one another created a vacuum for independent musicians in Wellington, a situation that has persisted. No other live music venues of comparable size have opened in the city. In fact, by the end of 2016, another landmark live music site, The Bodega, was also shuttered after twenty-five years, and The Matterhorn, the original owners of which started Mighty Mighty, where Fat Freddy's Drop got their start, and where many international DJs have played, will be shut due to ongoing refurbishments happening on Cuba Mall. This has left significantly fewer mid-size venues for live acts in the central city, a situation that has also engendered a palpable atrophying of the city's independent music scene.

The wax and wane of the city's music scenes raises salient questions regarding the city's current ethos, one which I refer to here as a kind of urban melancholy. It is worth asking, for example, how the aspirations and imperatives which helped shape this ad's particular packaging of Wellington as a revelation in hip are themselves revelatory with regard to the relation of the scene to the city, as a meaningful agglomeration of social and cultural spaces, as a branding tool, as accomplice to and pretext for the packaging and promotion of the city's culture, but also, more importantly, as an ethical space. In what ways, then, might the health and the vitality of the music scene be seen as a provocation, an invitation to debate and discuss what is made to matter in the city, what is valued, by and to whom and why, in terms of urban policy as well as those active in the city's musical life? More broadly, how might this local story, as full of differing visions of what matters in the city as it is, be instructive to us as a parable of the lifecycles of a creative city, literally and figuratively a tale told of (and to) a cultural capital, what the *Lonely Planet Travel Guide* referred to in 2010 as "the coolest little capital" (Wood 2010)?

The low-level, lo-fi constellation of industries, media institutions, artists and bands that make up the independent music scene in Wellington underpins an allegiance to local music-making that has lately entrenched the music scene as a definitive aspect of Wellington's urban identity. What distinguishes the current indie scene in the country's "cultural capital" is its place in a city that has worked hard to refashion itself as a "creative city" (Wellington City Council 2006). As a backdrop against which the current music scene and its various engagements with Wellington are set, many music-makers' commitment to a musical life in the city has to be seen in relation to a regime of cultural management and urban branding bound to notions of innovation and creativity found in the generic template of the "creative city" and its neoliberal imperatives.

This notion of creative, entrepreneurial solutions to the problems of modern urban economies has encouraged cities to look to culture to ameliorate the disappearance of other key economic drivers. Like many other cities, Wellington has increasingly come to rely on its cultural life as another mode of revenue generation. The "culturalization" (Lash and Urry 1993) of the Wellington economy is geared primarily to a middle-to-upper middle class demographic, made up of civil servants, bureaucrats, university students and faculty, and a host of cultural producers and a class of knowledge workers; in other words, members (and members-to-be) of an aspirational professional-managerial class that possesses the kind of education and training, the cultural capital, best suited to the diverse, yet refined, types of cultural consumption the city now offers. This class of consumer's enthusiastic engagement with the "entrepreneurial," "creative city" functions to affirm the role of culture envisioned by urban policy makers. Their primary motivation is the transformation of Wellington into an invigorating, captivating space of cultural consumption.

In this context, the independent music scene takes on a different, more ambiguous meaning in terms of consumption in Wellington. Broadly understood as one site of "event-fulness" in this new urban context, the scene becomes a vehicle to discursively inscribe on the city's imaginary a signature sense of place. This is symptomatic of the imperatives of the entrepreneurial city to capitalize on sociability as symbolic capital, and the promise of a certain kind of cultural experience, that can translate into economic return. The scene also provides the semiotic sheen that might also draw in an aspirational class of consumer, leading to hoped-for multiplier effects, such as property development and real estate investment.

For many music-makers, independent and otherwise, the connection to Wellington is offered via a range of highly sociable cultural spaces, cultivating a sense of community, with attention focused on creating a distinctive urban context that better nourishes their incipient entrepreneurial interests, forms an uneasy overlap with the directives of the Wellington City Council (WCC). As part of its policy objectives and strategic planning, for example, the WCC has sought to underpin the city's cultural vibrancy by implementing a cultural mandate that includes direct references to the music scene as part of its overall aim to make the city "more eventful":

> Wellington will be recognised as the arts and culture capital, and known for its exciting entertainment scene and full calendar of events, festivals, exhibitions and concerts. . . . Wellington is . . . known for its vibrant contemporary music scene, innovative art, architecture, literary, film and design communities . . . Wellington will attract and create new national cultural events, and promote arts and culture as a key part of the economy.
> (Wellington City Council 2006, 6)

The notion of "the event"—the fantasy of a phantasmagoria of cultural production and consumption at work here—forms part of the official view of the city as a potential site for the accumulation and expenditure of cultural, symbolic, and, hopefully, economic capital. The event(ual)-city has become the model many cities have adopted as a way to gain leverage in a global symbolic economy, using culture as a means to brand places and market their histories, packaged to appeal to a well-heeled demographic that has the discretionary income and consuming habits that, it is hoped, will lead to adequate returns on "quality" cultural investments (Elsaesser 2005). A city's "eventfulness" in this context becomes an index of its ability to realize and maintain a certain form of cultural livelihood, shorthand for its creativity, that can be parsed out in the number of events staggered throughout the year. In Wellington, a litany of local food, film, literary, art, and theater festivals attest to a willingness to celebrate and consume the local as well as deepen the branding of Wellington as a "cultural capital" which draws in cultural tourists as well. These festivals and events are designed to signal and signpost a way in which "the social" might be better mobilized as part of the arsenal assembled for urban branding. They carry significant discursive weight and thus also have material consequences, tied as they are not only to marketing campaigns, but also to a narrowly specific image of the city held by those that shape policy in terms of offering what they refer to as "quality" cultural production and consumption.

The hegemony of the eventful, "creative city" in Wellington is difficult to challenge or undermine; a local version of a global juggernaut that has taken over policy and planning in cities around the world. Richard Florida (2005), among others, has done much to promote this model, citing Wellington as a case study and underlining this with his visit to the city in 2003 (Volkerling 2009; McGuigan 2009). It is hard to argue against this view of the city,

124 • Geoff Stahl

in part because novelty, drama, and intensity are currently seen as the best means to put a city on the map: what city, particularly a capital city, does not want to imagine itself as culturally relevant or up-to-date? And while many of Florida's ideas are by now quite dated, in the Council's recent ten-year plan there are still traces of Florida, courtesy of his three "Ts" (talent, technology, tolerance). The "Florida thing" that Wellington enthusiastically adopted in some of its policy some years ago, which has been critiqued as "the articulation of neoliberal economics with cool culture" (McGuigan, 298), persists through to today. It is part of the Council's strategic vision for how Wellington will be shaped over the next decade: "Wellingtonians also tell us that 'creativity' is an important part of Wellington's identity and an important reason for why they choose to live here" (Wellington City Council 2012, 70).

Wellington has come to rely on the kinds of symbolic economies that are a defining characteristic of Florida's creative cities, through filmmaking and post-production producing images for Hollywood blockbusters, mainly through the efforts of filmmaker Peter Jackson and the production studios at Weta. Along with being branded the hipster capital of Aotearoa/New Zealand by Air New Zealand, and being saddled with monikers such as the "innovative capital," these recent developments point to the ways in which neoliberal entrepreneurial discourses are now entrenched on individual, municipal, and national scales. For Wellington, and elsewhere, this is a hegemonic bloc, the rhetoric of which is increasingly marked by empty buzz words such as "talent" and "creativity," designed to attract the right kind of creative producer and consumer. As detailed below, this is a strategy lately challenged by the waning status of the city's claim to be Aotearoa/New Zealand's cultural capital.

Urban Melancholy

The moving about that the city multiplies and concentrates makes the city itself an immense social experience of lacking a place—an experience that is, to be sure, broken up into tiny countless deportations, compensated for by the relationships and intersections of these exoduses that intertwine and create an urban fabric.

(de Certeau 1984, 103)

The aura of impermanence suggests that the city is always on the verge of losing itself and, so, can always be approached as if poised for an ethical collision over the question of who and what it is, that is, by the question of its identity.

(Blum 2003, 235)

The culture of the city is bound up in and defined by the way it is seen to engage with the generative tensions found between the city's presences and absences, its admixture of permanence and impermanence, fixity and flow, arrivals and departures, and the variegated multiplications and concentrations that de Certeau is alluding to here. They may be seen to lend depth and suppleness to its imaginary at any chosen point in its history, and give the city its characteristic rhythmic pulse and pullulations, its atmospheres. It is around and through these tensions, and how they are taken up in debates and discussions within it, that a city collectively carves out the contours of its identity. In what follows, I want to point to some of the issues that emerge in relation to these tensions through the closure of two music venues in Wellington—Mighty Mighty and Puppies—and the ensuing discussions about the state of the city's musical health. These events are the culmination of a particular civic discourse and discourse on the city that has been unfolding over the last few years. It has come to cast a lingering, anxious pall over the city, courtesy media stories focusing on the movement upward and outward of the city's "creative class" (Florida 2005), but reached its peak when the then Prime Minister John Key referred to the capital as a "dying city" (Wood 2014). I aim to situate the closure of these two venues as crystalizing into a moment of reflection, wherein a particular discursive envelope emerges, containing competing and sometimes complementary species of rhetoric. These are espoused by various interested parties and stakeholders in Wellington, from music-makers to policy makers, from fans to bar owners, and to local, national, and international media and social media. This discursive envelope delineates the boundary of an ethical approach to the city, inviting those interested to weigh in on the life and death of a nearly-great Aotearoa/New Zealand city. In moments like this, we can witness what Blum refers to as a city's "ethical collisions," cited above, as an animated call and response happening in different contexts, rejoinders to the feeling borne out by the sudden lack of a place, all of which can well be seen as an identity crisis. This anxious activity brings into focus a city's structure of feeling, which in the case of Wellington has lately been one of melancholy.

In one sense, the use of melancholy here draws and extrapolates from work done on states of mind and being associated with individuals, which has been taken up by a wide variety of thinkers, extending from the Greeks to Freud. Melancholy can be variously described as a kind of sadness, sorrow, and inward withdrawal, attributes which are usually framed negatively, though these are not melancholy's only dimensions. In fact, it could be argued that to reduce melancholy to only these qualities diminishes its power to point toward more promising openings, one which Aristotle, for example, characterized as "thoughtful being" (1957). In another sense, melancholy's relationship to the city is a similarly complex and rich one and has long inspired poets, songwriters, authors, filmmakers, songwriters, philosophers, sociologists, and others reflecting upon the affective dimensions of the city. It is in the essays and poetry of Baudelaire and sociological studies of Georg Simmel alike, where it is inextricably linked to modernity and the modern city as an alienating, atomizing space, in which the mental or emotional response is one of withdrawal, indifference, isolation, a feeling of existential drift, or anomie. However, much like the individual instance of melancholy, there are ways of approaching urban melancholy which redeem it much more along Aristotle's consideration, as opening up a space for a personal as well as a more collective mode of elegiac rumination, and it is in this broader sense that I want to put it to use here.

In a more fruitful formulation, melancholy facilitates and at times compels us to consider the way it frames meditations on the state of things as a more purposeful means through which a city's identity takes on a distinctive discursive and meaningful shape as a work in progress even when in decline. Describing this moment as melancholic is meant to capture a structure of feeling, in Raymond Williams' (1977) evocative term, dealing with more elusive qualities of city life such as atmospheres, moods, textures, ambiences, and the emotional life of the city. These become manifest in the city as it collectively comes to terms with loss, in this case the music scene in Wellington, where two vital hubs deemed by some as central to the city's collective life have gone dark.

Mighty Mighty and Puppies

Mighty Mighty, which opened in late 2006 and closed in mid-2014, was a venture established by owners of Wellington's renowned Matterhorn restaurant, which in its early days was itself a musical hub that nurtured the so-called "Wellington Sound" of the late 1990s and early 2000s. It was designed in part as both an homage to and pastiche of Berlin bars, notably the infamous Bar 25 and White Trash, Fast Food. These Berlin bars themselves have entered in the mythology of post-Wende Berlin as late or all-night (or all-week) party spots, where artists, musicians, new media workers, and tourists alike could indulge in late-night/early-morning parties, complete with DJs, food, and seemingly no end to decadence and bohemian flare. Mighty Mighty attempted to relocate aspects of that party spirit and aesthetic to Wellington. A mid-sized venue, the wood-paneled interior gave the place the warm feeling of a community hall, with one of the city's longest bars, arcade and pinball games, a low-rise stage, DJ booth, and walls dotted with artfully arranged vintage kitsch. It hosted local bands and DJs primarily, but gave itself over to a variety of functions, parties, including burlesque nights, Fringe festival events, monthly markets, magic shows, art openings, etc. The owners never envisioned it as a venue proper; instead, building on its community hall feeling, they saw it more as a larger social hub where good things happened, where people could let loose. It was situated up a few flights of steep, rickety stairs, at the crossroads of the city's two main arteries, Cuba Mall and Courtenay Place, where bars, clubs, galleries, restaurants, and cafes are found in abundance and guaranteed it a generous amount of foot traffic. In this respect, its distinctiveness was found in the way it brought together an eclectic array of patrons, from the well-heeled, professional, thirty-something civil servant, the over-worked, Weta computer coder, the feral punks, the Newtown bohemians, artists and activists, and university students (and academic staff), a space in which unfolded a weekly spectacle resulting from the bringing together of, in a tolerant and energized atmosphere, disparate lives of desperation, dissipation, and aspiration.

Puppies, open from 2012 until mid-2014, a venue that the owner, Ian "Blink" Jorgensen, had deemed an experiment. The goal was to get many of the city's other bars to re-think their policies, such as standardizing start times for bands, introducing a flat fee door charge of NZD$10, offering food to bands, among other things. It sat away from the city's main thoroughfares, in the basement of a nondescript bunker-like, brutalist building. Blink has a longstanding commitment to the local indie scene, beginning with his zine and concert photography, and later through his annual summer music festival, Camp a Low Hum. He prides himself on his DIY aesthetic, lately exemplified in a recent book on indie music, *The Problem with Music in New Zealand and How to Fix It & Why I Started and Ran Puppies* (2014), in which, manifesto-style, Blink outlines what he thought Puppies could bring to recalibrating Wellington's approach to music-making. If Mighty Mighty tended towards the rockier and raunchier side of live music and performances, Puppies catered more to a younger, mid-twenties indie scene which was local, national, and international in scope and character, and took advantage of Blink's extensive history with the city's scene and many of the bands he had encountered while managing tours for NZ bands locally and overseas. For Blink, Puppies was an ethical intervention; a strategy designed to prescribe new rules for how the music scene should better cater for audiences and bands alike. In its brief life, it allowed him, in the end, another opportunity to reflect on salient aspects of local music-making:

> Puppies was a success. Though I got a few things wrong that come with running a bar for the first time and having no understanding of the alcohol industry, I developed a pretty easily workable model where I could open only nine hours a week and specifically as a live music venue only and run a profitable, sustainable business with a huge earning potential. You don't need to charge bands to hire the venue, you can treat the public with respect and let them know how shows are running and run them to that format without any difficulty. You can provide bands with a service to make their shows cheaper and easier. You can take a venue associated with small profile acts and present large profile acts there. You can make drinks affordable. You can build a solid base for the future by avoiding doing cheap shows, staunchly monitoring guest lists and never reducing door-charge during an evening. People will turn up on time if you prove that you can run shows on time and keep to your word, and you can use that ability to run multiple shows in an evening, maximising the earning potential on any given evening. Maybe, I might do it all again sometime.
>
> (Jorgensen 2014, 139)

In contrast, Mighty Mighty's closure was due to a different set of factors: the majority shareholders had left Wellington; the introduction of new city by-laws trying to curb excessive drinking began affecting the night-time economy of the city more generally (with a number of after-hours bars also closing their doors); the global recession was sinking in, with punters and landlords beginning to feel its effects, the former not going out as much or much later, and the latter seeing the resale value of their property investments start to decline precipitously; the building's landlord underwent economic restructuring; the section of Cuba Mall where Mighty was based, which had long been targeted for redevelopment, was now going ahead; and there was an order to seismically strengthen the building. All of this meant there was a certain inevitability to its closure, beyond the story told by some that it had run its course.

Mighty Mighty and Puppies were fêted by local, national, and international media, so their closure took on a certain kind of poignancy among musicians, fans, and the media, signaling for many that an era had come to an end. Its closure was picked up on by Wellington lifestyle magazine, *Capital Magazine: Tales of the City*:

> Wellington likes its reputation for a vibrant music scene, but with San Francisco Bath House closed, and Mighty Mighty and Puppies set to close later this year, the question must be asked—is this the end of Wellington's reign as live music capital? Or is the closure of beloved old favourites anunavoidable necessity if the scene is to continue revived and refreshed.
>
> (Thomas 2014, 33)

The sentiment is echoed in the city's major newspaper, the *Dominion Post*, by local music critic Simon Sweetman:

> Something needs to change. The culture needs to be reworked. And though Puppies had a tight space, an annoying pole in the middle of the room and a slackness at the bar that was both endearing and, er, criminally vulgar, it was at least an attempt to offer something different. To put the onus (back) on the music. Wellington venues are dropping like flies. Each nail in the coffin like this one – well, it's always a sad day.
> R.I.P. Puppies.
>
> (June 2014)

As Blum reminds us, these moments of reflection are a sign of the existential fragility of the city:

> The impermanence of the city affirms the active capacity of the collective to be self-fashioning and, simultaneously, its anomic recognition of the perishable character of all that comes to be, showing in this way the limits of a finitude which is typically celebrated for its works and achievements, while being denigrated for its failure to master creation itself.
>
> (2003, 233)

The city measures the strength of its character through its ability to best actualize its self-fashioning, which at moments such as this are bound up in how it responds to its failures as much as its successes (ibid). In his recent book, *Why Music Matters* (2013), David Hesmondhalgh considers music's relationship and contribution to civic life in part as a way to reclaim music's ability to remind us of the collective power as a corrective or antidote to the currently dominant neoliberal ideology, but also outlining the ways in which music adds to a collective human flourishing in the form of either, what he calls, social publicness and/or deliberative publicness. The former considers strangers gathering together and sharing the same experience, while the latter is borne out by collectives working through issues germane to communities, nations, and/or the world. There is something in these modes of flourishing that gets at how these places resonate for Wellington as sites where both forms of publicness become manifest. The sorts of values, attachments, and identifications Hesmondhalgh discusses, enunciated and enacted in both these formulations of publicness, are realized in the closing of both Puppies and Mighty Mighty. While the former was an experiment that charged its brand of aesthetic politics with recalibrating Wellington's music scene and worked to reimagine it along the lines of a more ethically minded community, the latter was characterized by a more inchoate politics of pleasure and its own brand of excess. Each managed to channel social energies in such a way that the larger scene, and, by extension, the city further marshaled together in a way to give thrust to its semantic force, and more notably, its solidity, not only in terms of the ritual, eventful, and spectacular massing together of performers, audiences, and markets, but also in terms of its existential weight.

Conclusion

> The uncanny aura which impermanence casts over the city is dramatised in its relentless building and rebuilding initiatives, its endless circulation of things, goods, spaces, and people, and even more, through the very nature of the city as an artefact experiencing deterioration and revitalization marked by its mixing and matching of times and spaces that imparts an eerie ontological eclecticism to everything that is made.
>
> (Blum 2003, 203)

Sketched out here is a way of thinking about the kinds of discursive spaces the disappearance of musical and performance sites bring into view, melancholic moments of thoughtful being and glimpses of the city being thoughtful. They serve as temporary invitations to engage with what makes a city matter—to music-makers, policy makers, local fans, and tourists alike—and how it touches on matters beyond the city's scenes. "Change" is a city's modus operandi: a primordial axis and foundational axiom of urban life, socially, culturally, materially, an aspect of the ineluctably inevitable in the city, which people may rally against but to which they also must ultimately find ways to reconcile themselves. Embrace it or reject it, change persists as an energizing style of fraught restlessness that is a mark of a city's willingness to contemplate how it calls into being, owns up to, answers to, and ultimately measures, its "cityness." The exoduses and deportations that de Certeau described above are at the heart, existentially, demographically, materially, and symbolically, of the city's "moving about," indices of the "ontological eclecticism" Blum refers to above, and serve as barometers of the dynamics of change.

During their respective lifetimes, Puppies and Mighty Mighty lent yet more texture to Wellington's urban imaginary through their iconicity, acting as flagships for various music and creative scenes. Like previous music venues now gone, their passing connects to the present moment and projects beyond it via vectors of inquiry as to why music and music venues matter as they are tethered to urban memories and hitched to civic desires. These limn the urban imaginary such that certain views on the city gain a discursive purchase for different interested and differently invested parties. During these melancholic occasions, Wellington's urban character comes into focus, and different modes of civic engagement once more do a kind of identity work through which is created an ethical space wherein the collective deliberates, seeks clarity, sometimes ratifies, but more often grapples with, both the city's limits and its potential to flourish.

Bibliography

Aristotle. 1957. *Problems II, Book XXX*. Translated by W.S. Hett. London and Cambridge, MA: Heinemann and Harvard University Press.

Blum, Alan. 2003. *The Imaginative Structure of the City*. Montreal and Kingston: McGill-Queens University Press.

de Certeau, Michel. 1984. *The Practice of Everyday Life*. Berkeley: University of California Press.

Elsaesser, Thomas. 2005. "Film Festival Networks: The New Topographies of Cinema in Europe." *European Cinema: Face to Face with Hollywood*. Amsterdam: Amsterdam University Press, 82–106.

Florida, Richard L. 2005. *The Flight of the Creative Class*. New York: Harper Business.

Hesmondhalgh, David. 2013. *Why Music Matters*. New York: John Wiley & Sons.

Jorgensen, Ian. 2014. *The Problem with Music in New Zealand and How to Fix It & Why I Started and Ran Puppies*. Wellington: A Low Hum Publishing.

130 • Geoff Stahl

Lash, Scott and John Urry. 1993. *Economies of Signs and Space*. London: Sage.
McGuigan, Jim. 2009. "Doing a Florida Thing: The Creative Class Thesis and Cultural Policy." *International Journal of Cultural Policy* 15 (3): 291–300.
Sweetman, Simon. 2014. "Wellington Music Venues: Another Dead Dog." *Dominion Post*, June 23. www.stuff.co.nz/entertainment/blogs/blog-on-the-tracks/10189068/Wellington-music-venues-Another-dead-dog (accessed March 10, 2017).
Thomas, Melody. 2014. "The Sounds of Change." *Capital Magazine: Tales of the City*. Wellington, 33–39.
Volkerling, Michael. 2008. "Wellington as a 'Creative City': After Florida and Before." *Asia Pacific Journal of Arts and Cultural Management* 4 (2): 296–306.
Wellington City Council. 2012. *Long-Term Plan, 2012–2022*. Wellington. http://wellington.govt.nz/~/media/your-council/plans-policies-and-bylaws/plans-and-policies/longtermplan/2012-2022/files/ltp-final-entire.pdf (accessed March 10, 2017).
Wellington City Council. 2006. *Cultural Wellbeing Strategy: Shaping Wellington's Unique Identity*. Wellington. http://wellington.govt.nz/~/media/your-council/plans-policies-and-bylaws/plans-and-policies/a-to-z/cultural/files/cultural.pdf (accessed March 10, 2017).
Williams, Raymond. 1977. *Marxism and Literature*. London: Oxford University Press.
Wood, Stacey. 2014. "Wellington Cool with a Capital C." *Stuff*. November 10. www.stuff.co.nz/travel/destinations/nz/4292331/Wellington-cool-with-a-capital-C (accessed March 10, 2017).

Videography

"The Kiwi Sceptics: Hipster." Promotional video. YouTube, 2012, posted by David Smith. https://youtu.be/2z4RCttgEhU (accessed April 10, 2017).

PART **IV**

Global Sounds, Local Identity

The final part of this collection signals a change from an inward-looking perspective of Australia and Aotearoa/New Zealand to an outward-looking view, by exploring in more detail some of the contemporary instances of hybridization and syncretism that have long been a part of both countries' musical traditions. In doing so, these final chapters consider the complex set of relationships that shapes how the circulation of particular popular music genres is refracted through local contexts, and vice versa. Placing a city "on the map" through the inflection of global musical flows points to the many complicated and nuanced ways in which genres become domesticated, how they function to bind together scenes and communities locally and also how these sounds and musical practices might be articulated back into those global musical flows.

Another look at the Australian city of Hobart comes courtesy of co-authors Andrew Legg, Carolyn Philpott, and Paul Blacklow. Their chapter examines the role and function of the Southern Gospel Choir: how it contributes to the city's distinct national and international profiles, how the city in turn influences the sound of the choir, and what these findings can tell us about how the choir has adapted a globally circulated genre of popular music within an Australian local context. Chiara Minestrelli's chapter looks at a different kind of local identity—one that is articulated by Indigenous youth in various urban Australian centers via the global genre of hip hop. Her study brings to light how Indigenous rappers consolidate and enunciate their status as "urban Indigenous people," how they respond to the challenges imposed by an interconnected and globalized society, and the ways in which they relate to their lived experience in urban settings. Another global genre, techno, is the focus of Cathy Adamek's chapter. She presents a case study of the rise of this electronic dance music genre in Adelaide, South Australia; a capital city that has often been overshadowed by neighboring Sydney and Melbourne in the national musical hierarchy. Through local examples of music stores, DJs, and record labels, Adamek argues that there are distinct links between Adelaide and Detroit, and although they are very different cities with distinctive histories, techno is tied to their respective automotive industries. In Australia and Aotearoa/New Zealand, the strength of hip hop as a global musical force (particularly its racial politics) has been an important part of what underlines its continued success and relevance. In her chapter, April K. Henderson discusses the ways in which the local version, as filtered through the lives and experiences of Maori and Pasifika musicians based in Wellington, Aotearoa/New Zealand, challenges the by-now clichéd claim that it is just another form of cultural imperialism. With reference to specific cultural practices, Henderson offers a compelling argument that there is a kind of reciprocity that needs to be situated in relation to local tradition. Part IV concludes with Shane Homan's chapter on the "music city." Unlike many of the other chapters in this book, which focus on individual cities, Homan looks at the notion of a "city of culture" and deems it to be a commonplace concept that is based upon older understandings of how art and place-making have been entwined. Homan suggests that popular music has become part of a branding arsenal for cities trying to compete in a global market filled with other entrepreneurial cities which use culture as their point of difference. As part of this, Homan takes into account a selection of recent policies that have been put in place to develop various versions of "music cities" in a select number of Australian cities.

10

Singing the Lord's Song in a Strange Land

An Examination of the Nexus Between the Southern Gospel Choir and the City of Hobart, Tasmania

Andrew Legg, Carolyn Philpott and Paul Blacklow

Introduction

The Hobart-based Southern Gospel Choir (hereafter referred to as SGC), established by Tasmanian-born musician and academic Andrew Legg in 2000, has a unique and powerful voice within the local community, as well as within the wider Australasian popular music scene. Drawing on contemporary African American gospel music traditions, the Australian Record Industry Association (ARIA) award nominated choir has produced international-selling CDs and DVDs and has been recognized for its distinctive sound and significant impact upon the sociocultural life of its home city. With the support of the University of Tasmania's Conservatorium of Music, the Tasmanian Symphony Orchestra and the Museum of Old and New Art (MONA), the SGC has attracted some of the biggest names in gospel music from the United States to Hobart and has also played a key part in the establishment of two of Tasmania's largest music festivals—Festival of Voices and Standing in the Shadows of MONA. In turn, Hobart and its community have played pivotal roles in shaping the choir's sound and experiences—most recently by assisting the SGC to accept invitations to tour some of the largest venues for gospel music in the United States. By bringing African American gospel music performers to Tasmania, and by taking a Tasmanian choir to the country where African American gospel music originated, Andrew Legg and the SGC have demonstrated that it is possible for a popular genre of music to *travel* across cultural boundaries and to develop local traits that are ultimately acceptable to, and celebrated by, audiences in both places.

In this chapter, we explore the nexus between the Southern Gospel Choir and the city of Hobart, showing how the SGC has given the "global sounds" of gospel music an identifiable "local identity." In particular, we focus on the role and function of the SGC within Australia's southernmost city, why the SGC resonates with the people of Hobart and how the city in turn has influenced and supported the growth of the SGC, in order to reveal how the SGC has adapted what is now a globally circulated genre of popular music within its local context. We begin with a brief overview of the city of Hobart and its unique demographic profile in order to show the value of the arts, and popular music in particular, to the people of Hobart. This, in turn, provides a context for the discussion of the beneficial reciprocal relationship between the city and the SGC.

This is Our City: Hobart

Hobart is the capital city of Tasmania, Australia's island and smallest state. It is Australia's second-oldest capital city, having been founded in 1804 by the British Empire, initially as a penal settlement. The city is situated on the west bank of the estuary of the Derwent River in the southeast of the state and its forested skyline is dominated by Kunanyi, or Mount Wellington (Figure 10.1). Hobart's historic beauty, excellent agricultural produce and proximity to Tasmania's breath-taking scenery and wilderness attract and support a thriving tourism industry, which in turn provides support for the city's many cultural activities, including concerts and music festivals.

According to the Australian Bureau of Statistics (2011), Tasmanians generally spend more time on cultural activities, including listening to and/or participating in the production of music, than their mainland counterparts. Hobart's population of approximately 220,000 is slightly older than the population of Australia as a whole, with fewer people aged twenty-five to forty-four years and a median age of thirty-nine years, compared to a median age of thirty-seven for Australia as a whole (Australian Bureau of Statistics 2011). Its older population can partially explain the lower participation rate of its labor force and possibly why there is a lower proportion of full-time and a higher proportion of part-time jobs compared to Australia as a whole. The higher proportion of Hobartians not working or, at least, not

Figure 10.1 Victoria Dock, the city of Hobart and Kunanyi (Mount Wellington). Photograph by David Hay, used with permission.

working full-time gives them more time to devote to artistic and cultural pursuits. Even those working have more leisure time than their mainland counterparts due to short commute times related to the abundance of land and low population density.[1] In 2013–2014, 28.1 percent of Tasmanians aged fifteen years and over participated in cultural activities,[2] which is the third highest cultural participation rate amongst the eight states and territories and is above the Australian average of 26.8 percent (Australian Bureau of Statistics 2015a). Tasmanians generally attend more performing arts events than other Australians, with 57 percent of Tasmanians attending one or more performing arts events in this period, compared with 53 percent of all Australians (Australian Bureau of Statistics 2015b). In particular, during 2013–2014, Tasmanians attended more popular music concerts (34 percent) than Australians as a whole (33 percent), despite the fact there are generally fewer opportunities for Tasmanians to attend popular music concerts locally than there are for Australians living in the country's major cities. These figures suggest that Tasmanians tend to engage with and show support for the arts—including popular music—to a greater extent than mainland Australians. The support that the arts receive from Tasmanians is particularly obvious in Hobart and its surrounds, where almost half of the state's population is based (Australian Bureau of Statistics 2011), and where a number of successful arts festivals have been established in recent years These festivals include Ten Days on the Island (first held in 2001), Festival of Voices (established in 2005), the two festivals of the Museum of Old and New Art: MONA FOMA (held annually since 2009) and its winter counterpart Dark MOFO and Standing in the Shadows of MONA (held annually since 2012). These festivals, all of which include forms of popular music, have not only contributed significantly to the state's economy (*Tasmanian Times* 2014), but they have also played an important role in building a festival culture within the city of Hobart. This has led travel writers to observe that the country's southernmost capital city has experienced Australia's "biggest cultural shift in the last decade" (Del Pozo 2014, 48).

The Tasmanian Government has also recognized the value of the arts to Tasmania's economy and society in recent years. The Premier Will Hodgman acknowledged in the *Tasmanian Government's Events Strategy 2015–2020* that the state is now "renowned for hosting events of extraordinary quality and distinctive flair that entice more than 70,000 visitors to our state every year" (Tasmanian Government 2015, 2). He declares, "We want Tasmania to become Australia's boutique events capital, and one of the world's greatest event destinations" (Tasmanian Government 2015, 2). In addition the State Government has recognized that these events and activities provide positive social outcomes that help to enrich "Tasmania's keen sense of community" as well as enhance residents' "sense of place, engender pride, and promote participation," and create "excitement, entertainment and employment" (Tasmanian Government 2015, 3, 6). These benefits are similar to those identified by various scholars who have asserted arguments about the value of arts and culture to cities, including Zukin (2004), Silvanto and Hellman (2005), Currid (2007) and Richards and Palmer (2010). The nurturing festival and arts culture within Hobart has provided an ideal environment for the successful establishment and growth of the city's Southern Gospel Choir.

Background to the Establishment of the Southern Gospel Choir in Hobart

Andrew Legg founded the Southern Gospel Choir in Hobart in January 2000. Prior to this, he was a familiar face within African American gospel music as a gospel piano and Hammond player. During the 1990s, he worked, toured and performed with some of the finest gospel songwriters, musicians and choral directors in the United States, including Myron Butler (Levi and Potter's House), Kirk Franklin, Khristian Dently (Take 6), Jamar Jones, Eric Dozier and Dr Horace Clarence Boyer. Within a few years, Legg's reputation had grown to such an extent that in 1997 he was invited to be a "Featured Performer" at the Thirtieth Anniversary Gospel Music Workshop of America in Cincinnati, where he led workshops and performed in front of 30,000 African Americans. Many of the artists with whom he crossed paths at this time had been actively pushing the musical boundaries of African American gospel music—revolutionizing (and, in some cases, dividing) the genre within the United States. Inspired by their progressiveness, and hot on the heels of touring up and down the East coast of the USA with Myron Butler, Legg returned to Australia and decided to form a gospel choir in Hobart, under the auspices of the University of Tasmania.

The Southern Gospel Choir had very modest beginnings: its first performance took place in the University of Tasmania's Conservatorium Recital Hall in May 2000 with a choir of thirty, a ten-piece band and a capacity audience of around 160. During its earliest days, the SGC received significant support from the University. Housed within the Conservatorium's contemporary music program, "Gospel Choir" was an elective unit of study, and was used to connect students with, and reinforce for them, the fundamental principles of contemporary popular music-making—that is, the essence of what Craig Werner (2006) describes as the "gospel impulse." As a training choir based at a university, the SGC was established with the intention of performing African American sacred gospel music within a predominately secular context. Although other choirs in Hobart performed a small amount of gospel music as a component of their repertoire, the SGC was the first dedicated "gospel choir" to be established in the city. Through the University, the SGC grew its market and audience base over its first five years with performances on national radio and television (hosted by the Australian Broadcasting Corporation [ABC] and the Special Broadcasting Service [SBS], and with key performances as part of the Tasmania-based international arts festivals, Ten Days on the Island and Festival of Voices.

A Reciprocal Relationship: Hobart and the Southern Gospel Choir

It is undeniable that Legg's international reputation, combined with the intense local interest in the SGC, underpinned and drove the success of the inaugural Festival of Voices in 2005. The festival had been designed to attract large numbers of visitors to Tasmania during its traditional off-peak winter season and, in order for it to be a success, it was determined that it would need an international "draw card." Three workshop sections (Classical, *A Cappella* and Gospel) were established; however, in light of the growing success of the SGC, the "Gospel" component was given additional funding and a priority marketing profile in order to provide the inaugural festival with a distinctive focal point. In essence, the large numbers of participants and audience members who attended the festival were drawn to it primarily as a result of the involvement of Andrew Legg, the SGC and, most importantly, the international guest artist that Legg was able to secure for the event, Dr Horace Clarence Boyer.

Boyer (1935–2009) had been the first African American PhD graduate from Eastman School of Music in Rochester, New York, and by the time he visited Hobart in 2005, he had long been considered the "grandfather" of gospel music and was recognized as one of the leading choir directors and scholars of gospel music in the USA. Unlike the younger generation of gospel music artists, Boyer had been born early enough to have had strong connections to the very roots of African American music. During his week attending Festival of Voices, Boyer heard the SGC perform and then, in an interview that was broadcast nationally, declared:

> There is no reason in the world why you [the SGC] should sound like you sound. It's far too great a distance from Montgomery, Alabama, to Hobart. So I am beside myself because I've done a lot of travelling and I've worked with a lot of white people who cannot forget for a minute that they're white. They've been white for so long, everything that they do is white. This is black . . . . Right now, [African-American gospel music] is in [Legg's] blood, it's in his system.
>
> (Australian Broadcasting Corporation 2005)

Boyer's laudatory comments about the SGC on Australian national television proclaimed a credibility for the ensemble that increased its reach exponentially, and not only nationally but, most importantly, within its own home community of Hobart. In just one interview, Boyer laid waste to the "cultural cringe" and the conventional limitations of so-called "small town" thinking and as a result the SGC found a new legitimacy, respect and acceptance within the collective hearts and minds of its own people. Although the SGC had been steadily building an audience for itself within the Hobart community, these comments from one of the foremost scholars and practitioners of African American gospel music not only reached a much larger audience within Hobart, but also effectively gave that audience permission to believe, collectively, that the SGC was internationally accepted and acclaimed, and at the same time still "local."

Together with Legg, the SGC and the festival's gospel choir, Boyer launched the Festival of Voices onto the national scene and set a precedent for future iterations of the festival, establishing a mechanism through which Legg could bring more stars of African American gospel music to Hobart, including James Abbington, Eric Dozier (Harlem Gospel), Myron Butler (Levi and Potter's House), Alvin Chea and Khristian Dentley (Take 6). Although the involvement of these high-profile guest artists was facilitated by Legg and the SGC, it would not have been possible without the support of the city of Hobart. It has also had a profound and lasting impact upon the community of Hobart, the SGC and those who participated in the festival. As Tables 10.1 and 10.2 indicate, the Gospel components of the Festival of Voices have, overall, attracted considerably more participants than any other stream offered. Table 10.1 shows the total number of participants who enrolled in the Gospel stream in the first three years of the festival's operation, while Table 10.2 provides the total enrolment figures for the workshop streams offered in 2007, as a point of comparison, and then all workshop streams offered annually since 2010.

138 • Legg, Philpott and Blacklow

Table 10.1 Total numbers of participants who enrolled in the Gospel stream of Festival of Voices, against all enrollments 2005–2007. Data supplied to the authors by Festival of Voices.

Year	Number of participants in Gospel Workshops	Number of participants in weekend Gospel Workshops	Total number of participants in Gospel stream of Festival of Voices	Total enrollments in all streams in Festival of Voices
2005	58	50	108	280
2006	45	52	97	190
2007	135	NA[1]	135	208

[1] "NA" indicates the year/s in which specific workshops did not run at the festival.

Table 10.2 Total enrollment numbers for each of the Festival of Voices workshop streams offered in 2007, and from 2010–2014.

Year	Participants in Ritual workshop	Participants in Theatre workshop	Participants in Classical workshop	Participants in A Cappella workshop	Participants in Gospel workshop
2007	NA[1]	10	15	32	135
2010	NA	NA	80	65	130
2011	NA	40	73	140	164 (56)[2]
2012	NA	NA	79	260	152 (32)
2013	NA	NA	85	100	252 (32)
2014	33	NA	150	90	167 (67)
Total participation	33	50	482	687	1,000

Source: Data supplied to the authors by Festival of Voices.[3]

[1] "NA" indicates the year/s in which specific workshops did not run at the festival.
[2] The numbers shown in brackets in this column indicate the number of members of the Southern Gospel Choir who enrolled in the Gospel stream of *Festival of Voices* in the given years. Even without the SGC members included in the total, the Gospel stream still attracted more participants overall in the years shown than any of the other streams.

As the SGC's performances accumulated over time and the significance and impact of the Choir's activities increased, so too did its connection to, and impact upon, the city of Hobart. The Choir's debut album, *Great Day*, was nominated for an ARIA award in 2005 and this led to a number of major performances which attracted significant national attention. For example, the Southern Gospel Choir performed with the Tasmania Symphony Orchestra and the celebrated Australian vocal ensemble The Idea of North (2008); was featured in Broadway to Australia (2009) with Lyn Ahrens and Steven Flaherty (Melbourne Recital Hall; Angel Place, Sydney; City Hall, Hobart); and the Festival of Broadway (2010) with Stephen Schwartz (Melbourne Recital Hall; Angel Place, Sydney; City Hall, Hobart); and gave a standout performance with the Tasmania Symphony Orchestra and Torres Strait Islander singer Christine Anu in 2011. Demand from independent Australian recording artists for the SGC's sound increased during this time, as the Choir recorded tracks for high profile Australian popular music artists Guy Sebastian, Paulini Curuenavuli and Lindsay Field, and released its second studio CD, *High on A Mountain* (2009), with Badloves' key figure Michael Spiby,[4] followed by the live concert DVD, *Brighter Day* (2012).

Following on from these events, the SGC began to give a series of large-scale outdoor concerts on the lawns of Hobart's internationally celebrated MONA. MONA was established in 2011 by local philanthropist David Walsh and comprises one of the most significant private art and antiquities collections in the world, leading it to be hailed as the "most important addition to the Australian cultural landscape since the opening of the Sydney Opera House" (Franklin 2014, back cover; see also Hill 2011; Siegel 2012). The SGC's concert series Standing in the Shadows of MONA has been held annually at MONA since 2012 and in its first three years attracted in excess of 8,000 patrons (see Figure 10.2). The SGC's association with this world-leading venue for arts and culture has been significant because it has helped to bring the Choir squarely into the mainstream of Hobart's cultural, musical and social life. Walsh openly self-identifies as "atheist" and MONA itself has a strong and almost hedonistic framework centered on the themes of "sex and death" (Stewart 2014). The establishment of the partnership between the SGC and MONA has helped the Choir to reach an even wider audience within Hobart, which has been an extremely important part of the Choir's mission since its formation. Although African American gospel music has quite specific spiritual and religious origins as an expression of community, life and faith within the African American Christian community, the genre continues to penetrate non-African American global contexts and markets—in many ways spurred on by the vast reach of Hollywood and films like *Sister Act* (1992). The original Christian context for the music does not necessarily translate as easily as the music itself does. The SGC does not actively promote itself as a religious choir

Figure 10.2 Andrew Legg and the audience at Standing in the Shadows of MONA, November 2012. Photograph by Dean Stevenson, used with permission.

and, as such, the majority of SGC singers do not identify themselves as "Christian," although some do.[5] Through the support and encouragement of Walsh and MONA's music curator, Brian Ritchie (Violent Femmes), the SGC has been able to reach and be accepted within a far broader market than Hobart's Christian community alone.

The Resonance of the Southern Gospel Choir within the City of Hobart

It may, at first, seem highly unusual for people living on an island at the bottom of the world to develop such a strong interest in a musical genre that is so deeply embedded in a culture from the opposite side of the globe. It is perhaps more understandable in light of the impact that the genre has had upon the foundations of Western contemporary popular music and culture. African American gospel music, in all of its forms, is widely recognized as one of the most direct, powerful and influential musical genres of the twentieth and twenty-first centuries (Legg 2008). Like a benevolent *force majeure*, the genre has given birth to, nurtured, underpinned and inspired the whole of Western contemporary music, and further, Western popular culture in general. As the prominent African American gospel singer and scholar Bernice Johnson Reagon (1992) writes:

> it is African-American music, in structure and often in content, that drives mainstream popular culture worldwide ... Whether the community of musicians and audience is American, European, or Asian, or whether the audience crosses class or culture, the way the voice is used, the way instruments are held and played, the way instruments sound when played, the way an audience responds in a contemporary concert, the way in which a performer has dialogue with the audience, all can be traced to the African-American worship tradition created within the Black church.
>
> (4–5)

Although the genre is iconically African American, it seems to find a significant resonance within Australia, despite the fact that its defining cultural touchstones appear to have little obvious connection to Australian culture. The essential elements of the "gospel sound" (Legg 2010; Legg and Philpott 2015) contained within imported and home-grown contemporary popular music have laid some significant trans-cultural musical foundations that continue to provide a context within which Australians can find musical connections with gospel music. Gospel choirs such as Melbourne Mass Gospel Choir, Melbourne Singers of Gospel, Adelaide's GospoMusic, the Perth Gospel Choir and Australia's premiere *a cappella* gospel choir, Café of the Gate of Salvation, founded by Tony Backhouse, regularly attract large audiences and choir memberships and have done so for over a decade. Furthermore, a very large number of choirs and *a cappella* groups throughout the country include African American spirituals and gospel music as part of their repertoire.

Another reason why the genre of African American gospel music "travels" is that much of the music is genuinely uplifting. Notwithstanding the references to a specific set of religious beliefs, the lyrics speak strongly to widely relatable themes of hope, love, and overcoming and triumph over adversity. It is not surprising, therefore, that the genre resonates strongly with a broader, multi- and non-religious framework and worldwide audience, including with Tasmanians. In fact, this is particularly relevant to Tasmanians, especially those living in the south of the state, many of whom have experienced their own unique sense of "poverty" and a culture of violence that connects them to this music (Legg 2008). The Tasmanian community continues to tell and re-tell the often-violent stories of their convict and indigenous histories. Interestingly, the specific acts of violence are regularly depicted with great attention to detail, and many of the original penal settlements such as Port Arthur, the Women's Prison at South Hobart and Port Macquarie on the state's west coast have become more than simply beautifully maintained sites of historical and educational significance; they have become shrines of remembrance, a graphic reminder and an institutionalized reinforcement of the violence embedded in Tasmania's rich and colorful history. Whether or not (and to what extent) contemporary Tasmanian society and culture continue to be directly informed by this historical/cultural memory is debatable. However, more recent tragic events such as Martin Bryant's shocking massacre of thirty-five innocent people in and around the Port Arthur site on April 28, 1996, and the murder of the four Shoobridge girls in 1997,[6] whilst obviously abhorrent by any definition, have also certainly and dramatically reinforced the Tasmanian community's awareness of the violence simmering beneath their culture. The earliest African American responses to the violence of slavery and their existence in general are recorded and encoded in the lyrics of their religious music, and these messages seem to speak to many Tasmanians, particularly those living in the south—geographically closest to the most prominent reminders of Tasmania's violent past. Spirituals and gospels alike describe the immense hardships of life: the cruelty of slavery; the inevitability of early death; the need for and reliance on communal support, an eternal hope and a just God; and even the covert defiance of authority. Ultimately, these songs acknowledge the suffering of the past, provide comfort in the present and give an eternal assurance and hope of a just redemption in the future.

Tasmania's island culture and its unique and distinctive past—reinforced through the re-telling of its stories, continually reconnecting this community with its often violent history—provides the foundation for an emotional and even "spiritual" connection for many Tasmanians with African American gospel music. Gospel music not only embodies the feelings and attitudes of African Americans towards violence and oppression, but loudly and powerfully proclaims their eventual and inevitable victory over it. Although it is undeniable that the great majority of Hobartians cannot have complete access to the depth and influence of African American community and culture because they are not born into that culture and do not live within its defining geographical, ideological or cultural boundaries, the "resonance" that African American gospel music evokes in many people who live in Australia's southernmost city is still powerful. It establishes a unique "local" set of emotional, physical, musical and spiritual connections to the music and culture from which it has evolved and these are, of course, felt by those who experience them with varying degrees of depth and intensity.

These factors—including the resonance of African American gospel music due to its relationship to contemporary popular music and its uplifting message, as well as the quality of Andrew Legg's and the SGC's musicianship—have led to the success of the SGC in Hobart and abroad. Through the high-profile performances and recordings described earlier, the SGC was able to attract such a wealth of support, and engender such genuine feelings of pride and "buy-in" from the people of Hobart, that in November 2014, seventy-five members

Figure 10.3 The Southern Gospel Choir at the Potter's House Church in Dallas, with (front row, left–right) Myron Butler, Maria Lurighi (the Southern Gospel Choir's vocal coach) and Andrew Legg. Photograph by Robert Heazlewood, used with permission.

of the choir and ten staff (including band members) were able to undertake a fifteen-day tour of the United States (see Figure 10.3). During this tour, the SGC performed at significant African American churches in Dallas, Texas, Tuskegee, Alabama and Los Angeles, California, for concert audiences in excess of 25,000 and television audiences of over 25 million.[7] These international performances were exceptionally well received by African American audiences and congregations and have brought an authenticity and global reach to the SGC that is rare and would have been impossible to orchestrate without the support of the Hobart community. The tour costs tipped over AUD600,000 with the vast majority of the funding coming from the Hobart community itself, including one significant fundraising event that raised AUD120,000 in one evening alone. Given the relatively small size of Hobart in comparison to Melbourne and Sydney and the smaller number of philanthropic opportunities that its size could proffer, the fact that the people of Hobart were so prepared to colloquially "put their money where their hearts and minds were" provides a strong indication of the impact of the SGC upon the people and cultural fabric of the city of Hobart.

Conclusion

Tasmania's unique cultural history, environment and people have helped to shape the SGC from its earliest days, while Hobart's vibrant arts scene has provided a supportive home for the Choir and enabled its performance of what is now a globally circulated genre of contemporary music within a local and primarily secular context. Although the SGC initially relied heavily on the support of the University of Tasmania and the wider Hobart community, over time the nexus between the Choir and the city has developed into a relationship that is mutually beneficial, with the Choir playing a vital role in driving the success of a number of locally held international festivals and bringing esteem to the city through the national and international recognition it has received. This reciprocal relationship between the SGC and the city of Hobart ultimately underpins the ongoing success of the Choir. In turn, the success of the SGC in Hobart, and at the national and international levels, feeds back into the lifeblood of those who live in or visit Tasmania's capital—enhancing their overall experience of, and sense of connectedness to, Australia's southernmost city.

Notes

1 Flood and Barbato (2005) report that Tasmanians' average weekly time travelling to work is the lowest of all capital cities at 2.67 hours compared to a national average of 3.62.
2 This estimate has a relative standard error of 4.5 percent. Please note that many of the differences in reported participation rates mentioned in this chapter are not statistically significant.
3 In 2012, the *A Cappella* stream of Festival of Voices received a significant boost due to two of the organizers employing two high-profile *a cappella* acts (The Idea of North; and Moira Smiley and VOCO) to try to expand this particular component of the festival.
4 Spiby was the main songwriter and driving force for the Badloves, which was one of Australia's most successful bands during the 1990s, and now shares a songwriting partnership with Andrew Legg. Together, they are writing a new gospel-inspired repertoire for the SGC.
5 A survey of SGC members who participated in the Choir's tour to the United States in November 2014 showed that 42.59 percent of members identify themselves as "Christian."
6 On June 26, 1997, Tasmanian poet Peter Shoobridge murdered his four daughters while they slept. The girls attended two local schools and were mourned by the greater Hobart community.
7 The SGC and band performed at St Luke's Methodist Church, Dallas (November 14, 2014); Potter's House Church, Dallas (November 16, 2014); Tuskegee University (November 18, 2014); Greater St Mark's First Missionary Baptist Church, Tuskegee (November 18, 2014); and Breath of Life Church, Los Angeles (November 22, 2014). The SGC worked with Myron Butler (Levi), Khristian Dently (Take 6) and the Potter's House Choir in Dallas; Clarence Nobel and Dr Wayne Barr in Tuskegee; and Alvin Chea (Take 6) and Jerry Warren in Los Angeles.

Bibliography

Australian Broadcasting Corporation. 2005. "Tas Gospel Singer a Celebrity in US." *ABC: The 7:30 Report*, July 6. TV Program Transcript. www.abc.net.au/7.30/content/2005/s1408560.htm (accessed April 19, 2015).
Australian Bureau of Statistics. 2015a. *ABS 4921.0 Participation in Selected Cultural Activities, Australia, 2013–14*. Canberra: Australian Bureau of Statistics.
Australian Bureau of Statistics. 2015b. *ABS4114.0 Attendance at Selected Cultural Venues and Events, Australia, 2013–14*. Canberra: Australian Bureau of Statistics.
Australian Bureau of Statistics. 2011. *Census Quick Stats 2011—Greater Hobart (Code 6GHOB GCCSA)*. www.censusdata.abs.gov.au (accessed August 3, 2015).
Currid, Elizabeth. 2007. *The Warhol Economy*. Princeton, NJ: Princeton University Press.
Del Pozo, Joshua. 2014. "Why Tasmania is the Place to Be." *Travel Weekly Australia*, September 1: 48–49.
Flood, Michael and Claire Barbato. 2005. *Off to Work: Commuting in Australia*. Discussion Paper 78. Canberra: The Australia Institute.
Franklin, Adrian. 2014. *The Making of MONA*. Melbourne: Penguin.
Hill, Kendall. 2011. "Happening Hobart." *Australian Gourmet Traveller* 11(March). www.gourmettraveller.com.au/travel/travel-news-features/2011/2/happening-hobart (accessed January 25, 2018).
Legg, Andrew. 2008. "The Transculturalisation of African-American Gospel Music: The Context and Culture of Gospel Traditions in Australian Gospel Music." PhD diss., University of Tasmania.
Legg, Andrew. 2010. "A Taxonomy of Musical Gesture in African American Gospel Music." *Popular Music* 29 (1): 103–129.
Legg, Andrew and Carolyn Philpott. 2015. "An Analysis of Performance Practices in African American Gospel Music: Rhythm, Lyric Treatment and Structures in Improvisation and Accompaniment." *Popular Music* 32 (2): 197–225.

144 • Legg, Philpott and Blacklow

Reagon, Bernice Johnson, ed. 1992. *We'll Understand It Better By and By. Pioneering African American Gospel Composers*. London: Smithsonian Institute Press.

Richards, Greg and Robert Palmer. 2010. *Eventful Cities: Cultural Management and Urban Revitalisation*. Oxford: Butterworth-Heinemann.

Siegel, Matt. 2012. "Museum at the End of the World." *Bloomberg Businessweek* March 5: 1–3.

Silvanto, Satu and Tuomas Hellman. 2005. "Helsinki—the Festival City." In *Arts and Culture in Helsinki*, edited by Leila Lankinen. Helsinki: City of Helsinki, 4–9.

Stewart, Cameron. 2014. "David Walsh: From Shy Misfit to Big-Time Gambler Who Founded MONA." *The Australian*. October 4.

Tasmanian Government. 2015. *Tasmanian Government's Events Strategy 2015–2020*. Hobart: State of Tasmania.

Tasmanian Times. 2014. "A Truly Global Arts Festival for Tasmania," September 23. www.tasmaniantimes.com/index.php/article/a-truly-global-arts-festival-for-tasmania (accessed July 16, 2015).

Werner, Craig. 2006. *A Change Is Gonna Come: Music, Race and the Soul of America*. Ann Arbor: University of Michigan Press.

Zukin, Sharon. 2004. "Dialogue on Urban Cultures: Globalization and Culture in an Urbanizing World." World Urban Forum, Barcelona, September 13–17. www.barcelona2004.org/www.barcelona2004.org/esp/banco_del_conocimiento/docs/PO_31_EN_URBANCULTURES.pdf (accessed July 20, 2015).

Discography

Southern Gospel Choir. *High on A Mountain*. Spark in the Dark Music MMSGC002, 2009, compact disc.

Filmography

Ardolino, Emile (director). 1992. *Sister Act*. Touchstone Pictures/Buena Vista Pictures Distribution.

Southern Gospel Choir. 2012. *Brighter Day*. Hobart: University of Tasmania.

11

"I Rep for My Mob"
Blackfellas Rappin' from Down-Unda[1]

Chiara Minestrelli

In an era of decentering globalizing forces that continuously shift the locale of cultural production and consumption from global markets to local realities and vice versa, music has come to play a crucial role in redefining the value of regional discourses. Hip hop music,[2] with its long and solid history of indigenization in different parts of the globe, has provided marginalized and stigmatized communities around the world with accessible "artistic tools" of self-expression. Tony Mitchell (2001), Samy H. Alim, Awad and Pennycook (2009), Sujatha Fernandes (2011) and more recently Christopher Malone and George Martinez (2014), amongst others, have explored the multifaceted and compelling expressivity of "glocal" discourses articulated through hip hop. Many are the local stories of struggle and empowerment that have gained global recognition thanks to the new media. Recent emblematic cases of this movement from the local to the global are well represented by three distinct and yet interrelated cases that testify the power of hip hop as an amplifier for unique stories.

The first example is Sonita Alizadeh, a young Afghani girl who used her personal experience to convey a message of dissent against the issue of child marriage with a hip hop track called "Brides for Sale" (2014). In a similar fashion, with the track "Kodaikanal Won't" (2015) a young Indian Tamil woman, Sofia Ashraf, launched her protest against the pollution of Kodaikanal (India) caused by the multinational company Unilever. Fitting into a similar template, Kylie Sambo, a young Indigenous activist from Australia's Northern Territory, released the track "Muckaty" (2010),[3] where she lamented the Australian government's decision to create a nuclear waste dump on Indigenous land. Thanks to the visibility acquired on the social media, Sambo was invited to several events to raise awareness about the issue.

Sharing a view of hip hop as a vehicle of social change, these three "improvised' hip hop artists have gained notoriety across the Internet, and their stories have mobilized public opinion within and outside their respective countries of origin. Like them, many other artists have productively experimented with new technologies to reach international audiences, despite the particularities of their messages. In Australia, a significant number of Indigenous youth have found in hip hop an adaptable framework for the articulation of narratives grounded in the locale of their place of origin, but often projected towards international publics. Transnational connections are thus enhanced by the systematic use of new media, the strategic adoption of the American accent and the Indigenous artists' frequent collaborations with American rappers (see Minestrelli 2014; 2016). Reflecting on these spatial trajectories

146 • Chiara Minestrelli

(both virtual and real), and with a focus on the relationship between Indigenous hip hop artists and their surrounding urban environments, this chapter investigates the discursive techniques adopted by some prolific Australian Indigenous rappers in their negotiation of notions of place and cultural values in tension with the colonial history[4] of the country. In this regard, I have engaged with the artists' global views and local discourses by examining their music and testimonies. The material collected from secondary sources, participant observation[5] and thematic analysis of music allowed for an understanding of issues pertaining to identity and attachment to place as expressed by Yorta Yorta rappers Briggs and Darah, who are both from Shepparton, a country town in north-eastern Victoria, as well as Larrakia MC Jimblah,[6] who lives in Adelaide, South Australia. Even though these artists' music fulfills several communicative and entertaining purposes, it is their counter-hegemonic narrative of resistance and place that is of interest here, for it conveys the rappers' deepest feelings.

Twenty-First Century "Aboriginal Style" in the City

Since its beginnings in the 1980s, hip hop in Australia immediately found fertile ground amongst disadvantaged strata of the population. In particular, the language of hip hop appealed to those youths who were struggling to assert their presence within urban contexts. Second-generation immigrants[7] and Australian Indigenous people were very receptive to the influences coming from the USA, as they could relate to the messages of stigmatized groups from other parts of the world. Yet, even though Indigenous people had been actively involved in hip hop since its inception in Australia, their presence was often relegated to the margins of the so-called "Australian hip hop community," gaining public recognition and access to mainstream music channels only over the last ten years. Thanks to experienced and currently active artists such as The Last Kinection, Street Warriors, A.B. Original (Briggs and Trials) Jimblah, Impossible Odds and Yung Warriors, who have made a name for themselves within the national and international music industry, Indigenous hip hop has witnessed a greater exposure to avenues once exclusively dominated by Anglo-Australian voices. Such a change within the Australian cultural landscape is clearly suggested by the 2017 Triple J Hottest 100,[8] which saw for the first time an Indigenous hip hop group—A.B. Original in this case— securing a position within the top twenty songs in one of the most popular charts in Australia. This result is even more significant considering the title and content of the single, "January 26" (A.B. Original 2016), which addresses political themes with an overtly polemical tone.

Yorta Yorta rapper Briggs, who gained a privileged position within the Australian music industry thanks to his talent and the strategic branding of his artistic persona as "detached" from the politics of identity, later in his career embraced political tones by promoting his public figure and music as overtly "Indigenous." This is further evidenced by his collaboration with Trials for the album *Reclaim Australia* (2016). Indeed, in an interview for *The Age*, Briggs declared:

> "There is a time for a message ... now I've infiltrated [into the 'Australian hip hop community'] as far as I have I'm saying, all you younger [black] rappers you can be here, too ... rap music and success isn't just for white fellas"
>
> (Vincent 2015)

The rapper's statement, as well as his personal story, voice unspoken racial politics within the Australian music industry, and reiterate the idea that the only way for Indigenous people to succeed in (Australian) society is by "infiltrating" its most exclusive socio-cultural contexts. Strategic performances of "passing" (as non-Indigenous) have characterized the history of how most "racialized bodies" could gain recognition within predominantly "White" and patriarchal socio-political configurations, and music is no exception.[9]

Indigenous rappers have thus proved that, beyond sheer purposes of entertainment, hip hop music also functions as a vehicle for ideological representations aiming to disrupt conventional portrayals of "Indigeneity." In this regard, social media have been playing an important role in diffusing the stories of these artists. The Facebook pages *Australian Aboriginal Hip Hop* (2017), later named *Indij Hip Hop Show* (2017), as well as the YouTube channel AboriginalRap (2017), have further reinforced the creation of symbolic sites for the negotiation and promotion of transnational dialogues between international users with similar experiences. The accessibility of these digital platforms and the opportunity to start a virtual communication between geographically disconnected music lovers is in fact a new dimension to consider in relation to the promotion and distribution of music through non-conventional channels.

By embracing hip hop, Indigenous artists from the most disparate walks of life and areas of Australia have found a productive way to articulate the challenges of being Indigenous in the twenty-first century, defying prejudices on race, gender and culture. The album *Against All Odds* (2011a) by Brisbane-based hip hop group Impossible Odds clearly exemplifies this attitude through tracks like "Identity," "Soul of the Troubadour," "Take this Message" and "What Do You See." These songs represent different stories of discrimination through stereotyping, marginalization, personal and collective struggles. Fred Leone, also known as Rival MC, the voice of the band, explains that "mainstream media . . . only want to portray Murris as a black man in the bush, painted up, they don't acknowledge that we come in all colours" (Ward 2013). Nevertheless, as Rival MC has demonstrated throughout his successful career as a musician, producer, manager and mentor, these songs are also testimonies of positive outcomes through music, where Rap provides a means of channeling negative feelings, towards healing.

With hip hop as their preferred tool of communication, between the received knowledge of their Elders[10] and the aesthetics of modernity, many Indigenous rappers have created discursive spaces within what I have called "the Indigenous counter-public sphere" (see Minestrelli 2014, 2016), the Australian public sphere and beyond.[11] Researching Indigenous cultural performances in the global and globalized context of (Indigenous) cultural festivals, Peter Phipps (2010) argues that "[t]he emergence of a global 'indigenous' identity enables (and is symptomatic of) a reordering of the 'national' in the cultural sphere" (219). Phipps's assertion is relevant here, as it points to a growing "global indigenousness" (220) that exceeds the boundaries of locality through the politicization of a "pan-Aboriginal" identity. Hip hop, as both a domain of the Indigenous counterpublic sphere and a pan-Aboriginal movement, as I have mentioned in the introduction to this chapter and argued in depth elsewhere (Minestrelli 2014, 2016), has helped Indigenous rappers spread local messages to wider international audiences through social media. In fact, the underlying political vein of most Indigenous hip hop acts has mostly constituted a hindrance to achieving mainstream airplay within a profit-driven music industry that caters for the market's trends. Thus, Briggs' case clearly reflects this situation and the challenges of meeting the demands of a prevailing "White" hip hop consumer base (see Arthur and Quester 2006).

Indigenous hip hop artists have been actively participating in public debates by using their music to engage with the Australian government's political agenda in relation to Indigenous, national and international affairs. During the 1960s and 1970s, in the wake of the global ferment around civil and human rights, Indigenous people from some of the biggest Australian cities took a strong stance against the inequalities they had to face and voiced some of their concerns also through music genres such as rock and reggae (see Connell and Gibson 2004; Dunbar-Hall and Gibson 2004; Minestrelli 2014). Today, hip hop has taken that place through the many releases that tackle some of the most cogent local and global questions, ranging from the discrimination of Australian Indigenous people, to issues of global resonance. These discussions are clearly exemplified by A.B. Original's album *Reclaim Australia* (2016), Jimblah and Nooky's track "Treaty 2015," a hip hop rendition of Yothu Yindi's iconic protest song "Treaty" (1991), as well as Briggs and Dewayne Everettsmith "The Children Came Back" (2015), a remake of Archie Roach's classic song "Took the Children Away" (1990). Released on the occasion of the celebrations for the 2015 edition of NAIDOC Week (National Aboriginal and Islander Day Observance Committee), "The Children Came Back" is a clear demonstration of how Indigenous rappers actively engage with current social issues. The song's lyrics are a tribute to the dramatic history of child removal across Australia,[12] and the video clip, which is set in the Fitzroy Gardens in Melbourne, acknowledges past and present Indigenous heroes and leaders.

Nestled within this narrative of remembrance is a critique of current social debates related to acts of racism in Australia. In fact, Briggs is also using his song to tell a story of racial abuse against an Aboriginal child who was verbally attacked during a Disney event in country Victoria.[13] When the accident was made public, Briggs decided to have the child star in his latest video, declaring: "[t]his is a history lesson, a monologue, a celebration and an education in one song" (Booth 2015). The Shepparton rapper, who commemorates his predecessors in his lyrics, also addresses Australia's former Prime Minister Tony Abbott (2013–2015) by rapping: "Now Mr. Abbott, think about it / Me and you we feel the same / That might sound strange / I'm just saying / We both unsettled when the boats came" (Briggs 2015). Briggs' ingenious pun creates an ironic effect based on the fact that he shares the same feelings as the former Prime Minister, a controversial politician known for his conservative views and politics of exclusion. However, while the term "boats" is invested with a colonial meaning from Briggs' Indigenous perspective, Abbott's apprehension is directed at the refugee boats,[14] thus addressing both a national and global current issue. The passage from personal to public realm is further suggested by a shift from first and second person singular pronouns to the use of an inclusive "we," which stands for the Aboriginal population and, at the same time, the government. They both have similar feelings, but different concerns.

"Urban Blackfellas": Unsettling Categories

Indigenous hip hop artists are thus prolifically utilizing the medium of hip hop to participate in discussions on national affairs, continuing their Elders' legacy to speak out against injustices. Kabi Kabi rapper Weno from The Last Kinection confirms this view stating:

you talk to our Elders and they talk about how the young fellas have got to take up the battle, I guess, take up the fight and, I guess, this is kinda of our development, this is where we are at"

(Local Knowledge 2003)

As Indigenous cultures in Australia have adapted to a changing geographical and socio-political landscape, they have also sought viable ways to articulate their identity as active local and global citizens. Indigenous people have been doing so through "strategies of cultural 'survivance'" (see Vizenor 1999)[15] and by dismantling stereotypes that confine "Indigeneity" to the realm of "tradition." In this sense, the performance of Indigenous "songlines" through the hip hop vernacular has allowed Indigenous people to further demonstrate their culture's vitality in many ways, beyond political activism. As a by-product of modern technologies, this type of "Indigenous modernity," or "digital modernity" is certainly a characteristic of "mutually contaminated times" (Lyons 2010, xi), yet this is not an isolated occurrence, as it is placed along a trajectory of consolidated practices, whereby the new generations of Indigenous musicians create original soundscapes rooted in the knowledge and experiences of their predecessors.

It is in this context that we need to understand the relationship Indigenous rappers have with place, which is depicted as both symbolic and lived space. For most rappers, the lived space is often represented by a city or town, whereas the Outback assumes the contours of the symbolic. Cities are frequently described as places of exile, dispersal from the community of origin, but also as productive loci. A problematic view of the city is expressed by Darah in the track "City on Fire," where the rapper from Shepparton raps: "Burn down cities, slums, commissions and prisons / Burn down mansions where rich folk living" (Darah 2012). These lines, like the rest of the song, put an emphasis on the socio-economic degradation experienced by lower-class city dwellers, where class often coalesces with "racial stigma." The image conveyed through Darah's lyrics is also part of a greater discourse rooted in Australia's history of colonialism and the ensuing displacement of Indigenous people who were forced to move into urban areas as a result of genocide and assimilationist policies.

Such a critical view of cities is reinforced in the track "Straight Outta Shepparton" (South Side Kings 2012), a rendition of the notorious track "Straight Outta Compton" (1988) by the Los Angeles gangster Rap icons N.W.A. The song, which is produced by Darah and performed by Big Luke, Morgie Morgz, Sel, T.R. and Young AK pushes and exaggerates the semantic field generated by the simile, where Shepparton (VIC) is associated to Compton, a Californian municipality rendered (in)famous by N.W.A. for its sweeping poverty and high rates of crime. Although the track is celebratory of the Indigenous rappers' street credibility, the comparison provides a clue about perceptions of their locale. In this particular instance, credibility can be seen in relation to hip hop, with its inscribed "street code" (see McLeod 1999). It can also represent a claim of an Indigenous identity that does not need to be justified by a rural and remote geographical location in the north of Australia. It is also for this reason that in "Aboriginal Style" Darah raps: "Where you from? / South Side / What you gonna do? / Hold it down," thus reinforcing understandings of "urban indigeneity" as ideological and implicitly questioning notions of authenticity as defined by imposed parameters of "remoteness" and "skin color."

150 • Chiara Minestrelli

The geo-(political and cultural) distinction between the north of Australia, where Aboriginal cultural practices have been less affected by the settlers' culture, and the more urbanized south, is also reflected in Richard Broome's (2010) articulation of "urban Aboriginality" along the lines of: "cultural maintenance; a sense of injustice; the acting out of a sometimes-negative oppositional culture; and the rebuilding of a positive Aboriginal identity" (188). In the southern parts of the country, where the colonial process left a deeper mark on the local Indigenous populations, the survival strategies adopted by these peoples demonstrate their ability to change and acquire new traits in order to keep certain traditions alive: "I'm from the south side, never been afraid" (Darah 2011). Today, hip hop has inspired young Indigenous people to re-engage with their culture in new ways, utilizing the most accessible and productive means at their disposal. For Indigenous people living in urban areas, the sense of "Aboriginality" is maintained and, in some cases, restored through a series of cultural practices (kinship relations extended out of the immediate family circle, gatherings and community events) that endeavor to assert their presence, their identity, their pride and their rights within cityscapes (see Barwick 1988 and Behrendt 1995).

Larrakia[16] rapper Jimblah espouses this view in his celebration of the city where he lives and works. According to Jimblah, the city, in his case Adelaide (South Australia), is a tough reality, but it is also the place where he can find some peace: "Whenever I rest my head, / I've got a place to call home, / it's my city" (Jimblah 2012). Adelaide thus becomes a less hostile place in Jimblah's verses and acquires a new liveable dimension. Similar to Jimblah, but sharing the same place of origin as Darah, Briggs celebrates his hometown in the album *Sheplife* (2014), where he depicts Shepparton through his double bond of love for family and friends and aversion for the town's parochial mentality. The different representations of the city as provided by Darah, Jimblah and Briggs are diverse, and yet complementary. Their worlds represent the "local," with its mechanisms, institutions and the socio-economic dynamics that reflect large-scale phenomena. But the local is not destined to remain silent, as more and more Indigenous rappers utilize social media to their advantage. Either sparking controversial comments or praises, A.B. Original's YouTube video clips, for instance, attract comments not only from Australian, but also from a wide variety of international viewers. The dialogic exchange facilitated by the global template of hip hop music, together with the affinities that emerge through this dialogue, help reduce the distance amongst various "localities," fusing once more the local with the global.

Conclusion

Within the cityscape of Australian urban centers, hip hop has provided Indigenous youth with a productive tool of self-expression and, in some cases, of political activism. This way this phenomenon can be read as a complex set of forces, needs and aspirations that all operate and cooperate at a personal and group level, shifting across the boundaries imposed by identification processes. The local reality of Australian Indigenous hip hop, with its struggle over visibility, recognition and access to the Australian public sphere, has gradually encouraged a cross-cultural debate where specific local practices are fostered and re-shaped by different urban geographies. Localized forms of knowledge with their counter-hegemonic discourses are also produced in small centers like Shepparton, which are thus invested with new cultural power.[17]

Notes

1 The colloquial term "Blackfella" (Australian English) is composed of "black" and "fellow" and refers to Aboriginal Australians. The expression appears with great frequency in the lyrics of most Indigenous rappers. *Blackfellas* is also the title of a 1993 Australian film directed by James Ricketson. In contrast, the compound "Whitefella" ("white" and "fellow") is often used by Indigenous people to identify non-Indigenous people. In the 1980s, the Indigenous group Warumpi Band released a song called "Blackfella/Whitefella" (1985). "Down-Unda" is an alternative spelling for the term "Down Under" which is colloquially used to describe Australia (see the Introduction of this book).

2 By hip hop, I refer to a cultural movement traditionally identifiable through its four core elements (rapping, djing, breakdancing and graffiti writing). Over the years, notorious hip hop pioneers and artists have added other elements (street knowledge, beatboxing, street fashion, street language, street entrepreneurialism) to the "foundational ones." Hip hop music, or rap, refers to one of the artistic forms of the phenomenon, namely the combination of music and lyrics.

3 Sonita Alizadeh's "Brides for Sale," Sofia Ashraf's "Kodaikanal Won't," a politicized rendition of Nicki Minaj's "Anaconda," and Kyle Sambo's "Muckaty" are available on YouTube. There are no official recordings of these tracks, apart from those found on the Internet.

4 Australia's history of colonization with its political assimilationist legacy throughout the nineteenth and twentieth centuries and the ensuing removal of many Indigenous children from their families is at the root of forms of collective trauma, which is handed down from generation to generation.

5 This chapter stems from four years of doctoral research in Australia (from 2010 until 2014). It is thus part of a larger study (see Minestrelli 2016). Part of the data collected during fieldwork has been used in this chapter to corroborate some of my arguments.

6 James Alberts, Jimblah, is a Larrakia rapper from the Northern Territory, who grew up and currently resides in Adelaide. Darah and Briggs are Yorta Yorta rappers from Shepparton (VIC). This chapter will also incorporate testimonies from other artists, such as The Last Kinection, a band from Newcastle (NSW) formed by Kabi Kabi siblings Joel, "Weno," Wenitong, and Naomi, "Nay," Wenitong and Jacob Turner, DJ Jaytee. Nathan Bird, known as Birdz, is an artist of Butchulla and Nguburinji and Scottish and English heritage from Katherine (NT). Brisbane-based Rival MC, is a Murri man of Tongan and South-Sea Islander heritage, as well as Garrawa, Waanyi and Butchulla, he is the voice of the group Impossible Odds. Street Warriors are two brothers of Gamilaroi, Anaiwan and Dungutti background who, like The Last Kinection, live in Newcastle (NSW).

7 See for instance Tony Mitchell's (1998, 110) classification of various micro-communities of practice ("Falafel," "Wog" and "Ocker" hip hop) that reflect that cultural fragmentation of Australia.

8 The Triple J Hottest 100 is a public event hosted every year on Australia Day (January 26) by Radio Triple J, where the public is asked to vote for their favorite songs.

9 I am not using the word "society" here, as most societies are highly "multicultural." What I am referring to are governments, their constitutions and the bodies and institutions aiming to maintain dominant values and a status of inequality.

10 An Elder is a person who has gained respect in his/her community and who is highly regarded. Elders retain a great knowledge and provide guidance. The notion of Eldership varies according to the community, but it retains the above-mentioned common traits.

11 The "Indigenous counter-public sphere" combines Nancy Fraser's (1992) concept of "subaltern counter-publics" and Hartley and McKee's (2000) discourse on the "Indigenous public sphere."

12 The removals occurred roughly from 1869 to 1969 and probably during the 1970s.

13 In May 2015, a three-year-old Aboriginal girl was verbally assaulted in a racially motivated attack while she was lining up to attend *Frozen*, a Disney show which was taking place at a shopping center in country Victoria.

14 Tony Abbott's politics in relation to asylum seekers and refuges is manifest in his mantra: "Stop the boats!" In practical terms, his government's policy was to detain refugees, take them to offshore centers and relocate them somewhere else.

15 "Survivance" is a linguistic amalgam between "survival" and "resistance." It was coined by *Anishinaabe*-scholar Gerald Vizenor (1999).

16 *Larrakia* is the name of the Indigenous community from around Darwin in the Northern Territory.

17 Local Knowledge has a double meaning here. In fact, beyond its literal meaning, it also refers to the name of an Indigenous hip hop group from Newcastle (NSW).

Bibliography

Alim, Samy H., Ibrahim Awad and Alastair Pennycook. 2009. *Global Linguistic Flows: Hip Hop Cultures, Youth Identities and the Politics of Language.* New York: Routledge.

Arthur, Damian and Pascale Quester. 2006. "Defining Authenticity: An Ethnographic Study of Australian Hip Hop." In *AP: Asia-Pacific Advances in Consumer Research Volume 7*, edited by Margaret Craig Lees, Teresa Davis and Gary Gregory. Sydney: Association for Consumer Research, 112–113.

Australian Aboriginal Hip-Hop. 2007. Facebook. https://www.facebook.com/AboriginalRap/?fref=ts (accessed January 28, 2017).

Barwick, Diane. 1988. "Aborigines of Victoria." In *Being Black. Aboriginal Cultures in Settled Australia*, edited by Ian Keen. Canberra: Aboriginal Studies Press, 27–32.

Behrendt, Larissa. 1995. "Aboriginal Urban Identity: Preserving the Spirit, Protecting the Traditional in Non-Traditional Settings." *Australian Feminist Law Journal* 4: 55–61.

Booth, Andrea. 2015. "The Children Came Back: New Song Celebrates Indigenous Heroism Ahead of NAIDOC," *NITV News*, July 3, 2015. www.sbs.com.au/nitv/article/2015/07/03/children-came-back-new-song-celebrates-indigenous-heroism-ahead-naidoc (accessed July 5, 2015).

Broome, Richard. 2010. *Aboriginal Australians: A History Since 1788*. Sydney: Allen & Unwin.Connell, John and Chris Gibson. 2004. "World Music: Deterritorializing Place and Identity." *Progress in Human Geography* 28 (3): 342–361.

Connell, John and Chris Gibson. 2003. *Sound Tracks: Popular Music Identity and Place*. New York: Routledge.

Dawes, Glenn. 1998. "The Art of the Body: Aboriginal and Torres Strait Islander Youth Subcultural Practices." *Journal of Intercultural Studies* 19 (1): 21–35.

Dunbar-Hall, Peter and Chris Gibson. 2004. *Deadly Sounds, Deadly Places: Contemporary Aboriginal Music in Australia*. Sydney: University of New South Wales Press.

Fernandes, Sujatha. 2011. *Close to the Edge: In Search of the Global Hip Hop Generation*. London and New York: Verso Books.

Fraser, Nancy. 1992. "Rethinking the Public Sphere: A Contribution to the Critique of Actually Existing Democracy." In *Habermas and the Public Sphere*, edited by Craig Calhoun. Cambridge, MA: MIT Press, 109–142.

Hartley, John and Alan McKee. 2000. *The Indigenous Public Sphere: The Reporting and Reception of Aboriginal Issues in the Australian Media*. Oxford: Oxford University Press.

Indij Hip Hop Show. 2017. Facebook. https://www.facebook.com/IndijHipHop/?fref=ts (accessed January 28, 2017).

Local Knowledge. 2003. "Local Knowledge on Blaktrax (2003)." YouTube. https://www.youtube.com/watch?v=Bup5iC5Bwhs (accessed December 13, 2014).

Lyons, S. R. 2010. *X-marks: Native Signatures of Assent*. Minneapolis: University of Minnesota Press.

Malone, Christopher and George Martinez Jr., eds. 2014. *The Organic Globalizer: Hip-Hop, Political Development, and Movement Culture*. New York and London: Bloomsbury.

McLeod, Kembrew. 1999. "Authenticity within Hip-Hop and Other Cultures Threatened with Assimilation." *Journal of Communication* 49 (4): 134–150.

Minestrelli, Chiara. 2016. *Australian Indigenous Hip Hop: The Politics of Culture, Identity, and Spirituality*. London and New York: Routledge.

Minestrelli, Chiara. 2014. "'Are We There Yet?' The Political Power of Hip-Hop in Australia." In *See You at the Crossroads: Hip Hop Scholarship at the Intersections: Dialectical Harmony, Aesthetics, and a Panoply of Voices*, edited by Brad Porfilio, Debangshu Roychoudhury and Lauren M. Gardner . Rotterdam, Boston and Taipei: Sense Publisher, 129–146.

Mitchell, Tony. 2006. "Blackfellas Rapping, Breaking and Writing: A Short History of Aboriginal Hip-Hop." *Aboriginal History*, 30: 1–14.

Mitchell, Tony. 2001. *Global Noise. Rap and Hip-Hop Outside the USA*. Middletown, CT: Wesleyan University Press.

Mitchell, Tony. 1998. *Australian Hip Hop as a 'Glocal' Subculture*. Sydney: Ultimo Series Seminar, University of Technology, Sydney.

Morgan, George and Andrew Warren. 2011. "Aboriginal Youth, Hip-Hop and the Politics of Identification." *Ethnic and Racial Studies* 34 (6): 925–947.

Notarpietro-Clarke, Cristina. 2007. "Blackfella Beats and New Flows [A New and Distinctly Aboriginal Form of Hip-Hop Is Gaining Momentum]." *Arena Magazine* 87: 41–43.

Osumare, Halifu. 2001. "Beat Streets in the Global Hood: Connective Marginalities of the Hip-Hop Globe." *Journal of American Comparative Cultures* 2: 171–181.

Pennycook, Alastair and Tony Mitchell. 2009. "Hip-Hop as Dusty Foot Philosophy: Engaging Locality." In *Global Linguistic Flows: Hip-Hop Cultures, Youth Identities and the Politics of Language*, edited by Sami H. Alim, Awad Ibrahim and Alastair Pennycook. New York: Routledge, 25–42.

Phipps, Peter. 2010. "Performances of Power: Indigenous Cultural Festivals as Globally Engaged Cultural Strategy." *Alternatives* 35 (3): 217–240.

Sissons, Jeff. 2005. *First Peoples: Indigenous Cultures and Their Futures*. London: Reaktion Books.

Vincent, Peter. 2015. "Briggs Calls for Change in Australian Hip Hop Ahead of NIMA Awards: 'Time for a Message.'" *The Age*, July 21. http://m.theage.com.au/entertainment/music/briggs-calls-for-change-in-australian-hip-hop-ahead-of-nima-awards-time-for-a-message-20150721-gigwtp.html (accessed July 28, 2015).

Vizenor, Gerald R. 1999. *Manifest Manners: Narratives on Postindian Survivance*. Lincoln: University of Nebraska.

Ward, Matt. 2013. "Real Talk. Aboriginal Rappers Talk About Their Music and Country," Facebook. https://www.facebook.com/AboriginalRap (accessed January 18, 2015).

Warren, Andrew and Rob Evitt. 2010. "Indigenous Hip-Hop: Overcoming Marginality, Encountering Constraints." *Australian Geographer* 41 (1): 141–158.

White, Cameron. 2009. "'Rapper on a Rampage': Theorising the Political Significance of Aboriginal Australian Hip Hop and Reggae." *Transforming Cultures eJournal* 4 (1): 108–130.

Discography

A.B. Original. 2016. "January 26." *Reclaim Australia* [CD]. Adelaide: Golden Era Records.

Briggs. 2014. *Sheplife.* [CD]. Adelaide: Golden Era Records.

Briggs, Gurrumul and Dewayne Everettsmith. 2015. "The Children Came Back." [Single]. Melbourne: Kinnifish Music/Bad Apples.

Darah. 2011. "Aboriginal Style." *Aboriginal Style* [CD]. Melbourne: Darah Music.

Darah. 2012. "City on Fire." *I Believe in Revolution* [CD]. Melbourne: Darah Music.

Impossible Odds. 2011a. *Against All Odds* [CD]. Brisbane: Impossible Odds Records.

Impossible Odds. 2011. "Soul of The Troubador." *Against All Odds* [CD]. Brisbane: Impossible Odds Records.

Impossible Odds. 2011. "Take This Message." *Against All Odds* [CD]. Brisbane: Impossible Odds Records.

Impossible Odds. 2011. "What Do You See." *Against All Odds* [CD]. Brisbane: Impossible Odds Records.

Impossible Odds, KMT and G. Corowa. 2011. "Identity." *Against All Odds* [CD]. Brisbane: Impossible Odds Records.

Jimblah featuring Alex Truehl. 2012. "Capitol City." *Face the Fire*. Adelaide: Elefant Tracks.

Jimblah featuring Nooky, Ellie Lovegrove, Zachariiah Fieldieng X and Yothu Yindi. 2015. "Treaty 2015" [Single]. Adelaide: Elefant Tracks.

Nicki Minaj. 2014. "Anaconda." *The Pinkprint* [CD]. New Orleans: Young Money, Cash Money Republic.

N.W.A. 1988. "Straight Outta Compton." *Straight Outta Compton* [CD]. Los Angeles: Ruthless Records.

Roach, Archie. 1990. "Took the Children Away." *Charcoal Lane* [CD]. Melbourne: Mushroom Records/Liberation Music.

South Side Kings. 2012. "Straight Outta Shepparton." [Single]. Melbourne: Darah Music.

Street Warriors featuring Anthony Mundine. 2009. "I Rep for My Mob." *Unstoppable Force* [CD]. Sydney: GoSet Music.

Warumpi Band. 1985. "Blackfella/ Whitefella." *Big Name, No Blankets* [CD]. Brisbane: Parole and Powderworks Records.

Yothu Yindi. 1991. "Treaty" [Single]. Melbourne: Mushroom Records/Razor.

Videography

AboriginalRap. 2017. "AboriginalRap." YouTube. https://www.youtube.com/channel/UC1jAKMR1pJF29Y_hog BQxew (accessed January 28, 2017).

Alizadeh, Sonita. 2014. "Brides for Sale." YouTube. https://www.youtube.com/watch?v=n65w1DU8cGU (accessed January 28, 2017).

Ashraf, Sofia. 2015. "Kodaikanal Won't." YouTube. https://www.youtube.com/watch?v=nSal-ms0vcI (accessed January 28, 2017).

Indij Hip Hop Show. 2017. "AboriginalRap." YouTube. https://www.facebook.com/IndijHipHop/ (accessed January 28, 2017).

MoveItMobStyle. 2012. "Move It Mob Style Ep 5 Street Warriors." YouTube. www.youtube.com/watch?v=egy RKM--nQ8&list=PL1387848C46B20D67 (accessed October 23, 2014).

Sambo, Kylie. 2010. "Muckaty." YouTube. https://www.youtube.com/watch?v=nadlwfLapPg (accessed January 28, 2017).

Street Warriors. 2012. "Move It Mob Style Ep 5 Street Warriors." YouTube. (www.youtube.com/watch?v=egy RKMnQ8&list=PL1387848C46B20D67 (accessed May 15, 2012).

Filmography

James Ricketson. 1993. *Blackfellas*. Canberra: Ronin Films.

12
Technomotor Cities
Adelaide, Detroit and the Electronic Music Pioneers

Cathy Adamek

Introduction

In 1988, the "Second Summer of Love" was a dance music phenomenon that marked the global birth of new genres which were created with new technology: house, hip hop and techno.[1] In Australia, these genres proved a potent challenge to mainstream audiences who were used to Australian Rock (or "Oz Rock"), with its strong ties to notions of national identity. In the city of Adelaide, dance music culture had a substantial impact on the sociocultural landscape during the late 1980s to 1990s, and beyond. By examining dance music production, and placing it in the context of translocal formations of culture and economy, this chapter provides a counterpoint to the offerings of Part I in this volume on the role of place and music-making, by looking away from Australia for musical influence and inspiration. This chapter relates how dance music swiftly took root outside its place of inception (USA and UK) during a pre-Internet era, when global import markets were expanding. My findings reveal that a rapid reciprocal response of local production occurred—rather than a one-way flow of cultural influence, from the USA to Australia—demonstrating Adelaide's early contribution to the global formation of techno as a genre.

Detroit is credited as the birthplace of techno in the 1980s and by the early 1990s Adelaide had developed a reputation for its passionate engagement with dance music and particularly Detroit techno. During the 1990s, a key site for dance music was Adelaide's Central Station Records, which was well known locally as Australia's first dedicated dance music import record shop. The store, and the city of Adelaide, found international recognition via a center-spread in *International DJ* magazine which named Adelaide as the techno dance capital of Australia. Tony Caraccia, owner of Central Station, highlighted the importance of two local labels—Juice Records and its later incarnation as Dirty House—in earning this acclaim: "Without a doubt they led the way. They set the trend for Australia, at such an early stage. None of the DJs interstate were making the international mags. They put Adelaide on the map" (Caraccia 2011). In order to examine this cultural history of dance music in Adelaide via Central Station Records, and these two significant labels, Juice Records and Dirty House, I turn to interviews with two key artists/producers—Damien Donato and DJ HMC (Carmello "Cam" Bianchetti)—as well an online anonymous survey which attracted over fifty respondents from participants of Adelaide's early dance music scene. I also draw on scene theory

(Straw 1991) and the cultural geography work of Lloyd (2010), Walker (2009) and Wynne and O'Connor (1996), who link the specificity of place to creativity, in particular the dynamic and complex transnational flows that characterize contemporary cultural production.

Adelaide is the fifth largest city in Australia and the capital of the state South Australia. It is labeled with epithets (sometimes on car registration plates) such as "the Mediterranean of the South," "the City of Churches," and "the Festival State." Generally speaking, the media characterizes the city according to its low socio-economic status and substantial suburban sprawl, which lies in contrast to a gentrified but conservative CBD and inner-city suburbs. Genteel conservatism is a quality in keeping with South Australia as the only colony in Australia that was based on European free settlement rather than convict labor, and this has generally been taken to bestow upon it historical superiority. However, the city is also associated with a rich creative underground. These observations were supported by responses to my online anonymous survey:

> while Adelaide appears conservative on the surface, it has always had a large progressive and innovative element. Being the leader (or first mover) in the dance scene is consistent with Adelaide being the leader in most other cultural movements in Australia.
>
> (Male Survey Respondent 2011)

In the 1980s, the city center was sparsely populated and there were few incentives to encourage people to live there. The city was sectioned off from the suburban sprawl by a large green belt of parkland around all four sides of the city square. This created a crucial geographic and cultural divide between two worlds: "the suburban," as represented by the dominant Anglo-Celtic pub rock scene, and "the city" where new cultural forces existed to disrupt, revitalise and cosmopolitanise (Straw 1991, 361).

I argue here that techno production in Australia originated in the city of Adelaide, and is subsequently a missing link in the early global formation of EDM (Electronic Dance Music). Part of my argument rests on Adelaide's connections with another city associated with this genre: Detroit in Michigan. The two cities shared economic similarities through their car manufacturing industries, and form parallels as music-making cities despite their very different racial demographics. I posit that dance music creativity in Adelaide during the 1990s was greatly furthered via the small, local grassroots production label Juice Records which later, as Dirty House, had a significant impact on the international dance music market with its Detroit-influenced underground techno. In this chapter, I therefore ask "why music takes root in particular locations, and specifically why techno and Adelaide?" In addressing this question, I draw parallels between Adelaide and Detroit and I argue that the fates of the two cities were intertwined from the early years of the twentieth century in their relationship to Fordism and post-Fordism (Lloyd 2010; Walker 2009).

Translocal Genres: EDM and Techno

The history of dance music situates techno in Detroit and house in Chicago as part of a narrative of global dance music culture that was based in the USA and influenced by the UK. The anonymity and translocation of dance music production is often obscured by its origins, but since 2000 more detailed academic documentation of the musical form has revealed the unique contributions of specific scenes and locales. Straw compares the spatial and temporal dynamics of alternative rock and dance music, arguing that (at the time he was writing) the constantly evolving nature of EDM ensured the "simultaneous existence of large numbers of local or regional styles" (Straw 1991, 381). This particular phenomenon is referred to by Peterson and Bennett as "translocality," by which is meant "widely scattered local scenes drawn together in regular communication around a distinctive form of music and lifestyle" (2004, 3). This can result in an ambiguity regarding music authorship, an important part of the very make-up of EDM, which is often anonymous and has many producers.

What is it about Adelaide that made it unique as a space for musical translocality to take root? My interview data points to four answers: the people, the labels, the venues and the music itself. For example, Caraccia from Central Station emphatically states that "in no uncertain terms it was the people ... [they] put Adelaide on the map for techno with Juice and Dirty House. They led the way. People were more passionate here" (Caraccia 2011). My anonymous survey data also support this. When asked "How important was the music to you?" twenty-one of twenty-three respondents to this question included statements like: "as important as breathing" (Female Survey Respondent 2012); [it was] "an amazing parallel universe" (Male Survey Respondent 2011); and "I felt like I was part of a new movement" (Male Survey Respondent 2011). One respondent summarized the connection between dance music venues, the community and the music, saying:

> I found at [nightclub] Metro in particular a community of like-minded people, it was all about the music and the dancing for me ... we weren't there to pick up or get drunk, but to dance to this new and really good music.
>
> (Male Survey Respondent 2011)

This very brief summary of respondents points to a musical phenomenon taking place in Adelaide at that time. Techno sounds flourished. The following sections outline how this development occurred, with a focus on the early relationship between Adelaide techno music-makers—DJ HMC (Cam Bianchetti) and Damien Donato—with Detroit techno: a sound which informed and influenced their practice and early music-making experiments.

Adelaide's Juice Records (1991–1994) and Dirty House (1995–2001)

In 1989, Bianchetti heard the first Detroit electronic record "The Chase" by Model 500 (1989)—a blueprint of the early Detroit sound—and was hooked. At this time, Bianchetti and Donato started work at Tony Caraccia's aforementioned import record shop, Central Station Records, and Caraccia was equally enthusiastic about dance music and changing the musical tastes of the Australian rock-dominated youth culture. Bianchetti and Donato were responsible for ordering in new music for Adelaide and the shop was also the source of all their music buying. Central Station Records developed a reputation for buying exclusively for local DJs who would get first pick, "Tony brought in heaps of this music: 1990 UR [by Detroit techno collective Underground Resistance] and Plus 8 [a label credited as building the Detroit scene], and Detroit DJ pioneers Robert Hood and Jeff Mills" (Donato 2011), all

158 • Cathy Adamek

of which Bianchetti cites as musical influences. In our interview about that period in Adelaide, Donato spoke of the avant-garde and transcendent nature of techno back then. He explained that his impetus was to communicate ideas and visual imagery through sound, believing that electronic music should go beyond the hedonistic or the social. Moreover, he pointed to the influence that the situationists and Alvin Toffler's book *The Third Wave* (1980) had on the Detroit artists and himself: the idea of the techno rebel is to take discarded objects, in this case old synthesizers, and find a new musical use for them as a form of technological empowerment. Donato remained true to this aesthetic, using only second-hand instruments such as Roland drum machines such as "the 808 and 303 as well as [the] 707 [and also synthesisers such as] the 909" (Donato 2011). This philosophy and these instruments were the initial inspiration that propelled Donato and Bianchetti (under his moniker as DJ HMC) into ten years of producing Adelaide techno and house under two labels—Juice Records and Dirty House—which fed into international markets at an influential time during the growth of techno as a global genre.

The label Juice Records emerged in 1991 as a collaboration between Bianchetti, Donato and techno producer Theo Bambacas (who worked under the name Cinnaman), with the intention of releasing their own music. They composed separately in rudimentary studios, exchanged cassette tapes and also played at Adelaide venues. Bianchetti remembers playing a lot of hard Detroit techno at the nightclub Metro: musical choices that led to ongoing tensions within the club owners who were anxious about the success of their Friday night. Donato recalls that on some nights there were only twenty punters, as the confronting experimentalism of the music was initially a barrier to drawing a bigger crowd. Indeed, the techno sound was described by leading Detroit techno exponent Richie Hawtin as "futuristic music, sounds that you'd never heard before" (Lee and Shapiro 1998): dark sounds with no familiar formula. Metro let them go, only to rebook them months later when techno began to gain a larger crowd in Adelaide and Bianchetti became a huge success at another underground club in town, Control. When Bianchetti, Donato and Bambacas were not playing in clubs they performed at house parties, turning lounge rooms into warehouses with lighting and sound systems. Donato remembers walking into their own lounge late at night to see what record Bianchetti was playing and realizing it was coming from the tape deck and that "we were starting to make music like they [the Detroit artists] did." The track was "Life Support System," Bianchetti's first track produced with Bambacas as Vitamin HMC and Thee. In 1991 they released this track as their first record, launched at the local club Control, then at Metro. It sold 500 copies in Adelaide. Their approach to the European market was followed by a fax from a Belgian label which sent AUD3000 to license the track. Underground techno label Music Man also licensed the track, progressively becoming a bigger underground success throughout Europe. Bianchetti describes the track as having a unique sound despite its European and Detroit influences. The next record did not make much money for Juice but by this stage they were operating as a full-time techno label. A few months later Juice received an order from New York for 900 records. By 1993 their work was being reviewed internationally next to UR (Underground Resistance). Their underground connections were global, not national—a common characteristic of dance music according to Straw (1991). By this time, they were licensing to the Netherlands, the UK and other parts of the world—a significant achievement considering their distant origin.

In 1994, many DJs in Europe were playing music from Juice Records. HMC (Bianchetti), Donato and Bambacas (Cinnaman) were asked to do a set at the May Day rave in Dusseldorf: the first time an Australian act had been asked to play there and Bianchetti's first gig in Europe. Bianchetti performed to 25,000 people alongside early dance music exponents Laurent Garnier and Carl Cox. He also played at the Fridge in Brixton with Detroit artists Jeff Mills and Robert Hood. People could not believe that music like this was coming out of Australia. Eventually the two record-pressing plants they used in Australia closed down (due to the vagaries of a limited market) and they were forced to manufacture records in Canada at the pressing plant owned by Richie Hawtin and John Aquaviva (bought as a result of the success of their label Plus 8). Although the effect of the Juice label was widespread, the sales had been small. With Hawtin they maintained their own licensing while he manufactured and the sound of the music improved because of the better facilities in North America. Juice released about 1000 records between 1991 and 1994 but with Hawtin's worldwide distribution this increased to between 5000 and 10,000 between 1994 and 1996.

Dirty House was born in 1995, an invention of Bambacas, in collaboration with Donato, Bianchetti and musician Paddee Butavicius (Figure 12.1). The lessons learnt from running the label Juice were the foundations on which Dirty House was built, also defined by a different and more accessible sound which was less hard-edged, sparse and industrial, and more inspired by house music. Inspired by the European tour, Bianchetti became heavily involved in producing music on his return and made some of Dirty House's most successful

Figure 12.1 Theo Bambacas and DJ HMC (Cam Bianchetti), *The Face*, July 1995.

Figure 12.2 Claude Young DJing at the "toxic" dance party at Le Rox, Adelaide, 1993.

tracks, such as "Phreakin," "LSD," and "107." As UR had impressed upon them, they owned intellectual copyright on everything. But the focus was still on taking this local product out to the world; in Donato's words, their "markets are everywhere with the fax machine going 24/7" (Donato 2011). However, Plus 8 wanted to include "Made in Canada"—to denote Canadian authorship—on the label even though all the artwork was from Adelaide. Sticking to their principles of underground independence, they left Plus 8 and found another pressing plant in the USA. Both labels were driven by the underground ideology of UR who were militant towards the governing music industry and about maintaining creative freedom.

This case study of Adelaide's Juice Records and Dirty House is richly illustrative of Straw's (1991) analysis of the dance music scene as a polycentric culture that takes root in other places and is transformed and reworked. Indeed, global cities such as Adelaide are not self-contained hubs of creativity, and cityscapes are "continually fashioned through social webs that operate across different geographical scales simultaneously" (Waitt 2006, 171). Between 1991 and 1994 there was a particularly fruitful period of transnational collaboration and inspiration between Detroit and Adelaide, where the ideology of UR and the techno movement in general was augmented by key techno artists who toured to Adelaide. Sicko's American book, *Techno Rebels* (1999) documents the first international gig in Australia (in Adelaide) of Detroit artist-producer Claude Young (DJ 2120) (see Figure 12.2) in 1992:

> Young stumbled on a vibrant underground scene-anchored by DJ HMC and the Juice label—and turned his junket into an extended stay to learn more about it. Young's impact

Technomotor Cities • 161

was immediately followed by a legendary live performance of Underground Resistance which was intent on making its World Power Alliance concept a reality.

(Sicko 1999, 178)

As well as the Detroit artists traveling to Adelaide, the Dirty House artists spread their influence while touring to other parts of the world. Bianchetti recounted that during the "Phreakin" European tour, he DJ'd the same show as Thomas Banghalter, from Daft Punk, who was eager to meet him and asked Laurent Garnier to be introduced. Bianchetti gave him a copy of the track. Some claim that Daft Punk created their sound from that record (Bianchetti 2011). Beyond the Detroit and Adelaide interface, this is also an example of direct transfer between artists from different global locales, illustrating how musical ideas were communicated at the time and the potential influence of this transmission in a pre-Internet era. In answer to my question "How aware were you of being influenced by overseas trends?," one respondent noted that that they were influenced by

Music ... but on the whole I think we were quite isolated. A lot of fashion around then in Adelaide was individual, there was still the "Stussy & Nike" brands ... Another way of answering would to be to ask in reverse, how aware are we of how much HMC was influencing overseas?

(Female Survey Respondent 2011)

The case study of these two labels also reveals that Adelaide techno reached a substantial underground audience in the UK and Europe, and was also influenced by tech sounds outside the Detroit canon. DJ Angus recalled taking Bianchetti to an international music industry conference in Belgium in the later 1990s and witnessing his musical impact: "It was amazing to walk around with him for a week and watch people worship him ... falling at his feet, going you're HMC, you're a god" (Sanders 2012). Not only did Juice Records, and later Dirty House, transform the practice of music-making, it is also an example of how a successful small business developed an innovative product embedded in transnational networks.

Post-Fordism and Music-Making

Late twentieth-century music scenes grow, according to Silver, Clark and Yanez, in less industrial, contingent societies where traditional constraints fall away and leisure and amenities become a more central feature of social cohesion and interaction (2010, 2294). During this time, Henry Ford's car assembly line and its particular division of labor provided a template for factory work, mass production and mass consumption. Even so, Ford crumbled in the 1970s as a result of international competition from the rebuilding of Germany and Japan that created trade deficits for the USA (Lloyd 2010, 34–48). A number of writers have commented on the connections between Ford's methods of mass production, organization and promotion, and the change in the organisational structure of the music industry during the 1980s. Examples of what are referred to as "post-Fordist methods" include more fragmented niche markets, short-run batch production and multi-skilled workers (Longhurst 2007, Negus 1999). It is possible, then, to suggest that the breakdown of older industry led to the

162 • Cathy Adamek

flourishing of new creative scenes. Toynbee, for example, argues that the increasing fragmentation and plurality of mainstream markets as a result of globalisation during the 1980s ended "the hegemony of the rock mainstream" (2000, 157). In a global backlash, rock—which dominated the music charts in the USA, UK and Australia—was challenged first by disco, then by punk (Hebdige 1979; Shapiro 2009; Collin and Godfrey 1998), and in the late 1980s to early 1990s by house, hip hop and techno. In this context, the independent production and distribution methods of Adelaide's Juice and Dirty House records influenced international markets from the ground up.

Cars, Space and Place

Both Adelaide and Detroit were sites for vehicle production as well as techno production and it is pertinent to outline some of these connections here. In 1914, the Australian government supported the expansion of General Motors (now Holden) and Ford (the two big Detroit car manufacturers) into Australia as, at that time, there was no domestic car industry (Walker 2009, 20). Holden started as an Adelaide firm in suburban Woodville and mechanical parts were exported there to be assembled, leading to significant economic expansion and growth of working-class jobs. The importance of this enterprise was noted by Walker who observed that "the creation of General Motors Holden was the single most significant thing to happen to the Australian economy, and for Australian-American relations between the two wars" (Walker 2009, 21). Moreover, the car industry became imbedded into Adelaide's character as a city:

> Holden's story is Adelaide's story. It's a truism that Australian cities were designed by and for the motorcar. But it's hard to imagine any city where this is more true than Adelaide. The growth of Holden/GMH, and its integration in to Adelaide's urban form and its collective psyche is a perfect parallel for the growth of Adelaide itself from the 19th to the 20th and 21st century.[2]
>
> (Horton 2013)

In the 1950s, Adelaide's increasing level of car ownership and declining use of public transport occurred concurrently with vehicle manufacturers' establishment of factories on the cheap, flat land to the north and south of the city. This urban plan, with its focus on the motor car but lack of infrastructure, produced a disconnected suburban sprawl—a north, south, west, east divide; a city versus hills divide with an overreliance on cars to get around; and a depopulated city center. It also created distinct characteristics in the minds of musicians related to these areas. Artist and DJ Driller Jet-Armstrong reflects on the role of the car in providing a teenager from the north in the 1970s with freedom and simultaneously with a connection to the city in place of public transport:

> I sort of made that break from the northern suburbs, big time. Like my driver's licence was my key to freedom. Once I got my driver's licence at 16 I was free to go into town. It was impossible to get into town, once you got there, how would you get home? People used to walk, how's that, it's bizarre when you think about it.
>
> (Jet-Armstrong 2011)

Detroit's rich musical tradition was inextricably bound up with the automotive industry and its historical contours parallel the car's progress.

> If Detroit is notable for anything other than making cars and cornflakes, it is making tracks. Berry Gordy, Motown's founder was working on the Ford production line when he composed "reet petite." This sound went all around the world; what underlined it was the beat, metronomic, loping and unyielding, it was very easy to dance to.
>
> (Walker 2009, 27)

The aesthetic appeal of techno's sound directly echoes the transition to a technological base in factories and the automotive industries. The Detroit techno artists recall, in a documentary interview, their parents coming home from work and telling them they worked with robots. They cite this influence as a source of imaginative inspiration (Bredow et al. 2006). DJ/ producer Theo Parrish (2012) comments on this relationship between the techno artists in Detroit and the machine. It was not, he argues, a love affair with mechanization, as interpreted by European techno musicians. Instead, it involved the use of machines to make music, as a method of escape. The idea was to invert and transcend the power relationship between man and machine, mastering it for individual and creative ends, independent production rather than the routinised cog-in-wheel factory work where machines dictated how people worked (Parrish 2012). Parrish's thoughts can be read as a critique of Ford's mechanization, from the standpoint of a new generation. This was also expressed musically through the techno pioneers' rejection of the Motown influence that had come to define Detroit internationally. They felt oppressed by Motown's omnipresent musical legacy, which Walker (2009) relates to the Fordist mass production line and a world of individual artistic disempowerment as opposed to new methods of independent production.

Similarly, I suggest that the "pub-rock" stereotype in Australia emerged from this era of the standardized factory world of Ford, which reached its zenith during the two decades after World War II. Ford factory culture was a large part of industrialized work practice in Australia particularly amongst post-war migrant populations. Walker (2009, 27) suggests that the car created suburbia and, in Australia, Cold Chisel represented the voice of suburbia. Further, I would argue that this is the sound many dance music participants were running away from—musically as well as geographically—into the glamorous pockets of the empty 1980s Adelaide CBD. The mock sophistication of European-inspired new wave was central to the sound and style of Hindley Street West clubs Toucan and Le Rox. The new wave scene was also very influential in Detroit's high school social clubs such as Charivari (Sicko 1999, 33)—cliquey, fashion conscious and upwardly mobile and an indirect influence on techno, where the early artists played and partied as they did in Adelaide. Reynolds (1998, 5) describes the elitism of young black Detroit clubbers (a legacy of the Ford assembly line, which granted equal pay across race in factories). These descriptions of the early Detroit techno scene draw parallels with the middle-class location of the early techno scene in Adelaide. Europe at the time was still the imaginative heart of the emergent EDM scene in both Adelaide and Detroit, where the sounds of Kraftwerk, British new wave and Italo disco reflected similar musical pathways. Italo disco caught on in Detroit like nowhere else in America; in Australia it was found exclusively in the Greek, Italian and gay discos (Sicko 1999, 48).

164 • Cathy Adamek

Economic downturn and recession meant Detroit in the early 1980s was in a state of decay and characterized by racial tensions. By the early 1990s, the collapse of Adelaide's State Bank plunged Adelaide into a recession that lasted for most of the decade at the same time as the dance music scene flourished. However much it was plagued by small city blues, Adelaide, as Damien Donato said, was still a "cosmopolitan paradise" (Donato 2011). In certain shared respects, the middle-class location of the early EDM scene in the two cities, both small and elite, protected them from some of the harsher realities of social unrest.

Techno: Sonic Landscapes and Origins of Sound

The ambience of techno and rave music has been linked as a response to place, using "sound and rhythm to construct psychic landscapes of exile and utopia" (Reynolds 1998, p. xxvi), Detroit techno was contextualized by the press as coming from a forgotten city with an empty CBD, abandoned as a result of the flight to the suburbs. The sparse electronic minimalism of techno has been described as a "deprived sound, trying to get out" by Detroit techno artist and pioneer Juan Atkins in an interview (Bredow et al. 2006). Techno artist Derrick May affirms "you can only dream what the rest of the world is like and, whatever you believe, it will help you get out of that city" (ibid.). Atkins talks about a love/hate relationship with the city where "something happens on a creative level here that you won't find anywhere else." He attributes the existence of a rich underground to boredom, forcing people to make their own entertainment, observations that are also true of Adelaide at the time, where music was an escape from an insular city.

Although these comments suggest music can be a response to prevailing conditions, does music produced in a certain place actually sound like the place, or is this quality imposed retrospectively by commentators? In a 2012 article in Adelaide street magazine *Onion*, DJ HMC points out the connection between Detroit and Adelaide but questions the literalness of music sounding like a place (Onion 2012). Nevarez (2013, 58) describes this notion as part of a myth-making discourse about place and its effect on music. In particular, he discusses the attribution of Mancunian qualities to the music of Joy Division and New Order. The relationship between sound and place is not straightforward: the rhetoric of the local can indicate the ways in which place and the local are imagined by music scenes and it is often journalists and fans who link sound to locale (Cohen 1991, 340). However, the philosophical connection of the city to its sound was a conscious construction by the Detroit artists who wanted to emphasise the uniqueness of their musical project, and was embraced enthusiastically by music critics (Brewster and Broughton 2000, 332). I would argue that the industrial motor-city characteristics shared by Adelaide and Detroit were reacted to by developing and echoing a shared musical aesthetic.

Conclusion

This chapter has explored the creative relationship between Detroit and Adelaide techno, in light of the broader set of characteristics and history shared by the two cities. My analysis indicates that the car manufacturing industry formed a backbone to Adelaide's identity, revealing an interconnection with Detroit through the car manufacturer Holden from the early twentieth century also sharing musical affinities. A survey participant reflects on his engagement with the nascent dance music scene and his relationship to Adelaide:

> For me there was a feeling of being somewhere, doing something that was so completely off the mainstream radar, it felt like the growth of new ways of existing. Somewhere those who were searching for more than the status quo could go to create something totally new. I don't think this was specific to Adelaide, I think it was happening all over the world but I think perhaps the size and isolation of Adelaide helped to create a critical mass. Personally it was a search for myself as an individual separate from all external influence. There was nowhere else in Adelaide at that time that I felt I fitted in or belonged.
>
> (Male Survey Respondent 2013)

He acknowledges the impact that the Adelaide scene had on him, expressing an awareness of participating in a globally connected phenomenon which altered his experience of place by paradoxically making him feel more at home. This sentiment echoes Stahl's observation that "the movement and distribution of people, ideas, money and technologies through this global cultural economy take hold in both the imaginations of individuals as well as in concrete contexts" (2003, 34). Such transfers are not only a way of transforming the local and personal, but also indicate that the local can powerfully influence transnational culture, as demonstrated in this example of Adelaide's early and passionate engagement with techno and dance music.

Acknowledgments

Thanks to Professor Susan Luckman, Associate Professor Geraldine Bloustien, and Deirdre Adamek.

Notes

1   The "Second Summer of Love" was a reference to 1960s hippie counterculture known as the (first) "Summer of Love" or the "Age of Aquarius," which influenced much of EDMs early psychedelica.
2   Much has been written in the media about the effect that Holden's withdrawal from South Australia will have on the state: "Culture is not separate from an economy but one that grows and grafts on to the other. Adelaide's industrial economy and its culture has been built on auto making ever since those big decisions were made in the short window between recovery from the greatest depression the world had ever seen, and a war that supercharged the making of machinery, armaments and material." (Horton 2013).

Bibliography

Bianchetti, Carmello. 2011. Interview with author. Digital pen recording. Adelaide, January 24.
Brewster, Bill and Frank Broughton. 2000. *Last Night a DJ Saved My Life: The History of the Disc Jockey*. New York: Grove Press.
Caraccia, Tony. 2011. Interview with author. Digital pen recording. Adelaide, February 23.
Cohen, Sara. 1991. "Popular Music and Urban Regeneration: The Music Industries of Merseyside." *Cultural Studies* 5 (3): 332–346.
Collin, Matthew and John Godfrey. 1998. *Altered State: The Story of Ecstasy Culture and Acid House*. Second edition. London: Serpent's Tail.
Donato, Damien. 2011. Interview with author. Digital pen recording. Adelaide, March 16.

166 • Cathy Adamek

Hebdige, Dick. 1979. *Subculture, The Meaning of Style*. London: Methuen.
Horton, T. 2013. "How Holden Shaped Adelaide." In *Daily*, 19 August. http://indaily.com.au/opinion/2013/08/19/horton-how-holden-shaped-adelaide (accessed September 2013).
Hutchings, A.W. ed. 2007. *With Conscious Purpose: A History of Town Planning in South Australia*. Second edition. Adelaide: Planning Institute of Australia (SA Division).
Jet-Armstrong, Driller. 2011. Interview with author. Digital pen recording. Adelaide, May 14.
Lee, Iara and Peter Shapiro (directors). 1998. *Modulations*. DVD. Caiprihina Productions USA.
Lloyd, Richard D. 2010. *Neo-bohemia: Art and Commerce in the Postindustrial City*. Second edition. New York: Routledge.
Longhurst, Brian. 2007. *Popular Music and Society*. Second edition. Edited by M.A. Malden. Cambridge: Polity.
Negus, Keith. 1999. *Music Genres and Corporate Cultures*. London: Routledge.
Nevarez, Leonard. 2013. "How Joy Division Came to Sound like Manchester: Myths and Ways of Listening in the Neoliberal City." *Journal of Popular Music Studies* 25 (March): 56–76.
Onion 2012, 'Interview with HMC', Adelaide.
Parrish, T. 2012. *Electronic Beats TV* YouTube Interview, 14.30, posted May 4, 2012, https://www.youtube.com/watch?v=-5USZQ97l9s.
Peterson, Richard and Andy Bennett. 2004. *Music Scenes: Local, Translocal and Virtual*. Nashville, TN: Vanderbilt University Press.
Reynolds, Simon. 1998. *Energy Flash: A Journey through Rave Music and Dance Culture*. London: Picador.
Sanders, Angus. 2012. Interview with author. Digital pen recording. Adelaide, January 30.
Shapiro, Peter. 2009. *Turn the Beat Around; The Secret History of Disco*. Second edition. London: Faber.
Sicko, Dan. 1999. *Techno Rebels: The Renegades of Electronic Funk*. New York: Watson-Guptil.
Silver, Daniel, Terry Clark and Clemente Jesus Navarro Yanez. 2010. "Scenes: Social Context in an Age of Contingency." *Social Forces* 88 (5): 2293–2324.
Stahl, Geoff. 2003. "Tastefully Renovating Subcultural Theory: Making Space for a New Model." In *The Post-Subcultures Reader*, edited by Rupert Weinzierl and David Muggleton. 1st ed. Oxford: Berg, 27–40.
Straw, Will. 1991. "Systems of Articulation, Logics of Change: Communities and Scenes in Popular Music." *Cultural Studies* 5 (3): 361–375.
Toffler, Alvin. 1980. *The Third Wave*. London: Collins.
Toynbee, Jason. 2000. *Making Popular Music: Musicians, Creativity and Institutions*. London: Arnold.
Waitt, Gordon. 2006. "Creative Small Cities: Cityscapes, Power, and the Arts." In *Small Cities: Urban Experience Beyond the Metropolis*. Edited by David Bell and Mark Jayne. Abingdon: Routledge, 169–185.
Walker, Clinton. 2009. *Golden Miles: Sex, Speed and the Australian Muscle Car*. Second edition. Kent Town, South Australia: Wakefield Press.
Wynne, Derek and Justin O'Connor. 1996. *From the Margins to the Centre: Cultural Production and Consumption in the Post-Industrial City*. Aldershot: Arena.

Discography

DJ HMC. "107." In *Dirty Acid Trax Vol. 1*. Dirty House Records – DAT1, 1996, 12", 45 rpm.
DJ HMC (as C. Bianchetti). "LSD," In *House of Joy*. Sub Terranean T-43, Sub Terranean SPV 089-47092 – SPV 089-47092, 1996, compact disc.
DJ HMC. "Phreakin." Dirty House Records DIRT 01, 1995, 12", 33⅓ rpm.
Model 500. "The Chase," Metroplex M-014, 1989, 12", 33⅓ rpm.
Vitamin HMC and Thee. "Life Support System," Juice Records EP limited edition numbered, 1991, 12", 45 rpm.

Videography

Bredow, Gary, Juan Atkins, Derrick May and Kevin Saunderson (directors). 2006. *High Tech Soul*. DVD. New York: Plexigroup.
Lee, Iara and Peter Shapiro (directors). 1998. *Modulations*. DVD. Caiprihina Productions New York.

13
Giving Back in Wellington
Deep Relations, *Whakapapa* and Reciprocity in Transnational Hip Hop

April K. Henderson

It is mid-2011, and the acclaimed Bronx DJ Jazzy Jay relaxes into deft manipulation of two turntables in a warehouse flat in Wellington's Newtown neighborhood. Behind him, tables of another kind are draped in Pacific-themed *lavalava* fabric along with remnants of meats and salads, chicken wings, curry, rice, cakes and pie. It is a communal feast hosted by local hip hop artists, their families and friends for an international DJ who played a memorable cameo role in the initial global spread of hip hop.

A year later, a different touring hip hop artist, the Bronx MC KRS-One, leans in for a photo backstage at Wellington Town Hall. He's surrounded by a dozen mostly local hip hop artists. They are a mixed group with mixed talents: there are DJs, graffiti artists, MCs, bboys and a bgirl. Most identify as Māori, Samoan and Pākehā,[1] with a Wellington-raised Cambodian and a visiting indigenous Australian also in their midst. It is easy to see black and white amulets on beaded strings hanging from most necks. However, the American star doesn't wear a necklace, nor is he adorned with the flashy gold chains associated with other American hip hop artists. Instead, he dons an '*ulafala*: the distinctive red lacquered garland of dried pandanus fruits associated with Samoan orator chiefs.

That same year, the Harlem MC Immortal Technique begins a speech as part of a *pōwhiri*—an indigenous formal welcome ceremony—at Kāpiti Marae, a Māori meeting ground (*marae*) outside of Wellington. Surrounded by rows of local hip hop artists and fans, he acknowledges his indigenous ancestry through his Peruvian parentage. In keeping with the staunchly anti-establishment lyricism that gained him fame in the 2000s, he also offers passionate English and Spanish language commentary in prose and rhyme on colonialism, activism and the power of hip hop artistry. As he concludes, local bgirl Silas raises her voice in a *waiata*, a Māori language song form that functions as a customary closing support to his formal speech.

These three anecdotes about three generations of quintessentially New York hip hop artists illustrate the honor afforded to their distinctive contributions to hip hop musical arts in Wellington, Aotearoa/New Zealand. Jazzy Jay, KRS-One and Immortal Technique are of widely divergent ancestries and disparate geographies to these Aotearoa artists, yet in these exchanges the local hosts recognize something beyond fandom and beyond artistic respect. They recognize a kinship with their American visitors and demonstrate a sense of

168 • April K. Henderson

connection in ways locally meaningful and culturally significant. For local hip hop artists, these are opportunities to "give back" not only to specific artists but also to a broader hip hop culture that has shaped them.

This chapter explores how Wellington artists live hip hop culture in ways that explicitly and implicitly resonate with local indigenous Pacific cultures. In doing so, it also reveals their understanding of what "real" hip hop is. Key to this understanding is the concept of reciprocity or "giving back," as played out in the three examples described above. Reciprocity acknowledges the receipt of past gifts and, in this case, Wellington artists feel that hip hop culture (and these New York artists) have given them a great deal. Equally, reciprocity understands that the reciprocators, too, have gifts to offer.

This reciprocity articulates and affirms bonds of kinship. Metaphors of kinship and genealogy need to be understood in locally and indigenously specific ways in Aotearoa, and they offer ways to move the conversation about transnational hip hop beyond discussions of a global/local dichotomy. These metaphors offer specific examples of how local hip hop is lived in Aotearoa, providing an entry point to understand the "deep relations" (Shilliam 2015) between New Zealand and American artists. These relationships respect the *mana*— the power, dignity and efficacy—of multiple points of originary influence and value artists' own powerfully felt hierarchies of deference and respect.

Wellington

Aotearoa has an impressive history of hip hop participation dating back to 1982. Published and oral accounts from that time document a young Samoan man returning from a visit to the Samoan islands with elements of urban American dance forms such as popping, locking and breaking: dances brought to Samoa by diasporic youth visiting or returning from the USA (Henderson 2006; Scott 1985; Wright 2006). Wellington, the small harbor-hugging capital, holds a singular place in this history. It was home to this first hip hop dancer, as well as the first DJs to regularly spin hip hop music in nightclubs and the country's first regular (and still running) hip hop-devoted radio program. Wellington also produced many of the country's early graffiti writers, and Upper Hutt Posse's Māori nationalist anthem "E Tu" ("Stand"), Aotearoa's first recorded hip hop single, emerged from a group whose name unequivocally declared their origin in the Wellington region's Hutt Valley. Throughout their evolution, hip hop forms in Wellington and Aotearoa more generally have been avidly (though not exclusively) practiced by people of Polynesian descent, drawing together both indigenous Māori—Aotearoa's first Polynesian settlers—and more recent Pacific Islands migrants and their descendants.

Over the decades, a core group of Wellington artists have persisted in teaching the foundations of their craft to aspiring artists and the public. Such efforts have sometimes taken the form of publications, workshops, performances and symposia coordinated with support from a variety of local, regional and national institutions. Perhaps of equal or greater significance to knowledge transmission during this period has been the informal instruction between established and emerging artists via hip hop's "innate and intuitive mentoring system," as described by Wellington-based graffiti artist and dancer SpexOne (Tamati 2004, 56). Efforts to transmit essential information about histories and artistic genealogies alongside practical techniques have ensured that Wellington's community of artists are into their second and even third generation. In some cases, these generations are blood relatives. For example, among those gathering backstage with KRS-One at Wellington Town Hall were bboy Swerv, who first began dancing in the early 1980s and has been a fixture as a competition organizer and judge since the revival of breaking in Aotearoa in the late-1990s and his daughter bgirl Silas, who was raised on hip hop culture from birth and is now in her late 20s with a daughter of her own.

For the many Wellington artists not genetically related, strong ties are generated by mutual support that extends across ethnic, religious, gender and generational divides. Such connectedness was evident when I conducted interviews and focus groups during 2009–2010 with forty artists who were, or had been, active participants in hip hop art forms in Wellington. Their self-identified ethnic backgrounds included (in whole, part or combination): Samoan, Māori, Fijian, Tongan, Greek, Pākehā, Filipino, Cambodian, Chinese, Indian, Scots-Irish, Chilean and Brazilian. This research was designed to explore what I called their "community of interest": the networks and bonds between artists that I keenly observed over nearly a decade of residing in Wellington and an even longer period of researching Aotearoa hip hop. Although all participants agreed that the term "community" was appropriate, many also declared that "they often use the term 'family' or other metaphors of kinship instead of the term 'community'" (Henderson 2010a, 15). I had offered one way of characterizing their sense of relationship to each other and they had responded with something deeper.

Importantly, this sense of hip hop kinship extended beyond Wellington peers. These same artists also identified that their

> sense of connectedness through hip hop can and often does extend to people from other geographic regions locally, nationally, and internationally, and can prompt and facilitate the development of connections and relationships across geographic regions through recognition of shared interests.
>
> (Henderson 2010a, 15)

For many Wellington hip hop artists, this sense of shared kinship, and its demonstration through acts of mutual support, is integral to their understanding of "real" hip hop. In fact, senses of kinship and senses of "realness" operate co-constitutively. Artists recognize kinship with other artists that they deem "real," but their recognition of realness is in part informed by their sense of whether other artists—locally or internationally—will recognize and enact kinship with them. As argued in more detail later, such selective recognition of kinship underpins the moments of exchange described at the start of this chapter.

Thinking About "Local" Hip Hop in Aotearoa

Much of the academic literature on Aotearoa hip hop to date has determinedly refuted a position that it is simply a debased mimicry of African American forms. Although Tony Mitchell has been selective in ascribing degrees of localization to various musical examples, he generally affirms that "Maori and Pacific Islander rappers have attempted in convincing fashion to substitute Maori and Polynesian cultural expressions for the Black American cultural context of hip hop, while borrowing freely from the U.S. musical styles of the genre" (Mitchell 2001, 295). Kirsten Zemke-White has been more effusive in her celebration of localization

> New Zealand artists take globalised American rap, converting it to suit specific local sites, peoples and struggles. Rappers in Aotearoa/New Zealand, reinforce, explode and re-present essential hip hop tropes, using them to celebrate and negotiate complex contemporary identities and locations.
>
> (Zemke-White 2005, 1)

In defense of the localness of Aotearoa hip hop, academic analyses have often marshalled lyrical texts, music video imagery and artist interviews as evidence that it is obviously indigenized through reference to local languages, idioms, histories, politics and place-based understandings.[2]

Over the past decade, scholars have attempted to develop this argument about relationships between global and local forms further. Alistair Pennycook argues that even when the language and musical forms of non-American hip hop closely resemble American forms, and are potentially therefore read as "mimicry," this is to ignore how those languages and forms may be *enacted* differently in specific local contexts (Pennycook 2007). In subsequent writing, Pennycook and Tony Mitchell elaborate a desire to craft

> an image of localization that goes beyond appropriation of sounds or references to local contexts. It speaks to a particular groundedness, a relationship to the earth that is about both pleasure and politics . . . this is a much more significant issue to do with the ways in which our histories, bodies, desires, and localities are intertwined.
>
> (Pennycook and Mitchell 2009, 25–26)

Pennycook and Mitchell push us to think about specific local hip hop examples as instances of local, indigenous knowledge systems and practices being globalized through their transmutation into hip hop cultural vehicles, rather than solely as American hip hop being localized into an indigenous context. This subtle recentering of localness is, in part, to offer an anecdote to an unintentional residue of Western- or American-centrism in prior analyses of what the localization of hip hop involves and how it occurs. In short, if we continue to think of American hip hop as the originary form that then gets (and gets to be thought of as) globalized—as universally circulated and locally indigenized—then the local form is forever cast as subsidiary: a derivative even as we try to deny its derivativeness.

Thinking about Aotearoa hip hop through this shifted frame, there are certainly numerous examples of Māori and other Pacific artists explicitly articulating their hip hop artistry as resonant with pre-existing indigenous Pacific performing arts practices. For example, Wellington-raised artist Tha Feelstyle has referenced the special oratorical language of Samoan chiefly society (*gagana fa'afailauga*) as a means of understanding and rationalizing his chosen vocation as a hip hop MC. Speaking to a US-based journalist at Auckland's Pasifika Festival, he explained how

During a wedding or funeral in Samoa the village chiefs recite long oratories in the chiefly language, which is rich and complex in metaphors, not spoken by the commoners. One chief goes first, then another—who might be in opposition to him—gives a different sort of speech. It's just like an MC battle!

(Verán 2002, 88)

He echoed such statements in my own interview with him, likening the *fa'atau* (the process by which Samoan orators skillfully deploy *gagana fa'aifailauga* to establish who has the authority to speak in a formal context) to the verbal duels of hip hop MCs. Tha Feelstyle's comments stress a narrative of hip hop culture that posits it as something not alien, or even necessarily new, to Samoan culture: "It ain't like we just came off the boat and we're picking it up now ... It's been there. When I go to weddings, there's always some guy going off [and] battles between orators" (Tha Feelstyle 2003).

Other Pacific hip hop MCs in Aotearoa have similarly referenced Pacific oral traditions to justify their participation in an art form reliant on verbal dexterity. Scholars and journalists have likewise discussed linkages between Pacific and hip hop cultures' shared emphases on orality, dance and visual art (Drago 1998; Ho'omanawanui 2006; Imada 2006; Verán 2006; Zemke-White 2001). In the mid-1980s, celebrated Samoan novelist Albert Wendt even published an epic poem where the mythical Polynesian hero utilizes a "brand new beat" gleaned from contemporary African American popular music to win an oratorical contest against a powerful foe (Wendt 1986; Henderson 2010b). Such articulations indicate not just a commensurability between hip hop and pre-existing indigenous practices, but an ability to understand the former as a valid extension of the latter. Reflecting on how Tha Feelstyle can view his hip hop artistry as about globalizing a pre-existing indigenous form (hip hopping *gagana fa'afailauga)* as much as it is about indigenizing a pre-existing global form (Samoanizing American hip hop), it is understandable that Pennycook and Mitchell would take issue with a "still common" understanding of "the global spread of Hip Hop as if this were only the global take-up of a particular cultural form." They argue that what's happening is more complex than simply "the global spread of (African) American culture" (2009, 28).

But what of the politics of too vociferously *not* viewing hip hop as the global spread of African American culture? When taken to an opposite extreme, reading hip hop outside of (African) American contexts as "already local," as continuous with pre-existing local or indigenous knowledge and performing traditions rather than a newly adopted imported culture, runs the risk of obscuring African American genealogies in their development and ignoring African American critiques of appropriation and disenfranchisement. African American music dominates mainstream pop music in the USA and beyond, yet African American populations remain marginalized and vulnerable to systematic racialized abuse. In this tense cultural terrain, politics of recognition are fraught. Indigenous Pacific hip hop artists are keen to have their histories and experience respected and the validity and worth of their hip hop practices acknowledged, while acutely aware that their existence does not typically register in the USA, including among many African American hip hop artists. By turn, many African Americans, whether they are active participants in hip hop art forms or not, continue to lay claim to hip hop as African American popular culture and see its global spread in precisely the way Pennycook and Mitchell attempt to counter (Perry 2004): any

172 • April K. Henderson

attempt to downplay this diffusionist understanding, however well-intentioned or theoretically adept, can potentially feel like a disavowal of forebears.

"Deep Relations" and *Whakapapa* as Metaphors and Methods of Enactment in Transnational Hip Hop

Calls for a more nuanced politics of recognition and relationality are emerging. Robbie Shilliam's (2015) term "deep relations," mentioned previously, is especially helpful in this context. In his writing about the late-twentieth century history of Pacific, and particularly Māori, engagements with Afrodiasporic cultures, political movements, philosophies and peoples, Shilliam offers the phrase to characterize what he understands as "a deep, global infrastructure of anti-colonial connectivity" (2015, 3). Shilliam argues for a politics of relationality or a "decolonial science" that he hopes can "redeem the possibilities of anti-colonial solidarity between colonized and (post)colonized peoples on terms other than those laid out by colonial science" (11). In doing so, he highlights the Māori concept of *whakapapa* as an indigenous Pacific way to encompass such relationality. Sometimes glossed simply as "genealogy," *whakapapa* translates more literally as "to make a ground/foundation" (25, citing Hudson et al. 2007). A whakapapa framework can establish how

> all entities—tangible and intangible—are therefore related as part of creation [and it is] less a passive rehearsal of genealogy [and] much more an intentional and creative (re-) cultivation of relations that constitute the cosmos, announced to the world in the form of storytelling (*whaikōrero*).
>
> (Shilliam 2015, 27)[3]

Pacific models of understanding genealogy and kinship, such as whakapapa, are useful for understanding how hip hop is enacted in Aotearoa. Pacific scholars highlight their flexibility and creativity, in contrast to Western models of biological descent, as well as their important condition of being stories told in the present—stories that are both an enactment of relationship and preparation for further forms of enactment (Tengan, Ka'ili and Fonoti 2010; Teaiwa 2014). A concept such as whakapapa has the capacity for recognizing and respecting the *mana* and integrity of local artists' multiple originary lines of influence—the fact that both indigenous Pacific ancestors and African American progenitors of hip hop, funk and soul were all necessary for their present moment to exist.

In existing literature on Aotearoa hip hop, the concept of whakapapa is linked to the ways local artists narrate and pay respect to their hip hop genealogies. Both Zemke-White (2002) and Gibson (2003) cite the song "Autahi" (which the artist translates as "The Lone One") (2000), a solo release by Upper Hutt Posse co-founder Te Kupu, as a pertinent example. The track is a rapped recitation of Te Kupu's political, cultural and musicological influences, ranging from iconic US hip hop tracks and black nationalist texts to New Zealand history programs and the Roland TR 808 drum machine. Te Kupu explicitly introduces the track with the words "*Ko toku whakapapa Hip Hop tenei*" (my hip hop whakapapa/genealogy). Te Kupu's former UHP bandmate, DLT, similarly relayed what he called his "hip hop whakapapa" to a curator at the Museum of New Zealand Te Papa Tongarewa as part of contextualizing the personal archive he donated to the museum in 2000 (Mallon 2014). As these examples illustrate, thus far the discussion of whakapapa in scholarly work on Aotearoa hip hop has focused on it as a way of conceptualizing and narrating *influences*—a way of understanding how artists such as Te Kupu and DLT recount the media, people and artistic tools and experiences that were formative in their personal journeys in hip hop. This parallels how, in English, people might refer to their "artistic genealogy."

Recalling Shillam's (2015) discussion, whakapapa is not just about reciting lines of descent from the past, however: it is also about articulating relationships in the present. How might we use the concept of whakapapa to think not just about overseas—and particularly American—*influences* on Aotearoa artists, but to further think about how these deeply felt and cherished genealogies are drawn on to prepare a "ground for relating" to US and other international artists in person? In the three moments of transnational hip hop encounter recounted at the start of this chapter, Wellington artists recognized each of their New York guests DJ Jazzy Jay, KRS-One and Immortal Technique as holding a particular place of prestige in a shared, transnational hip hop genealogy. Although each visitor's status and historic contributions to hip hop ensured local artists' respect and deference, the latter's gifting of food, garland and a song-laden ceremony of welcome bespoke a more deeply felt sense of connection. The bestowal of such gifts required extended moments of shared intimacy—the time needed to welcome someone into a home and feed him; to place a weighty necklace over a bowed head and explain its meaning; to guide visitors through all the perfunctory parts of a *pōwhiri*, from the intimidating initial challenge, called the *wero*, to the lengthy exchange of speeches and waiata to the final lifting of *tāpu* (freeing from restrictions) over shared food—and were premised on local artists' knowledge, and faith, that such moments would be afforded them. In other words, local artists trusted that if they prepared a ground for relating, that their international guests would meet them and recognize them in that relational space.

For Wellington artists, DJ Jazzy Jay was treated as a venerated elder or *kaumātua*, someone with deep and intimate knowledge of a revered spatial and temporal homeland of sorts for them and for hip hop artists all over the world: the South Bronx as it existed for the first generation of hip hop's creators in the 1970s and early 1980s. Local artists connected with Jazzy Jay through a network of human relationship: someone they knew was married to a friend of Jay's, and alerted them to an opportunity to host him on an upcoming visit. They were honored to host Jay in the home of Māori DJ and graffiti artist KERB1 and his Samoan wife, graffiti artist and dancer SpexOne, in a converted industrial building emblazoned, outside and in, with meticulously crafted aerosol letters and characters in the New York graffiti tradition. Over the course of an evening, Jazzy Jay amiably shared knowledge and food with the two dozen or so local artists and their family members and friends who had gathered. When he good-naturedly took his place on the turntables in the corner of the room, his DJ set was received as a gift by those assembled. Local artists had prepared the ground for relating to someone they considered part of their hip hop genealogy, and DJ Jazzy Jay reciprocated their display of kinship through the giving of his time, positive energy and the sharing of his artistic gift.

When KRS-One visited in 2012 for a concert at Wellington Town Hall, he was enthusiastically greeted by Wellington hip hop community members. The Bronx MC was part of the generation of New York artists that followed Jazzy Jay and achieved fame with his group Boogie Down Productions (BDP) in the late 1980s and later as a solo artist in the 1990s. Known equally for the influential gritty storytelling of BDP's first album, 1987's *Criminal Minded*, and later for his refashioned politically conscious persona, KRS-One is also notable for his consistently outspoken championing of hip hop culture. For Wellington artists, he is a respected elder, but less a *kaumātua* and more like a high-profile tribal spokesman— someone who inspires respect and more than a little awe, whose specific opinions some may question but whose commitment to and work on behalf of the extended family is beyond doubt. Their sense of connection to him was further deepened by their shared membership, at the time, in the Universal Zulu Nation (UZN), a global network characterized as "hip hop's oldest and largest organization." (Davey D n.d.) Among the local artists who greeted KRS-One was JUSE1, a talented MC, graffiti artist and tattooist of Samoan and Pākehā ancestry. It was JUSE who gave the African American artist the *'ulafala*, the distinctive red garland that is particularly associated with Samoan *tulafale* or orator chiefs.[4] While seemingly unusual as a hip hop accouterment, JUSE had deliberately bestowed the *'ulafala* to honor someone he considers the hip hop equivalent of an influential orator chief. JUSE's gift was also fostered by his faith that KRS-One would make time to engage with local artists and would recognize kinship with them through their shared membership in UZN, specifically, and through their shared commitment to and participation in hip hop more generally. In other words, JUSE had a sense that his gift would be received with dignity, and it was: the African American artist, often referred to by others and himself as The Teacha due to his capacity to articulate ideas, subsequently wore the *'ulafala* on stage for a significant portion of his performance.

Immortal Technique was raised in Harlem of Afro-indigenous Peruvian heritage. The youngest of the three international visitors, he consolidated his reputation in the early 2000s through releases that brought the aggression and devastating lyrical precision of a battle MC to fiercely political content that was anticolonial, anticapitalist and pro-indigenous. As Wellington MC KOS-163 joked after listening to Immortal Technique's 2003 album *Revolutionary Vol. 2*, "he makes conscious hip hop sound gangsta!" Immortal Technique regularly backs up his rhetoric with free performances supporting activist causes. Of the three international visitors, the Māori welcome organized for Immortal Technique was the most extensive gesture: the "ground for relating" prepared for him was, quite literally, the meeting ground of Kāpiti Marae, a 30-minute drive north of Wellington. Those from the Kāpiti area with existing connections to the marae took part in the *pōwhiri* on the hosting (*tangata whenua*) side, but artists from central Wellington accompanied Immortal Technique on the *manuhiri* (visitors) side, appropriately indicating that they were both visitors to this specific marae and part of a collectivity with the visiting artist. When he spoke, they rendered support (*tautoko*) in the form of song.

Immortal Technique wasn't the first international hip hop artist to be given a pōwhiri in Wellington, but local artists are selective in their desire to extend the honor to visitors: they are aware of unsatisfactory attempts to "give back" to international artists by honoring them with indigenous welcome formalities, only to have the gesture ignored or received with apparent disinterest or bemusement.[5] A common complaint is that promoters who facilitate tours by "mainstream" artists don't bother ensuring they are briefed on Māori protocol.

Local artists also express doubt that major international artists have any interest in fostering deeper connections with counterparts in Aotearoa; their sense of kinship with such acts is therefore ambivalent.[6] They hold more hope for connection with "oldschool" artists, or the younger international artists who profess respect for the oldschool in their lyrics or interviews—those who whakapapa to some of the same hip hop ancestors as Wellington counterparts. This is true of Immortal Technique, but his vocal commitment to indigenous causes gave Wellington hip hop artists added assurance that he would greet them as kin.

Conclusion: A Genealogy that Binds

Over the past fifteen years, positive exchanges with a number of visiting US hip hop artists have bolstered Wellington artists' confidence. This is not only because the American artists have passed along insights and techniques to augment local knowledge and practice, but also because they have repeatedly commended the spirit of the local hip hop community. Indeed, it is not unusual for older New York artists such as Afrika Bambataa to remark, more generally, that the excitement in hip hop communities outside the USA is "more true to the hip hop culture than America itself" (Fricke and Ahearn 2002, 336). Wellington artists hear such statements, and observe themselves the value of their specific cultural context when opportunities for comparison arise. A particularity of that context is the influence of Māori and Pacific cultures—even on community members not themselves of Polynesian ancestry. In the KRS-One encounter described earlier, for instance, it is indicative that the three local artists not of Māori or Pacific ancestry are either married to, in a domestic partnership with or in decades-spanning hip hop crews with Māori; Māori are inextricably part of their whakapapa. So, when one of those Wellington artists, Sen Thong (bboy Khmer), explained to a reporter in 2013 how Wellington artists have "inherited a culture," hip hop, but "developed our own angle and take on it" and "injected our own personal and ethnic cultures" (Johnstone 2013), I have no doubt that Thong—the son of a Cambodian refugee—implicitly accords a special place for Māori and Pacific cultures in his statement.

For Wellington artists, encounters with visiting US hip hop artists offer rich and complex opportunities for articulating relationship. Certainly, such encounters provide an opportunity for validation—for having their own hip hop practices acknowledged and commended by international artists whose opinions matter to them. But it would be wrong to *only* understand these exchanges as about seeking validation. Wellington artists also feel like they possess much to offer back to hip hop and to international artists. As SpexOne articulates,

> Like Samoan pride, being proud to be Maori—I felt we had something to give, rather than just to connect or take from. There's something we can offer in the way that we have kept our cultures but still connected into society.
>
> (Johnstone 2013)

In moments of encounter between local and international hip hop artists, a sense of "deep relations" manifests when both sides recognize and respect that each has something to offer from the rich particularity of their experience, while also understanding their overarching commonality—that they are all offspring of a shared genealogy that binds them.

Notes

1   The term Pākehā technically applies to all non-Māori New Zealanders, but in common usage is understood to mean those of European descent.
2   See Bennett 2002; Gibson 2003; Henderson 2006, 2010b; Mitchell 2001; Pearson 2004; Zemke-White 2001, 2002, 2005.
3   Shilliam also draws on an interview with Darcy Nicholls, and Roberts *et al.* 2004. The opening example of his monograph theorizes a 1979 moment of encounter between British-based Afrodiasporic performance troupe Keskidee and Māori from Ngāti Kuri in the far north of Aotearoa. Shilliam writes of the moment when both sides of this cultural encounter articulate relationship with one another—a mutual recognition of each other's ancestors, dignity and *mana.* Excited by the possibilities that a *whakapapa* approach can offer to understanding moments such as these, and the interrelatedness of Pacific and Afrodiasporic peoples more generally, Shilliam concludes, "Perhaps, then, oceans (Pacific and Atlantic) and racial categorizations (black and brown) are only manifest barriers to peoples that can be bound back together at deeper levels. A ground can always be creatively prepared for relating" (2015, 27). Further consideration of relationality emerged in a panel coordinated by Teresia Teaiwa at the 2016 Pacific History Association Conference in Guam, "Afro-Diasporic Women Artists on History and Blackness in the Pacific," featuring Teaiwa, Ojeya Cruz Banks, Joy Enomoto, Courtney Savali-Andrews and Alisha Lola-Jones. Cruz-Banks, a dance studies scholar, subsequently offered further cogent analysis in her paper "Māoritanga Sampling Hip Hop: The Poiyonce Example" (2016).
4   Samoan history records how particular *tulafale* have, through their powerful oratory, exerted influence on swaths of the Samoan population. See Davidson (1970).
5   For example, news media widely reported that US artist Bow Wow ignored the Māori performers arranged by the promoter of his 2012 tour to welcome him when he arrived at Auckland Airport.
6   Teaiwa and Mallon offer the rich phrase "ambivalent kinships" to characterize flexible and contextual articulations of relationship between New Zealand's Pacific migrant populations and Māori, Pākehā and those in island homelands (2005, 207).

Bibliography

Bennett, Edgar Tamieni. 2002. "Scratchin' the Surface: Hip-Hop and the Social Construction of Auckland's Polynesian Youth Identities." MA thesis (Geography), University of Auckland.

Cruz-Banks, Ojeya. 2016. "Māoritanga Sampling Hip-Hop: The Poiyonce Example." Paper presented at Te Kōkī New Zealand School of Music's Music Forum, October 7.

Davey D. n.d. "Zulu Nation: From Gang to Glory." www.daveyd.com/zulunationhistory.html (accessed January 24, 2018).

Davidson, J.W. 1970. "Lauaki Namulau'ulu Mamoe: A Traditionalist in Samoan Politics." In *Pacific Island Portraits*, edited by J.W. Davidson and Deryck Scarr. Canberra: ANU Press, 267–299.

Fricke, Kim and Charlie Ahearn. 2002. *Yes Yes Y'all: The Experience Music Project Oral History of Hip-Hop's First Decade.* Cambridge, MA: De Capo Books.

Gibson, Lorena. 2003. "Versioning for the Love of It: Hip-Hop Culture in *Aotearoa.*" MA thesis (Anthropology), Massey University.

Henderson, April K. 2006. "Dancing Between Islands: Hip-Hop and the Samoan Diaspora." In *The Vinyl Aint Final: Hip Hop and the Globalization of Black Popular Culture,* edited by Dipannita Basu and Sidney J. Lemelle. London: Pluto Press, 180–199.

Henderson, April K. 2010a. "Connectedness and Identity in a Multiethnic 'Community of Interest.'" In *Youth Voices, Youth Choices: Identity, Integration and Social Cohesion in Culturally Diverse Aotearoa/New Zealand,* by Colleen Ward, James Liu, Tagaloa Peggy Fairbairn-Dunlop and April K. Henderson. Wellington: Centre for Applied Cross-Cultural Research and Va'aomanū Pasifika, Victoria University of Wellington, 12–19.

Henderson, April K. 2010b. "Gifted Flows: Making Space for a Brand New Beat." *The Contemporary Pacific* 22 (2): 293–315.

Ho'omanawanui, Ku'ualoha. 2006. "From Ocean to O-Shen: Reggae, Rap and Hip Hop in Hawai'i." In *Crossing Waters, Crossing Paths: Black and Indian Journeys,* edited by Tiya Miles and Sharon P. Holland, 273–308. Durham, NC: Duke University Press.

Hudson, Maui L., Annabel L.M. Ahuriri-Driscoll, Marino G. Lea and Rod A. Lea. 2007. "Whakapapa—A Foundation for Genetic Research?" *Journal of Bioethical Enquiry* 4 (1) (March): 43–49.

Imada, Adrian. 2006. "Head Rush: Hip-Hop and a Hawaiian Nation 'On the Rise.'" In *The Vinyl Aint Final: Hip-Hop and the Globalization of Black Popular Culture,* edited by Dipannita Basu and Sidney J. Lemelle. London: Pluto Press, 85–99.

Johnstone, Tessa. 2013. "Hip-Hop Don't Stop for Zulus." stuff.co.nz, 7 May. www.stuff.co.nz/entertainment/music/8630334/Hip hop-don-t-stop-for-Zulus (accessed June 15, 2017).

Mallon, Sean. 2014. "Hip-Hop Was Here … from Day 1." [blog] Museum of New Zealand Te Papa Tongarewa. http://blog.tepapa.govt.nz/2014/12/02/hip-hop-was-herefrom-day-1 (accessed January 24, 2018).

Mitchell, Tony. 2001. "Kia Kaha! Māori and Pacific Islander Hip-hop in Aotearoa-New Zealand." In *Global Noise: Rap and Hip-Hop Outside the USA*, edited by Tony Mitchell. Hartford, CT: Wesleyan University Press, 280–305.

Pearson, Sarina. 2004. "Pasifik/NZ Frontiers: New Zealand–Samoan Hip-Hop, Music Video, and Diasporic Space." *Perfect Beat: The Pacific Journal for Research into Contemporary Music and Popular Culture* 6 (4): 55–66.

Pennycook, Alistair. 2007. "Language, Localization and the Real: Hip-Hop and the Global Spread of Authenticity." *Journal of Language, Identity, and Education* 6 (2): 101–115.

Pennycook, Alistair and Tony Mitchell. 2009. "Hip-Hop as Dusty Foot Philosophy: Engaging Locality." In *Global Linguistic Flows: Hip-Hop Cultures, Youth Identities, and the Politics of Language,* edited by H. Samy Alim, Awad Ibrahim and Alistair Pennycook. New York: Routledge, 25–42.

Perry, Imani. 2004. *Prophets of the Hood: Politics and Poetics in Hip-Hop.* Durham, NC: Duke University Press.

Roberts, Mere, Bradford Haami, Richard A Benton, Terre Satterfield, Melissa L. Finucane, Mark Henare and Manuka Henare. 2004. "Whakapapa as a Māori Mental Construct: Some Implications for the Debate over Genetic Modification of Organisms." *The Contemporary Pacific* 16 (1): 1–28.

Scott, Mark. 1985. *StreetAction Aotearoa.* Auckland: Arohanui Publications.

Shilliam, Robbie. 2015. *The Black Pacific: Anti-Colonial Struggles and Oceanic Connections.* London: Bloomsbury.

Tamati, Sara [SpexOne]. 2004. "A Window to OUR WORLD." In *The Next—An Impression of Hip-Hop Expression,* co-authored by Yadana Saw, Sara Tamati and Danica Waiti. Wellington: Global Education Centre, 15–74.

Teaiwa, Teresia. 2014. "The Ancestors We Get to Choose: White Ancestors I Won't Deny." In *Theorizing Native Studies,* edited by Audra Simpson and Andrea Smith. Durham, NC: Duke University Press, 43–55.

Teaiwa, Teresia and Sean Mallon. 2005. "Ambivalent Kinships? Pacific People in New Zealand." In *New Zealand Identities: Departures and Destinations,* edited by J.H. Liu, T. McCreanor, T. McIntosh and T. Teaiwa. Wellington: Victoria University Press, 207–229.

Tengan, Ty P. Kāwika, Tevita O. Ka'ili and Rochelle Tuitagava'a Fonoti. 2010. "Genealogies: Articulating Indigenous Anthropology in/of Oceania." *Pacific Studies* 33 (2/3): 139–167.

Tha Feelstyle. 2003. Interview with author. Digital recording. Newtown, Wellington, April 15.

Verán, Cristina. 2002. "Hip Hop's Pacific Promised Land," *Oneworld* (April/May): 84–91.

Verán, Cristina. 2006. "Native Tongues." In *Total Chaos: The Art and Aesthetics of Hip hop,* edited by Jeff Chang. New York: Basic Civitas Books, 278–290.

Wendt, Albert. 1986. "The Contest." *Landfall* 40 (2): 144–153.

Wright, Andrew. 2006. Interview with author. Digital recording. Newtown, Wellington, December 2.

Zemke-White, Kirsten. 2001. "Rap Music and Pacific Identity in Aotearoa: Popular Music and the Politics of Oppression." In *Tangata O Te Moana Nui: The Evolving Identities of Pacific Peoples in Aotearoa/New Zealand,* edited by Cluny MacPherson, Paul Spoonley and Melani Anae. Palmerston North: Dunmore Press, 228–242.

Zemke-White, Kirsten. 2002. "Keeping It Real (Indigenous): Hip-Hop in Aotearoa as Community, Culture, and Consciousness." In *Cultural Studies in Aotearoa New Zealand: Identity, Space and Place,* edited by Claudia Bell and Steve Matthewman. Oxford: Oxford University Press, 205–228.

Zemke-White, Kirsten. 2005. "'How Many Dudes You Know Roll Like This?': The Re-Presentation of Hip-Hop Tropes in New Zealand Rap Music." *Image & Narrative* 10 (March): 1–16. www.imageandnarrative.be/worldmusica/kirstenzemkewhite.htm (accessed June 16, 2016).

Discography

Boogie Down Productions. 1987. *Criminal Minded.* New York: B-Boy Records.
Immortal Technique. 2003. *Revolutionary Vol. 2.* New York: Viper Records.
Te Kupu. 2000. "Aotahi," On *Ko Te Matakahi Kupu* [album]. Wellington: Kia Kaha Productions.
Upper Hutt Posse. 1988. "E Tu," [non-album single] Wellington: Jayrem Records.

Filmography

Drago, Carla (director). 1998. *Island Style: Young People Forging a Unique Identity.* West Brunswick, Victoria: FrontRow Distribution.
Silver, Tony (director). 1983. *Style Wars.* New York: Public Art Films.

14
The Music City
Australian Contexts

Shane Homan

Introduction

> We built this city on rock'n'roll ... and apartments ... Just once wouldn't it be great if some apartments were knocked down to build a music venue.
>
> (O'Neil 2014, 2)

A few blocks from the pleasant English seaside, one hundred and twenty delegates from fifty cities attended a one-day forum investigating global examples of the "music city." The Music Cities Convention in Brighton on 13 May 2015 hosted a series of presentations on the role of music in Barcelona, Melbourne, Liverpool, Mannheim, Groningen, Addis Ababa, Adelaide, Capetown, Berlin and Montreal. Although the competition among presenters (and, by extension, their cities) for global branding status was explicit at times, the mix of industry and government strategies on display was impressive.

Understandings of the "cultural" or "creative" city may have a longer history, but the "music city" has certainly arrived in the halls of government and industry as a central plank of social, cultural and economic policy for both art and popular music. In this chapter, I want to first examine how popular music has come to be considered as important to cities in a range of contexts, and the central urban, industrial and cultural precepts for its uses. I will then explore the ways in which the "music city" has been understood and developed in Australia in the last decade, and the localized peculiarities of Australian experiences and policies. As we shall see, although the concept has entered into common usage by fans, musicians and policy-makers, it remains contentious in the development of strategies and in meanings constructed by different music industry sectors and levels of government. As such, the "music city" is a fascinating concept in which to assess the cross-currents between the social, cultural and economic meanings of urban life.

The Music City: Culture as Primer

We can envisage the "literature city," the "information city" or the "film city" (Hall 1998). The "music city" promises an abundance of activity: music in the streets, in the classrooms, at the airport, on our turntables and smart phones, on the local airwaves and in the civic theater and hall. In contrast to the older high art conceptions of the "cultural city," it involves busking as much as the professional concert; the club DJ as much as the orchestra cellist.

180 • Shane Homan

Above all, whether music or sculpture, museums or theater, culture holds the promise of constructing unique civic, industrial and individual identities. In relation, although they are not interchangeable, the conditions for producing the "knowledge economy city" (e.g. Clifton 2008; Communian and Faggian 2011) or the "bohemian city" (Florida 2002a) have been useful in emphasizing the interconnected nature of different sectors and activities. The "creative city," and by extension, the "music city," can be mapped across three broad themes connecting the cultural to the urban.

First, spatial structure is important. Clusters of capital and labor have been argued to provide distinctive agglomeration and complementarity of music services, labor and products. New York, for example, draws upon its rich and intimate mix of recording, venue, agency and music retail infrastructure (Gendron 2006; Currid 2007). Music Row in downtown Nashville is a famous conglomeration of publishing, recording, radio and licensing businesses which "cross-pollinat[e] with other parts of the economy, be it healthcare or media, that rely heavily on information technology workers" (IFPI/Music Canada 2015, 28). Particularly close proximity of music businesses and workers that facilitates face to face contact can also be a further driver of innovation (Watson 2008).

Secondly, the uses of culture, high and low, to drive economic growth, and in many cases to recover "lost" urban areas and economies, have been well documented in popular music contexts (e.g. Cohen 2007). This may take the form of a lift in city/regional outputs, increased sector investment, workforce skills development or direct and indirect employment. To return to the Nashville example, its "home of country" status produces "more than 56,000 jobs within the Nashville area, supports more than US$3.2bn of annual labor income, and contributes US$5.5bn to the local economy for a total output of US$9.7bn" (IFPI/Music Canada 2015, 22).

Thirdly, both spatial and economic structures are clearly entwined with promotional strategies and outcomes. In some cases, music heritage is deployed to further tourism, where cities play to their historic strengths as symbolic foundational sites in popular music (Liverpool, London, Detroit). Others have promoted sector strengths: Austin as the world's live music capital, Berlin as dance party capital. Wellington, New Zealand is a good example where its city leaders have constructed a purposeful narrative since the 1990s. This has included music business skills development, a festivals strategy, greater use of city buildings and spaces for music and more funding to connect music education institutions with training and performance (Wellington City Council 2014). This represents the shift from managerial to entrepreneurial strategies, with the state as active cheerleader:

> The types and extent of state intervention remain tricky, yet Wellington's desire to continue to roll the dice on the digital and cultural industries shows what is at stake. Here, notions of the self-actualised musician have been transferred to the self-actualised city. Wellington's promotional campaigns have thus addressed itself as a positive, self-motivated person, 'Positively'[1] not allowed to fail through sheer good humour and persistence. This has been visibly successful, in making the right connections between lived material cultures at one end, and increasingly sophisticated digital and media entrepreneurialism at the other. This has also involved implementing a reverse advocacy model at times, with the state actively seeking input.
>
> (Homan, Cloonan and Cattermole 2016, 112)

These three themes accord with a recent report outlining the shopping list for a music city: "Artists and musicians; a thriving music scene; access to spaces and places; a receptive and engaged audience; and record labels and other music-related businesses" (along with state support, infrastructure and education programs) (IFPI/Music Canada 2015, 13). Cross-pollination is also evident in merging the technological, cultural and creative in Quebec City's claims as a "techno-cultural capital" (Gouvernement du Québec 2014, 25), or Berlin's "Smart City" status, with music start-ups and hubs playing important roles. The accentuated notions of music creativity and the re-imagining of city branding reflect the influence of Richard Florida's "creative class" thesis among city leaders, where it is sometimes difficult to separate the hyper-promotional from the economic and spatial outcomes. The effect of Florida's work has also produced a circular effect: the production of global league tables for consumption by politicians and cultural strategists ("is my city doing well?") meant a greater likelihood that cities would engage with the central prescriptions in an endless competition for status.

The recent global music city report produced by Music Canada and the International Federation of Phonographic Industries (IFPI) in 2015 also outlined future strategies which can be regarded as retrospective markers: "music-friendly and musician-friendly policies; a Music Office or Officer; a Music Advisory Board; engaging the broader music community to get their buy-in and support; access to spaces and places; and audience development" (IFPI/Music Canada 2015, 13–15). If we delete "music," we could arguably insert (for example) "fashion," "gaming" or "film." Why has popular music, in contrast to ministerial responses to other cultural industries to "sink or swim" (McRobbie 2012, 81), found favor? There is a view that musicians' entrepreneurial instincts afford them a better fit with governments' neo-liberal emphases, as a natural small business community. In some instances, cities have chosen to exploit what was already there, in existing organic music scenes and micro-hubs of music businesses, refining "unique component[s] of the final product as well as an authentication of substantive and symbolic quality" (Scott 2006, 10). This also perhaps speaks to the ubiquity of popular music, which makes it easier to leverage both internal and external uses and specializations.

A trawl through the academic and policy/strategy literature can enforce the idea that the music city is a natural and inevitable one for many locations. It can be argued that there now exists a global policy template in terms of strategic action. Edinburgh, for example, seeks input from Glasgow and Austin as to best live music strategies, while seeking to adopt Melbourne's agent of change principle (see below) (City of Edinburgh 2014, 4; City of Edinburgh 2015, 13). The success and visibility of popular music policies within wider city policies has attracted both bemusement and envy among other cultural sectors, even as classical music retains the majority of available funding at national levels. However, the rise of the music city has not been without its problems, and in the next section I wish to briefly canvas the recurring points of tension, where the cultural/creative must be reconciled with much wider issues of regulation and governance.

Governing the Music City

It is useful to remember that cultural policy, including music policy, is always politically framed (no pun intended). As successful as cultural/creative industry advocates have been in ensuring the flow of commensurate policies, cultural policy, like all others, enters into contested terrain on several fronts. Music "*embodies* political values and experiences, and *organizes* our responses to society as political thought and action . . . [it] does not just provide a vehicle of political expression, it *is* that expression" (Street 2010, 1; emphasis in original). The *value* of popular music to fans, musicians, industry workers, governments and other city populations is obviously important. Is access to music a human right, as argued by some (including UNESCO)? Further, those advocating for popular music policies and funding must contend with the finite economic resources of government, and the competing demands of health, education, transport, environment and the like on public expenditure and emphasis.

One means of dissecting such tensions between the political and the cultural is through ideas and practices of "the market" as they apply to music city policies. Historically, music has symbolized the distinctions between the market and the state: "the preservation of art and classical music can be regarded as neo-conservatism, where older definitions of 'culture' and 'heritage' provide mutual reinforcement" (Homan et al. 2016, 6), with commercial musics (pop, rock, country) left to fend for themselves. Here, discourses can be revealed by inverting their central logic. If the city can happily contemplate the construction of new concert halls for classical music (Higgins 2015), even in times of austerity, why does this not apply to other music forms? The "market failure" thesis can no longer be solely applied to classical/art music. The well-rehearsed industrial and regulatory obstacles precipitating venue closures for all forms of music performance attest to this. In this sense, music city proponents have had to contend with older values of "excellence" that have prioritized high art music, and its related concert and education infrastructure.

"Market forces" have also played a role in the greatest source of tension in the music city: land use policy. Rising property values in key CBD areas have threatened or eliminated music venues. The original Florida thesis—that attraction of the funky and the creative to rundown downtowns would foster an urban renaissance—in many cases has worked too well.[2] In London, one of the most fervent believers in the "animal spirits" of the free market, former Mayor Boris Johnson (2013), has expressed concern: "it's so worrying that we're seeing the pressure from property prices, the pressure from development, take away so many of those venues across town" (Johnson 2015): cause and effect neatly compartmentalized.

This, in effect, is driving new clusters of residential zones to replace older cultural ones. (In)famous Soho in London, through redevelopment, sees "identikit gimmicky pop-up hipster venues replacing cafes, restaurants, bars and shops that have been in situ for years" (Vaines 2015, 9). More appropriately, a London pub—the foundational home of UK garage— is to become a real estate agent's office (Khomami 2015). The wider industrial effects have been profound: a 38 percent reduction in London's music venues, accompanied by a reduction in the length of UK tours for artists (Davyd 2015). The anger among musicians can be considerable: at the 2015 launch of Edinburgh's creative city plan, the "dynamic city-wide conversation" (City of Edinburgh 2015, 5) quickly narrowed into fierce questions from the floor about the loss of music and theater venues, and the absence of town planners and developers from the "conversation."

We need to be careful here to distinguish between the types and causes of displacement involved with gentrification. There is property displacement—the familiar swap of cultural/

commercial for residential, where local councils and state governments profit from the "rent gap" in conversions of older venue sites to apartments. There is also displacement of modes of cultural activity in the rise of "festivalization and the role of festivals in agendas of culture as a resource and expedient" (Holt and Wergin 2013, 6) that can smooth away other micro-music activities. And, of course, there is displacement of peoples, with artist as shiny prophet (evidence of new populations of middle class consumerism) or villain (evidence of new populations of middle class consumerism!). As Paton has observed, more work is needed on the shifts and effects upon working class populations (which includes musicians excluded from the regeneration "miracle"). Culture, and music, is implicated not only in gentrification as urban regeneration, but in managing the "decline of people and place" (Paton 2014, 40).

Further, if "gentrification foregrounds the relationship between property and propriety" (Paton 2014, 40), other regulatory codes matter. New York's "three musician rule," designed to eradicate black jazz combos and venues (Chevigny 1993), was first and foremost a gentri-fication strategy. Noise disputes related to music venues are deeply implicated in the property-gentrification nexus, as significant contributors to urban "improvement." They are often the trigger for redevelopment or rezoning. We also have to consider liquor licensing and build-ing code laws that enforce different combinations of acoustic, drinking, crowd management and building capacities.

For many cities, the options vary according to histories and politics. Zoning—areas desig-nated as music or cultural zones/precincts/clusters—has been proposed as one means of protection (explored below). Discourses of heritage are emerging as the central weapon in battling combinations of regulatory change. Again, preferences seem to be based on class and market indicators:

> It's a lot easier to make a case for ornate places because they have stature, but heritage doesn't always have to be pretty ... Sometimes the grotty needs to be protected. Some people think The Silver Dollar is a hole.
> (Mary MacDonald, Toronto Heritage Preservation Services, cited in IFPI/Music Canada 2015, 39)

We can thus begin to see how particular mixtures of heritage, licensing, noise and land use planning underline competing discourses of cultural city "vibrancy" (underpinned by an unleashing of market forces), and the centrality of law and order. In this sense, the music city cannot become too successful, for its presence may become literally too audible and visible. I will now turn to examining recent Australian urban contexts, and how the state city capitals have sought national and global advantage through discourses and strategies of the music city.

The Australian Experience

Are there particularly Australian aspects to constructions and meanings of the music city? The state capitals have engaged in some forms of "flexible specialization" (Scott 2006, 3): Melbourne's strengths in public music radio, concert infrastructure and music education; Sydney's housing of globally recognized recording studios and as headquarters to major international labels, for example. All have privileged live music as the primary economic, spatial and promotional mechanism. Indeed, Melbourne, boasting more venues per capita than London or Austin, is staking a global claim as the world's live music capital to promote a cachet of direct origin.[3]

The choices are informed by history and necessity. The ability to "deliver" to live audiences has been particularly important for older "Oz Rock" mythologies, steeped in the connections between pub rock fans, bands and venues. Australians favor the live experience in general: "78 tickets to performing arts events were sold for every 100 Australians in 2013" (Australia Council 2015, 11). A 2011 study found 41.97 million attendances at 3,904 music venues across Australia, generating revenues of AUD$1.21 billion (Australasian Performing Right Association 2011, 4). In the Victorian context, more people attend live venues than other dominant leisure forms, including horse racing and the premier winter sport, the Australian Football League (Arts Victoria 2011, iii). The wealth of live venues has not transposed, however, to the individual wealth of musicians. Various studies have revealed professional musicians' wages to be below creative artist medians, and below national average incomes (Parker 2015; Throsby and Zednik 2010). Musicians, even famous ones, make less than AUD$600 per week from their local live circuits (Salmon 2011, 17).

The Australian advantage in live music infrastructure has arguably placed its cities as global innovators in several ways. In Brisbane, the local and state government established Fortitude Valley as an entertainment precinct, based on existing clusters of recording, rehearsal, music agency and venue businesses. The primacy of live music is maintained through planning, policing and liquor licensing laws that reverse city norms: the city explicitly calls out the *resident* as unnatural fit with the cityscape.

In Sydney, the recent *Live Music and Performance Action Plan* (City of Sydney 2014) found liquor licensing, noise and planning controls were still the primary factors impeding venue growth, despite earlier reforms, notably the introduction of a live music liquor licence, and the abolition of the burdensome Place of Public Entertainment licence.[4] A recent Sydney University/City of Sydney *Creative Spaces and the Built Environment* forum outlined the challenges for new creative spaces. After taking out mortgages with five co-investors to purchase a disused garage, Penelope Benton required AUD$165,000 in compliance costs and a further AUD$50,000 in general set-up costs to establish a music/exhibition space, The Red Rattler, in Marrickville in Sydney's inner west (Benton 2015). Instead of encouragement to develop an exciting new venue from the city's abandoned spaces, Benton faced conflicting advice and regulation from the City Council, and regulation that did not apply to configuration or use.

Situated in the middle of the southern coast, Adelaide has been proactive, commissioning its *Future of Live Music in South Australia* (Elbourne 2013), followed by a Music Development Office to broker funding, regulatory and industrial networks in the state. Some aspects of licensing reform have been achieved, with a 2015 amendment to the *Licensing Act* removing the need for Entertainment Consent Applications and its AUD$500 fee (Marsh 2015). Like Adelaide, Hobart and Perth, lacking economies of scale, have employed other points of difference. Perth has promoted its "outsider" status, employing the "tyranny of distance" as enabling strategy (e.g. Brabazon 2005). Hobart, the capital of Tasmania in the more remote south, has leveraged the success of MONA (Museum of Old and New Art). Funded by MONA, MOFO has been a successful music/performance festival since 2009, curated by Violent Femmes' bass guitarist Brian Richie in keeping with the "eccentric" branding motif of the museum.

Finally, it is worth returning to Melbourne's recent innovations, where the promotional rhetoric is complicated by the spatial and economic. The city's 1980s "doughnut syndrome of an empty central core" (Adams 2005, 58) has been too successfully reversed. Heeding the call to "pay attention to the historical sweep of a form of urban restructuring that dates in many cities to the late 1960s" (Ley 2003, 2536), Kate Shaw has mapped relationships between land use planning, gentrification and cultural activity that reveal a considerable emptying out of "indie" creative businesses from the Melbourne CBD and its surrounding suburbs (Shaw 2013). The council has imitated other cities in providing a Creative Spaces program that converts unwanted city spaces into creative studios. Yet this has to be regarded as a Band-aid solution in attempting to redress the flight of musicians and other creative workers.

The city has been busy in other respects, especially the vexed question of music venue noise. The agent of change principle, first suggested in 2003 (Carbines 2003), is simple in its premise, but promises to be complex in its implementation. The "agent" is that (either resident or venue) which has changed the environment. The corollary effects for venues changing their provision of music (extended hours, increased sound volume, room capacities) is to take steps as the change agent in their neighborhood to ameliorate its adverse effects. For residents or developers, building or moving next door to an existing venue might mean adequate soundproofing of houses/apartments as the change agent. Introduced as legislation in September 2014, Melbourne's music industry awaits a test case dispute to validate the State government's *bona fides*.

In addition, the new Victorian Labor government has granted extended night-time trading hours for small venues, and allocated AUD$1.48 million in its four-year Music Works package to its Good Music Neighbours program, to assist venues with acoustic design, soundproofing and related improvements. The heritage contexts of a "Good Music Neighbour" are interesting here. St Kilda's Palais Theatre was promised AUD$13.4 million by the incoming Labor government during the 2014 state election after local rock star Tex Perkins offered himself as a single-issue candidate on its restoration (Cook 2014, 19). There seemed to be inter-governmental consensus in fixing a beautiful 1927 theater that is a mainstay of international touring. In contrast, the Palace Theatre in downtown Bourke Street, a "mishmash of different building styles since 1912," has struggled to make a heritage case on its significance to music and touring circuits (Dow 2015). Problems in finding willing developers to take on the venue, which requires significant expenditure, have been exacerbated by one developer's (shelved) plans to build a seven-storey hotel on the site (Dow 2014). Despite claims to heritage status from the National Trust and Melbourne City Council, the Victorian Civil and Administrative Tribunal ruled for its demolition in April 2016 (Dow 2016).

Even in announcing further "good news"—that small venues could now trade after midnight and weren't beholden to the licensing hours "freeze" visited upon other sites—the binary between the market and public order is always there: "The Andrews Labor government is committed to ensuring a safe and responsible drinking culture while also supporting a vibrant nightlife in our city" (Garrett 2015). This speaks to a longer history than 2009, and the unsubstantiated claims of the previous Labor government of the role of venues in propelling "alcohol-fuelled violence" (Homan 2010). This followed previously unsuccessful strategies such as a 2 a.m. "lockout" for entertainment premises, which had many exemptions, and was legally challenged (Reece 2014, 18).[5]

Conclusion

What I have attempted to describe and analyze is a series of reifications of the city: notions of the "music city" are hyper-idealized representations of cultural and urban forms. In such representations, "only some aspects are given to be seen, while others remain out of sight" (Shields 1996, 246). The "music city" descriptor is both self-referential and self-enabling: proof of at least some of the accepted components is followed by demands for more policy and funding resources. How popular music flits across the city is the source of both its flaws and strengths. It reinforces the need for a holistic view that properly accounts for the full range of activities, from land use to transport, professional to amateur music-making, education to liquor law. The now accepted wisdom of a city music office to ride shotgun across the entire city policy machinery attests to this.

Music city debates also reflect the increasingly global nature of policy discourse in the context of established western nations with accompanying cultural policies. Canada, Britain, the United States and New Zealand are learning from Australia's renewed focus on urban planning and licensing laws to address the vulnerability of its venues that in many ways reflect late capitalism's sharp outcomes from particular mixes of capital, property and labor flows. The current solidarism of local peak bodies and policy networks are also being replicated internationally, as cities come to recognize that they must match the global reach and shared knowledge of not just the larger music-media corporations, but to also acknowledge the increasing list of "local" problems that are now self-evidently global, including a music precariat that increasingly relies on established touring networks (and not the trickle of streaming revenue) for their viability.

Yet it is also clear that in many cases, the Australian "music city" simply amounts to the "music venue city." Historical emphases upon live music policy have masked other struggles and other components of music city ecologies. City leaders are used to the grand statement in physical infrastructure; it does the "small, quirky, innovative cultural business" (City of Sydney 2013, 34) less well. It is here that Australian policy-makers could learn from the European and North American experiences, in beginning to examine the linkages between macro- and micro-scenes, the localized threads that ensure the best means of supporting the "subcultural entrepreneurs" (McRobbie 2012, 80), those running "indie" labels, community radio, rehearsal rooms, local recording studios or (diminishing) record stores. This includes the "toilet circuit" of small venues, where the musical experience takes precedent over (and enhances) the apparent lack of suitability of the building (Hann 2014).

In one sense, the Australian contexts outlined here reflect popular music's role in the ever-increasing global competition between cities in attracting labor and capital. Perversely, renewed attention to the intensely local sets of infrastructures described above remains the best means for small-to-medium music trading nations (such as Australia and New Zealand) to offset the globally complex networks of rights and intersections within the broader music

The Music City • 187

industries. Yet there is something else going on here. At its base, the renewed attention on music city scenes is not simply a response to the prevailing economic discourses, but an insistence by residents that music remains vital to neighborhoods and street life.

Notes

1 This refers to the "Absolutely, Positively Wellington" promotional campaign of 2013.
2 Florida (2013) has qualified his earlier findings by asserting that "On close inspection, talent clustering provides little in the way of trickle-down benefits," and notes the adverse effects of higher housing costs in "larger, more skilled metros."
3 The author is also guilty of engaging in this process: *The Music Capital: City of Melbourne Music Strategy* (Homan and Newton 2010).
4 The author was part of the Live Music Taskforce leading up to the publication of the report.
5 In contrast, the moral panic surrounding "one-punch" deaths in Sydney's CBD drew a swift response from then NSW Premier Barry O'Farrell, who established 1 a.m. "lockout" and 3 a.m. "last drinks" laws in February 2014. Media reports have discussed falling rates of violence and hospital emergency traffic in the city at weekends (Olding 2015). However, it has adversely affected nightclub profits, and others have argued that it has simply moved patron management problems to those venues and suburbs located just outside the CBD boundary (Skalrud 2014).

Bibliography

Adams, Rob. 2005. "Melbourne: Back from the Edge." In *Cityedge: Case Studies in Contemporary Urbanism*, edited by Esther Charlesworth. Oxford: Elsevier, 50–64.
Arts Victoria. 2011. *The Economic, Social and Cultural Contribution of Venue-Based Live Music in Victoria*. Report prepared by Deloitte Access Economics. Melbourne: Victorian Government.
Australasian Performing Right Association. 2011. *Economic Contribution of the Venue-Based Live Music Industry in Australia*. Report prepared by Ernst and Young. Sydney: Australasian Performing Right Association.
Australia Council. 2015. *Arts Nation: An Overview of Australian Arts*. Sydney: Australia Council for the Arts.
Benton, Penelope. 2015. "NFP Artist and Activist Run Initiative in Marrickville, NSW," *Creative Spaces and Built Environment Forum*, June 12. Newtown: University of Sydney.
Beth, Jehnny. 2014. "Show Us the Money: How the Music Industry Can Save the UK's Small Venues." *Guardian*, December 18.
Brabazon, Tara. 2005. *Liverpool of the South Seas: Perth and Its Popular Music*. Crawley: University of Western Australia Press.
Carbines, Elaine. 2003. *Live Music Taskforce: Report and Recommendations*. December 5. Melbourne: Victorian Government.
Chevigny, Paul. 1993. *Gigs: Jazz and the Cabaret Laws in New York City (After the Law)*. New York and London: Routledge.
City of Edinburgh. 2015. *Desire Lines: A Call to Action from Edinburgh's Cultural Community*. Edinburgh: City of Edinburgh Council.
City of Edinburgh. 2014. *Encouraging Live Music in Edinburgh: Update*. December 16. Edinburgh: Culture and Sport Committee, City of Edinburgh Council.
City of Sydney. 2014. *Live Music and Performance Action Plan*. Sydney: City of Sydney. www.cityofsydney. nsw.gov.au/__data/assets/pdf_file/0007/232783/Live-Music-and-Performance-Action-Plan.pdf (accessed June 6, 2017).
City of Sydney. 2013. *Creative City: Cultural Policy Discussion Paper*. Sydney: City of Sydney.
Clifton, Nick. 2008. "The 'Creative Class' in the UK: An Initial Analysis." *Geografska Annaler: Series B, Human Geography* 90: 63–82.
Cohen, Sara. 2007. *Decline, Renewal and the City in Popular Music Culture: Beyond the Beatles*. Aldershot: Ashgate.
Communian, Roberta and Faggian, Alessandra. 2011. "Higher Education and the Creative City." In *Handbook of Creative Cities* edited by David Andersson, Åke Andersson and Charlotte Mellander. Cheltenham and Northampton, MA: Edward Elgar, 187–207.
Cook, Henrietta. 2014. "Labor Promises $13.4m to Save Palais Theatre." *The Age*, November 18. www.theage.com.au/victoria/victoria-state-election-2014/labor-promises-134m-to-save-the-palais-theatre-20141117-11orss. html (accessed January 24, 2018).

188 • Shane Homan

Currid, Elizabeth. 2007. *The Warhol Economy: How Fashion, Art, and Music Drive New York City*. Princeton, NJ: Princeton University Press.

Davyd, Mark. 2015. "Small Venues, Big Developers: The Case For and Against Small Venues and What It Means for the United Kingdom." Music Cities Convention, May 13, Brighton.Dow, Aisha. 2016. "Palace Theatre to be Demolished: VCAT." *The Age*, April 22. www.theage.com.au/victoria/palace-theatre-to-be-demolished-vcat-20160422-goczqz.html (accessed January 24, 2018).

Dow, Aisha. 2015. "Palace Theatre Appeal 'Test Case' for Melbourne Heritage Battles." *The Age*, March 30. www.theage.com.au/victoria/palace-theatre-appeal-test-case-for-melbourne-heritage-battles-20150330-1mb35a.html (accessed January 24, 2018).

Dow, Aisha. 2014. "Palace Theatre No Longer Worth Protecting After Recent Damage: New Report from Independent Heritage Consultant Graeme Butler." *The Age*, December 2. www.theage.com.au/victoria/palace-theatre-no-longer-worth-protecting-after-recent-damage-new-report-from-independent-heritage-consultant-graeme-butler-20141202-11yapt.html (accessed January 24, 2018).

Elbourne, Martin. 2013. *The Future of Live Music in South Australia*. Adelaide: Don Dunstan Foundation/University of Adelaide.

Florida, Richard. 2013. "More Losers than Winners in America's New Economic Geography," *The Atlantic*, January 30. www.citylab.com/work/2013/01/more-losers-winners-americas-new-economic-geography/4465 (accessed September 14, 2017).

Florida, Richard. 2002a. "Bohemia and Economic Geography." *Journal of Economic Geography* 2: 55–71.

Florida, Richard. 2002b. *The Rise of the Creative Class: And How It's Transforming Work, Leisure, Community, and Everyday Life*. New York: Basic Books.

Garrett, Jane. 2015. "The Big Freeze Extended to Keep Melbourne Safe and at Its Best." Media Release, Minister for Consumer Affairs, Gaming and Liquor Regulation, State Government of Victoria, June 7.

Gendron, Bernard. 2006. "The Downtown Music Scene." In *The Downtown Book: The New York Art Scene 1974–1984* edited by Marvin Taylor. Cambridge, MA: Princeton University Press, 41–66.

Gouvernement du Québec. 2014. *Quebec Panorama*. Quebec City: Government du Québec.

Hall, Peter. 1998. *Cities in Civilization*. Michigan: Pantheon.

Hann, Micha. 2014. "Don't Flush Our Toilet Venues Away!" *Guardian*, May 30. www.theguardian.com/music/musicblog/2014/may/29/small-venues-live-music-petition(accessed September 2, 2017).

Higgins, Charlotte. 2015. "Simon Rattle is Waving His Baton at the Wrong Cause." *Guardian*, February 23. www.theguardian.com/commentisfree/2015/feb/22/new-concert-hall-classical-music-simon-rattle (accessed September 2, 2017).

Holt, Fabian and Carsten Wergin. 2013. "Introduction: Musical Performances and the Changing City." In *Musical Performance and the Changing City: Post-Industrial Contexts in Europe and the United States*, edited by Fabian Hold Holt and Carsten Wergin. New York and London: Routledge, 1–26.

Homan, Shane. 2010. "Governmental as Anything: Live Music and Law and Order in Melbourne." *Perfect Beat: The Pacific Journal for Research into Contemporary Music and Popular Culture*, 11 (2): 103–118.

Homan, Shane, Martin Cloonan and Jen Cattermole. 2016. *Popular Music Industries and the State: Policy Notes*. London and New York: Routledge.

Homan, Shane and Dobe Newton. 2010. *The Music Capital: City of Melbourne Music Strategy*. Melbourne: City of Melbourne.

IFPI/Music Canada. 2015. *The Mastering of a Music City: Key Elements, Effective Strategies and Why It's Worth Pursuing*. London: IFPI and Music Canada with MIDEM.

Johnson, Boris. 2015. "Mayor of London Boris Johnson Announces Live Music Venues Taskforce." *Music Australia*, March 17. http://musicaustralia.org.au/2015/03/mayor-of-london-boris-johnson-announces-live-music-venues-taskforce (accessed September 6, 2017).

Johnson, Boris. 2013. "Boris Johnson's Speech at the Margaret Thatcher Lecture in Full." *Daily Telegraph*, November 28. http://www.telegraph.co.uk/news/politics/london-mayor-election/mayor-of-london/10480321/Boris-Johnsons-speech at the Margaret Thatcher-lecture-in-full.html (accessed September 6, 2017).

Khomami, N. 2015. "South London Birthplace of UK Garage to be Turned into Estate Agents." *Guardian*, June 5. www.theguardian.com/music/2015/jun/04/south-london-birthplace-of-uk-garage-to-be-turned-into-estate-agents (accessed September 6, 2017).

Ley, David. 2003. "Artists, Aestheticisation and the Field of Gentrification." *Urban Studies*, 40 (12): 2527–2544.

Marsh, Walter. 2015. "Liquor Licensing Reform to Remove Barriers to Live Music." *Rip It Up*, February 18. http://ripitup.com.au/music/liquor-licensing-reform-remove-barriers-live-music (accessed June 8, 2017).

McRobbie, Angela. 2012. "Key Concepts for Urban Creative Industry in the UK." In *Artists and the Arts Industries*, edited by Ingrid Elam and Lars Tunbjörk. Stockholm: The Swedish Arts Grants Committee, 78–129.

Olding, Rachel. 2015. "Lockout Laws: Assaults Down 40 Per Cent in Sydney City, but No Evidence We are Drinking Less." *Sydney Morning Herald*, April 16. www.smh.com.au/nsw/lockout-laws-assaults-down-40-per-cent-in-sydney-city-but-no-evidence-we-are-drinking-less-20150416-1mm70x.html (accessed June 8, 2017).

O'Neil, Dave. 2014. "Dave O'Neil." *The Age*, May 23, 2.

Parker, Stacey. 2015. *Results of the Musicians' Well-Being Survey: Creative Realities for Music Professionals in Australia*. Brisbane: School of Psychology, University of Queensland.

Paton, Kirsteen. 2014. *Gentrification: A Working-Class Perspective*. Farnham: Ashgate.

Reece, Nicholas. 2014. "The Lockout: New Location, but the Same Old Mistakes." *Sydney Morning Herald*, February 24, 18.

Salmon, Kim. 2011. "Spare a Dollar for the Maker, Music Doesn't Play Itself." *The Age*, August 10, 17.

Scott, Allen J. 2006. "Creative Cities: Conceptual Issues and Policy Questions." *Journal of Urban Affairs*, 28 (1): 1–17.

Shaw, Kate. 2013. "Independent Creative Subcultures and Why They Matter." In *Popular Music and Cultural Policy*, edited by Shane Homan, Martin Cloonan and Jen Cattermole. London and New York: Routledge, 59–78.

Shields, Rob. 1996. "A Guide to Urban Representation and What to Do about It: Alternative Traditions of Urban Theory." In *Re-Presenting the City: Ethnicity, Capital and Culture in the 21st-Century Metropolis*, edited by A.D. King. Basingstoke: Macmillan Press, 227–252.

Skalrud, Sasha. 2014. "Why Lockouts are Wrong for Sydney Nightlife." *Inthemix*, January 21. www.inthemix.junkee.com/why-lockouts-are-wrong-for-sydney-nightlife/22470 (accessed September 7, 2017).

Street, John. 2010. *Music & Politics*. Cambridge and Malden, MA: Polity Press.

Throsby, David and Anita Zednik. 2010. *Do You Really Expect to Get Paid? An Economic Study of Professional Artists in Australia*. Sydney: Australia Council for the Arts.

Vaines, Colin. 2015. "Soho Stories." *Observer*, May 17, 8–9.

Watson, Allan. 2008. "Global Music City: Knowledge and Geographical Proximity in London's Recorded Music Industry." *Area*, 40 (1): 12–23.

Wellington City Council. 2014. *Our 10-Year Plan: Wellington City Council's Draft Long Term Plan 2015–2025*. Wellington: Wellington City Council.

Coda

15

Site-ing the Sounds
Discovering Australia and New Zealand's Popular Music in the United States

Kyle Barnett and Robert Sloane

Introduction

Moments of music consumption always emerge from specific sites and contexts of cultural production, and yet listeners are not necessarily aware of them. As music and media scholars, the two of us have devoted effort to examining and explaining these contexts, especially through cultural intermediaries' scholarship and cultural industries' research writ large.[1] In addition, we have our own memories of discovering the music of Australia and New Zealand as fans. In what follows, we consider our own roles in a much larger cultural circuit, as bit players in the US reception of Australia and New Zealand's popular music. Although our roles were small, the experiences were lasting and meaningful. This conversation also stands as recognition that many of our interests and concerns as scholars began through our roles as intermediaries: music fans, record store clerks, and rock musicians.

We only later discovered popular music studies research that addressed Australia and New Zealand on its own terms. Although there were diverse research agendas and paths, popular music studies from the region has been defined by a pronounced interest in national identity and transnational flows of music, culture, and commerce (Breen 1987; Hayward 1998; Johnson 1995). And Dan Bendrups (2013) has convincingly argued for a strong link between ethnomusicology and popular music studies in Australasia, which may be part of the larger negotiation between indigenous versus migrant identities in a variety of ways. As participants in these identity formations and cultural circulations, the long-time usefulness of such research is strongly evident, particularly in the varying ways its local and regional identities play out in differing contexts quite far away.

What follows, then, is a conversation held online and in person during August and September of 2015, wherein we discuss our first encounters with the music, various sites of mediation and the role of intermediaries, and the circulation of the recordings we heard as material objects. We want to reflect on moments that we experienced as fans, but which we can now interpret as meaningful in the context of popular music studies, and especially in the work on intermediaries that both of us have found useful in our own work. In doing so, our discussion highlights differing flows of information before and during the popularization of the Internet, when knowledge about the music also meant studying music videos for clues, using record stores as libraries and record store clerks as tutors, poring over music magazines and looking for town names on maps (where is Dunedin, exactly?), and talking to friends who shared our enthusiasm. We relied at times on word of mouth via those who had their own encounters with music from Australia and New Zealand. However, this observation is itself indicative of the partial and contextual ways in which music often hits our ears for the first time. Factors contribute, but we often don't see, know, or think about them.

What might be lost in our conversation is our deep and abiding love for the music, which is perhaps difficult to transmit amid our concerns about how the music got to us and how we understood it. We're also aware that we got a particular version or versions of music from these places, through our interest in rock and pop music. If releases from Australia and New Zealand were sitting in the "international" or "world music" sections of our record stores, we were largely unaware of them, suggesting the ways that our understandings of music and the broader world map onto the legacies of linguistic and colonial domination.[2] Thinking through this conversation overall, we are left with an enduring fascination in recorded music's cultural circulation and recording culture's low economic barriers to entry that has ensured this music not only as a site of consumption, but also as a starting point for more cultural production— as quickly as some fans of The Clean might work up a cover of "Tally Ho" on the other side of the world.

To give context to our conversation, and to our listening and music fan histories, we offer this brief biographical information. Kyle Barnett grew up in west suburban Indianapolis, where he played in bands influenced by the music discussed here. He also served as music director at his high school radio station, before graduating high school in 1984. Rob Sloane grew up in the Virginia suburbs of Washington, DC, graduating from high school in 1986. He attended the University of Virginia from 1986–1990, where he helped to start a new student radio station. From 1988–1994, he worked at four different record stores in Manassas, Richmond, and Charlottesville, Virginia. The two of us met in 1995, in an MA program in American Culture Studies in Bowling Green, Ohio, where we both hosted radio shows on WBGU-FM until 1997.

In Conversation

Barnett: When was your first interaction with music from Australia or New Zealand? Do we count Olivia Newton-John, for instance? The Bee Gees? AC/DC? I didn't think of any of them as Australian. For me, MTV was the start.

Sloane: We definitely knew artists from Australia, but didn't know them as such, and didn't experience them as "Australian." In college, I think Midnight Oil was the first band I thought of as "Australian," mainly because of their lyrics, videos, etc.

Barnett: I saw Men at Work and INXS on a US tour as a teen. I don't think I understood that INXS was from Australia, even after seeing them together.

Sloane: Right, Men at Work. That's earlier than Midnight Oil. I wonder if some sense of the "alternative" that American MTV helped usher in made it easier to identify this. As we know, much of the early content on MTV was British, so I wonder if that made Australia a sort of "auxiliary" market.

Barnett: Nor did I have a grasp on Split Enz as a New Zealand band. Since Europe popularized music videos first, the assumption was "They must be British."

Sloane:	Some bands highlighted their association with their home, others didn't. Like the mention of "Vegemite" in Men at Work's "Down Under." I was like, "What the heck is Vegemite?"
Barnett:	US FM radio was locked down tight by the 1980s. MTV opened up musical possibilities, along with college radio. But context was often lost. If we knew a band was Australian, that was as far as it went.[3]
Sloane:	How did Men at Work, INXS, etc. make their way to the USA? With the scenes, I can see how underground media, scenesters, etc. could pass music and info on from there to here.[4] But were these other bigger bands part of scenes? Was there a "Sydney" scene? I mean, I don't know.
Barnett:	I'm also a little older than you. Outside the booth at my high school radio station, the anti-punk and anti-new wave forces threatened to beat us up. But MTV did impact our local FM rock stations. Those stations still played American rock acts like Aerosmith and Ted Nugent, but they also added Split Enz's "I Got You."
Sloane:	Yes, MTV was big, although I remember our Top 40 stations (and another oddball station in DC, such as W(WHFS), playing lots of things that were big on MTV. Again, mostly British stuff, but I have to assume that this was a significant part of Men at Work's success.
Barnett:	There were moments that got me thinking about faraway contexts. A video from New Zealand band The Swingers on early MTV, "One Good Reason," was made up of footage from the film *Starstruck* (Gillian Armstrong 1982). They were a New Zealand band in Australia, though I didn't know that then. Information came from the record shop, liner notes, or magazines. I heard "One Good Reason" on radio. It was exciting when songs got through.
Sloane:	As I think about it, I guess I thought of "Australian" artists as having a bit of exotic cachet, but not too terribly different than others. Again, Men at Work seemed odd, but when Kylie Minogue came around while I was in college, I did not know or care that she was Australian, much like Olivia Newton-John before. However, I think as we go on, that "otherness" becomes a signifier of taste, knowledge, etc. Again, if you know something about Indigenous Australians, then Midnight Oil's 1987 album *Diesel and Dust* is more meaningful. And then later, far-flung scenes were even "better" than US scenes, because, y'know, "not American."
Barnett:	Anything else was preferred. Hearing X or REM or Rank and File actually convinced me it was OK to be American. You could even like country music!
Sloane:	As far as New Zealand goes, I can honestly say that I did not really cue into that until the 90s—after college, and just before I met you.
Barnett:	We've talked about this before, but New Zealand really became a place of curiosity via our discovery of Flying Nun Records. By then, The Clean had fractured into all these wonderful bands (The Bats, The Great Unwashed, The Mad Scene). And since New Zealand bands were often associated with either Flying Nun or Xpressway, there was a cohesion—a sense of place. Unlike Australia, we associated New Zealand music with labels.[5]
Sloane:	Again, I don't think it mattered much to me where someone is from, until college, when I started learning more about it. Then I learned about the music scenes from

	Athens, GA, then later Seattle, etc. Then I realized why New York was so important for punk. This was something that meant more to me the more I learned.
Barnett:	Flying Nun, Xpressway, I thought of it separately, not tied to MTV at all. I don't think I ever saw a Go-Betweens video on MTV in the USA, though I would have associated them with London, not Brisbane, in Australia. I was in a band called the Lovemeknots in Indianapolis and we studied the Dunedin bands. We identified with the close-knit and somewhat isolated feel of the so-called "Dunedin Sound." I had some sense that these bands existed in a scene. And they weren't hip Londoners. They seemed closer to who we were.[6] I'm struck at how long some of the music took to get to us. How did I not really hear the Go-Betweens until the 1990s? Their 1988 album *16 Lovers Lane* floored me. I learned more via a book by The Cannanes' David Nichols, *The Go-Betweens*.[7]
Sloane:	This is an easy segue to Plan 9 [Records, in Charlottesville, Virginia] for me, where I learned about a ton of stuff.[8] That was where I first heard The Bats, The Go-Betweens, etc.
Barnett:	How did your musical education benefit from your record store experience at Plan 9? How much was your knowledge a necessary cultural capital for the job? Did clerks develop reputations for knowing certain national contexts?
Sloane:	The thing I remember is standing at the register, usually with one other person, and we would take turns putting stuff on the store stereo. Naturally, we'd talk about it, listen to it, go to something related, etc. Plus, there was a ton of great stuff to choose from. We could play anything from the used CD stock (which, in a literate college town with a great college radio station, was pretty great), plus already-opened CDs for sale, promos. I heard The Go-Betweens' iconic single "Streets of Your Town" on a Beggars Banquet Records (label) promo, celebrating one of their anniversaries or something, along with "Hit the North" by The Fall and other things.[9] I can't remember how or why I heard about The Bats; it's likely that I had read something about them and/or Flying Nun/New Zealand. But I put a used copy of their 1991 album 'in my "hold" bin (we could stash stuff to buy on payday), then put it on one day. Whoa! I don't know what I was expecting, but the melodies and the tone immediately caught me. I thought of it like a more lo-fi R.E.M.; I bought it, of course.
Barnett:	I heard The Clean (via *Compilation*) before The Bats, but the two were sold concurrently in the USA. The Bats being signed to Mammoth here made a difference. I loved the Bats' *Daddy's Highway*, which was probably my first proper Flying Nun release, via mail order. The Clean's *Vehicle* was on Rough Trade in the USA. The Cakekitchen's *Time Flowing Backwards* came out on Homestead. These labels impacted a given release's distribution. Was there a point as clerks or perhaps as managers—where record store clerks felt you were being "pitched" Australian or New Zealand bands in a concerted way, focused on national borders?
Sloane:	I do not remember getting pitched in this way, probably for a couple of reasons. One, it was still early in the alterna-boom [1993–1994], or perhaps more precisely,

in the development of marketing "indie" materials. The pitches I remember usually revolved around major label artists, and were more common at the big store I worked at in Richmond (second largest in the then-Southeastern-only Peaches chain). At Plan 9 Records in Charlottesville, we'd get promos of lots of stuff, even small stuff, but I don't remember a concerted effort to package it as, say, "New Zealand" music.

Regarding the labels and their US marketing, this was probably inescapable, especially in the days before the Internet: we heard about stuff because, on some level, it was being marketed to us as US consumers.

Another track that really hooked me in at this point was "Heavy 33" by the Verlaines. I heard it on the (Red Hot) *No Alternative* compilation, which I got as a promo and played at Plan 9. I did not know the Verlaines were from New Zealand, but I was familiar with most everyone else on that compilation except them. So in a material way, that album introduced me to a New Zealand band, by putting them with other stuff I liked.

Barnett: Friends were and are an important influence. Gary Koehl, a mutual friend of ours, was so enamored with New Zealand pop music, he spent a few weeks in the country, seeing sites and going to see New Zealand's 3Ds live. Fandom meets tourism [Duffett 2014].

Sloane: It seems like New Zealand gained more cachet, if only because the people from there seemed less well known. Also, for me, my associations with New Zealand are influenced by knowing you, Geoff Stahl, Craig Robertson (who is from there) ... people I met in grad school whom I like and admire, and whose tastes I admire. It's like, "Hey, all of my cool friends like New Zealand bands, so New Zealand bands must be cool."[10]

Barnett: This rings true. My friend and bandmate Evan Finch and I fell in love with the 3Ds. He had heard them before, but my introduction was their 1993 Merge Records album *The Venus Trail*—and I may not have heard them otherwise. We mentioned that album in a song of ours. Labels as well as distributors were crucial.

Sloane: Right. Speaking of distributors, that reminds me that, at both Peaches and Plan 9, there was a bit of a thing among the employees to pursue an "import" of CDs not readily available in the USA. I think both stores worked with companies that essentially specialized in imports, so we would look through printed catalogs, and scan our computer inventory, to find bands and labels we wanted to procure (although imports, of course, were way more expensive, not incidental when you're making US$5/hr.). I don't recall pursuing any Australian or New Zealand bands in this way, mostly because I didn't know of many. This sounds similar to ordering from the mail order catalogs, which is something I didn't really do.

Barnett: By the early 1990s, I would go to local record shops with a pointed interest in what clerks at a given store might stock. Record stores were so important to me hearing this music, but at some point I realized I could order directly. I suspect this was via my discovery of fanzines, some of which listed music mail order listings. It was quite exciting to get those packages in the mail.

I'd read Tim Adams' zine *The Pope*, which he did at the University of Notre Dame. At some point, he switched from the zine to a mail order operation called Ajax. Later, I learned about Parasol in Champaign-Urbana and some others. But Ajax's love of New Zealand stuff had a particular impact. Later he launched an Ajax record label and shop in Chicago, putting out bands from New Zealand and Australia. He eventually stocked recordings from my own band, which meant a lot.

Sloane: We're always (perhaps unconsciously) asking ourselves, "What makes a good shop?" and to me, it's one that: (1) aligns well with our already-existing taste, (2) introduces us to things that are cool, but unknown, or (3) both.

Barnett: Hearing this has made me realize that I was sizing up shops as much as employees size up customers.

Sloane: However, through the people I met in Richmond and Charlottesville, I became increasingly aware of local music. Our tech consultant at Plan 9 had been in the Washington, DC punk band The Teen Idles; the girl I dated in Richmond had friends in the band Fudge (who signed to Caroline Records); a guy who worked at Plan 9 in Richmond was in Labradford (signed to Kranky Records); and then a bunch of staffers and customers were into, among other things, the Teen Beat Records and Northern Virginia/DC scenes/nexus. When I moved back to northern Virginia from 1994–1995, I started checking more of this out: ordering from indie label SpinArt Records (another favorite of the Richmond girlfriend), or visiting an indie rock festival in Alexandria (and talking to Unrest member and Teen Beat Records founder Mark Robinson at the Teen Beat tent). However, this was all in the service of finding off-the-beaten-path stuff, and directly; I didn't find any Australian or New Zealand stuff this way, as you did.

Barnett: Word of mouth was so important. A friend's older brother would order directly from labels and mail order from various countries. I loved looking at the labels and stamps on the packages. There was a certain fascination in how the music got to us. And local scenes were huge and sometimes unexpectedly connected to the national and transnational. Some bands were more tuned in. But really it was the mail order catalogs.

I really came to trust him through the catalog descriptions, in the way that readers trust critics as they become familiar. This was particularly true of his New Zealand band listings, from Look Blue Go Purple to the Dead C and Tall Dwarfs and so on.

I had trustworthy sources. *Popwatch* magazine was important to me and had a lot of information about New Zealand, often couched in Flying Nun or Xpressway frameworks. *Popwatch* sometimes had illustrations from the Tall Dwarfs' Chris Knox.

Sloane: Some of these bands are completely new to me.

Barnett: Well, I knew some of them only in passing. Case in point: The Look Blue Go Purple compilation released in the USA. I always had the sense that we might only be getting part of the story.

It occurs to me that these small operations—mail order catalogs, zines, etc.— were doing what smaller record companies have always done: looking for niche

Site-ing the Sounds • 199

genres and sub-genres, under-explored avenues of music that could be brought to light and introduced to new constituencies.

Sloane: Yeah, I tend to think of Australia as providing much "bigger" artists, in terms of stardom and marketing, although not exclusively, while New Zealand seemed to reside solely in the indie world.

Barnett: True. Australian music receded in terms of major acts, but not completely. I recall Pip Proud being framed in the USA as a Syd Barrett figure of sorts.

We should note that most of the music being exploited was from the Anglophone world—which leads back to that perennial question about what counts as "world music" depending on where one in a given time and place. In US record shops, we rarely if ever found Australian or New Zealand releases in world music sections. At the same time, traditional music from Anglophone countries might end up there (I'm thinking of traditional Irish music in particular). And the colonialist connections in world music are well known.[11]

Sloane: Right, yes. Timothy Taylor has a good riff on this in his book, *Global Pop: World Music, World Markets* [Taylor 1997]. It occurs to me here that we were interested in a certain type of rock/music first, and the fact they were from Australia or New Zealand second. I don't think we were seeking out any and all music from there, because we weren't necessarily interested in "world music."

Barnett: Right. We understood the New Zealand scene as part of a group of artists (right or wrong). Australian music seemed much more about individual efforts (we clearly lacked the greater context). We heard Radio Birdman and the Saints, but I didn't really see relationships. And in Australia, there seems to be a greater tradition of artists relocating to the UK to make a greater impact. The Go-Betweens did some globetrotting too.

I should say that interest in imports led to a certain amount of waste and overstep, to music that didn't sell, to releases in cut-out bins, which we also scoured and passed around between friends.

Sloane: Cut-out bins: the great treasure troves of capitalist overproduction.

Barnett: Exactly. I think I got some of The Clean stuff via cut-outs; The Bats stuff via Mammoth. I honestly anthropomorphized these objects a bit, thinking to myself: I need to give these a good home. Will Straw writes on the afterlives of media commodities in and out of circulation, in "The Thingishness of Things," which applies here [Straw 1999].

Sloane: Although, to be fair, indies/imports didn't show up as much in them, because: (1) the stores with cut-out bins didn't often deal with indie distributors, (2) they ordered such small numbers, and (3) indie labels didn't "cut out" as much as the majors. However, those majors or low-level/"indie" majors that signed foreign bands would have been well represented. That was the kind of stuff that they signed because someone thought it was cool, but they didn't know how to sell it (or care to try).

Barnett: What I got in the cut-out bins were all US releases or re-releases of New Zealand or Australian releases. We rarely if ever got imports in cut-out bins (I think I recall a stray EP or two). I'm pretty sure my copy of the US release for The Clean's *Vehicle* has a little nick taken out of it, denoting "cut out."

Sloane: There are a few factors that create cut outs. First, they are "cut out" of a label's catalog. This happens far more frequently with major labels than with indies. However, as we talked about earlier, the majors that distributed indies may have made too many, or later dropped a band, etc. Second, there is overproduction: there were just too many made, and they're taking a bath on them, so write them off and get rid of them, rather than having them take up inventory value. Third, there are promos that stores get and then re-sell as "used"; these usually have the "cut" in the spine, or a line through the UPC (Universal Product Code), to indicate that they are not meant to be sold as new.

Barnett: Perhaps we're talking too much about New Zealand, which speaks to our tastes. But we should distinguish between Flying Nun Records and Xpressway, the latter being a cassette label that was a bit less song-based, more experimental. Xpressway releases often appeared to be home recordings—self-produced affairs. This didn't always mean "lo-fi." This Kind of Punishment's music certainly wasn't.

I'm struck at how our reception was catch-as-catch-can. Certain US bands championed those from Australia or New Zealand.

Sloane: Yeah, I was going to ask you about that. My friend Craig was delighted when the American band Yo La Tengo played "Bad Politics" (by New Zealand band The Dead C) at one of their shows in Champaign; I can't remember how it came about, but he may have suggested it to [Yo La Tengo bassist] James [McNew], who was milling about at the merch table before they went on.

Barnett: Yo La Tengo sang the praises of The Clean. James McNew recorded The Go-Betweens' "Dive for Your Memory" under his Dump moniker. Touring and relocations made further connections. When The Clean's Hamish Kilgour moved to the New York City area, it cemented connections with Yo La Tengo and other bands.

Sloane: Right. So it may be that certain bands themselves serve as kinds of intermediaries, by passing their tastes on to their fans. I wonder what the overlap is between fans of Yo La Tengo and fans of New Zealand bands.

Barnett: Yes. Another appeal of New Zealand bands was their response to Australia's cultural strength. It echoed our own feelings in the Midwest and South, against the US coasts. I interpreted two songs by The Chills as a dialogue about staying home or going abroad. "Come Home" had a chorus that ended with "we still need you," while "Sunburnt" seemed to understand the need to emigrate. The Bats sang about similar issues.

Sloane: In addition to what I've talked about already, meeting you, then Gary, then Craig, solidified New Zealand as a place for people who like good music, or at least shared my tastes. Gary made me a cassette with The Paisley Underground compilation *Rainy Day* on one side, and the other side was titled "Kiwi Tracks." I can't remember what's on it, but the important equation for me was: Gary likes good music + I admire Gary's taste = This is good music that I will (or should) like.

Barnett: Good point. Beyond commercial compilations, we all made mixtapes for each other, which led to further connections.

Sloane:	There's another connection I now make in retrospect. Some of the guys from the American indie rock band Pavement went to the University of Virginia, a couple years ahead of me, and they worked at the radio station. I think Craig pointed out to me, after I met him, that the band's vocalist, Stephen Malkmus, is credited as playing "Guitar (Nz git)" on "Box Elder" from the band's *Slay Tracks: 1933–1969* EP, and later included on *Westing (By Musket and Sextant)*. I don't know if this is a reference to "New Zealand guitar," or "noize guitar" (or both), but I accepted Craig's interpretation of it as the former. I bought the *Westing* collection when I worked at Plan 9 (1993–1994), so I guess I assume that the New Zealand influence was kinda "hanging in the air" in Charlottesville, or at least certain parts.

So then Pavement gets signed by Matador, Matador forges a major-label deal, we're all reading about what Pavement likes, etc. It's artist-as-intermediary. Cobain did the same with American bands The Breeders and The Melvins, the English band The Raincoats, etc.

Barnett: I love this. Stephen Malkmus' "New Zealand guitar." Jangly and shambolic, no doubt. I'm sure there are discursive histories to be written about how the taste-making process, how music was defined, what words were used as qualifiers. One review begets another review. And then labels respond, perpetuating, or quibbling with the stakes of the game, the descriptors, etc.

Sloane: Recently, I went back to try to make Spotify playlists of some of my homemade tapes from that era, and I realized that I put a lot of promo-only tracks on some of them—stuff that is not available now, especially on Spotify. If this relates to what we're talking about, it is in the curation by knowledgeable types, and their subsequent spreading of it, either physically (on recordings) or through word of mouth. And, finally, if our system is no longer set up to facilitate this—who makes compilations to give out anymore?—then this may be going away in the current industry/context.

Barnett: We have been trying to map the music's circulation: How did popular music from Australia and New Zealand land in our hands? How did it travel and in what ways did we encounter it?

Sloane: Well, as I think I've suggested, I still am reasonably ignorant of all the precise connections. What's interesting to me, though, is this process of, "Oh, New Zealand and Flying Nun are these cool, unknown places, but the intelligentsia know about them." For me, they're proxies for people and tastes I appreciate and admire. That said, I like most of the music, too; but I'm interested in this topic for what it says about the associations we make, how and why we follow through with certain explorations, etc.

Barnett: Yes, absolutely. I got mixtapes with Christchurch, New Zealand's Roy Montgomery and his affiliated groups (Pin Group, Dadamah), but then learned more when we were both DJs at Bowling Green State University's WBGU-FM (another site of mediation). By the mid-1990s, I think the New Zealand music was just part of what we were hearing, though we remained ignorant about city scenes: Dunedin, Christchurch, Wellington, Auckland.

Sloane: Yes. On the diversity of the place thing: there is a great point made in *Hype!*, the documentary about Sub Pop and the Seattle scene. They point out that the Seattle bands were much more diverse than what got distilled/categorized/marketed to the wider audience.

Barnett: And searching out that diversity changes one's reception. In the fan's work we did (also a kind of pleasure), our fandom became a kind of connoisseurship. And the remoteness of the music made for cultural capital. Now, it just seems part of my musical DNA.

Conclusion

The memories evoked by our conversation suggest that the North American reception of Australia and New Zealand's popular music in the 1980s and 1990s was shaped by a number of socio-cultural realities. During the 1980s, American MTV and cable television was crucial in opening up pipelines to US listenership. These encounters via music video sent us to record shops, where clerks furthered our knowledge of such music as they mediated between industry and consumer, as well as differing national contexts. Even in the emerging Internet culture of the early-to-mid-1990s, mail-order sources were also crucial in the reception and understanding of Australian and New Zealand's music and culture, however imperfectly we understood both.

In remembering this highly specific and (we believe) important period for the US reception of Australia and New Zealand's popular music, we'd like to end with recent trends that suggest an ongoing interest and renewed chances for understanding (and misunderstanding). Australian Iggy Azalea and New Zealander Lorde have both been significant in mainstream pop music in recent years, while in indie rock, Melbourne's Courtney Barnett has been a ubiquitous presence, appearing in some of our country's biggest musical festivals and media outlets.

In addition, a variety of reissued recordings are allowing for reassessments. The Go-Betweens are the subject of Domino Records' lavish multi-volume box set, *G Stands for Go-Betweens*. The first volume, released both in the USA and the UK, covers the years between 1978 and 1984. Online music magazines such as *Pitchfork, Consequence of Sound,* and *Tiny Mix Tapes* have been key in publicizing such reissues for consumers. Perhaps the most ambitious label-based reissue project is the agreement between US-based Captured Tracks and New Zealand's Flying Nun to reissue classic and lesser-known albums, as well as legendary singles and EPs, for the US market. This activity suggests that enough time has passed for a generational reconsideration of the music that first appealed to us decades before, within very different contexts of production, distribution, and consumption than today's now ubiquitous digital culture, with its myriad triumphs and foibles. It is too soon to gauge how that reassessment will proceed, but is likely that current trends will lead to some of the same epiphanies and distortions that marked our reception.

Acknowledgments

Thank you to the editors of this collection for their insightful and generous comments on this chapter.

Notes

1 See Nixon and du Gay (2002), as well as David Hesmondhalgh's *The Cultural Industries* (2012), although the latter takes issue with the term "intermediaries."
2 Timothy Taylor (1997, 5) tells a story about a Tower Records in Mexico City, which houses US and UK pop music on its first floor, and then a much larger section of Mexican music in the "world music" section on its second floor.
3 Rob Tannenbaum and Craig Marks' oral history, *I Want My MTV: The Uncensored Story of the Music Video Revolution* (2012), provides useful context for this era.
4 Michael Azerrad's *Our Band Could Be Your Life: Scenes from the American Indie Underground 1981–1991* (2002) discusses the ways such circulation took place in the US underground in the 1980s, but he does not consider the international context.
5 Geoff Stahl has addressed some of these topics in "Citing the Sound: New Zealand Indie Rock in North America" (1997).
6 In *Site and Sound: Understanding Independent Music Scenes* (2003), Holly Kruse thoroughly examines the constitution of specific music scenes. See her theoretical discussion in Chapter 5, "Locating Subjectivity in Independent Music."
7 See David Nichols (2003).
8 Plan 9 Music was (and still is) a small chain of stores operating primarily in Richmond and Charlottesville, Virginia. Robert Sloane worked at one of the Charlottesville stores 1993–1994, after being a customer since he started college there in 1986.
9 On the influence of record stores on music consumptions, see Paul du Gay and Keith Negus (1994) and Will Straw (1998).
10 See Robertson's (1991) Honors thesis on "the Dunedin Sound."
11 While editing this conversation, we recalled Yothu Yindi, a band comprising Aboriginal (and non-Aboriginal) Australians that incorporated indigenous styles into their music (see the Introduction in this book). They were promoted in "alternative" US circles in the late 1980s and early 1990s, and while we heard the band at the time we didn't remember them when first thinking about "Australian" music for this project. We attribute this to a variety of dynamics, among them the bifurcated categories of world music and indie rock, which impacted the band's influence in the indie rock world despite boundary crossing attempts in Australia and elsewhere, as well as the course of our own musical tastes, focused less on place and more on indie rock's stylistic critique of and debt to the pop-rock tradition. For more on Yothu Yindi, see Hayward (1998).

Bibliography

Azerrad, Michael. 2002. *Our Band Could Be Your Life: Scenes from the American Indie Underground 1981–1991*. New York: Back Bay.
Bendrups, Dan. 2013. "Popular Music Studies and Ethnomusicology in Australia." *IASPM@Journal* 3 (2): 48–62. doi: 10.5429/2079-3871(2013)v3i2.4en (accessed June 22, 2016).
Breen, Marcus, ed. 1987. *Missing in Action: Australian Popular Music in Perspective*, Volume 1. Melbourne: Verbal Graphics.
Duffett, Mark. 2014. *Popular Music Fandom: Identities, Roles, and Practices*. New York: Routledge.
Du Gay, Paul and Keith Negus. 1994. "The Changing Sites of Sound: Music Retailing and the Composition of Consumers." *Media, Culture & Society* 16 (3): 395–413.
Hayward, Philip, ed. 1998. *Sound Alliances: Indigenous Peoples, Cultural Politics and Popular Music in the Pacific*. London and New York: Cassell.
Hesmondhalgh, David. 2012. *The Cultural Industries*. Third edition. Thousand Oaks, CA: Sage.
Johnson, Bruce. 1995. "Towards a New Cartography—Rethinking Australia's Musical History." In *One Hand on the Manuscript: Music in Australian Cultural History 1930–1960*, edited by N. Brown, P. Campbell, R. Holmes, P. Read, and L. Sitsky. Canberra, ACT: Humanities Research Centre, 243–257.
Keil, Charles and Steven Feld. 1994. *Music Grooves: Essays and Dialogues*. Chicago: University of Chicago.
Kruse, Holly. 2003. *Site and Sound: Understanding Independent Music Scenes*. New York: Peter Lang.
Nichols, David. 2003. *The Go-Betweens*. Expanded and Revised Edition. Portland, OR: Verse Chorus Press.
Nixon, Sean and Paul du Gay. 2002. "Who Needs Cultural Intermediaries?" *Cultural Studies* 16 (4): 495–500.
Robertson, Craig. 1991. "'It's OK, It's All Right, Oh Yeah': The 'Dunedin Sound'?" B.A. Honors thesis, University of Otago.
Stahl, Geoff. 1997. "Citing the Sound: New Zealand Indie Rock in North America." *Perfect Beat: The Pacific Journal for Research into Contemporary Music and Popular Culture* 3 (2): 60–76.
Straw, Will. 1999. "The Thingishness of Things." *Invisible Culture* 2. https://ivc.lib.rochester.edu/the-thingishness-of-things (accessed July 6, 2016).

204 • Kyle Barnett and Robert Sloane

Straw, Will. 1998. "Organized Disorder: The Changing Space of the Record Shop." In *The Clubcultures Reader: Readings in Popular Cultural Studies*, edited by Steve Redhead, with Derek Wynne and Justin O'Connor. Malden, MA: Blackwell, 57–65.
Tannenbaum, Rob and Craig Marks. 2012. *I Want My MTV: The Uncensored Story of the Music Video Revolution*. New York: Plume.
Taylor, Timothy D. 1997. *Global Pop: World Music, World Markets*. New York: Routledge.

Discography

3Ds. *The Venus Trail*. Merge Records, MRG065, 1994, compact disc. Originally released in 1993.
Lambchop: Dump, "Dive For Your Memory," *Dump/Lambchop* Third Gear Records, 3G23, 1999 33⅓ split single.
Look Blue Go Purple. *Compilation*. Flying Nun Records FNCD171, 1991, compact disc.
Men at Work. "Down Under." In *Business as Usual*. CBS 85423, 1982, 33⅓ rpm.
Midnight Oil. *Diesel and Dust*. Columbia CK 40967, 1988, compact disc. Originally released in 1987.
Pavement. *Slay Tracks: 1933–1969*. Treble Kicker Tk001, 1989, 33⅓ rpm.
Pavement. *Westing (By Musket and Sextant)*. Drag City DC14CD, 1993, compact disc.
Phillipps, Martin and The Chills. *Sunburnt*. Flying Nun Records FNCD303 / Festival Records D31538, 1996, compact disc.
Split Enz. "I Got You." In *True Colours*. A&M Records SP 4822, 1980, 33⅓ rpm.
The Bats. *Daddy's Highway*. Flying Nun Europe FNE 23, 1987, compact disc.
The Bats. *Fear of God*. Flying Nun Records/Mammoth Records, MR0040-2, 1992, compact disc.
The Cakekitchen. *Time Flowing Backwards*. Homestead Records HMS 156-2, 1991, compact disc.
The Clean. *Compilation*. Flying Nun Europe FNE 3, 1988, compact disc. Originally released in 1986.
The Clean. *Vehicle*. Rough Trade VICP-56, 1990, compact disc.
The Dead C. "Bad Politics." In *Making Losers Happy: Xpressway NZ Singles 1988–91*. Drag City DC24, 1992, compact disc.
The Fall, "Hit the North (Pt. 1)." In *The Collection*, Beggars Banquet Germany 076-05452, 1991, compact disc.
The Go-Betweens. *16 Lovers Lane*. Beggars Banquet BEGA 95CD, 1988, compact disc.
The Go-Betweens. *G Stands for Go-Betweens Volume One*. Domino REWIG89X, 2015, 33⅓ rpm and compact disc.
The Swingers. "One Good Reason." In *Counting the Beat*, Backstreet Records BSR-5328, 1982, 33⅓ rpm.
The Verlaines. "Heavy 33." In *No Alternative*, Arista ARCD 8737, 1993, compact disc.
Various artists. *Rainy Day*. Llama Records E1024, 1984, 33⅓ rpm.

Filmography

Armstrong, Gillian (director). *Starstruck*. Australian Film Commission /Palm Beach Pictures, 1982.
Pray, Doug (director). *Hype!* Helvey-Pray Productions /Lions Gate Films, 1996.

Afterword

16
Negotiating Trans-Tasman Musical Identities
Conversations with Neil and Tim Finn

Liz Giuffre

Brothers Tim and Neil Finn are songwriter/performers who were born in the small North Island town of Te Awamutu, New Zealand, in 1952 and 1958 respectively. They began working in the music industry as teenagers, starting in New Zealand and then Australia, where they spent significant parts of their careers. Both continue to write and perform today, and are claimed equally by the Australian and New Zealand music industries and their fans. The brothers have each driven internationally successful popular music groups (Split Enz for Tim and Crowded House for Neil), as well as folk projects as *The Finn Brothers* and *Finn*, and their own solo and other collaborative work. These contributions have earned both men an OBE (Order of the British Empire) for their services to music. In addition to this Commonwealth award, the brothers have each been honoured by the Australian and New Zealand music industries, including by APRA (the Australasian Performing Rights Association), ARIA (the Australian Record Industry Association) and RIANZ (the Recording Industry Association of New Zealand, now known as Recorded Music New Zealand). In November 2016, Crowded House was inducted into the ARIA Hall of Fame, seeing the work of the Finn Brothers recognized alongside other Australian icons like AC/DC, Men at Work, INXS and Kylie Minogue. Tim and Neil Finn are recognisable to international audiences as musicians from the Australia/New Zealand region, having performed widely across the USA, UK, Europe and Asia, as part of their own tours and on major international festival bills, including Coachella and Glastonbury. Each have also had their music used in various film and television soundtracks, as well as for live theater, and have collaborated with international artists including members of Radiohead, Pearl Jam and The Smiths as part of 2009's *7 Worlds Collide* concerts in Auckland.

Their activity in both Australia and New Zealand has led academics such as Tony Mitchell to describe artists like Neil and Tim Finn as "transnational musician[s] with an Australasian and global identity" (2010, 25), and these complex relationships are reflected in the musicians' comments which feature below. The Finn brothers are clearly tied to their New Zealand ancestry; however, their activity and success in Australia has allowed the industry and fans there to claim them as their own as well. This is a tension that the media has played up over the last few decades. A recent example of this unfolded during the ARIA Hall of Fame induction, where New Zealand comedy duo Flight of the Conchords were invited to present

208 • Liz Giuffre

the award to the band, but instead offered a joke "protest" against the award on behalf of the New Zealand government, seeking to reclaim the musicians from the Australian industry (*New Zealand Herald* 2016).

Claims to a national ownership are based on where artists were living while making music, as well as who they were collaborating with (with each having worked with Australian musicians Paul Hester and Nick Seymour, in particular). The Finns have tended to either downplay this tension by laughing off suggestions that they should 'choose one or the other', or they have made fun of the tug-of-war between the nations with cameo appearances on comedy programs including the animated *Bro' Town* (2006, 2009), a comedy series focused on a Pacific Island community, and the internationally broadcast *Flight of the Conchords* (2005).[1] Tim and Neil Finn's influence has also been keenly felt by the music industries in Australia and New Zealand. This dual nationalism was demonstrated most markedly in the album and concert series dedicated to their music, "They Will Have Their Way", where Australian and New Zealand musicians of various genres and generations performed covers of Tim and Neil's works,[2] and recently where Crowded House's 'encore' shows on the steps of Sydney Opera House were broadcast as a main feature of the ABC's (Australian Broadcasting Corporation) AusMusic Month (Chamberlin 2016), which features the best of new and iconic Australian music.

This chapter presents a series of interviews I conducted between 2006 and 2016. The introduction to each section provides the time and location of the discussion, as well as details of the musical release the musicians were promoting. Although I published sections of the original interviews soon after each was conducted, the interview material presented in this chapter has not been published before. Interestingly, some of the same territory is covered a few years apart, with slightly different responses as each artist has continued to evolve.

The interviews shed light on issues that have arisen for Tim and Neil Finn as musicians claimed by both Australian and New Zealand industries and audiences. The artists explain how location informs their music making and its performance; how fan communities have contributed to their sustained music making; and the place of Australia and New Zealand artists in the international music market.

Phone Interview with Neil Finn, Conducted in 2006

Neil Finn was speaking from "a little village just outside of Bath" in the UK, and was promoting the CD/DVD release of the Crowded House Farewell to the World *concert: an Australian concert staged ten years earlier, in 1996, that featured both Tim and Neil Finn performing on the steps of the Sydney Opera House. Even today, the significance of that farewell concert resonates with the band and is fans; ten years after this interview was conducted, Crowded House commemorated the twenty-year anniversary of the Farewell to the World concert by staging a series of 2016 concerts at the same location. This interview demonstrates Neil's perspectives at that time on the band's connections with Australia and New Zealand, and how its music is received beyond this region.*

Giuffre: So, this has got to be a bit weird for you, doing Crowded House promotion a decade after the band's farewell performance?

Conversations with Neil and Tim Finn • 209

Neil Finn: Sort of, although essentially it's not that different to any kind of promo[tion] really. And I've been talking about other things too, and it's just been a catch up really. The whole year [2006] has been about the past, really: the Split Enz tour earlier this year, and now the Crowded House reissue [*Farewell to the World*, 2006]. But it's a good thing to take in, but also a good thing not to labour on otherwise it's too hard to work on new stuff.

Giuffre: It was interesting seeing that commentary that you and [Crowded House bass player and founding member] Nick [Seymour] were doing as part of the DVD release—talking about the whole production of the Farewell concert—can you remind me what the word was you used to describe the event and its scale?

Neil Finn: I think Nick jokingly mentioned something about the whole thing being "vulgar." But I think what I was getting at, when the idea came around to do this whole sort of final show, I was inclined to think it was too grandiose. I would rather just play in the lounge room like we did when we were just starting off. But I'm stupid sometimes, and to give credit to Grant Thomas, who was our manager at the time, he convinced me it was a great notion and he talked me into it, then pulled it together brilliantly and I think it stands as a great document.

Giuffre: Did you cop flack [criticism] at the time about not having the concert event in New Zealand?

Neil Finn: Yeah, there was a bit of rumbling in New Zealand at the time, and I can understand that, but it really wouldn't have made sense in New Zealand. I am a New Zealander obviously, there was never any secret about that, and in fact the band started in Melbourne, and there was some grumbling in Melbourne about that too. But that setting, that Opera House setting is an international setting in many ways. To me it says "Sydney," but it also says "this is the world", it was a glorious opportunity to play somewhere so beautiful and to play to the world.

Giuffre: Maybe we're spoiled being here in Australia and New Zealand, but it's easy to take for granted just how far your music has actually gone. It hit home to me with the *7 Worlds Collide* release [a live album of a collaboration concert filmed at the St James in Auckland] you did in 2001 with all these amazing musicians, like members of Radiohead and The Smiths and Pearl Jam. They all came together to record and play with you in New Zealand because they knew you and how far your work has gone. Do you ever get surprised by how far your music has stretched and who has responded to you in return?

Neil Finn: Well it's the wonderful mystery of what music is really. It can end up in the darkest places and you find the most unlikely people are aware of your stuff. Not just famous people but just unlikely people, people from like Columbia or something saying "Oh, I really loved that song." And I think "Wow, my song made it to Columbia!" I've never really been able to judge it because we were never really "fashionable, man", but we had our movements where they [the audience and other musicians] gave us lots of respect. There's something that endures for a lot of musicians, and I don't know how many people take into account what's fashionable or what isn't. I think 90 per cent of the public decide, and I thank them for it, on a combination of factors. The most important thing

210 • Liz Giuffre

is "Does the song mean something or does it touch them in some way?" And I think that's central to why the songs endure, and that's why there's so much good will out there—why they've hung around.

Giuffre: When it comes to people performing cover versions of your work, do you get a bit defensive?

Neil Finn: No, I've had to let to go. To use a slightly well worn analogy, and it's not always entirely appropriate, but [the songs] are like your children and you can't really chose who your children sleep with when they leave home; you've just gotta back them up. It's great, whatever gets the song getting sung by people is fine with me, it's the ultimate. I'm a traditionalist, so if a good song moves on then I don't mind who sings it.

Interview with Neil Finn and Nick Seymour, Conducted in Person in Sydney, 2007

The interview was to promote the re-formation of Crowded House as a band, notably with a new member following the death of founding Melbourne-based musician, Paul Hester, who passed away in 2005. Neil Finn and Seymour had started playing music together again after an extended break, and the re-formation of the band developed from their initial explorations with other collaborative work. This interview, and subsequent new Crowded House album and tour, took place relatively shortly after the band's re-launch performance at the iconic Coachella festival in the USA, and was the beginning of a new life for the band after an eleven year hiatus.

Giuffre: How did the decision to come back together again come about?

Neil Finn: I was going to do another [solo] record anyway and I wanted Nick to come and do it with me, because we enjoyed hanging out in the last couple of years, and we did Homebake [a Sydney based Australia/New Zealand music festival] together and I thought "it feels good to be playing with him again." So what began as just a natural collaboration led to a realization that this was something I wanted to continue on. Just naturally Nick got more deeply involved in the record I was working on, and I loved having him to do it, so we didn't talk about [getting the band back together] until the original solo record was almost done, and then we did some extra recording once that realization came. But before then it was just hanging around and playing together.

Giuffre: Was there a temptation to just start a new band, rather than using the Crowded House name?

Neil Finn: All these things crossed my mind, I thought about it before and talked to Nick about it, and said "I really want to be in a band and it feels good to have Nick there, and maybe we should just form a new band and be a new name," and then I thought "Why would we do that? We've got this name that we're proud of and we worked hard on and in essence what it felt like with Nick was Crowded House. And in essence we've probably confused the public enough—Crowded House, Split Enz, Finn Brothers, Neil Finn,

Conversations with Neil and Tim Finn • 211

	Tim Finn, now we've got [Neil's son, musician] Liam Finn, you may as well just stick to it.
Giuffre:	I've read recently reviews of your gigs at Coachella [Crowded House performed at the 2007 American festival Coachella] as part of the re-launch, of sorts, of the band. Is it true you were pelted with bottles by some of the fans waiting to see [Los Angeles rap metal band] Rage Against the Machine while you were playing on the main stage?
Nick Seymour:	There was a photograph in the newspaper that I think was me just after I got hit, and I was convinced it was just one guy, because the accuracy was pin point. It [a flying object] took out Neil's microphone first, just as he was about to sing, then it took out my microphone, and it was just too good a shot I thought this can't just be random people in the audience. Then there was a rebound shot that hit my bass and fell and bounced on the beat, and I think it was at that point I turned to Neil with this big smirk on my face, saying "How ironic, this guy's got impeccable timing." But, they stopped throwing bottles of water after a while, and I'm not sure if we won them over or the crowd stopped them, or they just ran out of water (laughs).
Neil Finn:	I think they warmed to us, and we got more relaxed in the middle of our set and got better and better. And you could see their heads starting to go and the music was starting to draw them in. Obviously it was a very challenging position to be in, performing two songs in before Rage Against the Machine, but it was also a glorious position to be in and we wanted to enjoy it, and we did, we really enjoyed it.
Giuffre:	So you think your folk/pop/rock audience braved the metal fans to be there?
Neil Finn:	It's amazing what people will endure. And we won't have that kind of challenging situation that many times this year so it's good for us, good for our mental approach.
Nick Seymour:	I saw one Kiwi [New Zealand] flag down the front but it disappeared after a while. I don't know if it was snatched or if a Rage fan with a lighter got a hold of it.
Giuffre:	It's so weird—I could understand if it was a crossover in terms of genre, but surely you're not competing with Rage Against the Machine for fans, necessarily.
Neil Finn:	I think people thought that the organizers had done the wrong thing by us by scheduling the bill like that, but to be honest they offered us a spot and we said "yes, we want that." So we were either foolish or brave or a mixture of both. The sense of occasion of it was too much to pass up—Willie Nelson, Manu Chao, Crowded House and Rage Against the Machine—I thought "that sounds right."
Giuffre:	So you were "the festival find" [meaning, the band that audiences discover for the first time at the festival]?
Neil Finn:	Well not only us, but we were well represented in the favorites list, so that's nice to know.

212 • Liz Giuffre

Nick:	It's a great festival. And it's become the festival that a lot of other festival organizers seem to go to, to assess. They seem to be setting the standard for comfort zone and cultural anomalies, and the blend of that. And I think they all go just to check out each other's toilets, really. If you're a festival organizer who has to ask "how do we do this?"

Interview with Tim Finn in 2008, in Person in Sydney

Tim Finn was talking about his new album The Conversation, *as well as an upcoming theater production* Poor Boy", *which used his back catalogue to develop "a play with songs" for the Sydney and Melbourne Theatre Companies. Poor Boy went on to be staged by the Sydney, Melbourne and Auckland Theatre Companies, drawing on songs by Finn to develop an original story. Academy Award nominated Australian actor Guy Pearce played the lead in* Poor Boy *for the Melbourne production in 2009, and as of 2016 is reportedly working on a film production of the work (Rosser 2016).*

Giuffre:	When you write, are you a "piece of pen and paper" person or do you use tape, or is just "if it comes back to me I'll keep it"?
Tim Finn:	A bit of two of those, a bit of "pen and paper", a bit "if it comes back to me then it must have been ok." There's one song I remember, I was very drunk about twenty-five years ago, walking through a small city in New Zealand, because I couldn't sleep. And I found this hotel that was open, wondered into the hotel lobby, there was no one around, wondered over to their piano and wrote this brilliant song, and I've never been able to remember one thing about it. Perhaps it wasn't brilliant, but at the time I thought it was. But if they are good they tend to hang around. And I don't have them all recorded as demos, just fragments, which makes me a bit forgetful. I am quite a forgetful person and I sometimes excuse myself by thinking that I've probably got quite a lot of musical junk dangling around up there, but then you've only got so much memory, you realize as you get older too (laughs). It's finite; you tend to forget people and things. Neil doesn't, but then he demos everything.
Giuffre:	Neil always struck me to as someone who was much more methodical than you.
Tim Finn:	Yes, to a point … but do you mean in terms of cataloging ideas and being clear about what he wants?
Giuffre:	Having seen you both a few times as well, he seems very structured, where I really do get a sense that you're more spontaneous at times.
Tim Finn:	Yeah, [those feelings] are great for an audience.
Giuffre:	Not to say that it's not great to see Neil and think "this ship is being steered very clearly and masterfully" …
Tim Finn:	Yeah, and he can move in and out of that if he's got the right sparring partner—like Paul [Hester] used to be, or like I can be. Then Neil's very adept at moving in and out. There are certain things that you'll never go below, beneath a certain level [when experimenting], but you like to think there's always a bit of danger and room for the unexpected. I was thinking about that the other day actually

Conversations with Neil and Tim Finn • 213

	because I'm about to do [Split Enz song] "Poor Boy" as a theater piece, and when you go and see a theater show it's never quite like that because you know something's been written, so it's encased within this very controlled environment, so it can never be as wild and dangerous as a rock show. But it can be something else, something equally as wonderful. It can be separate to what I know well.
Giuffre:	How did that come about?
Tim Finn:	A friend who's a producer, who lives here in Sydney, knew this writer Matt Cameron, and suggested to me that I write with him, to try something. So I threw something at him and he responded straight away, and he wrote a synopsis and it turned into a first draft. And it happened really organically and naturally, and Matt knows a lot of my stuff. He knows really obscure B-sides and you know, it was just meant to be. So he was just putting songs in throughout his first draft, and they were really good ideas, so I trusted him to weave this skeleton through with the songs. I've added a couple of new ones and changed a few things here and there, but basically it's his feel for my songs, and his story. It's great, it's exciting.
Giuffre:	I imagine that's what it feels like when someone covers your songs. Is that right?
Tim Finn:	Yeah. I had to go along to these auditions and listen to actors singing my songs, and sometimes to great affect, and sometimes it just didn't quite work. I find it quite hard to get a feel for them, to do that in the audition. But it's part of an actor's world, they just have to do it. But it's really bold to just come into a room with a director and composer and writer, who are all waiting to hear what you've got to offer. But actors know that I suppose, and the really good ones can make that experience quite spine tingling when they get that right. As a songwriter, this isn't false humility, but you're never quite sure you've written a proper song until you've heard someone else sing it. I mean, you know you've done it 100 times and with a crowd and know it works, but when you hear somebody else do it, it's like "wow, I've really written a song." I know that sounds a bit weird, but that's how it is for me.
Giuffre:	I love cover versions. To me, when people write they write in their own key in their own voice and never put themselves out of their comfort zones too much. But when you play someone else's songs, all of a sudden you need to step into their range and their abilities. It's interesting that having someone else play your song.
Tim Finn:	A cover makes the song feel real. I think any songwriter loves that. Even if you don't like the version that much, there's still something about it. One of the weirdest ones was [American country folk artist] Jimmy Buffett doing "Weather with You" [a 1992 Crowded House song released on Buffet's 2006 album *Take the Weather with You*]. It was just so unlikely, and he does it really well! Then there was the *She Will Have Her Way* album [comprised of cover versions of Neil and Tim Finn's music], which we had nothing to do with, and some of them worked really well, and some not so much, but it was really interesting to hear it. You know, and I love Missy Higgins doing [Split Enz song] "Stuff and Nonsense"— I was so pleased with that.

214 • Liz Giuffre

Giuffre: Just finally: how do you feel about the Frenz of the Enz [the Tim and Neil Finn fan club]? [Frenz 2017]. It's been going for well over thirty years now under the same leader, Peter Green. How does that make you feel? Proud? Surreal? A bit of both?

Tim Finn: I suppose a bit of both. There's a great loyalty there, and when you go onstage you can sometimes see those faces, but it's often just more of a feeling that those people are there. Some of them have been there right from the start, from 1975, and people might come up to you occasionally and say "I was at that gig in 1975," and when they talk about it to you, you just know that time just doesn't exist. They saw you play yesterday and you were twenty-three, and they saw you play today and you're fifty-three, and it's still great and you're still having a great time of it. And it links it all up, and without that [connection to the audience] it can be really hard. In my mid-40s I lost that connection with playing live and connecting. That time was just before I met my wife and had my family, when I had lost that connection to that live [performance circuit]. Then her and I started listening to music again and being a fan again, then going to shows and playing shows, playing acoustic, and it just all started happening, and I realized unless you play live, unless you connect up, it somehow feeds into the writing—when you're playing live you're getting that connection. So in answer to your question, it's an unacknowledged source of inspiration I think—fans, who know you well. The part I occasionally hear about through Neil, or somebody will tell me, I don't go there but he goes there occasionally, and he'll say "they're talking about our shoes," you know that sort of stuff. And that's surreal. That's not what I'm talking about. I'm talking about the other sort of stuff.

Giuffre: It's an interesting group to be part of – I joined the Frenz [of the Enz] when I was about eleven years old and it's a really nice non hierarchical community—often in those types of groups there can be in-fights about who knows what and to what degree.

Tim Finn: Yeah, you know, at one level it's just silly fun, but on another level if you've been following the music and it's been part of your life for thirty years, then that's pretty big, that's a big chunk of somebody's life.

Phone Interview with Tim Finn, Early 2016

Tim Finn was talking on the phone from Auckland to promote his most recent Australian/New Zealand collaboration – a play called The Fiery Maze which was the result of work with Australian poet Dorothy Porter. Originally conceived as an album or performance, it remained unfinished when Porter died suddenly in 2008. Nearly a decade later and with the blessing of her partner, Finn returned to the work to resurrect what they had begun by tracing traces left on now-defunct technology and tried to rekindle the original creative spark without his collaborator. The theater production has toured Melbourne and Sydney as of March 2017 to very positive critical acclaim.

Giuffre: You started writing with Dorothy Porter in the mid-1990s, and now she's passed away and many other projects have come along. Also, you're now based back in

Conversations with Neil and Tim Finn • 215

	New Zealand rather than Melbourne when this started. How did you get back into the mindset you were originally in when you started this work?
Tim Finn:	It was trying to work out what I was thinking and doing at the time. I didn't write anything down, I don't write music anyway, so I could hear these songs on DAT tapes, those early digital tapes, and they were starting to degrade with funny glitches and things, so I became obsessed with trying to figure out what I'd actually played, because I really liked them. So I re-learned them all and then put them into my computer to be sort of safe, but I didn't change a single note. It was just trying to decipher, like ancient hieroglyphics or something
Giuffre:	Did the songs still feel like yours, or did they feel like someone else's, given they'd been "time capsuled" like that?
Tim Finn:	Well some songs are timeless, really, and they put me instantly back in that room, singing with Abi [Tucker, the young Australian vocalist on the demos]. I think that's what made me so convinced they deserved a hearing, was that every time I played them or thought of them they just seemed so fresh, you know.
Giuffre:	I notice Abi's coming back to the Malthouse [Melbourne theater venue] to perform then, too. Is there any translation happening there, given she's now a little older than she was the first time around?
Tim Finn:	Yeah, well she's really, we had a workshop, and she was able to get right back inside the songs. And sure, she's singing them with more maturity and authority, but you know, it's the same singer, she's got this magnificent voice and she just connects with the material. She sent me an email a few years ago just saying "What's happened to those songs?," so she didn't forget about them either.
Giuffre:	This must be something you've encountered a lot given how long you've been making music for, but do you find somethings that songs appear in the wrong time and place and they have to wait to get their turn? Or do you think that's a bit too philosophical?
Tim Finn:	No, no, that does seem to happen, even though I'm not sure why, but it definitely does. I've got pieces of music that are twenty or thirty years old and I finally find the lyrics for it, so it does happen. It doesn't happen often with fully-fledged, finished songs, usually if they're any good you're keen to get them down as soon as you can, but certainly good melodic ideas or good lyrical ideas can sit around for ages, you know.
Giuffre:	I wonder if it's got to do not just with a particular time but also with a particular place—that was Melbourne at a particular point and context?
Tim Finn:	I live in Auckland now, we moved back about seventeen years ago I guess. But you're right, these songs belong, and had their existence, in Melbourne. I feel they've lived beyond that, but they definitely do take me back to those days when I lived there, we all did. We all lived there and all loved it, and I have strong connections with friends and family and people still. But yeah, with Dorothy gone now, she was a great Australian voice, and yeah, went too soon. So her sort of presence and life in Melbourne is very much in those songs from that time.

216 • Liz Giuffre

Conclusion

The snippets of these interviews over the last decade of music making reveal engaging details about Australian and New Zealand work as it is continuing to develop. At the time of the first interview, in 2006, both Neil and Tim Finn were extremely well established. A decade later in 2016 each had continued to write, release and perform even more. This series demonstrates how both men have continued to passionately engage and evolve as part of, and beyond, the Australia and New Zealand industries over time. During the discussions each engaged with nostalgia in different forms (acknowledging their existing fans and their own legacies), but they were never looking backwards simply for its own sake. The impact of their musical legacy and the loyalty of their fans were to be respected, but never to be taken for granted. Tim Finn's commitment to exploring music, poetry and the stage builds on his very early theatrical take with the New Zealand band Split Enz back in the 1970s and 1980s. He explains on a number of occasions over time how this work has now evolved to allow him to inhabit others' voices and bodies through mixed media. Meanwhile Neil Finn's determination to take audiences with him on a new journey—by continuing to develop Crowded House beyond its greatest hits and towards new heights, is also inspired. His enthusiasm for the challenge of trying to win over hardened Rage Against the Machine bands with Antipodean pop/folk is not only hilarious when taken in the context of someone of his already established success, but also demonstrates the "thrill of the chase" he still feels in trying to inspire new listeners.

Notes

1   The full details of the *Bro' Town* and *Flight of The Conchords* programs can be found via www.imdb.com/name/nm0278154 and www.imdb.com/name/nm0278178 (each accessed 25 November 2016) and www.bbc.co.uk/programmes/b007k17r (accessed November 25, 2016).
2   Full details available at www.abc.net.au/local/stories/2011/10/11/3337146.htm (accessed November 25, 2016).

Bibliography

Chamberlin, Chris. 2016. "ABC Simulcasts Crowded House Live as Part of Ausmusic Month Celebrations", *ABC Online Media Release*, October 29. https://tv.press.abc.net.au/abc-simulcasts-crowded-house-live-as-part-of-ausmusic-month-celebrations (accessed November 26, 2016).
Frenz. 2017. The Frenz of the Enz Fansite. www.frenz.com (accessed March 30, 2017).
Mitchell, Tony. 2010. "'Kiwi' Music and New Zealand National Identity." In *Many Voices: Music and National Identity in Aotearoa/New Zealand*, edited by Henry Johnson, 20–29. Cambridge: Cambridge Scholars Publishing.
New Zealand Herald. 2016. "ARIA Awards 2016: Conchords Protest Crowded House Award," 24 November. www.nzherald.co.nz/entertainment/news/article.cfm?c_id=1501119&objectid=11754018 (accessed November 28, 2016).
Rosser, Michael. 2016. "Guy Pearce to Make Directorial Debut with 'Poor Boy'", *Screen Daily*, 13 May. www.screendaily.com/festivals/cannes/guy-pearce-to-make-directorial-debut-with-poor-boy/5103820.article (accessed March 30, 2017).

Discography

Buffett, Jimmy. "Weather with You" in *Take the Weather with You*. MBD 2118 Mailboat Records, 2006, compact disc.
Crowded House. *Farewell to the World: 10th Anniversary Edition*. 0946 3 7032992 EMI, 2006, DVD.
Crowded House. *Woodface*. CDP 7 93559 2 Capitol Records, 1991, compact disc.

Flight of the Conchords. *Flight of the Conchords: The Complete Radio Series*. 1846 070708 BBC Audio, 2006, compact disc.

Finn, Tim. *The Conversation*. 50999 265303 2 1 EMI, 2006, compact disc.

Higgins, Missy. "Stuff and Nonsense" in *They Will Have Their Way: The Songs of Tim and Neil Finn*. 7305842 EMI, 2011, compact disc.

Split Enz. "Poor Boy" in *True Colours*. D37167 Mushroom Records, 1979, 33⅓ record.

Various Artists. *7 Worlds Collide Live Album*, Parlophone Records, 2001, compact disc.

Various Artists. *7 Worlds Collide: Neil Finn and Friends Live at the St James*. F.PM.85 Parlophone Records/EMI, 2001, compact disc.

Various Artists. *She Will Have Her Way: The Songs of Tim and Neil Finn*. 0946 3 404952 8 EMI, 2006, compact disc.

Various Artists. *They Will Have Their Way: The Songs of Tim and Neil Finn* Capitol Records, 2011, compact disc.

A Selected Bibliography of Books on Popular Music in Australia and Aotearoa/New Zealand

Appleby, Rosalind. 2012. *Women of Note: The Rise of Australian Women Composers*. Perth: Fremantle Press.

Arrow, Michelle. 2009. *Friday on Our Minds: Popular Culture in Australia since 1945*. Sydney: UNSW Press.

Baker, Glenn A. and Roger Dilernia. 1982. *The Beatles Down Under*. Sydney: Wild & Woolley.

Bannister, Matthew. 2006. *White Boys, White Noise: Masculinities and 1980s Indie Guitar Rock*. London: Ashgate.

Bannister, Matthew. 1999. *Positively George Street: A Personal History of Sneaky Feelings and the Dunedin Sound*. Auckland: Reed.

Barney, Katelyn, ed. 2014. *Collaborative Ethnomusicology: New Approaches to Music Research between Indigenous and Non-Indigenous Australians*. Melbourne: Lyrebird Press.

Barrand, Janine, Margaret Marshall, Tim Fisher and Nick Henderson. 2010. *Rock Chicks: Women in Australian Music*. Melbourne: Victoria Arts Trust.

Bourke, Chris. 2013. *Blue Smoke: The Lost Dawn of New Zealand Popular Music 1918–1964*. Auckland: Auckland University Press.

Brabazon, Tara, ed. 2005. *Liverpool of the South Seas: Perth and Its Popular Music*. Perth: University of Western Australia Press.

Breen, Marcus. 1999. *Rock Dogs: Politics and the Australian Music Industry*. Oxford: University Press of America.

Breen, Marcus. 1989. *Our Place, Our Music: Aboriginal Music*. Canberra: Aboriginal Studies Press.

Chapman, Ian. 2010. *Kiwi Rock Chicks, Popstars & Trailblazers*. Auckland: Harper Collins.

Clare, John and Gail Brennan. 1995. *Bodgie Dada & The Cult of Cool*. Sydney: UNSW Press.

Connell, John and Chris Gibson. 2003. *Sound Tracks: Popular Music Identity and Place*. London: Routledge.

Desoto, Lucy. 2016. *Australia Rocks: Remembering the Music of the 1950s to 1990s*. Wollombi, NSW: Exisle Publishing.

Dix, John and Richard Symons. 2005. *Stranded in Paradise: New Zealand Rock'n'Roll 1955–1988*. Auckland: Penguin.

Downes, Peter. 1979. *Top of the Bill: Entertainers through the Years*. Auckland: AH & AW Reed.

Dunbar-Hall, Peter and Chris Gibson. 2004. *Deadly Sounds, Deadly Places: Contemporary Aboriginal Music in Australia*. Sydney: UNSW Press.

Eggleton, David. 2003. *Ready to Fly: The Story of New Zealand Rock Music*. Nelson, NZ: Craig Potton Publishing.

Garland, Phil. 2009. *Faces in the Firelight: New Zealand Folk Song & Story*. Wellington: Steele Roberts.

Harding, Mike. 1992. *When the Pakeha Sings of Home: A Source Guide to the Folk & Popular Songs of New Zealand*. Auckland: Godwit.

Hayward, Philip, ed. 1998. *Sound Alliances: Indigenous Peoples, Cultural Politics, and Popular Music in the Pacific*. London: Bloomsbury Publishing.

Hayward, Philip, ed. 1992. *From Pop, to Punk, to Postmodernism: Australian Popular Music and Culture from the 1960s to the 1990s*. North Sydney: Allen & Unwin.

Homan, Shane. 2003. *The Mayor's A Square: Live Music and Law and Order in Sydney*. Newtown, NSW: LCP.

Homan, Shane, Martin Cloonan and Jennifer Cattermole. 2015. *Popular Music Industries and the State: Policy Notes*, Vol. 8. London: Routledge.

Homan, Shane and Tony Mitchell, eds. 2008. *Sounds of Then, Sounds of Now: Popular Music in Australia*. Hobart: ACYS Publishing.

Johnson, Bruce. 2000. *The Inaudible Music: Jazz, Gender and Australian Modernity*. Sydney: Currency Press.

Johnson, Henry, ed. 2010. *Many Voices: Music and National Identity in Aotearoa/New Zealand*. Newcastle upon Tyne: Cambridge Scholars Publishing.

Keam, Glenda and Tony Mitchell, eds. 2011. *Home, Land and Sea: Situating Music in Aotearoa New Zealand*. Auckland: Pearson New Zealand.

Marks, Ian D. and Iain McIntyre. 2011. *Wild about You! The Sixties Beat Explosion in Australia and New Zealand*. Portland: Verse Chorus Press.

220 • Selected Bibliography

Martin, Toby. 2015. *Yodelling Boundary Riders: Country Music in Australia Since the 1920s*. Melbourne: Lyrebird Press.

McFarlane, Ian. 2017. *The Encyclopedia of Australian Rock and Pop*. 2nd edition. Gisbourne, Victoria: Third Stone Press.

McLean, Mervyn. 1995. *An Annotated Bibliography of Oceanic Music and Dance*. Sterling Heights, MI: Harmonie Park Press.

Minestrelli, Chiara. 2016. *Australian Indigenous Hip Hop: The Politics of Culture, Identity, and Spirituality*. London: Routledge.

Mitchell, Tony. 2001. *Global Noise: Rap and Hip Hop Outside the USA*. Middleton, CT: Wesleyan University Press.

Mitchell, Tony. 1996. *Popular Music and Local Identity: Rock, Pop, and Rap in Europe and Oceania*. Leicester: Leicester University Press.

Moffat, Kirstine and Patricia Prime. 2011. *Piano Forte: Stories and Soundscapes from Colonial New Zealand*. Dunedin: Otago University Press.

Neuenfeldt, Karl, ed. 1997. *The Didjeridu: From Arnhem Land to Internet*. Sydney: J. Libbey/Perfect Beat Publications.

Nichols, David. 2016. *Dig: Australian Rock and Pop Music 1960–1985*. Portland, OR: Verse Chorus Press.

O'Donnell, John, Toby Creswell and Craig Mathieson. 2011. *The 100 Best Australian Albums*. Melbourne: Hardie Grant Publishing.

Ottosson, Åse. 2017. *Making Aboriginal Men and Music in Central Australia*. London: Bloomsbury.

Priest, Gail. 2009. *Experimental Music: Audio Explorations in Australia*. Sydney: UNSW Press.

Russell, Bruce. 2009. *Left-Handed Blows: Writing on Sound, 1993–2009*. Auckland: Clouds.

Scott, Michael. 2013. *Making New Zealand's Pop Renaissance: State, Markets, Musicians*. London: Ashgate.

Shute, Gareth. 2005. *Making Music in New Zealand*. Auckland: Random House New Zealand.

Smith, Graeme. 2005. *Singing Australian: A History of Folk and Country Music*. Annandale: Pluto Press Australia.

Spittle, Gordon and Tony Ricketts. 2009. *Counting the Beat: A History of New Zealand Song*. Wellington: Royal New Zealand Foundation of the Blind.

Staff, Bryan and Sheran Ashley. 2002. *For the Record: A History of the Recording Industry in New Zealand*. Auckland: David Bateman.

Stafford, Andrew. 2004. *Pig City: From the Saints to Savage Garden*. St Lucia: University of Queensland Press.

Stratton, Jon. 2007. *Australian Rock: Essays on Popular Music*. Perth: Network Books.

Stubington, Jill and Raymattja Marika-Munuŋgiritj. 2007. *Singing the Land: The Power of Performance in Aboriginal Life*. Strawberry Hills, NSW: Currency House.

Thomas, Allan. 2004. *Music is Where You Find It: Music in the Town of Hawera, 1946: An Historical Ethnography*. Wellington: Music Books New Zealand.

Thomas, Allan. 2000. *Music in New Zealand: A Reader from the 1940s*. Christchurch: School of Music, University of Canterbury.

Walker, Clinton. 2014. *Buried Country: The Story of Aboriginal Country Music*. Portland, OR: Verse Chorus Press.

Walker, Clinton. 2005. *Inner City Sound*. Portland, OR: Verse Chorus Press.

Walker, Clinton. 1996. *Stranded: The Secret History of Australian Independent Music, 1977–1991*. Sydney: Pan Macmillan.

Watkins, Roger. 1995. *Hostage to the Beat: The Auckland Scene 1955–1970*. North Shore City, NZ: Tandem Press.

Watkins, Roger. 1989. *When Rock Got Rolling: The Wellington Scene, 1958–1970*. Christchurch: Hazard Press.

Whiteoak, John. 1999. *Playing Ad Lib: Improvisatory Music in Australia, 1836–1970*. Sydney: Currency Press.

Whiteoak, John and Aline Scott-Maxwell. 2003. *Currency Companion to Music and Dance in Australia*. Sydney: Currency House.

Notes on Contributors

Cathy Adamek was awarded her PhD thesis, "Adelaide Dance Music Culture, Late 1980s-Early 1990s," in 2017 from the University of South Australia through the Hawke Research Institute, where she tutors and guest lectures. She is an independent artist and producer who works extensively as an actor/dancer/director/choreographer for theater warehouse parties and festivals, film, TV and radio (voiceover). Her award winning original physical theater and dance music collaborations have toured Australia premiering at the Sydney Opera House and she is board secretary for Ausdance South Australia, Australia's peak national body for dance and a peer assessor for the Australia Council for the Arts.

Kyle Barnett is Associate Professor of Media Studies at Bellarmine University's School of Communication, United States. His work has appeared in *Music, Sound, and the Moving Image*, the *Journal of Popular Music Studies*, the *Journal of Material Culture*, and several anthologies. He recently co-edited a special issue of *Creative Industries Journal* on the recording and radio industries. He is currently completing a book on the transformation of the US recording industry between 1920 and 1935. His work focuses on media history, media industries, and sound across media.

Andy Bennett is Professor of Cultural Sociology in the School of Humanities, Languages, and Social Science at Griffith University in Queensland, Australia. He has written and edited numerous books including *Popular Music and Youth Culture* (Macmillan 2000), *Music, Style and Aging* (Temple University Press 2013) and *Music Scenes* (co-edited with Richard A. Peterson) (Vanderbilt University Press 2004). He is a Faculty Fellow of the Yale Center for Cultural Sociology, an International Research Fellow of the Finnish Youth Research Network, a founding member of the Consortium for Youth, Generations, and Culture, and a founding member of the Regional Music Research Group.

Paul Blacklow is Lecturer in Econometrics and Microeconomics at the University of Tasmania, Australia. Paul specializes in modeling the behavior and choices of individuals and households, particularly in how they allocate their money and time. He conducts research into prices, incomes and inequality, the cost of living, the cost of children, education performance, and labour markets. Paul also provides specialist consulting services for Tasmanian organizations and has examined such issues as illicit drug reform, workers compensation, and Antarctic services.

222 • Notes on Contributors

Shelley Brunt is Senior Lecturer in the Music Industry program at RMIT University, Australia. Her research interests lie in the field of popular music ethnomusicology, and she has published on community music and street festivals in Australia and New Zealand. She was Chair of the Australia-New Zealand branch of the International Association for the Study of Popular Music (IASPM-ANZ) from 2007–2013, and is currently the co-editor of *Perfect Beat: The Asia-Pacific Journal of Research into Contemporary Music and Popular Culture.*

Mara Favoretto is Senior Lecturer in Spanish and Latin American Studies at the University of Melbourne, Australia. She specializes in the intersections between politics, power, and popular culture in Latin America, with a special interest in popular music. She is the author of *Luis Alberto Spinetta: mito y mitología* (Gourmet Musical Ediciones 2017), *Charly en el país de las alegorías* (Gourmet Musical Ediciones 2014), *Alegoría e ironía bajo censura en la Argentina del Proceso* (Edwin Mellen Press 2010), and of numerous research papers published in peer-reviewed journals.

Liz Giuffre is Senior Lecturer in Communications at the University of Technology, Sydney, Australia. In addition to this she works regularly in the national independent arts press as a journalist and commentator, including work as the regular contributing editor for *Metro Magazine*, a regular contributor to *Critical Studies in Television*, and columnist for *The Conversation.*

April K. Henderson is Senior Lecturer in Pacific Studies and Programme Director of Va'aomanū Pasifika (Pacific Studies and Samoan Studies) at Victoria University of Wellington, Aotearoa/New Zealand. Her multi-sited research often involves tracking the movements of people, things, and ideas in, through, and beyond the Pacific, as well as contextualizing the aspirations of Pacific peoples involved in these movements. Hip hop music, dance, and visual art have featured prominently in this work for at least two decades.

Michael Holland is Professional Practice Fellow in the Department of Music, Theatre, and Performing Arts at the University of Otago, Aotearoa/New Zealand. His research focuses on the intersection of music, technology, and place, and spans the fields of ethnography, record production, and popular music studies. Michael's research is also informed by his work as a studio and live sound engineer, and he has recently completed several recording projects and international tours with prominent Aotearoa/New Zealand artists.

Shane Homan is Associate Professor in Media Studies at Monash University, Australia. He has completed commissioned reports on music industry strategies for the New South Wales government (2003), Melbourne City Council (2010), and the Australia Council (2013). His latest book is *Popular Music, Industry and the State: Policy Notes*, co-authored with Martin Cloonan and Jennifer Cattermole (Routledge 2016).

Andrew Legg is Director of the Tasmanian Conservatorium of Music and Deputy Head of the Tasmanian College of the Arts at the University of Tasmania, Australia. Associate

Professor Legg's career spans over thirty years in the USA and Australia as an award winning African American gospel music pianist, singer, choral conductor, and educator, and his research now focuses on the performance practices and transculturization of contemporary African American gospel music.

Tony Mitchell is honorary Research Associate at the University of Technology, Sydney, Australia. He grew up in Auckland, and is the co-editor of *Home, Land and Sea: Situating Music in Aotearoa New Zealand* (Pearson Education 2011), *Sounds of Then, Sounds of Now: Popular Music in Australia* (ACYS 2007), editor of *Global Noise: Rap and Hip Hop outside the USA* (Wesleyan University Press 2001), and author of *Popular Music and Local Identity: Rock, Pop and Rap in Europe and Oceania* (Leicester University Press 1996). He most recently co-edited the volume *Sounds Icelandic* (Equinox 2017).

Chiara Minestrelli is Associate Lecturer in Contemporary Media Cultures at the London College of Communication (University of Arts London). She also holds a Visiting Fellowship at King's College (Menzies Centre for Australian Studies) and London South Bank University (School of Arts and Creative Industries). Her first monograph, *Australian Indigenous Hip Hop: The Politics of Culture, Identity and Spirituality* was published by Routledge in 2016.

Carolyn Philpott is Senior Lecturer in Musicology and the Research Coordinator at the Conservatorium of Music within the School of Creative Arts at the University of Tasmania, Australia. She teaches a variety of undergraduate and postgraduate units across both classical and contemporary music programs and her research interests include Australian music, connections between music, place, and the environment, and the characteristics and globalization of African American gospel music.

Julie Rickwood is Visiting Fellow at the Australian National University's School of Music. She has published in peer reviewed journals and edited collections on popular music and community, popular music and gender, and in the field of ecomusicology. Julie has taught popular music in culture and in context, co-convened the Popular Music, Stars, and Stardom IASPM-ANZ Conference in 2015, and was an executive member of IASPM-ANZ from 2012–2014.

Ian Rogers is Senior Lecturer in the Music Industry program at RMIT University, Australia. He is the author of numerous articles on musician ideologies, music policy, and local music history and his latest publication is a monograph titled *Popular Music Scenes and Cultural Memory* (co-authored with Andy Bennett, Palgrave Macmillan 2016).

Robert Sloane is Instructor of American Culture Studies at Bowling Green State University, United States. His research and teaching interests include cultural theory, the cultural industries, and various forms of popular communication. He has published articles on popular music and animation.

Geoff Stahl is Senior Lecturer in Media Studies at Victoria University of Wellington, New Zealand. His publications include *Poor, but Sexy: Reflections on Berlin Scenes* (Peter Lang 2014) and *Understanding Media Studies* (Oxford 2009), as well as many articles on music-making in Montreal, Berlin, and Wellington.

224 • Notes on Contributors

Jon Stratton is Adjunct Professor of Cultural Studies in the School of Creative Industries at the University of South Australia. Jon has published widely in Cultural Studies, Popular Music Studies, Australian Studies, Jewish Studies, and on race and multiculturalism. His most recent books are *When Music Migrates: Crossing British and European Racial Faultlines 1945–2010* (Ashgate 2014) and, co-edited with Nabeel Zuberi, *Black Popular Music in Britain since 1945* (Ashgate 2014).

Catherine Strong is Senior Lecturer in the Music Industry program at RMIT University, Australia. Among her publications are *Grunge: Popular Music and Memory* (Ashgate 2011), and *Death and the Rock Star* (edited with Barbara Lebrun, Ashgate 2015). Her research deals with various aspects of memory, nostalgia, and gender in rock music, popular culture, and the media. Current projects include an ARC (Australian Research Council) Discovery on the history of popular music in Melbourne. She is currently Chair of the International Association for the Study of Popular Music (IASPM-ANZ) and incoming co-editor of *Popular Music History* journal.

Adam Trainer is a researcher, academic, and musician, who currently oversees Western Australian music projects at the State Library of Western Australia. He has taught film, cultural and popular music studies, and has published on film aesthetics, online music communities, and Western Australian popular music history. Adam has been involved in several research projects investigating specific music communities, including the Western Australian New Music Archive and a critical social history of popular music in the state. Adam is an Adjunct Lecturer at Edith Cowan University.

Emma Williams is Curator at Albury LibraryMuseum in regional New South Wales, Australia. She was Assistant Curator of "Head Full of Flames: Punk in the Nation's Capital 1977–1992" which was exhibited at Canberra Museum and Gallery from September 2013 until February 2014. With a keen interest in Australian popular music history in the museum and gallery context, previous work includes "'Taking the Next Step' with Web 2.0–Social Media as a Research Tool for Museums" (*Museums Australia Magazine* 2014) and "States-Minded: Local Identity in Australian Popular Music Scenes 1962–1971" (Honours thesis, University of Sydney 2007).

Oli Wilson is the Music Programme Leader in the School of Music and Creative Media Production at Massey University, Wellington, Aotearoa/New Zealand, and is the Co-Editor of *Perfect Beat: The Asia-Pacific Journal of Research into Contemporary Music and Popular Culture*. His research draws on his creative practice in popular music, and explores concepts relating to fandom, nostalgia, and community through his involvement as keyboard player in the iconic band The Chills. He has also studied Aotearoa/New Zealand popular music, and has conducted extensive ethnographic research on the impact that new media technologies are having on local cultures in Papua New Guinea.

Index

7 Worlds Collide 207, 209
16 Lovers Lane (Go-Betweens) 196
"107" (DJ HMC) 160

A.B. Original 146, 148, 150
ABBA 65
Abbott, Tony 148
ABC Concerts 33
Aboriginal people 2–4, 10, 91, 146–50
"Aboriginal Style" (Darah) 149
AboriginalRap (YouTube) 147
AC/DC 194, 207
AC/DC Lane (Melbourne) 62, 65
academia *see* universities
Adamek, Cathy 221; chapter 131, 155–66
Adams, Jessica 62
Adams, Tim 198
Adelaide 113, 131, 140, 146, 150, 155–65, 184
Aerosmith 195
Afghanistan 145
African Americans 6–7, 11; gospel 133, 136–7, 139–42; hip hop 171–2, 174
Afrika Bambataa 175
Against All Odds (Impossible Odds) 147
The Age 146
agent of change principle 181, 185
Ahrens, Lyn 138
Air New Zealand 52, 121, 124
Ajax 198
Albert Hall (Canberra) 33
alcohol 39, 127, 183–6
Alexandria 198
Alim, Sami H. 145
Alizadeh, Sonita 145
Allenby, Guy 25
alternative rock 23, 157
Amphlett Lane 59–60, 62–3, 65–7
And They Were Masked 47
DJ Angus 161
Antonoff, Jack 46, 53

Anu, Christine 138
Aotearoa/New Zealand 1–14, 131, 186; Auckland 45–54; Christchurch 97–108; cities as theme 13–14; colonialism 2–5; Dunedin 69–77; Finn brothers' interviews 207–9, 211–12, 214–16; key moments 9–12; music discovery 193–202; popular music histories/industries 5–9; Wellington 121–9, 167–76
appropriation 4, 171
Aquaviva, John 159
Architecture for Humanity 101, 104
Argentina 85
Aristotle 125
Arnhem Land 2
"Arsehole of The Universe" (Exterminators) 24
Art Beat 102
Ashraf, Sofia 145
Así es Peru 85
Asia 1, 6, 12, 14, 20, 113
Astro Children 74
Athens (GA) 196
Atkins, Juan 164
Auckland 10, 45–54, 104, 201, 207, 215
Auckland Anniversary Day 52
AusMusic Month 208
Austin (TX) 33, 59, 180–1, 184
Australasian Performing Rights Association (APRA) 207
Australia 1–14, 131; Adelaide/techno 155–65; Brisbane 111–19; Canberra 31–41; cities as theme 13–14; colonialism 2–5; Finn brothers' interviews 207–10, 212, 214–16; Hobart 111–19, 133–43; Indigenous rappers 145–50; key moments 9–12; Latin American music 81–91; Melbourne 59–67; "music cities" 183–7; music discovery 193–6, 198–202; "Oz Rock" 9, 155, 184; Perth 19–28; popular music histories/industries 5–9
"Australia Day" 3, 10
The Australian 25

226 • Index

Australian Aboriginal Hip Hop 147
Australian Broadcasting Corporation (ABC) 8–9, 136, 208
Australian Music Vault 59
Australian National University 34, 38
Australian Record Industry Association (ARIA) 133, 138, 207
"Autahi" (Te Kupu) 172
authorized heritage 59–61, 64–7
automotive industry 156, 161–4
Awad, Ibrahim 145
Azalea, Iggy 202

Backhouse, Tony 140
"Bad Politics" (Dead C) 200
Baillie, Russell 53
Baker, James 24–5
Bali 20
Balwyn 24
Bambacas, Theo 158–9
Bandcamp 99
Bandstand 9
Banghalter, Thomas 161
The Bank Holidays 21
Bank of New Zealand 47
Bannister, Matthew 51, 76
Bar 25 (Berlin) 126
Barnett, Courtney 202
Barnett, Kyle 194, 221; chapter 193–204
Barnett, Stephen 49
Barone, Stefano 112
Barrett, Syd 199
bars 126–7, *see also* pubs
Barter, Ben 52
Barton, Chris 50
Bass Strait 113
The Bats 196, 199–200
Baudelaire 125
BBC 8
Beat Magazine 90
Beat music 7
BEATBOX 100
The Beatles 60, 65, 75
The Bedford (Christchurch) 105–6
The Bee Gees 194
Beggars Banquet 196
Belgium 161
Bell, Thomas 19
Bell Tower (Perth) 22
Bemac 82
Bendrups, Dan 193
Bennett, Andy 61, 112–13, 157, 221; chapter 95, 111–20
Bennett, Barnaby 98, 101, 103, 107
Bennett, Tony 91

Benton, Penelope 184
Berlin 59, 126, 180–1
Bhabha, Homi 86
Bianchetti, Cam 155, 157–61, 164
Bicentenary 10, 22
Bicton 26–7
Big Luke 149
Big Sound 114
Billboard 49
Birnies 23
Blacklow, Paul 221; chapter 131, 133–44
Blackman, Guy 25
Blainey, Geoffrey 5
Blair, Tony 11
Blake, James 53
Blue Cheese 74
Blum, Alan 124–5, 128
The Bodega (Wellington) 121
"bohemian city" 180
Bolivia 85
Boogie Down Productions (BDP) 174
Booragoon (Perth) 26
Bootleg Sessions 31–2, 34–9, 41
Born Sandy Devotional (Triffids) 25
Bowie, David 12
Bowling Green State University 201
"Box Elder" (Pavement) 201
Boyer, Horace Clarence 136–7
Brabazon, Tara 21–2
branding 122–4, 132, 146, 179
Brass Knuckle Brass Band 34, 41
Brazil 85
breaking 168–9
"Breaking News" (Madre Monte) 90–1
The Breeders 201
"Brides for Sale" (Alizadeh) 145
Briggs 146–8, 150
Brighter Day (Southern Gospel Choir) 138
Brighton 71, 179
Brisbane 32, 95, 111–16, 118–19, 147, 184, 196
British Empire 3, 5, 134, *see also* United Kingdom (UK)
Brixton 159
Bro' Town 50, 208
Broadway to Australia 138
Bronx 167, 173
Broods 52
Broome, Richard 150
Bruce Mason Centre (Takapuna) 47
Brunt, Shelley 222; chapter 95, 97–109; introduction 1–14
Bryant, Martin 141
Buenos Aires 85
Buffett, Jimmy 213

built environment 23, 60, 63–4, 66, 104–5
Bull Creek (Perth) 27–8
"Burden of Relief" (The Nudge) 106–7
Butavicius, Paddee 159
Butcher, Bleddyn 26
Butler, Judith 50
Butler, Myron 136

Café of the Gate of Salvation 140
The Cakekitchen 196
California 149
Cambodia 175
Cameron, Matt 213
Canada 159–60, 186
Canberra 17, 31–41, 88
Canberra Musicians Club (CMC) 34, 38
The Cannanes 196
Canterbury (A/NZ) 97, 105
capital, cultural 122–4
capitalism 186, 199
Capital Magazine 127
Captured Tracks 202
Caraccia, Tony 155, 157
car industry 156, 161–4
Carlton 24
"Carlton North" (Sleepy Township) 25
Carniel, Jennifer 12
Carr, Barry 86
Carson, Nat 21
Carter, Shayne 75
Cathedral Square (Christchurch) 97–8, 106
CDs 100–3, 105, 196–7
celebrity 51–2
Celestino 87
Central Station Records 155, 157
change 61–2, 64, 67, 128; agent of 181, 185
Chapter Music 25
Charivari (Detroit) 163
Charlottesville (VA) 194, 196–8, 201
charts 102–3, 146
Chau, Rebecca 21–2
Los Chavos 89
Cheltenham Beach (Devonport) 49–50
Chick's (Dunedin) 74
children 3–4
"The Children Came Back" (Briggs and Everettsmith) 148
Chile 85, 88–9
The Chills 69–70, 72, 74–6, 200
Chipkiewicz, Eyal 88
Christchurch 52, 95, 97–108, 201
Christchurch City Council 98, 101
Christchurch Music Industry Trust (CHART) 97, 100–1
Cinnaman 158–9

cities 1, 13, 17, 49, 57, 77, 121; Canberra 31–5; "creative" 122–4, 179–82; fragility 128; heritage-making 59–60, 62–6, 69; hip hop 149–50; "music city" 132, 179–87; peripheral 112–13, 115, 118–19; Perth/suburbs 19–28; technomotor 156, 160, 162, 164; urban melancholy 121, 124–6, 128, *see also* urban
"City on Fire" (Darah) 149
"The City Is Too Small" (Bank Holidays) 21
Civic 31
Claremont Serial Killer 23
Clark, Helen 11
Clark, Terry 161
class 7, 21, 27, 61, 122, 162–4, 183
classical music 182
Clave Contra Clave (CCC) 81–3, 87–91
The Clean 72, 74, 194–6, 199–200
Cliff, Jimmy 10
Clohessy, Kieron 35
clubs 85, 158, 163, 168
C'Mon 8
Coachella 210–12
Cobain, Kurt 201
Cohen, Sara 39, 59–61, 64, 75, 77
Cold Chisel 9, 163
collective memory *see* memory
Cologne 71
Colombia 85, 87, 90, 209
Colón, Willie 87
colonialism 2–3, 5–6, 8, 12; hip hop 146, 149–50, 167, 172; music discovery 194, 199
"Come Home" (The Chills) 200
community 123, 157, 214; disaster fundraising 98–100, 105–7; gospel 135, 141–3; heritage-making 63–4, 66; imagined 5–6; of interest 169; Latin American music 83–5, 91; peripheral cities 117–18
compilations 73, 98–102, 117, 197–8, 200–1
Compton 149
concerts *see* touring; venues
Condon, Hilary 48
conga 85
Connell, John 19, 23
Consequence of Sound 202
conservatives 7, 21, 156
consumption 122–3, 193–4, 202
Control (Adelaide) 158
Cook, James 2–3
Cooke, Eric Edgar 22
Corinbank 34
Corroboree (Split Enz) 3
Countdown 9
country music 180
Courtenay Place (Wellington) 126
cover versions 194, 210, 213

228 • Index

Cox, Carl 159
The Cramps 50
Creation Records 72
"creative city" 122–4, 179–82
Creative New Zealand 98, 101
Creative Spaces 185
creativity 156
crime 114
Criminal Minded (Boogie Down Productions) 174
cringe 4–5, 121, 137
crowd-funding 101, 107
Crowded House 207–11, 213, 216
Cuba 88
Cuba Mall (Wellington) 126–7
cueca 85
cultural capital 122–4
"cultural city" 179, 183
cultural cringe 4–5, 121, 137
cultural imperialism 5, 7–8
cultural memory *see* memory
cultural nationalisms 4, 10
culturalization 122
culture: hybridization 91; survivance/ maintenance 149–50
cumbia 85
"Cumbia March" (Madre Monte) 90
Currid, Elizabeth 135
Curtis, Ian 71
Curuenavuli, Paulini 138
Custard 114
cut-out bins 199–200

Daddy's Highway (The Bats) 196
Daft Punk 161
Dahahoo 37, 39
Dallas, David 52
Dallas (TX) 21
dance 84–6, 88, 168; electronic 155–65
danger 88–9
Darah 146, 149–50
Davidson, Delaney 100
DD Smash 11
The Dead C 198, 200
de Certeau, Michel 124, 128
deconstruction 77
"deep relations" 172, 175
DeNora, Tia 111
Depot Artspace 48
Derrida, Jacques 77
Detroit 52, 131, 155–8, 160–4, 180
developing countries 112
development 10, 26, 182–3, 185, *see also* land use
Devlin, Johnny 7
Devonport (Auckland) 45–51, 53

Devonport Folk Club 48, 50
Devonstock 47, 50
"El Diablo" (Madre Monte) 90–1
didgeridoo 2
Diesel and Dust (Midnight Oil) 195
Dirty House 155–62
disasters 95, 100, 104–5, 107
disco 162–3
discourse 164, 182; "Dunedin Sound" 76–7; hip hop 145–6, 149–50; identity construction 81–2, 84, 87; Wellington 123, 125, 128
distance, tyranny of 5–6, 12, 184
distributors 197, 199
"Dive for Your Memory" (Go-Betweens) 200
diversity 83, 88
The Divinyls 62
DIY 98, 100, 107, 113, 115, 117, 126
DJs 99, 126, 155, 157–61, 164, 167–8, 173
DLT 172–3
Dominion Post 128
Domino Records 202
Donato, Damien 155, 157–60, 164
Doprah 52
"Down Under" (Men at Work) 195
Downes, Graeme 71, 75
Dragon 10
Drayton, Charlie 63
The Dreaming 2
Dreamtime 91
Dreisinger, Baz 28
drinking *see* alcohol
drum machines 158, 172
Drysdale, Ben 37, 39, 41
Dubba Rukki 37
dullness 20–3, 25
Dunedin 11, 13, 32, 57, 69–77, 98, 196, 201
Dusseldorf 159
Dux De Lux (Christchurch) 97

earthquakes 97–101, 104–7; Recovery Grants 98
East Row Rabble 41
The Eastern 98, 100
economy 9–12, 23, 57, 85, 134; heritage-making 63–4; manufacturing 156, 161–2, 164; music city 179–87; urban melancholy 122–4, 127
Edinburgh 181–2
EDM 156–7
Edrosa, Emily 76
Edwards, Ben 100
Elders 147–9
Electronic Dance Music (EDM) 163–4
electronic music 155–65
Elvis Presley 7
Empathy Recordings 100
entrepreneurialism 122–4, 180–1

Index • 229

erotic 88–9
ethnicity 6, 51, 57, 169, *see also* Indigenous people; racism
ethnomusicology 98, 193
"ethno-pop" 10
Eurogliders 24–5
Europe 7, 158–9, 161, 163, 186, 194
European Broadcasting Union 8
European Economic Community (EEC) 10
European Union (EU) 10
Eurovision Song Contest 12
Evans, Bob 27–8
eventfulness 57, 122–3, 128, 135
Everettsmith, Dewayne 148
excess 88–9
exotic 88–9
The Exterminators 24
Extreme 47

fa'atau 171
Facebook 36, 41, 45, 63, 147
factories 161–3
The Fall 196
fans 197, 200–2, 207–8, 211, 214, 216
Farewell to the World (Crowded House) 208–9
Farrugia, David 112
Fat Freddy's Drop 122
Faulkner, Dave 24–5
Favaretto, Mara 222; chapter 57, 81–93
Fawcett, Pauly 99
feeling, structure of 125
feminism 53
Fernandes, Sujatha 145
Festival of Broadway 138
Festival of Transitional Architecture 103–4
Festival of Voices 133, 135–8
festivals 34, 57, 116, 123, 183; Finn brothers 207, 210–12; Latin American music 85–6; Lorde 47, 50, 52; Southern Gospel Choir 135–8
Field, Lindsay 138
Finch, Evan 197
Finn 207
The Finn Brothers 207
Finn, Liam 211
Finn, Neil 207–12, 214, 216
Finn, Tim 5, 207–8, 211–16
Fishrider Records 73
Fitch 46
Fitzgerald Inquiry 114
Fitzroy Gardens (Melbourne) 148
Flaherty, Steven 138
Flight of the Conchords 98, 207–8
Florida, Richard 123–4, 181–2
The Floyd (Canberra) 34
Flying Nun 11, 69–72, 74–6, 195–6, 198, 200–2

FM radio 8, 195
Fonseca 87
food 167, 173
Ford, Henry 161
Fordism 156, 161–3
formats 99–100
Fortitude Valley (Brisbane) 114–15, 184
Fremantle 19
Frenz of the Enz 214
Freud, Sigmund 125
Fridge (Brixton) 159
Frith, Simon 90
Fudge 198
The Fuelers 37
Fugs 26
Fullbrook, Hollie 52
fundraising 41, 98–101, 103, 107, 142
funk 172
Furia 89
Futuro house 27

gagana fa'aifailauga 170–1
Gallan, Ben 38–9
Gap Filler 103
Garden City (Christchurch) 97
Garden City (Perth) 26–7
Gare, Pete 36–7
Garnier, Laurent 159, 161
Geier, Fiete 35
gender 48, 76
genealogy 168–9, 171–3, 175
General Motors 162
genres 4, 6, 38, 83–5
gentrification 28, 35, 156; Melbourne 64, 66; music city 182–3, 185
geography 106, 112–13, 156; isolation 69, 118–19
Germany 59, 71–2, 159, 161
Gevinson, Tavi 49, 53
Gibson, Chris 19, 23
Gibson, Lorena 172
Gift Abroad 82
gifts 167–8, 173
gigs see touring; venues
Giles, Roger 48
Giuffre, Liz 222; afterword 207–17
"giving back" 168, 174
glam 24
Glasgow 181
global 1–2, 4–6, 8–13, 131, 186; electronic music 161–2, 165; hip hop 145–7, 149–50, 168, 170–1
Global Pop (Taylor) 199
"glocal" 161
The Go-Betweens 114, 196, 199–200, 202
The Go-Betweens (Nichols) 196
Good Music Neighbours 185

230 • Index

Goodnight Bull Creek! (Evans) 27
Gordy, Berry 163
gospel 133, 136–43
Gotye 12
government 3–4, 8–11, 59, 148, 179–86, *see also*
   politics
graffiti 51, 168, 173–4
Grammy Awards 51–3, 98
Gramsci, Antonio 88
Great Day (Southern Gospel Choir) 138
Green, Peter 214
Greens 41
Greive, Duncan 50
Groovin The Moo 34
Grupo Niche 87
G Stands for Go-Betweens (Go-Betweens) 202
Guardian 69, 72
guitar 73–4, 201

Hadley, Adam 34, 37–8
haka (chant) 11, 52
Haley, Bill 7
Hall, Rodney 20–2
Hannigan, Sean 35, 38
The Harbour Union 100
The Harder They Come 10
Harlem 174
Hart, Stephen 48–9
Harvey, P.J. 47
Hawke, Bob 10
Hawtin, Richie 158–9
Hay, Colin 9
Heap, Imogen 106
"Heaven (Must Be There)" (Eurogliders) 24
"Heavy 33" (Verlaines) 197
Helena Pop 41
Hellman, Tuomas 135
Henderson, April K. 222; chapter 131–2,
   167–77
Henderson, Ian 73
Herbs 10
heritage 91, 114; Melbourne 59–67; music city
   180, 183, 185, *see also* history; memory
Hesmondhalgh, David 32, 128
Hester, Paul 208, 210, 212
Higgins, Missy 213
High on A Mountain (Southern Gospel Choir)
   138
hikoi 3
hip hop 11–12, 131, 145–50, 162, 167–76
hipsters 28, 121, 124
history 2–6, 91, 114, 141; "Dunedin Sound" 74–7;
   hip hop 146, 149, *see also* heritage; memory
"Hit the North" (The Fall) 196
DJ HMC 155, 157–61, 164

Hobart 184; music scenes 95, 111, 113, 116–19;
   Southern Gospel Choir 131, 133–43
Hodgman, Will 135
Holden 162, 164
Holland, Michael 74, 222; chapter 57, 69–80
Hollywood 85, 124, 139
Homan, Shane 32, 222; chapter 132, 179–89
Home (Hall) 20
Homebake 210
Homestead 196
homogeneity 88–9
Hood, Robert 157, 159
Hoodoo Gurus 25
house music 158–9, 162
housing 27, 46, 48–9, *see also* property markets
huayno 85
Hunger Games 12
Hutt Valley (Wellington) 168
hybridity 4–5, 86, 88, 91, 115–16, 131
Hyde, Adam 35
Hype! 202

"I Got You" (Split Enz) 195
The Idea of Latin America (Mignolo) 84
The Idea of North 138
identity 90, 105; hip hop 146, 149–50; national
   5–6, 155, 193; urban melancholy 125, 128, 131
imagination 87, 165
imagined community 5–6
immigration *see* migration
Immortal Technique 167, 173–5
imperialism: cultural 5, 7–8, *see also* British
   Empire; colonialism
imports 197, 199
Impossible Odds 147
In the Groove 8
"In the Still" (Jessie James and the Outlaws) 106
inclusion 83
independent music 11, 121–2, 160, 186
India 145
Indianapolis 194, 196
indie 76, 126, 197, 199–200
indie pop 75
indie rock 52, 69, 72–3, 198, 201
Indigenous people 2–6, 10–11, 90, 131, 141, 195;
   hip hop 145–50, 167–71, 173–5
Indij Hip Hop Show 147
Indonesia 1
industry *see* automotive industry; music industry
Indyfest 34
Inflatable Ingrid 37, 39
influence 173
infrastructure 7, 14, 33; earthquake impact 97,
   105; music city 181, 183–4, 186; peripheral
   cities 112, 115–16, 118–19

Ingall, Reuben 39
Inspire & Develop Artists (IDA) 82–3
Instagram 45
International Association for the Study of Popular Music (IASPM) 14
International DJ 155
International Federation of Phonographic Industries (IFPI) 181
Internet 45, 145, 193, 197, 202
INXS 9, 194–5, 207
irrationality 88–9
isolation, geographic 69, 118–19
Italo disco 163
iTunes 104
iwi 3

Jackson, Peter 124
James, Jessie 106
"January 26" (A.B. Original) 146
Japan 84, 161
jazz 6–7, 38, 183
Jazzy Jay 167, 173–4
Jealous, Virginia 21–2
Jebediah 27
Jessie James and the Outlaws 106
Jet-Armstrong, Driller 162
Jimblah 146, 148, 150
Jinshan Investments 63
Johannesburg 47
Johansson, Ola 19
Johnson, Boris 182
Johnson, Greg 106
Jorgensen, Ian "Blink" 126–7
Joy Division 71, 164
Juice Records 155–6, 158–62
Julia and the Deep Sea Sirens 37
JUSE1 174

Kabi Kabi 148
Kāpiti Marae 167, 174
Karami, Queenie 48
Kardinya 27
kaumātua 173–4
Kelloway, Paul 39
KERBI 173
Key, John 125
Khmer 175
Kilgour, Hamish 200
Kimbra 12
Kings of Leon 47
Kingsland 46
King Tut's Wah Wah Hut 35
kinship 71, 150, 167–9, 172–3, 175
Kirwan, Liz 36
Knight, Grace 24

Knives at Noon 75
"knowledge economy city" 180
Knox, Chris 198
"Kodaikanal Won't" (Ashraf) 145
Koehl, Gary 197
KOS-163 174
Kraftwerk 163
KRS-One 167, 169, 173–5

labels 11, 157–60, 162, 195–200
labor 134, 161, 180, 186, *see also* working class
Labor Party (Aus) 59, 185
Labour Party (A/NZ) 11
Labour Party (UK) 11
Labradford 198
"Land Down Under" (Men at Work) 9
Land March 3
land use 182–3, 185, *see also* development
language 3, 6, 10–11, 48; hip hop 167, 170–1; Latin American music 90–1; music discovery 194, 199
Larrakia 146, 150
The Last Kinection 148
Latin American music 81–91
Latinamericanism 81–2, 91
"Latino" 86
Legends of Cuba 87
Legg, Andrew 133, 136–7, 139, 141, 222–3; chapter 131, 133–44
Lemon Tree (Canberra) 34
Leone, Fred 147
Leslie, Rebecca 63
licensing 115, 158–9, 183–6
"Life Support System" (Vitamin HMC and Thee) 158
Life in Vacant Spaces 104
Lipshutz, Jason 49
liquor *see* alcohol
Little, Joel 46–7, 51–2
live music *see* touring; venues
Live Music and Performance Action Plan (Sydney) 184
Liverpool 21, 32, 60, 75, 118, 180
Living in the 70s (Skyhooks) 24
Lloyd, Richard D. 156
"Lo que hay" (Madre Monte) 91
local 34–5, 40, 70, 137, 186; electronic music 157, 161, 164–5; hip hop 145–7, 149–50, 168–71
London 22, 24–5, 180, 182, 184, 196
Lonely Planet 21–2, 122
Look Blue Go Purple 198
Lorde 12, 17, 45–54, 202
Los Angeles 51–2
Love Christchurch 100
The Love Club (Lorde) 47

232 • Index

Love in Bright Landscapes (Triffids) 25
Lovelock, Millie 74
Lowe, James 46
"LSD" (DJ HMC) 160
Lynch, Bernie 24
lyrics 81, 215; earthquake 106–7; hip hop 148–9, 167; Perth 19, 21–8
Lyttleton 100, 105

McComb, Dave 22, 25, 28
Macdonald, Jimmy 52
McDonald, Louis 47
McGee, Alan 72
Maclachlan, Scott 46–7
McLaney, Paul 97
McMillan, Paul Andrew 73
McNew, James 200
Macquarie University 14
McRae, Nigel 34–5, 38–9
Madre Monte 81–2, 90–1
mail order 197–8
Males 73
Malkmus, Stephen 201
Malone, Christopher 145
Mammoth 196, 199
Manchester 164
Mandurah (Perth) 21, 25
manufacturing 156, 161–4
Māori 3–4, 6, 10–12; Auckland 48, 51–2; Wellington 167–70, 172–5
marae (meeting house) 3, 174
market 127, 182–3, 185
marketing 6, 123, 196–7, 199
Marley, Bob 10
Marrickville (Sydney) 184
Martinez, George 145
mass production 161, 163
Massive Attack 47
Matador 201
The Matterhorn (Wellington) 121, 126
Maungauika (Devonport) 48–9
May, Derrick 164
MCs 37, 146, 167, 170–1, 173–4
media 8–9, 51–2, 156; Christchurch 103–4; Dunedin 69–70, 72–6; Melbourne 84–5; Wellington 125, 127–8, *see also* social media
melancholy 125, 128
Melbourne 13, 101, 140, 148; Brisbane/Hobart and 113, 115–16, 118–19; Canberra and 31, 33–4; Finn brothers 209, 214–15; heritage-making 57, 59–67; Latin American music 81–2, 85–91; music city 181, 183–5; Perth and 20, 23–5, 28
Melbourne City Council (MCC) 62–4, 66, 185
Melbourne Music Walk (MMW) 59–60, 65, 67
Melbourne Music Week 65

Meldrum, Molly 9, 62
The Melvins 201
memory 60–1, 111, 118, 141, *see also* heritage; history
Men at Work 9, 194–5, 207
Merge Records 197
metal 112; sludge- 74
Metcalf, Chelsea Jade 52
Metro 50
Metro (Adelaide) 158
Metropolitan Regional Planning Authority (MRPA) 26
La Mezcla 88
Mi Terra 88
Michigan 156
middle class 7, 21, 27, 61, 122, 163–4, 183
Midnight Oil 194–5
Mighty Mighty (Wellington) 121–2, 125–8
Mignolo, Walter 84
migration 5–7, 12, 84–7, 89, 112, 146
military 48
Mills, Jeff 157, 159
Milton Keynes 118
Minestrelli, Chiara 223; chapter 131, 145–54
mining 19, 28
Minogue, Kylie 9, 195, 207
"Miranda" (Madre Monte) 90
Mitchell, Elizabeth 50
Mitchell, Kevin 27–8
Mitchell, Tony 71, 106, 145, 169–71, 207, 223; chapter 17, 45–55
mixtapes 200–1
Moana and the Moahunters 11
Monash University 13
Montgomery, Roy 201
Montreal 118
moral panics 7
Morgie Morgz 149
Morningside (Auckland) 45, 50–1
Motown 163
Mount Victoria (Auckland) 48, 50
MTV 9, 194–6, 202
"Muckaty" (Sambo) 145
Multicultural Arts Victoria 82
multiculturalism 5, 57, 81, 86, 91
Museum of Old and New Art (MONA) 116, 133, 135, 139–40, 184–5
museums 48, 57, 172–3
Music Canada 181
"music cities" 132, 179–87
Music Cities Convention 179
Music Development Offices 184
music industry 11, 85; Finn brothers and 207–8; Fordism/post-Fordism 160–1; "music cities" and 179, 183–4; peripheral cities 114, 117

Music Man 158
Music Row (Nashville) 180
music scenes *see* scenes
Music Victoria 59
myths 19–20, 90, 118–19, 164

NAIDOC Week 4, 148
Naked and Famous 50
The Naked Samoans 51
Nashville 180
National Folk Festival (Aus) 34
National Youth Network 8
nationalism 4–6, 8, 10, 208; national identity 5–6, 155, 193
"Neglected Space" (Imogen Heap) 106
neoliberalism 122, 124, 181
Netherlands 158
networks 38–40, 45, 118–19, 169
Neuenfeldt, Karl 10
Nevarez, Leonard 164
New Musical Express (NME) 69–70, 72–3
New Order 164
New Orleans 32
New South Wales 23, 33, 38
new wave 163
New York 24, 196, 200; Dunedin and 70–2; hip hop 167–8, 173–5; music city 180, 183
New York Times 28
New Zealand *see* Aotearoa/New Zealand
New Zealand Herald 46, 48, 52
New Zealand Music Awards 52
New Zealand Music Commission 100–1
Newton-John, Olivia 194–5
Newtown (Wellington) 167
Ngāti Pāoa 48
Nichols, David 196
nightclubs 85, 158, 163, 168
No Alternative 197
noise 183–5
Nooky 148
North Head (Auckland) 48–9
North Shore (Auckland) 46–7
Northern Territory 145
nostalgia 71–3
Notre Dame, University of 198
The Nudge 106–7
Nugent, Ted 195
N.W.A. 149
NZ on Air (NZOA) 11–12
NZ Listener 47

O'Connor, Justin 156
O'Connor, Victor 46
"Ode To My Car" (Evans) 27
Ohio 194

O'Keefe, Johnny 7
"oldschool" 175
"One Good Reason" (The Swingers) 195
Onion 164
Operation Restore 100
Opposite Sex 73
oral tradition 2, 90–1, 171
organized crime 114
Orientalism 81–2
Orulas 87
Otago, University of 75
Othering 82
Outback 149
Oxford Tavern (Wollongong) 38–9
"Oz Rock" 9, 155, 184

Pacific 12, 113, 170–2, 175
Pacific Islands 1, 10, 51, 168–9, 208
Paisley Underground 200
Pākehā 3, 6, 10, 167, 174
Palace Theatre (Melbourne) 59–60, 62–7, 185
Palais Theatre (St Kilda) 185
Palma Violets 72
Palmer, Robert 135
Panda Band 22–3, 25
Parasol 198
Parrish, Theo 163
Paru 167
Pasifika 6, 10, 12
Patea Maori Club 11
patere 12
Paton, Kirsteen 183
Pavement 72, 201
Peaches 197
Pearl Jam 207, 209
Peking Duk 35
Peña, Mauricio 90–1
Pennycook, Alastair 145, 170–1
Perfect Beat 14
peripheral cities 112–13, 115, 118–19
Perkins, Tex 185
Perth 17, 19–28, 32, 112–13, 116, 118, 140, 184
"Perth is a Culture Shock" (Victims) 24
Peru 85, 88
Peterson, Richard 157
"Phantom" (Warner) 26
Phillipps, Martin 75–6
Philpott, Carolyn 223; chapter 131, 133–44
Phipps, Peter 147
The Phoenix (Canberra) 31, 33–41
"Phreakin" (DJ HMC) 160–1
A Picture Book of Old Auckland (Barnett) 49
pirate radio 8
Pitchfork 69, 74, 202
Piticco, Paul 114

234 • Index

place 17, 73, 149; electronic music 156, 164–5; venues 32, 45
Plan 9 Records 196–8, 201
planning, land use 182–5
PledgeMe 101, 105
Plesch, Melanie 83, 88
Plus-8 157, 159–60
"Poi E" (Patea Maori Club) 11
police 114
policy 21, 95, 122–5, 179, 181–6
politics 33, 148, 150; heritage-making 59, 64, 66; music city 181–2, *see also* government
Polynesians 6, 168, 170
Poor Boy (Finn) 212–13
pop 75, 91, 171, 197; indie pop 75, 114, *see also* popular music
The Pope (Adams) 198
PopMatters 72
popular music 1–2, 4–14, 19, 59–61, *see also* pop
Popwatch 198
Port Arthur 141
Porta, Gonzalo 87
Porter, Dorothy 214
post-Fordism 156, 161–3
Powderfinger 114
power 7–8, 76, 88, 128, 167
pōwhiri 167, 173–4
Prebble, Ryan 104–7
Presley, Elvis 7
Prince 65
The Problem with Music in New Zealand (Jorgensen) 126
property markets 127, 182–3, *see also* housing
Proud, Pip 199
publicness 128
pub rock 156, 163, 184
pubs 31, 34–41, 182, *see also* bars; venues
Puffin, Lindon 100
punk 19, 23–4, 162, 196, 198
punk rock 34
Puppies (Wellington) 121, 125–8
Pure Heroine (Lorde) 46, 51, 53
puritanism 6
Pus 26

Quebec City 181
Queensland 111
Queen Street riot 11

racism 84, 146–9, 163–4, 171, *see also* ethnicity; Indigenous people
radio 8, 11, 35, 194–5, 201
Radio Birdman 199
Radio Hauraki 8

Radiohead 207, 209
Radio New Zealand 47
Radio with Pictures 8–9
rag 11
rage 9
Rage Against the Machine 211, 216
The Raincoats 201
Rainy Day (Paisley Underground) 200
Randa 52
Randles, Alec 41
Rangitoto 49–50
Rank and File 195
rap *see* hip hop
Rattenbury, Shane 41
rave 159, 164
Raza Madre (Madre Monte) 90–1
Re:START 102
Ready to Roll 8
Reagon, Bernice Johnson 140
REAL NZ Festival 100
"realness" 169
rebellion 77
recession 10, 127, 164
reciprocity 168, 174
Reclaim Australia (A.B. Original) 146, 148
record stores 196–8, 202
recording 6, 51, 85, 183–4, *see also* labels; music industry
Recording Industry Association of New Zealand (RIANZ) 207
Red Cross Earthquake Appeal 99–100
Red Rattler (Sydney) 184
reggae 10–11, 90
Regurgitator 114
reissues 202, 209
Reith, John 8
relationality 172, 175
religion 139–40
R.E.M. 195–6
representation 117–19
Revolutionary Vol. 2 (Immortal Technique) 174
Reykjavik 112, 118
Reynolds, Simon 62, 163
rhythm 81, 83, 89, 164
Richards, Greg 135
Richmond (VA) 194, 197–8
Rickwood, Julie 41, 223; chapter 17, 31–44
Ritchie, Brian 140, 185
Rival MC 147
RMIT University 13
Roach, Archie 4, 148
Roberts, Les 59–61, 64

Index • 235

Robertson, Craig 71, 197
Robinson, Mark 198
rock 6–7, 9, 11, 114–16, 162, 199; alternative 23, 157; indie rock 52, 69, 72–3, 198, 201; pub rock 156, 163, 184; punk rock 34
rock'n'roll 6–7, 34, 179
Rogers, Ian 223; chapter 95, 111–20
Rolling Stone 50
Rookie 49
Rose, Lionel 65
Rough Skies Records 117
Rough Trade 196
Le Rox (Adelaide) 163
Royal, Marc 97–8, 100–1
"Royals" (Lorde) 46–7, 49–51, 53
Rudd, Kevin 4
rumba 85

Sackful of Squirrels 46
Said, Edward 81
Saiko Management 46
St Kilda (Victoria) 185
The Saints 114, 199
Salmon, Kim 25
salsa 83, 87–8
Sal Salvador All Stars 87
samba 85
Sambo, Kylie 145
Samoans 167–8, 170–1, 173–5
San Diego 21
San Francisco 101
San Lazaro 89
Santiago 85
Savage Garden 114
Save Live Australian Music (SLAM) 66
Save the Palace (STP) 63–5, 66–7
scenes: electronic music 155, 165; music cities 186–7; music discovery 195–6, 198, 201–2; peripheral cities 111–15, 118–19; urban melancholy 121–2, 127–8
Schulz, Chris 52
Schwartz, Stephen 138
Scientists 25
Scotland 35
Scott, Michael 11–12
Scribe 12
Seattle 118, 196, 202
Sebastian, Guy 138
Second World War 84
Sel 149
self, technology of 111
Seymour, Nick 208–12
Shank, Barry 32, 111
Shaw, Kate 23, 185

She Will Have Her Way 213
Sheffield 21
Shepherd, Roger 71, 75
Sheplife (Briggs) 150
Shepparton (Victoria) 146, 148–50
DJ ShiKung 99
Shilliam, Robbie 172–3
shops 196–8, 202
Sicko, Dan 160–1
Silas 167, 169
Silo Park 52
Silva, German 89
Silvanto, Satu 135
Silver, Daniel 161
Silver Bullets (The Chills) 69
Simmel, Georg 125
The Simpsons 51
Sinclair, John 86
Singapore 20
Sister Act 139
Sitting Room 100
"Six Months in a Leaky Boat" (Split Enz) 5
Six O'Clock Rock 9
Skyhooks 13, 23
slavery 90, 141
Slay Tracks (Pavement) 201
"Sleepy Little Deathtoll Town" (Panda Band) 22–3
Sleepy Township 25, 28
Slightly Odway (Jebediah) 27
Sloane, Robert 194, 223; chapter 193–204
sludge-metal 74
Smithies, Grant 73
The Smiths 207, 209
social media 45, 63, 88; Canberra 36, 40–1; Wellington 121, 125, 147
Soho 182
"Somebody I Used to Know" (Gotye/Kimbra) 12
"Someone So Much" (Evans) 27
Son Lux 53
songlines 2, 149
Songs for Christchurch 98–9, 101–2, 104–7
Sorry Day 4
soul 40, 172
Soundcloud 45
South Australia 156
South Park 51
Southern Gospel Choir (SGC) 131, 133, 135–43
Southern Sinfonia 75
"Spanish Blue" (Triffids) 22
Spartacus R 106
Special Broadcast Service (SBS) 8, 136
SpexOne 168, 173, 175
Spiby, Michael 138

236 • Index

SpinArt Records 198
Split Enz 3, 5, 10, 52, 194–5, 207, 209–10, 213, 216
Spotify 201
Springboks 11
"S.T. Song" (Sleepy Township) 25
Stafford, Andrew 114
Stahl, Geoff 165, 197, 223; chapter 95, 121–30; introduction 1–14
Standing in the Shadows of MONA 133, 135, 139
Starstruck 195
state *see* government; politics
State Bank 164
stereotyping 81–2, 85, 88, 91, 147, 149
Stolen Generation 3–4
"Straight Outta Shepparton" (South Side Kings) 149
Strang, Kane 74
Stratton, Jon 7, 224; chapter 17, 19–29
Straw, Will 45, 111, 118, 157–8, 199
Street, John 45
"Streets of Your Town" (Go-Betweens) 196
Strong, Catherine 224; chapter 57, 59–68
"Stuff and Nonsense" (Split Enz) 213
Styles, Reuben 35
Stylus 70
"Subidero" (Madre Monte) 90
Sub Pop 202
"Suburban Boy" (Warner) 26–7
Suburban Kid (Evans) 27
Suburban Songbook (Evans) 27
suburbs: Adelaide 156, 162–3; Auckland 45–6, 48, 50–1; Perth 21–8
"Sunburnt" (The Chills) 200
Sunday Star Times 51
"Survival Day" 3
Swan Bells 22
Sweetman, Simon 128
Swerv 169
Swift, Taylor 46, 53
The Swingers 195
Sydney 85, 121; Brisbane/Hobart and 113, 115; Canberra and 31, 33–4; Finn brothers 210, 212–14; music city 183–4; Perth and 20, 23, 25, 28
Sydney Opera House 208–9
syncretism 4–5, 10, 131

Takapuna (Auckland) 47, 50
Takarunga (Auckland) 48, 60
"Take Me to the Old Cathedral" (Johnson) 106
talent competitions 81–3
Tall Dwarfs 198
"tall poppy syndrome" 4
"Tally Ho" (The Clean) 194

tango 84–5
Tannenbaum, Rob 50
tāpu 173
Tasmania 111, 113, 116–17, 134–6, 140–3, 184
Tasmania, University of 133, 136, 143
Tasmanian Symphony Orchestra 133, 138
Taylor, Timothy 199
Te Awamutu 207
Te Kupu 172–3
te reo Māori 3, 6, 10–11, 48
Te Taua Moana marae 48
Teakle, Julian 117
"Team" (Lorde) 49
techno 131, 155–65
Techno Rebels (Sicko) 160
Teen Beat Records 198 The Teen Idles 198
television 8–9
Temporary: Selections from Dunedin's Pop Underground 73–4
Ten Days on the Island 136
Tha Feelstyle 170–1
theater 213–14, 216
Thee 158
"They Will Have Their Way" 208
third space 81–2, 86, 91
The Third Wave (Toffler) 158
"This is My City" (Skyhooks) 13
This Kind of Punishment 200
Thomas, Grant 209
Thong, Sen 175
time 61, 72
Time Flowing Backwards (The Cakekitchen) 196
tino rangatiratanga 12
Tiny Mix Tapes 202
Tiny Ruins 52
Toffler, Alvin 158
The Tomb (Canberra) 34
"Took the Children Away" (Roach) 34, 148
Toorak 24
Torres Strait Islanders 2–3, 138
Toucan (Adelaide) 163
touring 76, 105, 142, 186; Brisbane/Hobart 115–17; Canberra 33–5, 38
tourism 59–62, 121, 134, 180, 197
Toynbee, Jason 162
T.R. 149
Trainer, Adam 224; chapter 17, 19–30
Transitional City Projects Fund 101
translocality 157
"Treaty 2015" (Jimblah and Nooky) 148
Treaty of Waitangi 3
Treaty of Waitangi Act (1975) 10

"Treaty" (Yothu Yindi) 10, 148
Trials 146
The Triffids 22, 25, 28
Triple J 8, 35, 89, 146
Tucker, Abi 215
Tumblr 45, 50
Tunisia 112
Turangawaewae: Sense of Place (Depot Artspace) 48
tyranny of distance 5–6, 12, 184

Ukamau 85
'ulafala 167, 174
Underground Resistance (UR) 157–8, 160–1
"Unearthed" (Triple J) 8, 35, 89
Unilever 145
United Kingdom (UK) 6–8, 10, 53, 60, 101; Dunedin and 69–70; electronic music 156, 158, 161–2; music cities 182, 186; music discovery 194–5, 199, 202; Perth and 20–1, 24, *see also* British Empire
United States of America (USA) 6–7, 21, 53; electronic music 155–6, 160–3; gospel 133, 136–7, 142; hip hop 146, 149, 167–75; Latin American music 82–4, 86–9; music discovery 193–202
Universal Music 47
Universal Zulu Nation (UZN) 174
universities 13–14, 75; gospel 133, 136, 143; music discovery 194, 198, 201
Upper Hutt Posse 12, 168, 172
urban 149–50; melancholy 125, 128; policy 95, 122, *see also* cities
Uruguay 87

Vehicle (The Clean) 196, 199
venues and live music 74, 115, 135, 214; Canberra 31, 33–41; Christchurch 97–8, 105–6; Melbourne 63–6; music cities 179, 182–6; Wellington 121–2, 125–8
The Venus Trail (3Ds) 197
The Verlaines 71, 75, 197
Victims 24
Victoria 146, 148–9, 184–5
Victoria Theatre (Devonport) 47
Video Hits 9
videos 49, 104, 150, 194, 202
"Vincente" (Madre Monte) 90–1
violence 141
Violent Femmes 185
Virginia 194, 196, 198, 201
Vitamin HMC 158
Vorn Doolette 37

waiata (songs) 3, 167
Waiata (Split Enz) 3
wainua (attitude) 12
Waitangi, Treaty of 3, 10
Waitemata Harbour 50
Walker, Clinton 156, 162–3
Walsh, David 139–40
Warner, Dave 26–7
Washington (DC) 194, 198
Watercolours 52
WBGU 201
"Weather with You" (Crowded House) 213
Wellington 95, 121–9, 180, 201; Christchurch and 104, 106; hip hop 131, 167–76
Wellington City Council (WCC) 123–4
"Wellington Sound" 126
Wendt, Albert 171
Weno 148
Werner, Craig 136
wero 173
West 81–3, 88, 122, 140, 170
The West Australian 21
Western Australia 19, 23, 25, 28, 112
Westing (Pavement) 201
Weta 124, 126
whakapapa 172–3, 175
whakarongo (listen up) 12
Whish-Wilson, David 20, 22, 26
White Australia Policy 84
White Trash, Fast Food (Berlin) 126
"whitening" 6
Why Music Matters (Hesmondhalgh) 128
"Wide Open Road" (Triffids) 28
Williams, Emma 224; chapter 17, 31–44
Williams, Raymond 125
Williamson, Mary 48
Wilson, Oli 75, 224; chapter 57, 69–80
Wollongong 32, 38
women 48, 76
Woodville 162
working class 27, 162, 183, *see also* labor
World Expo 114
World Literary Quiz 47
"world music" 10, 199
Wunderbar (Christchurch) 105
Wynne, Derek 156
Wynyard Quarter 52

X 195
Xpressway 195–6, 198, 200

Yanez, Clemente Jesus Navarro 161
Yelich-O'Connor, Ella *see* Lorde
"Yellow Peril" 6

238 • Index

Yo La Tengo 72, 200
Yolngu 10
Yorta Yorta 146
Yothu Yindi 10, 148
Young AK 149
Young, Claude 160
Your Hit Parade 9

youth culture 7, 112, 157
YouTube 9, 45, 121, 147, 150

Zemke-White, Kisten 170, 172
zines 197–8
zoning 183
Zukin, Sharon 135